CHESTERTON
AND THE ROMANCE
OF ORTHODOXY

THE MAKING OF GKC
1874–1908

WILLIAM ODDIE

OXFORD
UNIVERSITY PRESS

OXFORD
UNIVERSITY PRESS

Great Clarendon Street, Oxford OX2 6DP

Oxford University Press is a department of the University of Oxford.
It furthers the University's objective of excellence in research, scholarship,
and education by publishing worldwide in

Oxford New York

Auckland Cape Town Dar es Salaam Hong Kong Karachi
Kuala Lumpur Madrid Melbourne Mexico City Nairobi
New Delhi Shanghai Taipei Toronto

With offices in

Argentina Austria Brazil Chile Czech Republic France Greece
Guatemala Hungary Italy Japan Poland Portugal Singapore
South Korea Switzerland Thailand Turkey Ukraine Vietnam

Oxford is a registered trade mark of Oxford University Press
in the UK and in certain other countries

Published in the United States
by Oxford University Press Inc., New York

British Library Cataloguing in Publication Data

Data available

Library of Congress Cataloging in Publication Data
Oddie, William.
Chesterton and the romance of Orthodoxy :
the making of GKC, 1874–1908 / William Oddie.
p.   cm.
William Oddie draws extensively on Chesterton's unpublished letters and notebooks,
his journalism, and his early classic writings, to reveal the writer's spiritual development,
from his early childhood in the 1870s to his intellectual maturity in the
first decade of the twentieth century.

ISBN 978-0-19-955165-1

Includes bibliographical references (p.   ) and index.
1. Chesterton, G. K. (Gilbert Keith), 1874–1936—Religion.   2. Chesterton, G. K. (Gilbert Keith),
1874–1936. Orthodoxy.   3. Authors, English—20th century—Biography.
4. Christianity and literature—Great Britain—History.
I. Title: Making of GKC, 1874–1908. II. Title.
PR4453.C4Z743   2008
823'.912—dc22   2008015119

Typeset by SPI Publisher Services, Pondicherry, India
Printed in Great Britain
on acid-free paper by
CPI Antony Rowe, Chippenham, Wiltshire

1 3 5 7 9 10 8 6 4 2

For my wife, Cornelia

Contents

PART II

Abbreviations for Works Most Frequently Cited

Autobiography	G. K. Chesterton, *Autobiography* (London: Fisher Press, 1992)
Cecil	Cecil Chesterton, *G. K. Chesterton: A Criticism* (London, 1908)
Collected Works	G. K. Chesterton, *Collected Works* (San Francisco: Ignatius Press, 1986)
Conlon	Denis Conlon (ed.), *G. K. Chesterton: The Critical Judgements* (Antwerp, 1976)
Return	Maisie Ward, *Return to Chesterton* (London, 1952)
Ward	Maisie Ward, *Gilbert Keith Chesterton* (London, 1944)

PART
I

Introduction

When Chesterton published *Orthodoxy* in 1908 he was 34 years old; and though he was by now one of the most successful writers of the age, many readers still did not know quite what to make of him. Even his religious views were not entirely clear at the time, strange though this may seem now. Despite his dogged two-year campaign, in three different newspapers, in defence of Christianity—which had begun five years before in response to the vociferously secularist assaults of the socialist writer Robert Blatchford—he was still seen as almost wilfully unpredictable, given to plunging into any topic that might occur to him on the spur of the moment, rather than as a writer with any consistency of purpose. His defence of Christianity had been conducted in three very different news-papers, each with its own specialised readership. His regular audience in *The Daily News*, his principal journalistic outlet, were acquainted by now with his views on the Christian religion (though his weekly column was by no means obsessively concerned with them); but the paper's readers tended to be not only Liberal in politics but Nonconformist in religion. *The Commonwealth* was the organ of the Christian Social Union, leftward leaning in politics and Anglo-Catholic in religion, edited by one of the great post-Tractarian theologians of the day, Henry Scott Holland. The controversy had been wound up with a series of articles by Chesterton in Blatchford's own paper, the socialist (and mostly atheist) weekly *The Clarion*. Those who read these papers were probably in no doubt as to Chesterton's views on religion. But those who did not (possibly a majority of those who had followed his literary career) were not necessarily acquainted with them, despite *Heretics* (1905), which one might have thought would have put the matter beyond doubt: three years later, nevertheless, *Orthodoxy*'s reviewer in the *Manchester Guardian* commented that 'not a few of his habitual readers, hearing that he has written a book about orthodoxy in religion, will be quite uncertain whether to look for a defence or an attack'.[1]

[1] B.S., 'Mr Chesterton on Orthodoxy', *Manchester Guardian* (29 Sept. 1908); Conlon, 167.

Orthodoxy was the book in which Chesterton first fully declared himself unmistakably. The very title, as he recalled in his autobiography, 'was provocative. . . . A serious defence of orthodoxy was far more startling to the English critic than a serious attack on orthodoxy was to the Russian censor. . . . Very nearly everybody, in the ordinary literary and journalistic world, began by taking it for granted that my faith in the Christian creed was a pose or a paradox. . . . It was not until long afterwards that the full horror of the truth burst upon them; the disgraceful truth that I really thought the thing was true. . . . Since then they have been more combative; and I do not blame them.'[2] The publication of *Orthodoxy* was the end of a journey. It was both the conclusion of a process of self-discovery and the key document (for there were others) in which, at this pivotal moment in his life, he assessed not only where it was that he now stood but how it was that his journey had followed the course that it did: *Orthodoxy*, he declared in the book's first chapter, 'is a kind of slovenly autobiography'.[3]

In the same year, 1908, he published *The Man who was Thursday*, a work in some vital ways even more self-revealing. It contains a lengthy and at times powerfully emotional dedication, in verse, to his closest friend, Edmund Clerihew Bentley. This dedication is centrally important to any history of Chesterton's mind (though most of his biographers ignore it), and it will be necessary to consider it in detail in a later chapter. It is enough, here, to note how it establishes 1908 as a year in which it seemed natural to this prolific—and by now almost extravagantly successful—young writer to pause and gratefully to take stock of his life; there is a sense here of profound relief, of coming into port after traversing perilous seas, of the danger of a personal shipwreck narrowly avoided:

> This is a tale of those old fears, even of those emptied hells,
> And none but you shall understand the true thing that it tells. . . .
> The doubts that were so plain to chase, so dreadful to withstand—
> Oh, who shall understand but you; yea, who shall understand. . . .
> Between us, by the peace of God, such truth can now be told;
> Yea, there is strength in striking root and good in growing old.[4]

Chesterton was not alone in seeing 1908 as a pivotal point in his career. Between *The Man who was Thursday* and *Orthodoxy,* his brother Cecil published an anonymous (and, though loyal, by no means entirely

---

[2] *Autobiography*, 180.   [3] *Collected Works*, i. 215.
[4] G. K. Chesterton, *The Man who was Thursday* (London: Penguin, 1986), 6–7.

uncritical) assessment of his brother's achievement thus far. Cecil's book *G. K. Chesterton: A Criticism* conveys accurately enough the extent of his brother's fame, though, as we shall see, he greatly exaggerates the dizziness of its steady rather than meteoric rise:

In the autumn of the year 1899 no one outside his own circle had ever heard of G. K. Chesterton. In the spring of 1900 everyone was asking everyone else, 'Who is "G.K.C."?' Before the year was over his own name and writings were better known than those of men who had made reputations while he was still an infant. I do not know any [other] example in the last fifty years of so dizzy a rise from obscurity to fame.[5]

In fact, he had published very little by the spring of 1900, and even by the end of the year, though he had produced two books of verse and a respectable number of articles, it cannot yet be said that 'everyone was asking everyone else, Who is "G.K.C."?' Even when his 'rise from obscurity to fame' had taken place, it still took some time (as we have seen) for his contemporaries to make out exactly what it was they had on their hands. Partly this was because of the confusing variety of the published works now appearing in rapid succession: comic verse with accompanying drawings (*Greybeards at Play*, 1900); poetry and doom-laden drama (*The Wild Knight*, 1900); campaigning journalism (*The Speaker*, *The Daily News*, and other outlets, 1899 onwards); the fine arts (*G. F. Watts*, 1903); literary criticism (*Robert Browning*, 1904; *Charles Dickens*, 1906); novels and short stories (*The Napoleon of Notting Hill*, 1904; *The Club of Queer Trades*, 1905), religious controversy (*The Daily News*, *The Commonwealth*, and *The Clarion* newspaper, 1903–4; *Heretics*, 1905). But the real reason why this abundant literary phenomenon was so difficult to make out was that all this chaotic output showed nothing more clearly than that Chesterton himself was still, in full view, undergoing a process of intellectual development and self-discovery. In the early years of the decade, indeed, he was becoming well known not only before he had become detectably 'orthodox', but at a time when he seemed still (on the evidence of his earliest published work) intellectually closer to Stopford Brooke, the celebrity modernist preacher—at whose feet he had sat in the Bedford chapel a decade before[6]—than to the 'doctrinaire' Roman Catholic Hilaire Belloc (whom he had met in the autumn of 1899) or to Conrad Noel, the left-wing Anglo-Catholic he had also met shortly before his emergence from obscurity. His first appearance, at the age of 26,

---

[5] Cecil, 30. [6] *Autobiography*, 174. See pp. 68–72 below.

was in the persona of the anti-clerical anti-dogmatist he had been ten years before as a prolific teenage poet and essayist. 'In a less tolerant age', wrote the literary critic James Douglas in his review of *The Wild Knight*, which appeared in November 1900, '"Gilbert Chesterton" might find himself arraigned as a blaspheming atheist. . . . Some of the most powerful lyrics in this volume I can hardly venture to quote, so terrible is their pessimism, so insurgently brutal their insurrection against orthodox idols and ideals.'[7]

The Wild Knight, however, is in some ways a regression to earlier periods in Chesterton's life. It is an incongruous ragbag of work he had been collecting over the previous five years: it recalls the raw anti-clericalism of his schoolboy verse, and the intermittent but traumatic pessimism of his time of crisis as a student at the Slade School of Art; it also contains poems which reflect the recovery of his underlying optimism, though these do not predominate. Interestingly, Rudyard Kipling, on reading this strange but powerful collection, suggested that Gilbert needed 'a severe course of Walt Whitman' so that he might be 'jolted out of' his tendency to depressive imagery.[8] But Whitman (together with Robert Louis Stevenson) was part of a literary cure he had already taken, and *The Wild Knight* also reflects Whitman's influence. What the collection demonstrates most vividly is that although the auspices under which his discovery of orthodoxy could now take place were assembled (his devout fiancée Frances, Belloc, Conrad Noel and other Anglican clergy), the serious intellectual business which had to be done before that discovery could be authentically his own was still in its early stages.

The starting point for this journey of discovery, however, has to be traced further back than the turn of the century, further back than his student days at University College, London, and the Slade School of Art, further back, even, than his precocious adolescence during the early 1890s. There are few other major writers whose literary and even political influences can be traced back to their early childhood, few whose childhood, indeed, remained with them throughout life in quite the same way, not—as with James Barrie, or A. A. Milne, perhaps—as something he never grew out of, but as a persistent source of literary vitality which in no way raises questions about lack of maturity or refusal to grow up. His childhood was not without its sorrows; it would not, nevertheless, be wrong to describe it as a cloudlessly happy one. And Chesterton's parents, in an impressively relaxed but

---

[7] Conlon, 30–1.　　　[8] Ibid. 28.

persistent way, took their children's intellectual growth seriously from their earliest years. They shared with them their values, they fed their growing minds by endlessly talking to them and reading to them, and by nurturing their capacity to learn for themselves, in short, by encouraging and making possible the attainment of that priceless Victorian ideal, the 'well-stocked mind'.

Thus, the whole of Chesterton's life so far has to be seen as the period over which we need to trace the process of intellectual discovery which comes to a fairly clear *terminus ad quem* in 1908 with *Orthodoxy*. To chart this journey of discovery involves a whole series of questions. How, born into what Carlyle had called, so many years before, an age of 'down-pulling and disbelief', did this child of Victorian modernist liberalism become, in the way that he did, such an icon of anti-modernist cultural counter-revolution? And what, having become an anti-modernist, was the logic which made it increasingly inevitable that he would embrace orthodox Christianity? This last question may seem a strange one: the general assumption has always been that Chesterton's reaction against the idea of progress was a consequence of his Christianity. But Chesterton's anti-modernism emerged independently at the same time as (and possibly even before) his Christianity. Partly, its origins were political, and had to do with his support for the pro-Boer cause in particular and for the independence of small nations in general: the anti-Boer party within South Africa described itself as 'progressive' in contrast to the Boers, who were defending their long-established traditions against the irruption of the modern world. Quite simply, the imperialists saw themselves as representing the forces of modernity and change: it is strange but true that at this curious juncture in English history, to be anti-imperialist was to be considered reactionary; the leading intellectual exponents of socialism, Shaw and most of the Fabian Society, supported the war, as did a large part of the Liberal party. In the same year as he concluded his defence of Christianity in *The Clarion*, Chesterton published *The Napoleon of Notting Hill* (1904), in which he imagines an explanation given to the former President of a small country, which has been forcibly absorbed by a larger one, of why his country's continued independence had been inconsistent with modern thought:

You misunderstand, I think, the modern intellect. . . . If I differ with the greatest of respect from your Nicaraguan enthusiasm, it is not because a nation or ten nations were against you; it is because civilisation was against you. We moderns believe in a great cosmopolitan civilisation, one which shall include all the talents of all the absorbed peoples.[9]

Chesterton's distaste for modernity and progress, however, was a recent volte-face, one which had its consequences, not all of them predictable: one result was that he felt inclined to defend anything that modernity was against. This included the Christian religion, though, as we shall see, he had other reasons for his increasingly pro-Christian views. The point is that these views (like his rejection of the cult of progress) were of recent date. Thus when, in 1903, Robert Blatchford published, in *The Clarion* news-paper, a series of attacks on the Christian religion, and Chesterton set himself to rebut them in a series of articles in various papers which came to an end only the following year, his defence, though spirited enough, was of something of which his understanding was still rapidly developing. Nevertheless, this was the first time that he had in a sustained way publicly avowed his belief in the Christian religion. He was beginning to approach the end of a long process of intellectual transition: Cecil called it his 'drift towards orthodoxy'.[10] The following year, he published *Heretics* (1905), a collection of attacks on literary figures of the day (Shaw, Wells, Kipling, George Moore, and others) in which, once more, there was no coherent defence of Christianity as such, but a wealth of evidence that he understood what it was. 'By showing what heresy implies', writes David Dooley, 'Chesterton illustrates what orthodoxy implies.'[11] Perhaps; but as we shall see (Chapter 7), discussions of the implications of orthodoxy in *Heretics* are more than once occasions for Chesterton to make it clear that he has come to the view that orthodox belief is identical with the teachings of the Christian tradition. By the time, three years later, that Chesterton published *Orthodoxy* itself, we have the sense of an arrival, of the attainment of an equilibrium newly won but now permanent: now, his Christianity is defined clearly as being a systematic body of belief held by a historical community of faith:

'When the word 'orthodoxy' is used here it means the Apostle's Creed, as under-stood by everybody calling himself Christian until a very short time ago and the general historic conduct of those who held such a creed.[12]

---

[9] G. K. Chesterton, *The Napoleon of Notting Hill* (London, 1904), 24.
[10] Cecil, 95–123.   [11] *Collected Works*, i. 22.   [12] Ibid. 215.

It is, more or less, the classic formulation of St Vincent de Lérins (dearly loved by Anglo-Catholics): 'that which was believed everywhere, always, and by all' ('ubique, semper et ab omnibus'). He had come a long way since his beliefs on such matters had been formed, nearly two decades before, by the Reverend Stopford Brooke, who taught him that 'Creeds . . . have been used in all ages as the weapons of spiritual tyranny' (a proposition the young Gilbert had passionately espoused).[13] His thinking was certainly not static from this point on; but we have the sense that all his writings on the Christian religion after 1908 were built on foundations now firmly established. When he died twenty-eight years later, T. S. Eliot pronounced that 'Chesterton's social and economic ideas were *the* ideas for his time that were fundamentally Christian and Catholic'.[14]

But how did he come by these ideas? Eliot insisted that he attached 'significance also to his development, to his beginnings as well as to his ends, and to the movement from one to the other'.[15] It is on that development, on those beginnings, and on the most important period of that movement that this book is focused. The first part of it deals with the years of Chesterton's obscurity—his childhood, his adolescence, his years as a student and a young adult—not least because this period has been, if not ignored by his biographers, certainly left behind with what seems to me an undue impatience to move on to a period in their subject's life in which the initials G.K.C. begin to count for something.

We need to understand not simply why Chesterton wanted to say *something* about the world (voluble young men always want to do that). The important question to answer, before we can fully elucidate *what* he said, is why he said it. It would, of course, be generally accepted that since his writings were from the beginning closely concerned with the world in which he lived, Chesterton's published works may legitimately be referred to their immediate social, religious, literary, and historical context (though, as a matter of observable fact, few books about him do anything of the sort). But if we accept that, we have to assume, too, that the period which preceded Chesterton's earliest published writings was also one in which social, literary, religious, and historical context is at least as important as isolated biographical detail to our understanding of how he came to write as he did.

---

[13] See pp. 69–70 below.   [14] Conlon, 532.   [15] Ibid. 531.

We must, of course, as all his biographers do, evoke Chesterton's early years as nearly as we can by recalling the happiness of his childhood and adolescence and the spiritual crisis of his student years. But that childhood, and that spiritual crisis, were deeply rooted in their times; we need to see more clearly than we do that the spirit of the age in which he grew to manhood had a deep effect on Chesterton's personal and intellectual development and on the kind of writer he became: for once we have seen that, we will be able to perceive more clearly, behind the Edwardian journalist, popular versifier, and minor novelist, a more substantial and more prophetic figure, whose proper place is not with such petty luminaries as Max Beerbohm and John Galsworthy, or even with H. G. Wells and George Bernard Shaw, but with those great Victorians who epitomised their age by standing in fundamental opposition to it. We can apply directly to Chesterton his own words about the painter G. F. Watts: 'He has the one great certainty which marks off all the great Victorians from those who have come after them: he may not be certain that he is successful, or certain that he is great, or certain that he is good, or certain that he is capable: but he is certain that he is right.'[16] My judgement is that of Ian Ker: that we need to see 'the non-fiction prose writer, the Chesterton who wrote such studies as *Charles Dickens* (1906), *The Victorian Age in Literature* (1913) and *St Thomas Aquinas* (1933), as well as the apologetic classics *Orthodoxy* (1908) and *The Everlasting Man* (1925), as a successor to the great Victorian "sages" or "prophets", who was indeed often compared to Dr Johnson in his own lifetime, and who can be mentioned without exaggeration in the same breath as Carlyle, Ruskin, Arnold, and especially, of course, Newman'.[17] This prophetic cast of mind, I hope to show, had been fully formed by the time he wrote *Orthodoxy*: with Ian Ker's judgement we can place that of another of Newman's biographers—the first, Wilfrid Ward—who in an extended review of *Orthodoxy*, significantly entitled 'Mr Chesterton among the Prophets', classed 'his thought—though not his manner—with that of such men as Burke, Butler and Coleridge',[18] and who also, more than once, made the inevitable comparison with Newman himself.

The aim of this book is to trace the growth of Chesterton's mind from early childhood to the point in his literary career at which, as I shall argue,

---

[16] *G. F. Watts* (London, 1904), 13.

[17] Ian Ker, *The Catholic Revival in English Literature, 1845–1961* (Notre Dame, Ind., 2003), 75.

[18] Wilfrid Ward, 'Mr Chesterton among the Prophets', *Dublin Review*, 144 (Jan. and Apr., 1909), 1.

he had fully established the intellectual foundations on which the massive oeuvre of his last three decades was to be built. My study is inevitably organised and written in biographical form, though there are differences to be noted from the biographies which have so far appeared. A general biography must inevitably be a kind of catch-all, organising chronologically any material which comes to hand: endearing anecdotes, love letters, holiday reminiscences, the posthumous memories of friends. Much of such material may be of value: but its cornucopian assembly inevitably brings, to a greater or lesser extent, a certain loss of focus on the one part of a writer which is of lasting importance: his writings. In the case of some biographies of Chesterton, his writings can seem like events in his life to be listed with all the other events: they somehow emerge and are published, and contribute to his growing reputation: but as to why they were written, or how they relate to each other as part of a growing corpus which more and more indicates the lineaments of a developing human intellect, hardly more than desultory enquiries have generally been made. With one exception, I have found existing biographies of little help in my own study. The exception, however, is an important one: *Gilbert Keith Chesterton*, by Maisie Ward, itself the principal source (whether acknowledged or not) for all subsequent biographies. This has been an indispensable source to those who have followed for two reasons. First, because of the closeness of biographer and subject. Maisie Ward knew Chesterton and his wife well; her father Wilfrid Ward had become a close personal friend; after his death, she had access to most of Chesterton's friends, who as she sat, notebook in hand, generously showered her with their personal reminiscences. Secondly, this closeness gave her the active cooperation of Chesterton's secretary Dorothy Collins, who acted, in a sense, as a kind of research assistant by making for her 'a selection...of the most important among the immense mass of notebooks and papers'. This was, comments Maisie Ward, 'well and truly done, despite falling bombs and over-warwork'.[19] From this selection, Maisie Ward made her own for the biography itself, often quoting copiously. This process of selection has governed the way in which the Chesterton papers have been used subsequently, for whenever they are quoted, it is generally from Ward rather than directly from the papers themselves. The reasons for this are not hard to understand: in this 'immense mass' of material, then uncatalogued and disorganised, it has been very difficult for

---

[19] *Return*, 4.

a researcher to find their way; even those biographers, like Michael Ffinch, who have worked directly on the notebooks and papers (living, in Ffinch's case, for several weeks in Chesterton's attic in Beaconsfield) have not managed to do more than skim the surface of what they contain, extracting from this lucky dip a valuable new insight here or there.

This situation, however, has now been transformed. After Dorothy Collins's death, nearly all the Chesterton papers were acquired by the British Library and catalogued by Dr R. A. Christophers. Dr Christophers's printed catalogue[20] (which, for instance, lists every item in each of the hundreds of notebooks, page by page) contains over 100 pages of indexes. This substantial labour, it is not too much to say, has established the foundations on which all future Chesterton scholarship will be built; it is now possible to conduct serious enquiries, topic by topic, into what new insights the papers may contain. I have been able to quote at length directly from the papers themselves as well as from Maisie Ward's selection of them, though this has not always been possible since, as Dr Christophers points out, 'it appears that some material, once it was used by Ward or copied into typescript, was not retained'.[21] This could be explained by the fact that the offices of Sheed and Ward (where Maisie Ward worked on the book) sustained a direct hit during wartime bombing, and many papers were destroyed. Whatever the reason, it is not always possible to find passages quoted from Chesterton's papers by Maisie Ward in the British Library's Chesterton collection. This matters less than it might seem. Wherever one can verify Ward's use of the papers, it seems faithful enough (though inevitably, as we shall see, her selection reflects her own perspective); and there is much left for future generations to work on. A good start has been made on the papers by Professor Denis Conlon, who has transcribed and published a good body of poems (mostly in the *G. K. Chesterton Quarterly*) and stories (in volume xiv of the Ignatius Press *Collected Works*): his discoveries include an entire novel, now published separately.[22] This new material is mostly from the 1890s, perhaps the decade with the greatest potential for new discoveries.

The establishment and cataloguing of the British Library's collection has come at a fortunate juncture, for Chesterton scholarship is, in a sense, in its

---

[20] ISBN 0 7123 4677 5.

[21] R. A. Christophers, *The British Library Catalogue of Additions to the Manuscripts: The G. K. Chesterton Papers* (London, 2001), p. x.

[22] G. K. Chesterton, *Basil Howe: A Story of Young Love* (London, 2001).

infancy. Though Gilbert Keith Chesterton died over seventy years ago, little serious work has been done on the implications of his writings. Although, especially in America, his reputation is growing, his works are even now rarely studied in university courses either in literature—despite such judgements as Shaw's of his 'colossal genius'—or theology—despite the clear and established phenomenon of his success as an apologist: Étienne Gilson called *Orthodoxy* 'the best piece of apologetic the century [has] produced'; it brought Dorothy L. Sayers back to Christianity, just as *The Everlasting Man* brought C. S. Lewis to his famous moment of conversion on Headington Hill. Much remains to be done before Chesterton's huge oeuvre can be adequately assessed as a major part of the cultural history of the last century. The academic embargo against recognition of Chesterton's stature remains in place, for reasons which remain a matter of speculation. Thus, despite the current growth of interest in his life and works, when, as late as 2007, the *Oxford Handbook of English Literature and Theology* appeared, it contained no chapter, or even a paragraph, on Chesterton.

Most writers on such a major figure, writing seventy years after his death, would at the outset find it appropriate to describe in some preliminary way an existing body of scholarly writing, to which they have been in some way indebted, and to which their own endeavour was intended either as a response or an addition. With the exceptions I have noted, however, I have not been able to build on any existing scholarly foundation. A handful of useful articles, introductions, even a few books (as well as the biographies already mentioned) have appeared over the years; to these, reference will be made at the appropriate juncture. Apart from Maisie Ward's, one work warrants mention here: Denis Conlon's *G. K. Chesterton: The Critical Judgements* (1976), on which most biographers who have written since it appeared have relied for their understanding of the contemporary response to Chesterton's works (though for obvious reasons, Professor Conlon was unable to include one notable critical essay because of its length, Wilfrid Ward's important thirty-two-page review of *Orthodoxy* in the *Dublin Review*). But there is little else which can be described as indispensable. To a writer whose first book was on Charles Dickens (about whom there was, even then, thirty-five years ago, a massive critical and scholarly literature to take into account), the contrast has been more than merely striking. In some ways, however, this is a situation which has been not entirely without its attractions. Much of this book's available basic materials—manuscript notebooks and correspondence, the diary

Chesterton kept for a short time as a boy, the files of *The Debater* (the magazine he co-founded at St Paul's School) to which he was the most frequent contributor, even, astonishingly, his uncollected journalism (far more extensive in terms of the number of words written than the books published over the same period)—have been (for the most part) either casually dipped into or virtually unused by others; this gives a certain freedom of action and choice to the writer who first draws on these unpublished or uncollected materials to anything like the extent necessary if the story of the growth of this extraordinary and unique mind is adequately to be told. A number of acknowledgements must be made here: above all to Dr Christophers for his catalogue and to the staff of the Manuscripts Room at the British Library for their unfailing courtesy and helpfulness, and to A. P. Watt Ltd on behalf of the Royal Literary Fund, for permission to quote unpublished material from the Chesterton Papers. I am grateful to the staff of the British Library's newspaper library at Colindale, and that of the Bodleian Library. I owe a special debt of gratitude to David Bussey, the archivist of St Paul's School, who not only gave me access to the school's Chesterton archive and carried out research on my behalf in the surviving records of Chesterton's school career, but also arranged for the photocopying of the bound volumes of the full run of *The Debater* magazine I am grateful, too, to Professor Denis Conlon and to Aidan Mackey, both of whom kindly read my typescript and made a number of invaluable suggestions. Finally, I have to thank Ian Ker, who read the book chapter by chapter as I produced its first draft, and who has been unfailing in his wisdom and in his kindness and encouragement.

I

The Man with the Golden Key, 1874–83

I regret that I have no gloomy and savage father to offer to the public gaze as the true cause of all my tragic heritage; no pale-faced and partially poisoned mother whose suicidal instincts have cursed me with the temptations of the artistic temperament. . . . I cannot do my duty as a true modern by cursing everybody who made me whatever I am. I am not clear what that is; but I am pretty sure that most of it is my own fault.[1]

> The ignorant pronounce it Frood,
> To cavil or applaud.
> The well-informed pronounce it Froyd
> But I pronounce it Fraud
>
> ('On Professor Freud')[2]

Gilbert Keith Chesterton was born on 29 May 1874, in Sheffield Terrace, Campden Hill. His father was by profession 'the head' as Chesterton later put it, 'of a hereditary business of house-agents and surveyors'—though signs of heart trouble early in life had led his medical advisers (including a Harley Street consultant) to insist that work could be fatal, and he had withdrawn from the active conduct of the firm's affairs. This probably came as something of a relief to him: Edward Chesterton had always regretted that he had entered the family firm rather than following his own ambition to become an artist; he spent the rest of his life, between occasional visits to the office, pursuing a wide variety of intellectual and artistic pursuits. If he had been a Frenchman, he would have been described as an intellectual; and he was, in this period of the Victorian era, by no means as unusual in this as we might suppose. 'During the second half of the nineteenth century', wrote Gilbert's younger brother Cecil, 'the middle class was absolutely bubbling over with ideas. . . . It was rioting in its new-found intellectual

---

[1] *Autobiography*, 26. [2] *Collected Works*, x. 508.

liberty as heartily as the men of the Restoration rioted in their new-found moral liberty. Everywhere you found households where new theories of politics, philosophy, religion, or science were eagerly welcomed, debated, and assimilated. Most of us have come across dozens of such households. Into such a household . . . G.K.C. was born.'[3]

No. 11 Warwick Gardens, where the family moved when Gilbert was 5, was not by some Kensington standards a large house, but it was clearly a happy one, which had about it an air of solid warmth and expansiveness. Cecil's wife Ada remembered it from a later time, but her description of it probably conveys accurately enough the appearance and atmosphere of the house as it was during much of Gilbert's childhood:

The Chestertons' house in Warwick Gardens, the home of Gilbert and Cecil for years, stood out from its neighbours. As you turned the corner of the street you had a glimpse of flowers in dark green window boxes and the sheen of paint the colour of West country bricks, that seemed to hold the sunshine. The setting of the home never altered. The walls of the dining room renewed their original shade of bronze green year after year. The mantel-board was perennially wine-colour, and the tiles of the hearth, Edward Chesterton's own design, grew more and more mellow.

Books lined as much of the wall space as was feasible and the shelves reached from floor to ceiling in a phalanx of leather. The furniture was graceful, a slim mahogany dining-table, a small sideboard, generously stocked with admirable bottles, and deep chairs.

The portrait of G.K. as a child smiled from a wall facing the fireplace. Walking with his father in Kensington gardens, the fair and radiant beauty of the boy, the flowing curls and graceful poise, held the eyes of the Italian artist, Bacceni, who did not rest until he had conveyed the vision to canvas. . . .

On party nights wide folding doors stood open and through the vista of a warm yet delicate rose-coloured drawing-room you saw a long and lovely garden, burgeoning with jasmine and syringa, blue and yellow iris, climbing roses and rock plants. The walls were high, and tall trees stood sentinel at the far end.[4]

There was a contrast between the image presented by Edward Chesterton to the outside world and the reality of the life he lived behind the dark green window boxes of 11 Warwick Gardens. 'He was known to the world', recalled Gilbert later, 'and even the next-door neighbours, as a very reliable and capable though rather unambitious business man.' But to his sons, Gilbert continued, he was 'the Man with the Golden Key, a magician opening the gates of goblin castles or the sepulchres of dead heroes'.[5]

---

³ Cecil, 6.
⁴ Ada Chesterton, *The Chestertons* (London, 1941), 19–20.   ⁵ *Autobiography*, 38.

Chesterton's father—known affectionately to the family as 'Mister' or 'Mr Ed'—had a huge, and in many ways definitive, intellectual influence on him, and this emerges unmistakably in the opening chapters of the *Autobiography*; but it is necessary to say, before anything else, that this influence was built on the foundation of Gilbert's emotional relationship with both his parents, the depth of which he himself—understandably—implied rather than stated. To acute observers like Edmund Clerihew Bentley— Gilbert's closest friend from the age of 9 until the end of his life—it was very clear. 'Family affection', Bentley wrote, in a memoir published in *The Spectator* immediately after Gilbert's death, '... was the cradle of that immense benevolence that lived in him. I have never met with parental devotion or conjugal sympathy more strong than they were in the exceptional woman who was his mother; or with greater kindliness—to say nothing of other sterling qualities—than that of his father, the business man whose feeling for literature and all beautiful things worked so much upon his sons in childhood.' The spell of 11 Warwick Gardens was felt beyond the family itself: Bentley adds that 'The parents made their home a place of happiness for their two boys' many friends, a place that none of them can ever have forgotten.'[6]

Chesterton's mother was a woman of strong character, and to those who did not know her, of slightly alarming personality. Gilbert's friends found her kind but somewhat forbidding in appearance, 'her clothes thrown on anyhow, and with blackened and protruding teeth which gave her a witchlike appearance'.[7] Marie Louise was not a stickler for order and cleanliness. The house was untidy. More to the point, she did not see it as any part of her duties to teach her boys orderly habits. As Maisie Ward puts it, 'They had not the training that a strict mother or an efficient nurse usually accomplishes with the most refractory. Gilbert was never refractory, merely absent-minded; but it is doubtful whether he was sent upstairs to wash his hands or brush his hair. . . . And it is perfectly certain that he ought to have been so sent several times a day.'[8] He was frequently late for meals, but never rebuked. One has the impression that though, in the words of Annie Firmin, one of Gilbert's childhood playmates, 'Aunt Marie was a bit of a tyrant in her own family',[9] her boys—especially, perhaps, Cecil, to whom

---

[6] E. C. Bentley, signed obituary, *The Spectator* (19 July 1936), 1125–6; Conlon, 525–7.
[7] Ward, 18.   [8] Ibid. 17.   [9] Ibid.

she was closest, just as Gilbert was closest to his father—were treated with a possibly excessive indulgence.

The Chesterton home must have been a magical place for a child to grow up in; and at the centre of it all was the benign and amazingly diverse creativity of Edward Chesterton. On special occasions, Ada Chesterton remembered him hanging up fairy lamps in the garden, 'in absurd and ravishing loops among the flowers and trees'.[10] 'His den or study', remembered Gilbert, 'was piled high with the stratified layers of about ten or twelve creative amusements; water-colour painting and modelling and photography and stained glass and fretwork and magic lanterns and mediaeval illumination.'[11] His many artistic and intellectual activities were described by Gilbert himself as his 'hobbies'; but he emphasised that this was not intended to diminish their dignity or importance: 'A hobby is not a holiday. It is not merely a momentary relaxation necessary to the renewal of work. . . . a hobby is not half a day but half a life-time. It would be truer to accuse the hobbyist of living a double life. And hobbies, especially such hobbies as the toy theatre, have a character that runs parallel to practical professional effort, and is not merely a reaction from it. It is not merely taking exercise; it is doing work.'[12]

'The permanent anticipation of surprise'

Gilbert in later life thought of himself as a bohemian, and this is probably as good a description of his parents as any. Gilbert remembered that his father one day 'remarked casually that he had been asked to go on what was then called The Vestry. At this my mother, who was more swift, restless and generally Radical in her instincts, uttered something like a cry of pain; she said, "Oh, Edward, don't! You will be so respectable! We never have been respectable yet; don't let's begin now." And I remember my father mildly replying, "My dear, you present a rather alarming picture of our lives, if you say that we have never for one single instant been respectable." Readers of *Pride and Prejudice* will perceive that there was something of Mr. Bennet about my father; though there was certainly nothing of Mrs. Bennet about my mother.'[13] Cecil, indeed, claimed of their mother that 'anyone who

---

[10] Chesterton, *The Chestertons*, 20–1.   [11] *Autobiography*, 37.
[12] Ibid. 39.   [13] Ibid. 6–7.

wishes to know from whence G.K.C. gets his wit need only listen for a few minutes to her conversation'; Gilbert, however, makes clear that his father, too, was a humorist of considerable stature:

He was rather quiet than otherwise, but his quietude covered a great fertility of notions; and he certainly liked taking a rise out of people. I remember, to give one example of a hundred such inventions, how he gravely instructed some grave ladies in the names of flowers; dwelling especially on the rustic names given in certain localities. 'The country people call them Sailors' Pen-knives,' he would say in an offhand manner, after affecting to provide them with the full scientific name, or, 'They call them Bakers' Bootlaces down in Lincolnshire, I believe'; and it is a fine example of human simplicity to note how far he found he could safely go in such instructive discourse. They followed him without revulsion when he said lightly, 'Merely a sprig of wild bigamy.' It was only when he added that there was a local variety known as Bishop's Bigamy that the full depravity of his character began to dawn on their minds. It was possibly this aspect of his unfailing amiability that is responsible for an entry I find in an ancient minute-book, of mock trials conducted by himself and his brothers; that Edward Chesterton was tried for the crime of Aggravation. But the same sort of invention created for children the permanent anticipation of what is profoundly called a Surprise. And it is this side of the business that is relevant here.[14]

This permanent anticipation of surprise was induced by Chesterton's father in a number of ways; and it was an aspect of his influence that encouraged what was to become an essential characteristic of Gilbert's adult intellect and imagination. It was at the root of his religious apologetic; and it was the driving force of his almost unconscious tendency towards the unearthing of paradox in apparently unfruitful soil. The expectation that the everyday is the gateway to the unforeseen, that normality is a kind of veil hiding the possibility of surprise, even of wonder, is the underlying theme of the first two chapters of the *Autobiography*; and as I shall show, the contemporary evidence is that, though these features of the Chestertonian imagination were not to become explicit until he was already an established writer in the early years of the twentieth century, and though Chesterton's memories of childhood were written nearly six decades after the period they so vividly evoke, they do convey the reality of what they describe: Chesterton's own version of his childhood is not a semi-fictional reconstruction (as his account of several episodes in his later life can be shown to be) but a sometimes profound meditation on a reality authentically recalled.

---

[14] Ibid. 36–7.

The view through the proscenium arch

The expectation of surprise was by no means the only way in which Chesterton's imaginative and intellectual inclinations were affected by his father's influence; another is represented—and according to Chesterton himself actually formed—by the huge toy theatre (about five feet high) his father made, which Gilbert preserved carefully throughout his life and used later on to give regular performances at the children's parties he gave in Beaconsfield (from which parents were rigorously excluded). The toy theatre symbolised something essential about his childhood that remained always with him as an adult; and at the most obvious level, the reason for this is clear enough. There is no sinister Freudian reason for it; as he insisted himself, 'If some laborious reader of little books on child-psychology cries out to me in glee and cunning, "You only like romantic things like toy-theatres because your father showed you a toy-theatre in your childhood," I shall reply...simply that I associate these things with happiness because I was so happy.... the question [is] why I was so happy.'[15] Cecil Chesterton cites his love of toy theatres simply as a symptom of his 'romanticism'.[16] Chesterton himself, in a passage of self-analysis that has about it the feeling of a long-pondered-over conclusion, takes the subject a good deal more seriously than that. The second chapter of the *Autobiography* opens with his famous vision, inspired by one of his father's toy-theatre performances, of 'The very first thing I can ever remember seeing with my own Eyes': this was 'a young man walking across a bridge' who 'carried in his hand a disproportionately large key of a shining yellow metal and wore a large golden or gilded crown. The bridge he was crossing sprang on the one side from the edge of a highly perilous mountain chasm, the peaks of the range rising fantastically in the distance; and at the other end it joined the upper part of the tower of an almost excessively castellated castle. In the castle tower there was one window, out of which a young lady was looking. I cannot remember in the least what she looked like; but I will do battle with anyone who denies her superlative good looks.' Chesterton makes two very different kinds of point about this memory. The first is the most obvious one: that by means of the toy theatre, his father could transform the home of a house-agent 'living immediately to the north of Kensington

[15] *Autobiography*, 29.   [16] Cecil, 251.

High Street' into 'a glimpse of some incredible paradise' which 'for all I know, I shall still remember...when all other memory is gone out of my mind'. But there is also in Chesterton's analysis a very different kind of perception of the toy theatre's formative intellectual influence on him. It is not simply that it gave him the entry into a fantastic alternative world of the imagination: it is also that it instilled a particular way of perceiving the world of everyday sense:

Apart from the fact of it being my first memory, I have several reasons for putting it first. I am no psychologist, thank God; but if psychologists are still saying what ordinary sane people have always said—that early impressions count considerably in life—I recognise a sort of symbol of all that I happen to like in imagery and ideas. All my life I have loved edges; and the boundary-line that brings one thing sharply against another. All my life I have loved frames and limits; and I will maintain that the largest wilderness looks larger seen through a window.

This 'love of frames and limits' was another essential feature of the Chestertonian imagination; it runs like a leitmotif throughout his intellectual life. Like the expectation of surprise, it was a guiding principle of his mature religious apologetic. It was also at the root of his first fully developed polemical attitude: his intensely anti-imperialist brand of English patriotism. 'An empire', he wrote in an essay published in 1904, is above all 'utterly undefined and unlimited. Not to see how this frustrates genuine enthusiasm is not to know the alphabet of the human heart. There is one thing that is vitally essential to everything which is to be intensely enjoyed or intensely admired—limitation. Whenever we look through an archway, and are stricken into delight with the magnetic clarity and completeness of the landscape beyond, we are realising the necessity of boundaries. Whenever we put a picture in a frame, we are acting upon that primeval truth which is the value of small nationalities.'[17] Gilbert's love of seeing things within a frame can be traced not only to his father's toy theatres but also in one quite specific way to his direct imaginative influence: Gilbert's fascination, throughout his life, with a book for children his father both wrote and illustrated, entitled *The Wonderful Story of Dunder van Haeden*:

One of the sports of the imagination, a game I have played all my life, was to take a certain book with pictures of old Dutch houses, and think not of what was in the pictures but of all that was out of the pictures, the unknown corners and side-streets of the same quaint town.

[17] Lucian Oldershaw (ed.), *England: A Nation* (London, 1904), 16–17.

This indicates a principle which was to become more and more evident to Chesterton: that the function of limitation, of 'frames and limits', was precisely that it made possible the imaginative transcendence of the area thus confined. The point about the frame or the archway was that what could be seen led on to what could be imagined beyond its confines: tangible and definable reality, that is, was the gateway to the intangible and the undefinable. This is a property of Chesterton's imagination which we can without exaggeration describe as quasi-sacramental—a tendency which we can see as being a kind of predisposing factor in what Cecil called the 'drift towards orthodoxy' which was to establish itself in Gilbert's mind during the first seven or eight years of the twentieth century.

Given his father's evident influence over Chesterton's imaginative development, *The Wonderful Story of Dunder van Haeden* is worth some attention at this point:

The book was one my father had written and illustrated himself, merely for home consumption. It was typical of him that, in the Pugin period he had worked at Gothic illumination; but when he tried again, it was in another style of the dark Dutch renaissance, the grotesque scroll-work that suggests woodcarving more than stone-cutting. He was the sort of man who likes to try everything once. This was the only book he ever wrote; and he never bothered to publish it.[18]

Why Chesterton should have thought that his father never bothered to publish his book is something of a puzzle, since it was indeed published, not privately, but by R. Brimley Johnson, a perfectly respectable commercial publisher, in 1901 (in fact, it was Frances, Chesterton's wife, who persuaded her father-in-law to have the book published: the copy with which he presented her is inscribed 'Frances Chesterton, with the author's love, Nov 1901. (All your fault!)'.[19] It is certainly true that at the time Chesterton, a newly successful writer who was already, at an energetic pace, profusely turning out books and articles to keep his head above water financially, had a lot on his mind: but he can hardly have missed the publication by his own father of a book which had meant—and by his own account was to continue to mean—so much to him, providing, as he recalled toward the end of his life, 'one of the sports of my imagination, a game I have played all my life'. What seems clear, though, is that he knew the book not from one of the printed copies but from its original manuscript (now in the British Library's Chesterton collection).

---

[18] *Autobiography*, 36.   [19] Now in the collection of Mr Aidan Mackey.

Whatever the solution of this puzzle, the book itself provides ample explanation not only for Chesterton's fascination with it, but for Edward Chesterton's intellectual and imaginative influence over his sons. We know little about 'Mr Ed' but what Gilbert wrote in the *Autobiography*, and what Cecil wrote in his own book about his brother—much of which, perhaps, we tend to explain away as being due to filial piety. We can see that he was an amusing and lovable man—as Gilbert suggests, rather after the manner of Jane Austen's Mr Bennet. This book, however, establishes something more: that he was seriously talented—an accomplished and painstaking draughts-man (possibly more accomplished, and certainly more painstaking, than his son), and a story teller of charm and imagination.

The Wonderful Story of Dunder van Haeden is a moral tale told with a light touch. Its hero, the father of seven daughters, is not unreminiscent of Mr Ed himself:

> . . . the worthy old man was so learned and clever
> That he always was reading and writing for ever,
> He was busier than any who work at a trade
> And had read all the books that had ever been made.[20]

The 'worthy old man' is writing 'an exceedingly wonderful book', in his study, which appears in the first of the book's eight beautifully drawn pen-and-ink illustrations, a room not unreminiscent of Mr Ed's study as Gilbert describes it: it is untidy, full of piles of books on tables and on the floor: a stuffed stork sits on a small shelf and other curious objects sit on the mantelshelf and on every other conceivable surface. Dunder van Haeden is seated before a huge open volume in which he is writing with a quill pen; he is smoking a large curly pipe and wearing a full-length garment, dark glasses, and a round smoking cap.

His seven daughters, though good and industrious, have a tendency to become noisy and hysterical whenever they make a mistake in their dress-making (by which they make their living):

> So Dunder van Haeden would quietly say
> To his daughters, that if they behaved in that way,
> Some day they would certainly scream off his head;
> He knew before long he should lose it, he said.
> Every shriek made it more and more loose on his shoulders,

---

[20] Edward Chesterton, *The Wonderful Story of Dunder van Haeden* (London, 1902), 1.

> It would come off at last to surprise the beholders.
> And then, if his head from his body they took,
> What was to become of his wonderful book?[21]

Predictably, the daughters continue in their noisy ways

> Till one day when a sister had made some great blunder,
> And the seven all began to shout louder than thunder;
> Then the head of Papa, what I tell you is true,
> Bounced off, and right out of the window it flew.[22]

The illustration facing this is very funny and beautifully drawn. We see one of the Dutch street scenes that Gilbert refers to, that made him 'think not of what was in the pictures but of all that was out of the pictures, the unknown corners and side-streets of the same quaint town'. Gabled houses and an elaborate roofscape with many spires on the left of the picture sit next to a close-up of the gable end of the van Haeden residence, on the right; crowded into one window, we see his seven daughters anxiously looking out; through the adjacent window we see the headless body of their father, seated at his desk with quill pen in hand; flying through the air is his head, still puffing away at his large curly pipe. A crowd (dressed in sixteenth-century costume) look up dispassionately. Interestingly, though Gilbert refers to his father's fascinating volume as 'a certain book with pictures of old Dutch houses', only two of its eight illustrations are street scenes, though one (which shows Dunder van Haeden's head flying back onto his shoulders again after a fairy has noted the girls' penitence) shows a gable and a church spire through the window. The verse on the facing page is as funny as the illustration; the head

> ... came down, to the wonder of all the beholders,
> Went in at the window, and stuck on his shoulders.
> Making no observation upon its alighting,
> He took up his pen and went on with his writing![23]

The tale has its moral ('Now, all little maidens should learn from this song | Not to scream when one thing or another goes wrong'[24]); Gilbert, of course, approved of moral tales for children, insisting that 'It is quite false to say that the child dislikes a fable that has a moral. Very often he likes the moral more than the fable.'[25]

---

[21] Edward Chesterton, *The Wonderful Story of Dunder van Haeden* (London, 1902), 5.
[22] Ibid. 7.　　　[23] Ibid. 13.　　　[24] Ibid. 18.　　　[25] *Autobiography*, 42.

'Literary Composition among Boys'

Dunder van Haeden undoubtedly captured Gilbert's imagination, and it is interesting for that reason; it is even more interesting, perhaps, for what it tells us about the mind and personality of Edward Chesterton. It is not simply the fact that his father wrote, drew, and painted (and made toy theatres and all the other things he created) which helps to explain why Gilbert should have wanted to write and draw from his earliest years; just as important, perhaps, was the fact that he did these things *well*. Even more important was a rather different feature of his father's intellectual influence over him, what Bentley meant when he referred to his 'feeling for literature and all beautiful things', which 'worked so much upon his sons in child-hood'. Most important of all, perhaps, was the fact that he read to him constantly before he could read for himself and then, when he could read, that he encouraged him to learn lengthy passages—particularly of poetry—by heart.

The idea has grown up among Chesterton's biographers that he was a backward child who learned to read unusually late. This notion probably originates with Maisie Ward, who states baldly that there was from his unusual childhood 'a result often to be noted in the childhood of exceptional men: a combination of backwardness and precocity. Gilbert Chesterton was in some ways a very backward child . . . He learnt to read only at eight.'[26] She gives no evidence for this; and it has to be said that there is good evidence directly to the contrary, which not only suggests that he was reading well before the age of 8, but which strongly indicates that he was writing stories at the latest by the age of 6 and probably sooner, and quoting poetry that he had learned by heart not long afterwards. By the age of 8, he was writing tidily in cursive script; there has survived an exercise book[27] which belongs either to his early days at prep school or (more likely) to the period immediately before it. Inside the cover, in the handwriting of Dorothy Collins, Chesterton's secretary, is inscribed 'With Miss Seamark | 8 years old' (information she was presumably given by Chesterton himself). Joseph Pearce assumes that Miss Seamark must have been Gilbert's form mistress at his prep school, Colet House; but contemporary evidence and later memoirs (such as those of H. A. Sams) do not suggest that Colet

---

[26] Ward, 14.   [27] BL MS Add. 73315A.

House was any different from other prep schools of the period in having an exclusively male teaching staff. It is much more likely that Miss Seamark was a private tutor, engaged by Edward Chesterton to teach Gilbert at home. The exercise book contains, among other exercises, a number of neatly written passages taken down from dictation; this alone disproves the notion that he was at this age still struggling to read. Spelling mistakes are underlined by Miss Seamark; some are then corrected by Gilbert:

Under this new feeling he built the church of St Michael at Scone and founded a Monstry there; driven by a tenpest to Acmona Isle, in gratitude for his presishalion and for his manetenance by the hermets he dedicated a church there to St Colomb
Monastery Monastery Monastery
Preservation, preservation,
Hermits, Hermits, Hermits,
Hermits, Hermits, Hermits

The book also contains exercises in grammar: for instance, 'Words which tell what anything does, or what is done to it, or in what state it is, are called Vearbs.' Later on, the verb 'to be' is written out in full, in its present, past, future, present perfect, and past perfect tenses. Other contents include the English counties with their principal cities. This exercise book gives an interesting insight into the disciplined nature of elementary education at the period; it also allows a comparative dating of three of Gilbert's notebooks which contain stories from different earlier periods, the earliest (judging by spelling and handwriting) being from two or even three years before the exercise book. There survives evidence, however, of creative endeavour taking place even earlier than that.

In 1892, when he was 18, Gilbert was to read a paper to the St Paul's School 'Junior Debating Society', which he had helped to found, entitled 'Literary Composition among Boys'. According to the Society's record of the event, 'He said that a creative instinct exists in [every child, who] has . . . a series of imaginary characters, whose proceedings he details at enormous lengths, while the desire to let off one's feelings in the form of composition, he said, comes somewhat later.'[28] Fifteen years earlier—in other words, when he was 3 years old—this 'desire to let off [his] feelings in the form of composition' was already expressing itself in the form of a swashbuckling story concerning a boy called 'Kids', which his Aunt Rose took down from little Gilbert's dictation, and faithfully preserved. It is

---

[28] G. K. Chesterton, 'Literary Composition among Boys', *The Debater*, iii. 89.

divided into two chapters; in the first he kills a giant (there are also boars and dragons). The second chapter, entitled 'The Boyhood of Kids', begins, 'He was dressed for fun in armour, with a short dagger by his side, and his father thought it would only be for fun, but Kids marched off and you could not see him except like a little speck a 100 miles off in the army. He fought and conquered.'[29]

The earliest surviving written composition by Gilbert (probably aged 5 or 6) appears to be a story entitled 'The Rolling Stone', and it demonstrates, among other things, a familiarity with the layout of printed books. It begins, on the notebook's first left-hand page, with a large, chaotic pencil drawing of several huge dragons confronting a tiny man in a long swallow-tailed coat, wielding an axe. Underneath, in large untidy capitals, is the caption: 'HE RASED HIS AXE', and below that, in larger capitals, the word 'FONTISPEECE'. On the right-hand page and overleaf, also in ill-formed capital letters, is the following:

THE ROLING STONE
AND OTHER TALES
CHAPTER I

TOMTAP GOT UP THE NEXT MORNING AT IV OCLOCK HE TOOCK WITH HIM A STICK ANDWENT OUT IN THE SNOW (IT WAS WINTER TIME). WHEN HE GOT A LITTLE WAY HE HAD NOTHING POTICULER TO DO HE WAS KICKING A STONE ALONG THE ROAD FOR AMEWSMENT WHEN IT WENT TO FAR AND IT WAS GOING DOWN A VALY AT TH BOTOM OF WHITCH WAS A CAVE I MUST NOT LET IT GO IN THERE SED HE AND HE RAN AS FAST A HE COOD AND SLIPED ON A BIT OF ICE AND ROLD DOWN THE VALY AND INTO THE HOLE AFTER THE STONE. WHEN HE GOT THERE HE FOUND HIMSELF

Here, the written story ends: but on the right-hand page opposite is a well-drawn illustration of a large monkey sitting on the branch of a tree, holding a round object and looking fiercely down at a small boy who is looking up at him. Underneath this is the caption:

R
'HE GASPED THE STONE'[30]
∧

Gilbert's childish imagination was undoubtedly fed not only by what he read, but also—perhaps even particularly—by what he learned by heart. His father, he recollected in the *Autobiography*, 'knew all his English literature

[29] G. K. Chesterton, 'The Story of Kids', *G. K. Chesterton Quarterly*, 1 (Oct. 1996), 1.
[30] BL MS Add. 73314B.

backwards, and . . . I knew a great deal of it by heart, long before I could really get it into my head. I knew pages of Shakespeare's blank verse without a notion of the meaning of most of it; which is perhaps the right way to begin to appreciate verse. And it is also recorded of me that, at the age of six or seven, I tumbled down in the street in the act of excitedly reciting the words,

> Good Hamlet, cast this nighted colour off,
> And let thine eye look like a friend on Denmark,
> Do not for ever with thy veiled lids
> Seek for thy noble father in the dust,

at which appropriate moment I pitched forward on my nose.'[31] It is likely that Gilbert at this age understood more than he claimed: the *Autobiography* has a persistent tendency towards retrospective self-underestimation; this may demonstrate an admirable humility but can be irritating to anyone attempting to discover the facts. Gilbert was also learning Latin by heart as well as Shakespeare, and though what may be the only known childhood attempt to quote it—in the second of his surviving early stories—may be incorrect in nearly every word, the quotation is still identifiable, and the story it inspired indicates that he had understood its meaning well. Like the earlier story already quoted, this one shows a familiarity with the organisation of printed books; judging by the handwriting (in slightly less chaotic upper and lower case lettering), it can be dated about six to nine months after 'The rolling stone', that is, at about the same period as the incident just quoted, which took place 'at the age of six or seven':

THE WANDERING MONKEY
CHAPTER I

> Sytere tu patulie
> Reculans sublegmine fugi
> virgil

O! the life of a monkey is wild O! he lives in the wood O! he ravages bird's nests O! the forests of tall parms and Orang trees such is the life of a monkey as he swings in the trees O! such was the life of the hero of my story he was sitting on a bough with his mother when he slipt and fell his mother did not see him fall and went off there he lay on the moss the tall pines waving above him and the beechs shedding their

---

[31] *Autobiography*, 12.

nuts like hail on him when a hand seized him he shrieked but was carried shrieking out of the forest he was brought to and taken to the zoological gardens where he was put in a cage

CHAPTER II

> stone walls do not a prism make
> nor iron bars a cage
> minds innocent and quiet take
> this for a hermitage
> if I have freedom in my love
> and in my sole am free
> angels that hover in the air
> know no shuck liberty

At the zoological gardens he was treated well and enjoyed myself. One day a respectable Rev put his finger in my cage which of couce was bitten

CHAPTER III
MASTERY

> he captured many thousand guns
> he wrote the great before his name
> and ageing only left his sons
> the recollection of his shame

Though at first they enjoyed themselves they soon got tired.[32]

Here the story ends; like most of Gilbert's childhood attempts, it peters out before coming to any conclusion: to adapt his one-sentence third chapter, at this age, when writing, though at first he enjoyed himself, he soon got tired. But the story does show that he was learning passages by heart, and that he was understanding them. His quotations are not, of course, correct. Incorrect quotation was a habit that persisted throughout life, and its explanation was always the same: that he was drawing from his vast memory and never verified his quotations: what is remarkable, perhaps, is that he got so many right. The passage from Virgil (from the opening two lines of the Eclogues) should read

> Tityre, tu patulae
> Recubans sub tegmine fagi

[32] BL MS Add. 73314A.

This means 'O Tityrus, you who lie beneath the covering of a beech': this must have suggested the first chapter of 'The Wandering Monkey', in which Gilbert's hero is seized, lying beneath 'the beechs shedding their nuts like hail'. His quotation from Richard Lovelace's famous poem 'Stone walls do not a prison make' (even more relevant to the story) is similarly flawed: 'angels that hover in the air', for instance, should be 'Angels alone that soar above'. Again, Gilbert's quotation bears all the marks of imperfect recollection of a passage learned by heart, of which, nevertheless, the general gist has been understood.

By the age of 6 or 7, then, he was learning passages of poetry by heart; he had already begun a habit which persisted throughout his youth and into his early manhood, of endlessly scribbling fragments of stories interspersed with sketches, normally in pencil. A little later, as well as stories he began to write verse; later still, little essays. And above all, he was expanding his imagination by reading avidly. His brother Cecil remembered that 'Reading, no less than discussion, was in the air of his home, and from his childhood he was a voracious reader. His memory was . . . almost as astounding as Macaulay's, and he always had pages of his favourite authors stored in his head. His taste, then as now, was always for the romantic school: Shakespeare, Dickens, Scott (both prose and verse), Macaulay, were the writers he devoured, I think, most eagerly in his boyhood.'[33] He was particularly attracted by Scott's romantic historical ballads: he later remembered 'running to school in sheer excitement repeating militant lines of "Marmion" ';[34] he was also fascinated by Macaulay's *Lays of Ancient Rome*.[35]

We do not know how early he was reading Macaulay's and Scott's historical poetry, but it could have been quite early, possibly before he went to prep school at 8 or 9 years old: certainly, we know of one very notable example of his close reading of verse in the same genre, which in one juvenile poem, possibly written about the age of 8,[36] strikingly influenced his own writing to the point of direct imitation. His inspiration for the poem was *Lays of the Scottish Cavaliers* (1849) by William Edmondstoune Aytoun, a romantic conservative and passionate Jacobite. *Lays of the Scottish Cavaliers* was vastly popular among readers of all ages throughout

---

[33] Cecil, 23–4.   [34] *Autobiography*, 67.   [35] Ibid. 12.

[36] I have been unable to find the manuscript of this poem in the British Library's Chesterton collection; but according to Maisie Ward, 'the very immature handwriting and curious spelling mark it as early'. She herself seems to assume that it belongs to the period before Gilbert went to prep school at 8 or 9 years old; the correctness of this impression is confirmed by a comparison with the spelling of the exercise book quoted on p. 26 above.

the second half of the nineteenth century—especially in Scotland, but in England too; it went into a new edition every year for thirty-two years. Its appeal is obvious: the ballads offer swashbuckling adventure, blood and glory, high ideals, heroism, and betrayal, themes which Gilbert was to relish all his life. One poem from the *Lays* that Gilbert clearly read was 'The Execution of Montrose', a poem about the dramatic end of James Graham, Marquess of Montrose, who opposed the alliance between the Scottish Covenanters and the Parliamentary forces at the beginning of the English Civil War, and joined King Charles at Oxford in 1643. The Covenanters put a price on his head, dead or alive. Early in 1645, Montrose led a successful campaign against his old enemy, Archibald Campbell, Marquess of Argyll. After years of military campaigning (during which he became a heroic figure throughout Europe) he was defeated and betrayed to the Covenanters. Montrose was taken to Edinburgh, driven by the hangman in a cart through the streets, and hanged at the Mercat Cross on 21 May 1650. His betrayal, death, and manner of dying became a Jacobite legend; as Aytoun chronicled it,

> ... when [Montrose] came, though pale and wan,
> He looked so great and high,
> So noble was his manly front,
> So calm his steadfast eye;—
> The rabble rout forebore to shout,
> And each man held his breath,
> For well they knew the hero's soul
> Was face to face with death ...
>
> [Then] onwards—always onwards,
> In silence and in gloom,
> The dreary pageant laboured,
> Till it reach'd the house of doom ...
> Then, as the Graeme looked upwards,
> He met the ugly smile
> Of him who sold his King for gold—
> The master-fiend Argyle![37]

The Jacobite politics of all this, of course, were not at all in accordance with the Gladstonian liberalism of the Chesterton household, of which even at this age Gilbert was clearly aware. 'The childhood of G.K.C.', states Cecil

---

[37] William Edmonstoune Aytoun, 'The Execution of Montrose', in *Lays of the Scottish Cavaliers* (Edinburgh, 1849), 36–7.

(himself an infant at the time), 'coincided more or less with the St. Martin's Summer of Liberalism, from 1880 to 1885 [Cecil was born in 1879]. Political controversy was so much in the air of the household that even as an infant he must have heard echoes of that last stand of Gladstonian Liberalism.'[38] What is interesting is that at the age of 8 or 9 Gilbert himself should not only absorb the political atmosphere of the household, but it should directly affect his own writing, so that, though he clearly enjoyed the blood and thunder of Aytoun's ballads, when it came to writing his own ballad under Aytoun's influence, he rather impressively inverted their political content:[39] throughout his childhood and (as we shall see) his schooldays, Gilbert was a fierce and polemical young anti-Jacobite. In his own ballad, the heroic James Graham becomes 'false Montrose', and Archibald Campbell, for Aytoun 'the master-fiend Argyle', becomes Gilbert's warrior hero. There is a religious dimension to note: Montrose, though not himself a Catholic, was something of a hero amongst Catholics: Aytoun quotes 'the eulogy pronounced upon him by the famous Cardinal de Retz... "Montrose, a Scottish nobleman, head of the house of Grahame... has sustained in his own country the cause of the King his master, with a greatness of soul that has not found its equal in our age".'[40] Gilbert's ballad shows, among much else, how very early in his life not only contemporary liberal politics, but the anti-papist views which sometimes (but by no means inevitably) accompanied them, were being absorbed by him from the endless discussion that was 'in the air of the household';[41] the spelling of the poem (reminiscent of the exercise book already quoted) confirms the impression that it could date from around 1882, when he was 8 years old:

> Sing of the great Lord Archibald
> Sing of his glorious name
> Sing of his covenenting faith
> And his evelasting fame.
>
> One day he summoned all his men
> To meet on Cruerchin's brow

---

[38] Cecil, 23.

[39] Cecil claims nevertheless that 'though Mr. Chesterton must have been tolerably familiar with religious and political controversies almost before he could speak, it can hardly be supposed that he had developed ideas of his own on these subjects until well on in his schooldays'. Gilbert's 'Scottish' ballad may prove him wrong (Cecil was himself only 3 or 4 when Gilbert wrote it). Ibid. 9–10.

[40] Aytoun, *Lays*, 29–30.   [41] Cecil, 9.

Three thousand covenenting chiefs
Who no master would allow . . .

And he creid (his hand uplifted)
'Soldiers of Scotland hear my vow
Ere the morning shall have risen
I will lay the trators low. . . .

Onward let us draw our clamores
Let us draw them on our foes
Now [w]hen I am threatened with
The fate of false Montrose.

Drive the trembling Papists backwards
Drive away the Tory's hord
Let them tell their hous of villians
They have felt the Campbell's sword. . . .

And we creid unto our master
That we'd die and never yield.
That same morn we drove right backwards
All the servants of the Pope
And Our Lord Archibald we saved
From a halter and a rope
Far and fast fled all the Graemes
Fled that cursed tribe who lately
Stained there honour and thier names.[42]

The realism of fairyland

What Gilbert was reading at this period, apart from Aytoun, must for the
most part be a matter of conjecture. Macaulay and Scott possibly (though
perhaps not until his schooldays). We know that he was learning passages of
Shakespeare by heart. He was also reading 'voraciously'; what else did he
read? He mentions having loved as a child *The History of Sandford and Merton*,
by Thomas Day, a collection of didactic stories about a very good child
called Harry Sandford and a naughty, disobedient, untruthful, lazy child
called Tommy Merton. The stories are a blend of adventure, practical
information, and moral teaching: at the end of the book, Tommy Merton
resolves to improve himself; no wonder Gilbert, with his love of stories with
a moral at the end, responded to Thomas Day's.[43] Probably somewhat later
(perhaps when he was 11 or 12) he read Charles Dickens and W. S. Gilbert:

[42] Ward, 21–2.   [43] *Autobiography*, 42–3.

at his first meeting with Bentley at prep school, he mentions that they talked
about literature: perhaps, he surmises, Dickens or the *Bab Ballads*.[44] In his
account of the same event in a letter to his fiancée, Frances, he specifies
Macaulay's *Lays of Ancient Rome*.[45] Apart from these hints, little firm evidence is to be had about what he read as a child, particularly before he went
to school. But one key milestone is clearly visible through the mist. We do
know that possibly the most important of all his childhood reading—
infinitely more important, certainly, than the likes of *Lays of the Scottish
Cavaliers*—was the Scottish writer George MacDonald. Certainly, this was
his own assessment in 1924, over forty years later: 'I for one', he wrote in the
introduction to MacDonald's biography by his son, 'can really testify to a
book that has made a difference to my whole existence, which has helped
me to see things in a certain way from the start; a vision of things which
even so real a revolution as a change of religious allegiance has substantially
only crowned and confirmed. Of all the stories I have read, including even
all the novels of the same novelist, it remains the most real, the most realistic
in the sense of the phrase the most like life. It is called *The Princess and the
Goblin*.'[46] Any book thus described has to be given more than passing
attention by anyone seeking to trace the growth of Chesterton's imaginative
and intellectual life.

George MacDonald's story evokes the same world of fantasy, adventure,
and moral certainty as Gilbert's memory of the Prince crossing the bridge in
one of Mr Ed's toy-theatre performances; even the plot and scenery are
similar: it has a Princess in a castle who has to be rescued; the castle is set on
'the edge of a highly perilous mountain chasm'. The perils of the castle,
however, come chiefly from a race of hideous and unspeakably wicked
goblins who live beneath the ground, and who are plotting to enter the
castle by means of a tunnel they are constructing, so that they can seize the
Princess and force her into marriage with the repulsive goblin prince,
Harelip, heir to the goblin throne: this abduction would, it is made clear,
involve the infliction on the Princess of unspeakable cruelties. The goblins
are also plotting to divert the course of an underground stream into the
workings of a mine, so that the miners, their natural enemies (who are as
virtuous as the goblins are depraved), will all be drowned.

[44] *Autobiography*, 56.
[45] Ward, 91–2.
[46] Introduction to Greville M. MacDonald, *George MacDonald and his Wife* (London, 1924), 9.

The King, Princess Irene's father (or 'King-papa'), has left her in the castle with a small household, under the care of a nurse and what seems on the face of it to be woefully inadequate protection; but Irene is protected by a magical fairy great-great-grandmother who lives in the attic, and who, despite her great age, has the beauty of a girl in her twenties. This fairy grandmother carries most of the weight of the story's underlying theme. *The Princess and the Goblin* is before anything else a parable about faith and unbelief. The fairy grandmother reveals herself only to those who are ready to believe in her existence, and even then is accessible only when she chooses. This leads even the Princess into momentary doubts: having failed to find her magical attic room again after her first discovery of it, 'sometimes she came almost to the nurse's opinion that she had dreamed all about her; but that fancy never lasted very long. She wondered very much whether she should ever see her again.'[47]

The story's brave Prince is Curdie, the son of a miner, whose heroic status is earned by his courage and acumen. George MacDonald makes it clear that high rank has to reflect not only bravery and virtue but also deeper moral qualities, including the capacity for self-examination and penitence; thus, Curdie having realised that he has been unjust to Irene by refusing to believe her stories of her grandmother and her magical powers, MacDonald democratically grants him princely status—because he has asked for forgiveness, 'you see there is some ground for supposing that Curdie was not a miner only, but a Prince as well'.[48] (In the sequel, *The Princess and Curdie*, he and Irene eventually become King and Queen.)

Belief in the fairy grandmother, Irene learns, means maintaining faith in and obedience to her, even when all the evidence seems to indicate that safety lies in some other course. The grandmother has woven from spiders' webs a thread so thin that it is invisible; this she has attached to the end of a ring which she gives to Irene, in such a way that it will always be there to guide her in time of danger. 'But remember', says the fairy grandmother, 'it may seem to you a very roundabout way indeed, and you must not doubt the thread. Of one thing you may be sure, that while you hold it, I hold it too.'[49]

In due course, the Princess's faith in the thread is sorely tried. When Curdie is in danger, having been captured by the goblin King and Queen,

---

[47] George MacDonald, *The Princess and the Goblin* (London: Puffin Classics, 1996), 28.
[48] Ibid. 200.
[49] Ibid. 119.

the fairy grandmother uses the thread to send Irene to the rescue, deep underground. At first, 'as she went farther and farther into the darkness of the great hollow mountain, she kept thinking more and more about her grandmother. . . . And she became more and more sure that the thread could not have gone there of itself, and that her grandmother must have sent it.' But the thread leads her to a huge heap of stones, through which it vanishes: 'For one terrible moment she felt as if her grandmother had forsaken her. The thread . . . had gone where she could no longer follow it—had brought her into a horrible cavern, and there left her! She was forsaken indeed!'[50] But she soon recovers, removes the stones, finds Curdie and leads him to safety. The goblins are in the end destroyed when the waters they have diverted to drown the miners are diverted back into their own underground kingdom; but not before they have terrifyingly broken into the castle from below. Again, Irene is preserved by her magical grandmother's protection and all ends happily.

What is it about this story which so affected Chesterton that, over four decades later, he could write that *The Princess and the Goblin* 'made a difference to my whole existence', and that it 'helped me to see things in a certain way from the start; a vision of things which even so real a revolution as a change of religious allegiance has substantially only crowned and confirmed'? What was this 'vision of things'? One obvious answer is suggested by MacDonald's use of the magic thread as a symbol for the contradictory nature of religious discernment—for the way in which the eye of faith so often leads in the opposite direction to that suggested by merely human instinct or reason. The central theme of MacDonald's story was thus consistent with other features of Gilbert's developing imagination that we have noted—the expectation of surprise and the 'love of frames and limits' which lead the mind on to realities beyond what can be immediately perceived—in helping to build up the counter-intuitive instinct which lies behind so much of Chesterton's adult controversial writing.

Chesterton himself appears at first to explain the appeal of *The Princess and the Goblin* rather differently (though consistently with what I have suggested), by identifying in this 'parable' what we have already seen from other sources to be a recurrent imaginative theme of his childhood: the imbuing of the everyday with magical properties, the turning of the Golden Key. Nevertheless, it is important to understand that this perception of

[50] George MacDonald, *The Princess and the Goblin* (London: Puffin Classics, 1996), 154–5.

the commonplace as gateway to magical realms is an essential part of the meaning of the fairy grandmother's thread; as Chesterton puts it in *The Victorian Age in Literature*, MacDonald 'could write fairy-tales that made all experience a fairy-tale. He could give the real sense that every one had the end of an elfin thread that must at last lead them to paradise.'[51] The essential breakthrough in perception is to see that there is a direct line of communication between the imprisoned world of everyday sense and another imaginative dimension in which anything might happen, a dimension that has the power to transform the element in which we ourselves must continue to move:

When I say [*The Princess and the Goblin*] is like life, what I mean is this. It describes a little princess living in a castle in the mountains which is perpetually undermined, so to speak, by subterranean demons who sometimes come up through the cellars. She climbs up the castle stairways to the nursery or the other rooms; but now and again the stairs do not lead to the usual landings, but to a new room she has never seen before, and cannot generally find again. Here a good great-grandmother, who is a sort of fairy godmother, is perpetually spinning and speaking words of understanding and encouragement. When I read it as a child, I felt that the whole thing was happening inside a real human house, not essentially unlike the house I was living in, which also had staircases and rooms and cellars.

MacDonald's fairy story differs from others, Chesterton argues, 'in achieving this particular purpose of making the ordinary staircases and doors and windows into magical things'. Not only doors and windows were thus transmuted: 'Another recurrent image in his romances was a great white horse; the father of the princess had one. . . . To this day I can never see a big white horse in the street without a sudden sense of indescribable things.' But there is more to be said:

the picture of life in this parable is not only truer than the image of a journey like that of the Pilgrim's Progress, it is even truer than the mere image of a siege like that of The Holy War [Bunyan's second spiritual chronicle]. There is something not only imaginative but intimately true about the idea of the goblins being below the house and capable of besieging it from the cellars. When the evil things besieging us do appear they do not appear outside but inside. Anyhow, that simple image of a house that is our home, that is rightly loved as our home, but of which we hardly know the best or the worst, and must always wait for the one and watch for the other, has always remained in my mind as something singularly solid and unanswerable; and was more corroborated than corrected when I came to give a more

---

[51] *Collected Works*, xv. 487.

definite name to the lady watching over us from the turret, and perhaps to take a more practical view of the goblins under the floor.[52]

At the risk of labouring the point, it is probably worthwhile to register in passing that this later identification of the protective fairy grandmother with the Blessed Virgin Mary, and of a 'more practical view' of how to deal with one's inner goblins (sacramental confession), was what he meant when he spoke of MacDonald's story as giving him 'a vision of things which even so real a revolution as a change of religious allegiance has substantially only crowned and confirmed'.

MacDonald, clearly, occupied a uniquely personal position in Chesterton's developing imaginative and spiritual life. In an article written about a quarter of a century before his 1924 analysis of *The Princess and the Goblin*'s meaning for him, he had expressed his sense of the higher truth of George MacDonald's imaginative world, in a way which seems to refer as much to himself as to his subject: the ordinary moral fairy tale, he argued, 'is an allegory of real life. Dr MacDonald's tales of real life are allegories, or disguised versions, of his fairy tales. It is not that he dresses up men and movements as knights and dragons, but that he thinks that knights and dragons, really existing in the eternal world, are dressed up here as men and movements. It is not the crown, the helmet or the aureole that are to him the fancy dress; it is the top hat and the frock coat that are, as it were, the disguise of the terrestrial stage conspirators.'[53] This may or may not be true of George MacDonald: it could hardly—in the year that it was written (1901)—be bettered as a description of the attitude to contemporary society of the young controversialist who was then emerging into the public arena with such panache, swordstick in hand.

'The white light of wonder'

The fairy grandmother of *The Princess and the Goblin* transforms the lives of those whom she protects by two sorts of guidance, both of which are invested by MacDonald with equal symbolic weight. There is the invisible thread; there is also a kind of supernatural lamp, which in times of danger shines out, through the walls, from the attic in which the grandmother lives.

---

[52] Introduction to MacDonald, *George MacDonald and his Wife*, 9–11.

[53] G. K. Chesterton, 'George MacDonald and his Work', *The Daily News* (11 June 1901).

When Irene is lost on the mountain in total darkness, terrified by grotesque creatures, 'She looked up, and for a moment her terror was lost in astonishment. At first she thought the rising moon had left her place . . . but she soon saw that she was mistaken, for there was no light on the ground at her feet, and no shadow anywhere. But a great silvery globe was hanging in the air; and as she gazed at the lovely thing, her courage revived.'[54] MacDonald's magical guiding light retained its potency for the adult Chesterton, not simply as a memorable visual image but as a symbol of transcendent truth, of something 'solid and unanswerable': 'Since I first read that story', he wrote in 1924, 'some five alternative philosophies of the universe have come to our colleges out of Germany, blowing through the world like the east wind. But for me that castle is still standing in the mountains and the light in its tower is not put out.'[55]

There is a sense in which we can see Chesterton's whole childhood as having been filled by the symbolic light he saw inextinguishably shining from MacDonald's mountain fortress. The early chapters of his autobiography seem to be full of the memory of it; and Chesterton's evocation of this light-filled childhood, six decades later—an account entirely devoid of sentimentality or false nostalgia—is written with such conviction that we cannot fail to see that if we are to understand the sources of his imaginative life, we must take his childhood as seriously as he did himself:

To me my whole childhood has a certain quality, which may be indescribable but is not in the least vague. . . . [it] was of quite a different kind, or quality, from the rest of my very undeservedly pleasant and cheerful existence.

Of this positive quality the most general attribute was clearness. Here it is that I differ, for instance, from Stevenson, whom I so warmly admire; and who speaks of the child as moving with his head in a cloud. He talks of the child as normally in a dazed daydream, in which he cannot distinguish fancy from fact. Now children and adults are both fanciful at times; but that is not what, in my mind and memory, distinguishes adults from children. Mine is a memory of a sort of white light on everything, cutting things out very clearly, and rather emphasising their solidity. The point is that the white light had a sort of wonder in it, as if the world were as new as myself; but not that the world was anything but a real world. . . . There was something of an eternal morning about the mood.[56]

[54] MacDonald, *Princess*, 107–8.
[55] Introduction to MacDonald, *George MacDonald and his Wife*, 11.
[56] *Autobiography*, 44–5.

The *Autobiography* was Chesterton's last book; it appeared after his death. For the most part, it tells us little, directly, about the course of his life. The anonymous reviewer of the *Times Literary Supplement* rightly commented that though it was one of his best books, he was not the ideal autobiographer, since 'the proper autobiographer is an egoist': '[Chesterton] recalls with pleasure his schoolmates; he gives the liveliest pictures of his friends . . . and the interesting public figures he encountered . . . what he is shy of producing is himself.'[57] Except, it has to be said, for two important chapters: that in which he recalls the spiritual crisis he underwent during his time at the Slade School of Art; and the book's second chapter, about his childhood, by common consent the best part of the book. This important chapter is at the heart of Chesterton's quest in the *Autobiography* for the understanding of his own life; indeed, there is a sense in which the rest of the book is mostly an entertaining way of filling up the pages. It vividly conveys his conviction that it was from the rediscovery of the clarity and solidity of his childhood perceptions, of what he elsewhere calls the 'white light of wonder'[58]—which he remembers as playing on the toy theatre and all the other keys to the opening of his mind—that his adult vision of life sprang forth as from an underground source. His account of his crisis at the Slade shows him emerging from a time of confusion and darkness by means of what seems at first to be a new discovery, but which turns out after all to be the re-emergence of something he has always known: as he recalls it, it seemed to him that 'At the back of our brains . . . there was a forgotten blaze or burst of astonishment at our own existence. The object of the artistic and spiritual life was to dig for this submerged sunrise of wonder; so that a man might suddenly understand that he was alive, and be happy.'[59] The *TLS* reviewer of the *Autobiography* concluded that 'The other articles of the Chestertonian creed fall into place once this ruling principle of "wonder in all things" . . . is firmly grasped'.[60] But he was thinking, not of the 20-year-old Chesterton's relieved discovery that after all he was an optimist, but of a key passage in his later evocation of early childhood:

I have never lost the sense that this was my real life; the real beginning of what should have been a more real life; a lost experience in the land of the living. It seems

---

[57] Unsigned review, *Times Literary Supplement* (7 Nov. 1936); Conlon, 540.
[58] *Autobiography*, 46.
[59] Ibid. 91–2.
[60] Unsigned review, *Times Literary Supplement* (7 Nov. 1936); Conlon, 542.

to me that when I came out of the house and stood on that hill of houses, where the roads sank steeply towards Holland Park, and terraces of new red houses could look out across a vast hollow and see far away the sparkle of the Crystal Palace (and seeing it was a juvenile sport in those parts), I was subconsciously certain then, as I am consciously certain now, that there was the white and solid road and the worthy beginning of the life of man; and that it is man who afterwards darkens it with dreams or goes astray from it in self-deception. It is only the grown man who lives a life of make-believe and pretending; and it is he who has his head in a cloud.[61]

Hence, the loss of the innocence of childhood, for Chesterton, means more than a mere sinking into the sins and compromises of adult life: it means also a fatal loss of clarity of vision. Innocence is thus to be recovered by confronting evil, not only with a soul protected from corruption by purity of heart, but also, and above all, with a mind focused by clarity of discernment and imagination: it is the Chestertonian paradox at the root of the Father Brown stories, in which it is the truly innocent man who has both the greatest knowledge of evil, and the greatest power to overcome it. Chesterton understood Christ's injunction to become 'as a little child' as being not a commandment to withdraw from adult reality but, on the contrary, a charge to confront life's complexities in such a way as to transcend them: above all, for Chesterton, this confrontation involves the perception of life with that 'white light' of childhood 'on everything, cutting things out very clearly'. Marshall McLuhan's judgement here is to the point: 'For the Victorians, the nursery was the only tap-root connecting them with psychological reality. But for Chesterton the rhetoric and dimensions of childhood had also their true Christian vigour and scope.'[62] Chesterton's account of the death of St Thomas Aquinas suggests itself irresistibly; for here, in his vision, was a great Christian mind whose involvement in theological controversy had towards the end of his life induced in him a longing for 'the inner world . . . in which the saint is not cut off from simple men', and whose intellectual grasp of great realities had led him, at the last, to the clarity and innocence of the child: 'In the world of that mind there was . . . a just and intelligible order of all earthly things, a sane authority and a self-respecting liberty, and a hundred answers to a hundred questions in the complexity of ethics or economics. But there must have been a moment, when men knew that the thunderous mill of thought had stopped suddenly; and that after the shock of stillness that wheel would shake the world no more . . . and the confessor, who had been with him in the inner chamber, ran forth as if in fear, and whispered that his confession had been that of a child of five.'[63]

[63] *Collected Works*, ii. 510–12.

2

School Days: St Paul's and the JDC, 1883–92

It is uncertain when Chesterton's schooldays began.[1] When, later, he went on to St Paul's School, he was in the same class as boys who were mostly one or two years his junior: this may indicate that it was later than was normal—perhaps when he was around 9 years old—that he was sent to Colet House. This was a preparatory school founded in 1881 at the request of the great F. W. Walker, High Master of St Paul's, by Samuel Bewsher, the school's Bursar.[2] The first headmaster of Colet House was Samuel Bewsher's brother James; in its early years the school was generally known simply as 'Bewsher's'. James Bewsher was seen by the boys as an essentially benign figure, but the eccentric 'Sammy' seems to have been a more sinister character: according to Digby D'Avigdor (later to be a friend of Chesterton's) this melodramatically Dickensian personage 'would come in, cane in hand, crash it down on the desk and exclaim loudly, "Now then"'.[3] Another friend remembered that he 'used to see him going a round of the

---

[1] Most of his biographers (except Maisie Ward, who is wisely silent on the matter) confidently give dates varying from 1880 when he was 6 years old to 1883 when he was nearly 9. Alzina Stone Dale says he went to Colet House in 1880; the school, however, was not founded until 1881. The fact is that we do not know.

[2] According to Maisie Ward (p. 23), Colet Court (as the school became known in 1891) 'is not technically *the* preparatory school for St Paul's': but this was only the case in its very earliest years. It was always intended to serve St Paul's, as its name (after the founder of the school, John Colet) indicates (until 1891 it was known as Colet House). According to H. A. Sams (*Pauline and Old Pauline* (Cambridge, 1933), 4), 'the facts that Mr Bewsher was known to be the Bursar of the big School and that the teaching in his "Prep" school was known to be on identically the same lines as those of St Paul's, gave his school a very great advantage ... Mr Bewsher never claimed that his school had any connection with St Paul's.' Nevertheless, its status soon became official, and when the school moved to new premises in 1890, the boys entered through a Gothic arch over which were carved the words 'St Paul's preparatory school'.

[3] *Return*, 13.

classes with a cane, picking out a boy here and there for questions about the work in hand, and dealing him a few hearty whacks if the replies were unsatisfactory'.[4]

Bewsher's, all the same, does not seem to have been an unduly inhumane establishment; and much of the teaching was imaginative and intelligent: 'The masters at "Bewsher's"', wrote H. A. Sams (another St Paul's friend),

stand out as vividly as those at St Paul's. Monsieur Devaux was French master who afterwards succeeded at St Paul's Paul Blouet, the witty author of *Drat the Boys*, among other amusing books. One day he took a batch of boys to the Hammersmith Baths. On the way back he told them about the Franco-Prussian War, in which he himself had fought not so many years before. Then there was Mr Birch, who in spite of his sinister name was a kindly martinet with mutton-chop whiskers. He introduced us to Greek and somehow robbed it of its terrors. Thanks to him, most of us, I think, imbibed a liking for that musical language expressed in its clear characters.[5]

'Most of us', perhaps; but not Chesterton, whose later reminiscences of his schooling begin with a diatribe against what he was taught at Bewsher's of the 'clear characters' of the Greek language, the 'small letters' at least, which seemed to him 'quite nasty little things, like a swarm of gnats'.[6] His explanation was significant, and explains a good deal about his later school career:

I believe that the explanation is that I learnt the large Greek letters, as I learnt the large English letters, at home. I was told about them merely for fun while I was still a child; while the others I learnt during the period of what is commonly called education; that is, the period during which I was being instructed by somebody I did not know, about something I did not want to know.[7]

It was towards the end of his time at Bewsher's that he met his greatest friend, Edmund Clerihew Bentley.[8] It was a memorable meeting for Chesterton:

When I first met my best friend in the playground, I fought with him wildly for three quarters of an hour; not scientifically, and certainly not vindictively (I had

---

[4] Edmund Clerihew Bentley, *Those Days* (London, 1940), 54.

[5] Sams, *Old Pauline*, 7.

[6] *Autobiography*, 53.

[7] Ibid. 54.

[8] Chesterton does not say whether he met Bentley at Bewsher's or at St Paul's, but Bentley seems to have no doubt that they met at prep school (Bentley, *Those Days*, 47).

never seen him before and I have been very fond of him ever since) but by a sort of inexhaustible and insatiable impulse, rushing hither and thither about the field and rolling over and over in the mud. . . . When we desisted from sheer exhaustion, and he happened to quote Dickens or the Bab Ballads, or something I had read, we plunged into a friendly discussion on literature which has gone on, intermittently, from that day to this.[9]

This is the account he gave half a century later in the *Autobiography*; it is more or less corroborated by the account he gave his fiancée Frances in a long autobiographical letter written about fifteen years after the event:

one day, as he was roaming about a great naked building land which he haunted in play hours, rather like an outlaw in the woods, he met a curious agile youth with hair brushed up off his head. Seeing each other, they promptly hit each other simultaneously and had a fight. Next day they met again and fought again. These Homeric conflicts went on for many days, till one morning in the crisis of some insane grapple, the subject of this biography quoted, like a war-chant, something out of Macaulay's *Lays*. The other started and relaxed his hold. They gazed at each other. Then the foe quoted the following line. In this land of savages they knew each other. For the next two hours they talked books. They have talked books ever since.[10]

Bentley had no precise memory of this occasion when he wrote his own memoirs, some years after Chesterton's death; but he 'had not the least doubt that we did signalize our instinctive liking for each other in the way that is usual among mammals of tender years—by struggling and tumbling about in imitation of a hostility that only the death of one of us could terminate. But the puppy stage cannot have lasted long: it must very soon have been followed by the opening of a conversation that was to last, with the minimum of interruption, for seven or eight years.'[11]

There was, though, about these puppyish struggles, something that was to persist into that long literary conversation—a certain 'inexhaustible and insatiable' vigour. The important thing to understand is that at the time they met, books did not occupy for either of them a different universe of the mind from their 'rushing hither and thither about the field and rolling over and over in the mud': reading was for them a natural boyhood activity, one as voraciously to be enjoyed, at the age of 12, as any other. Chesterton, as we have seen, had been for at least two or three years (and probably more) a habitual reader, and by the time he met Bentley was probably already

---

[9] *Autobiography*, 56.   [10] Ward, 91–2.   [11] Bentley, *Those Days*, 46.

unusually widely read for his age. As we have seen, apart from George MacDonald, W. E. Aytoun, and one or two others, we know little in detail of what he was reading when he went to school; but as he grew older, he read more and more avidly. Cecil Chesterton recalled that 'His taste . . . was always for the romantic school. Shakespeare, Dickens, Scott (both prose and verse), Macaulay, were the writers he devoured, I think, most eagerly in his boyhood. I do not think that he gave much attention to contemporary or even to later Victorian writers. Swinburne caught him in his later school-days; Browning, I believe, later still; Tennyson I do not believe he ever fully appreciated.'[12] This comes from Cecil's anonymous assessment, published in 1908, of his brother's literary achievement thus far; it has a photograph of Gilbert,[13] aged about 13, looking fiercely into the camera lens and some-what self-consciously holding a book; it was probably intended as a characteristic pose.

His schoolboy literary discoveries were not made alone, but with friends, and particularly with Bentley. It was not only books they shared, but the life of 11 Warwick Gardens, with its constant pageant of creative amusements, initiated in the early years by Mr Ed, but more and more by Gilbert himself. Throughout their boyhood, he and Bentley were to-gether most of the time; when they were not, they corresponded, 'at a length', Bentley remembered in later years, 'that now seems miraculous'.[14] Gilbert's earliest surviving letter to Bentley was written when he was 14:

November 10th 1888
11 Warwick Gardens
Dear Bentley,
Oh Yes! Oh Yes! Oh Yes! Know all whom it may concern that it is nearly certain that the festive gathering you wot of will be held on the Saturday following the end of the holidays. The tableaux we have arranged on will most probably include among others King John signing Magna Carta, Dream of Richard III, St George and the dragon, etc.
I am not on the whole sorry it is to be on the Saturday, as we have not too much time to prepare the Tableaux.
I am,
Your grovelling serf, villein and vassal,
G. K. Chesterton

---

[12] Cecil, 23–4.   [13] Cecil, facing p. 60; see also Ward, facing p. 25.
[14] Bentley, *Those Days*, 45.

Putting up a smokescreen

There is a conundrum about Gilbert's schooldays: why was it, when from his earliest years he was so fascinated by the world of books, so interested in ideas, that he was so resistant to being educated by others? From the beginning, Chesterton was perceived to be unusually unreceptive to instruction. It was at Bewsher's that one of the masters delivered the famous judgement: 'You know, Chesterton, if we could open your head, we should not find any brain, but only a lump of white fat.'[15] Both at this time and later at St Paul's, there tended to be on Gilbert's part, in the classroom at least, the erection of a kind of mental barricade against revealing any sign of intellectual enthusiasm. Only the most gifted masters, Chesterton remembered later, 'ever got past my guard in this matter'. One of them, Mr T. Rice Holmes, 'managed, heaven knows how, to penetrate through my deep and desperately consolidated desire to appear stupid; and discover the horrible secret that I was, after all, endowed with the gift of reason above the brutes. He would suddenly ask me questions a thousand miles away from the subject in hand, and surprise me into admitting that I had heard of the Song of Roland, or even read a play or two of Shakespeare.' There was for all the boys, but for Chesterton, perhaps, to an unusual degree, 'a horror of showing off':[16]

I can remember running to school in sheer excitement repeating militant lines of Marmion with passionate emphasis and exultation; and then going into class and repeating the same lines in the lifeless manner of a hurdy gurdy, hoping that there was nothing whatever in my intonation to indicate that I distinguished between the sense of one word and another.[17]

Digby D'Avigdor remembered that 'He meandered through school like a rudderless bark. *He put up a smokescreen over his real interests.* I remember him called up to construe. Standing up he would sway backwards and forwards, his head bowed over a hopelessly ragged book. He would hold it in one hand and clutch it with the other to prevent it disintegrating. He would construe adequately enough—but he would do the minimum. You wouldn't think he had an ounce of poetry in him.'[18]

'Almost all the anecdotes of his childhood', wrote his brother Cecil, turn on the fact that he was 'incredibly absent-minded'.[19] Once, his schoolmates

---

[15] *Return*, 12.   [16] *Autobiography*, 66.   [17] Ibid. 67.
[18] *Return*, 13–14. My italics.   [19] Cecil, 10.

filled his pockets with snow; he simply did not notice.[20] One school friend remembered him 'striding untidily along Kensington High Street, smiling and sometimes scowling as he talked to himself, apparently oblivious of everything he passed; but in reality a far closer observer than most, and one who not only observed but remembered what he had seen'.[21]

This tendency to create for himself a kind of private space, from which he could emerge and to which he could return at will, was not one he ever outgrew. Once he had been seized by a train of thought, the reality of the material world could without warning fade into oblivion. Such anecdotes are told of him not only in childhood but throughout his life. One of his friends once saw him

emerge from Shoe Lane, hurry into the middle of Fleet Street, and abruptly come to a standstill in the centre of the traffic. He stood there for some time, wrapped in thought, while buses, taxis and lorries eddied about him in a whirlpool and while drivers exercised to the full their gentle art of expostulation. Having come to the end of his meditations, he held up his hand . . . and returned to Shoe Lane. It was just as though he had deliberately chosen the middle of Fleet Street as the most fruitful place for thought.[22]

This legendary absentmindedness, suggests Ian Crowther,[23] demonstrates that 'here was a true contemplative, given (as few people are) to the habit of prolonged and concentrated thought'. It was a habit whose origins Maisie Ward correctly locates in Chesterton's childhood: 'I suppose it was in part the keenness of the inner vision that produced the effect of external sleepiness and made it possible to pack Gilbert's pockets with snow; but it was also the fact that he was observing very keenly the kind of thing that other people do not bother to observe. All the time he was seeing qualities in his friends, ideas in literature, and possibilities in life. And all this world of imagination had, on his own theory, to be carefully concealed from his masters.'[24]

The genius of St Paul's

It has become customary to say that the school to which Chesterton proceeded not long after his first meeting with Bentley (he moved to the 'big school' in January 1887) contributed little to his intellectual formation.

---

[20] Ward, 26.   [21] Ibid. 25.   [22] *Return*, 72–3.
[23] Ian Crowther, *Chesterton* (London, 1991), 11.   [24] Ward, 26.

Both at Bewsher's, and later at St Paul's, Chesterton's consistent resistance to 'what is commonly called education' has become generally assumed, and was certainly his own reminiscence. It was also his brother's, who evokes 'a picture of a tall, thin, rather good-looking boy . . . passionately fond of reading, covering all his school-books with drawings till the printing was unrecognisable, delightfully indifferent to ordinary schoolwork, and quite equally indifferent to athletics'.[25]

The truth about his schoolwork (though not about his indifference to athletics) was probably more complex. Where a teacher was able to engage his attention, he was capable enough of absorbing knowledge by the normal processes of formal education. Nor did he entirely manage to hide his intellectual calibre from those who taught him. But for most of his school career, he was an enigma to them. He went to St Paul's when he was 13, 'and stayed there some five years, interesting the more intelligent masters by his mental originality, and irritating the stupider ones by his refusal to take the routine of the place seriously'.[26] There is about his half-yearly form reports, from his first year at St Paul's to the time he left at the age of 18, an impression of a certain suppressed irritation:

December 1887. Too much for me; means well by me, I believe, but has an inconceivable knack of forgetting at the shortest notice, is consequently always in trouble, though some of his work is well done, when he does remember to do it. He ought to be in a studio not at school. Never troublesome, but for his lack of memory and absence of mind.
July 1888. Wildly inaccurate about everything; never thinks for two consecutive moments to judge by his work: plenty of ability, perhaps in other directions than classics.
December 1888. Fair. Improving in neatness. Has a very fair stock of general knowledge.
July 1889. A great blunderer with much intelligence.
December 1889. Means well. Would do better to give his time to 'modern' subjects.
July 1890. Can get up any work, but originates nothing.
December 1890. Takes an interest in his English work, but otherwise has not done well.
July 1891. He has a decided literary aptitude. But does not trouble himself enough about school work.
December 1891. Report missing.

---

[25] Ibid. 10. [26] Cecil, 10.

July 1892. Not on the same plane with the rest; composition quite futile, but will translate well and appreciate what he reads. Not a quick brain, but possessed by a slowly moving tortuous imagination. Conduct always admirable.[27]

Nevertheless, by July 1891 (when his form master thought that he did 'not trouble himself enough at school work') he had made enough academic progress in at least one subject to win a school prize, a *Dictionary of Roman and Greek Antiquities*. This volume has survived; on its flyleaf is the school's bookplate, printed 'Apposition [the school's name for its annual prize-giving ceremony] 1891', and inscribed 'G. K. Chesterton. French prize. Sixth form (A). Midsummer'.[28] 'I did not see you at the apposition,' he wrote to Bentley at the beginning of the long vacation, 'though I went up into the gallery, but I hear from Oldershaw that you saw me. I received a Dictionary of Antiquities for a prize—a very useful and interesting book to have, if not precisely light reading for a holiday.'[29]

The school's direct academic contribution to Chesterton's intellectual formation was probably greater than he himself later remembered. But the real genius of St Paul's at this period was more intangible than his school reports indicate. Certainly, its academic reputation was high, and was built on its solid achievement in scholarships to Oxford and Cambridge. But this was more than an intellectual forcing house: there was about the place a quite unique atmosphere and character, for which its High Master, the great F. W. Walker, was largely responsible. Walker was something of a prodigy: at Corpus Christi, Oxford, he took a first in classics and a first in literae humaniores (though only a second in mathematics); he then proceeded to gain postgraduate scholarships in Sanskrit and law. He was elected Fellow and Tutor of Corpus, and was called to the Bar at Lincoln's Inn. At the age of 29, he was elected High Master of Manchester Grammar School; eighteen years later, he became High Master of St Paul's, the only other school whose headmaster bore this splendidly grandiose title. He was a close friend of the legendary Master of Balliol, Benjamin Jowett, and his status as an

---

[27] Ward, 28.

[28] Aidan Mackey, 'Books from G. K. Chesterton's Library' (unpublished), item 124. Aidan Mackey comments: 'Dorothy Collins always firmly denied to me that Gilbert knew any French other than an odd word or two—because he had told her that. My pointing out that his books, perhaps especially *Chaucer*, show a good familiarity with the language, and that he had brilliantly translated a sonnet by du Bellay (see the *Collected poems*) could not shake her. She was not to know that in 1990 I was to discover two more of his translations from the French. The existence of this prize volume puts the matter beyond doubt... MORAL: Believe anything that G. K. Chesterton tells you—unless he's talking about himself.'

[29] BL MS Add. 73191, fo. 21.

eminent Victorian was reflected in a cartoon by Spy. Cecil Chesterton's memory of him is worth quoting at length: he was, wrote Cecil,

a man who left a deep impress of his personality, not only on the school over which he presided, but also on the characters of all those who came into contact with him. He was one of those forceful characters that instinctively suggest greatness. He was, I believe, a very fine scholar; he was certainly a remarkable organizer, and the school, moulded by his hands, won triumph after triumph. But it was neither scholarship nor organizing capacity that one thought of in connection with him; it was mere bigness and irresistible natural power. His head was leonine, and his voice, when raised in anger, was not unlike the roar of a lion. His geniality was scarcely less deafening than his wrath. His laughter, in particular, used to make the corridors rock, and it was currently believed that it could be heard at Hammersmith Broadway. I have sometimes wondered whether some reminiscence of his old High Master may be traced in Mr Chesterton's description of the huge personality of the terrible 'Sunday' . . . [30]

'He was the sort of man', wrote Chesterton in the *Autobiography*, 'who may live in anecdotes, like Dr Johnson; indeed, he was not unlike Dr Johnson.'[31]

The school he moulded was very unlike the other great public schools of the day. He saw it as no part of his purpose to train the prosperous middle class in the manners and deportment of the gentry. When one prospective parent wrote to enquire as to the social standing of the boys at St Paul's, he famously replied, 'Madam, so long as your son behaves himself and his fees are paid, no questions will be asked about his social standing.'[32] Corporal punishment in his time (in sharp contrast with the regime of his predecessors[33] and with public school practice elsewhere) was rare, though not entirely unknown. Occasionally, in serious cases, there were 'whackings' (carried out by the head porter) though never in public; but as Bentley remembered, 'any master would have regarded it as discreditable to himself if he could not maintain discipline in his own room without the use of the cane; and as far as diligence in learning was concerned, the idea that boys should be terrorised into it was practically dead'.[34] He added that this gave 'a complete answer to the whacking theory of education, for the period was the most brilliant in the history of St Paul's from the academic point of view'. The school in Walker's time was also entirely free of the public school cult of sporting prowess, so humiliating to the unathletic, and with such possibilities for the regimentation of the boys' free time.

---

[30] Cecil, 10–11.   [31] *Autobiography*, 68.   [32] Ibid.
[33] Bentley, *Those Days*, 55.   [34] Ibid. 54.

This comparatively relaxed regime was precisely what Gilbert needed; here, he could develop in his own way, uncrushed by a public school system designed to produce rulers for the empire. The school under Walker established a tradition, which continued well into the twentieth century, of nurturing creative and original minds. Its list of famous old boys is unusually rich in literary and artistic talent: Chesterton and Bentley, naturally; the poets Laurence Binyon and Edward Thomas; the novelist Compton Mackenzie; the artist Paul Nash; the philosopher Isaiah Berlin; the great horn player Denis Brain.[35] Even its solitary military man, Bernard Law Montgomery, was in his own way an anti-establishment figure. This unique Pauline ethos was the product of two main factors. The first was the genius of Walker himself, who created a school in his own image, one in which unconventional personalities could flourish. 'Mr Walker', remembered Cecil, 'could be a sufficiently stern and even terrible disciplinarian when he liked, but he had in his nature vast reserves of good humour and tolerance. Also there was in him a touch of unconventionality; he lived the kind of life he liked, and not the kind of life a schoolmaster was expected to live. With a little change in his circumstances he might almost have been a Bohemian. He had a shrewd sense of human character and a keen eye to types of talent alien from his own. He always liked G.K.C and prophesied great things of him.'[36]

Walker's unconventional personality dovetailed with the other major fact about St Paul's that made it entirely congenial to a personality like Gilbert's: that it was a day school and not a boarding school. This fact was crucial to his development for more than one reason. The first reason has been largely ignored by his biographers, perhaps because most of them have had no personal experience of what it is like to be sent away to a boarding school at the age of 8 or 9. Being sent to day schools spared Chesterton what would surely have been—for a contemplative, sensitive, unathletic, highly eccentric boy suddenly withdrawn from a secure and loving home and placed in what would undoubtedly have been for him the emotional desert of a repressively conformist and possibly quite brutal English boarding school—a major traumatic shock from which he might in time have partly recovered, but which also might well have undermined forever his essentially warm and secure personality.

---

[35] This is not to say that the school in pre-Walkerian days had no creative and original old boys; they include Thomas Gresham (founder of then Royal Exchange), John Milton, Samuel Pepys, Judge Jeffreys, Edmond Halley (the astronomer), and Benjamin Jowett, Master of Balliol.

[36] Cecil, 11–12.

Instead, he found himself in a benign environment during the day, from which he returned to his intelligent, literate, and affectionate parents in the evening and over the weekends. He described the effect of this combination of influences in an unpublished history (written when he was about 20) of the Junior Debating Club, which he founded in his sixteenth year together with his two closest friends. As we shall see, this was an event of crucial importance to his intellectual development; and, as he realised himself, it could really not have been achieved anywhere else:

In the atmosphere of St Paul's is found little echo of the dogma of the High Master of Christ's Hospital. 'Boy! The school is your father! Boy! The school is your mother! . . . Friendships formed in this school have a continual reference to home life, nor can a boy possibly have a friend long without making the acquaintance and feeling the influence of his parents and his surroundings. . . . The boys' own amusements and institutions, the school sports, the school clubs, the school magazine, are patronised by the masters, but they are originated and managed by the boys. The play-hours of the boys are left to their several pleasures, whether physical or intellectual, nor have any foolish observations about the battle of Waterloo being won on the cricket-field, or other such rather unmeaning oracles, yet succeeded in converting the boys' amusements into a compulsory gymnastic lesson. The boys are, within reasonable limits, free.[37]

'Don't you wish that you were me?'

The intellectual atmosphere of the home life of Chesterton and his friends is interestingly captured in a 'dramatic diary', kept tantalisingly briefly, mostly during the school holidays of December 1890 and January 1891, when he was 16. The diary begins by describing the arrival of his friend Oldershaw at the Chesterton home, for a rehearsal of a dramatisation, by Gilbert, of Scott's novel *Woodstock*:

December 30
Wednesday 2–15. 11. Warwick Gdns. Enter Oldershaw in superb hat and waterproof (The usual greetings pass. The superb hat and waterproof are hung up.)
Your Humble Servant. (loq.) Langdon coming?
Old. Yes. He said he'd be here about 2.30.
Y.H.S. Bentley—
Old. Is not coming.

---

[37] Ward, 24.

Y.H.S. No. he has accepted to go down to his uncle's. What are you laughing at?
Old. Bentley will do his duty at the performance but declines to come to rehearsals.
Y.H.S. Bentley hates anything systematic. So do I.
Old. (with terrific solemnity) You admit that it is necessary to be so
Y.H.S. Oh yes. Implicitly. I only say I hate it. I have just finished 'Philip'
Old. Do You like it?
Y.H.S. Yes very much. As well as anything of Thackeray's I have read except Esmond. The villain Dr Brand Firmin is splendid. So are the mean people, the Twysdens,
Old. Oh, Thackeray is so—
Y.H.S.—Cynical—I never can see that—(here ensues an argument on the imputed cynicism of the author of Vanity Fair, into which we need not go, the end of which is a compact never to mention the name of Thackeray again that afternoon)
Old. Well, shall we rehearse.
Y.H.S. All right, I'll go and get the foils.[38]

Thackeray's alleged cynicism had already arisen as a topic in the Junior Debating Club, which had been formed a month or two before (as club secretary, Oldershaw recorded that 'the matter being put to the vote he was exculpated from the charge of Cynicism by 6 to 4 votes'[39]).

After that Wednesday's rehearsal, Chesterton wrote to the absent Bentley:

You were not the only individual unavoidably absent from Wednesday's rehearsal.
     Towards the end of the evening I had a note from Langdon-Davies, announcing that his sister had the chicken-pox, and on Thursday evening, when I was at Oldershaw's, the latter gentleman received another note stating that that the great L.D. was a victim to the same reverse of fortune and would be unable to take the part.
     The books I had for Christmas were all satisfactory, with the slight objection that three of them were given me twice, in different editions and by different people on the same day. Two of these, however are remediable, being replaced by 'The Newcomes,' and Poems by Stopford A. Brooke.
     The books of which I received duplicates were (1) 'Our Mutual Friend, which I regret to say I have never before read. (2) 'Philip', by Thackeray, which I have just read, and like as well as anything by the author outside Esmond. (3) Shelley's Poetical works, which I wanted to possess.[40]

Discussions about books and ideas among this circle of friends seem to have been continuous whenever they were together. The Diary shows them talking, endlessly; and mostly, but not exclusively, they discuss literature and

---

[38] BL MS Add. 73317A, fos. 5–6.   [39] *The Debater*, ii. 96.   [40] BL MS Add. 73191.

history: 'walking home discuss Roman Catholicism, Supremacy, Papal, v. Protestant Persecutions. [Your Humble Servant] arrives at 11 Warwick Gdns. . . . Conversation about Frederick the Great, Voltaire and Macaulay.' And then: 'Cheerful and enlivening discourse on Germs, Dr Koch, Consumption, & Tuberculosis.'[41] When Chesterton's cousin Johannes comes to stay, they discuss the Bible:

> Johannes was showing me his Bible, which he reads every night, a duty I observe with less regularity, I fear, but with equal pleasure. Johannes plods religiously through a list of minute directions in the Epistle to Timothy. Y.H.S., I fear, skips about to the parts he likes best, the Book of Ruth, the Psalms & the Revelation. The other night I read Johannes the lament of David over Saul and Jonathan, the grandest poem I have ever read, & last night the vision of Ezekiel, the valley of dry bones, & thought what a marvellous allegory it was & what a splendid text it would have been for a preacher in a fallen & corrupt society just before a general revolution, such as the Church before the Reformation, or France before the Revolution. 'Can these bones live?' and I answered & said 'Lord, thou knowest'. My people never forced me, when a child, to read the Bible as a lesson, a sagacious plan I have known adopted by parents, to awake in their children a deadly & eternal loathing of the Scriptures, but let me find out the beauty of them for myself, & the consequence is, I am very fond of them. Johannes and Y.H.S. in bed discuss sleep, Coleridge & Bulwer Lytton till nearly 12 o'clock after which we agree to make a practical experiment of the first-named subject of conversation & sink into the arms of Morpheus.[42]

The diary was written some months after a development which Cecil described, with no exaggeration, as 'the most important event of [Gilbert's] school career, so far as its influence on his own future is concerned': the formation of the Junior Debating Club, or JDC. The official school debating society was open only to members of the highest form, the eighth; so Chesterton, Bentley, and the third member of Gilbert's inner circle, Lucian Oldershaw ('boys', wrote Chesterton, 'wander in threes'[43]), formed a society of their own. Its original purpose was to discuss Shakespeare, but this restricted remit was inevitably soon abandoned, and the JDC became a general debating society. What is striking now is the extraordinary seriousness with which its members (at first confined to twelve) regarded it. It was at the centre of their lives. As well as the main club, there were associated clubs for other activities: a Chess Club, a Naturalists' Society, a Sketching Club. As well as all this, a lending library was formed: each JDC member

---

[41] BL MS Add. 73317A, fo. 20.   [42] Ibid., fos. 50–1.   [43] *Autobiography*, 58.

drew up a list of books to which he had access, and Lawrence Solomon as Librarian compiled from these a catalogue and devised a system whereby books could be ordered and safely returned; a similar process was devised for the circulation of magazines. The JDC was more like an alternative culture than a debating society. One boy was expelled for rowdy conduct but asked to be readmitted, saying, 'I feel so lonely without it.'[44]

When they had all grown up, an annual JDC dinner (with humorous menus designed by GKC) was for some years held for former members and their bemused wives. Printed menus, toast lists, and guest lists survive for the years 1899, 1900, 1901, 1913, and 1925.[45] Maisie Ward (who was able to record the memories of several former members) comments that for Chesterton the JDC became a 'symbol of the ideal friendship. They were the Knights of the Round Table. They were Jongleurs de Dieu. They were the Human Club, through whom and in whom he had made the grand discovery of Man. They were his youth personified.'[46] But the club was more important even than that: its proceedings were for him an intellectual crucible; it is not too much to say that the JDC (and, just as importantly, its magazine, *The Debater*) represented for him the kind of intensive intellectual apprenticeship which is for most people served only at university. A good deal of his time was now spent, either in preparing papers to be read to the weekly Friday afternoon meetings, or in writing poetry and prose of various kinds for the magazine, literary activities to which he gave a degree of dedication only intermittently directed towards his formal schoolwork. Other JDC members got more out of normal academic education, and went on to successful university careers. Nevertheless, the JDC seems to have been just as powerful a continuing influence on many of them; Frances Chesterton recorded one of the club reunions over a decade later, when Chesterton was 30 years old and a brilliantly successful journalist and man of letters:

Words fail me when I try to recall the sensation aroused by a JDC dinner. It seems so odd to think of these men as boys, to realise what their school life was and what a powerful element the JDC was in the lives of all. And there were husbands and wives, and the tie so strong, and the long, long thoughts of schoolboys and schoolgirls fell on us, as if the battle were still to come instead of raging round us.[47]

---

44 Ward, 31.   45 BL MS Add. 73303B, fos. 161–194.
46 Ward, 31.   47 Ibid. 149.

The club was taken seriously enough by its members; but there was about its proceedings, too, a certain note of youthful—indeed, characteristically Chestertonian—festivity. These were, in one way, very solemn and exceedingly precocious young men; but they were also teenage boys, with teenage boys' appetites; as Sams recalled:

Picture a dozen healthy, boisterous schoolboys, beginning to leave their boyhood and to bud into young manhood, twelve apostles of Letters, straining at the leash on Friday afternoons and listening for the Head Porter to ring the big bell, which meant Liberty till 9.30 on Monday morning, the joyous release at five o'clock, the brisk walk with a pal or two to the House of our host for the evening, the gathering round a well-laden board, the pleasing consumption of cups of tea and of various sweet and sticky cakes, the chaffing and the joking, the gradual subsidence into a semblance of order, the running facetiae on a too serious paper, the gentle rebuke of our one and only G.K.C., the pleasing feeling that we had a holiday till Monday morning (forgive this repetition) and that . . . there was nothing to mar our happiness; the rush of high spirits following the restraint, if any, imposed by the meeting; the walk home, again with a pal as far as he could go. Picture all this and you will have some idea of the JDC. . . . We were definitely keen on knowing more about 'Letters' than we were likely to gather at School. But we were not going thereby to deprive ourselves of a thoroughly good weekly 'beano'.[48]

At these 'beanos' there would also be singing; invariably, the club song, to the tune of 'Clementine', would be roared out:

> I'm a Member, I'm a Member, Member of the JDC,
>   I'll belong to it forever,
> Don't you wish that you were me?[49]

A poem recited at a JDC dinner at Pagani's Restaurant in the mid-1890s (when most of his fellow members were still at university, and when Chesterton himself had just begun work as a publisher's assistant) nostalgically recalled the JDC's unique combination of high spirits and intellectual passion:

> Am I once again discussing all the old entanglements
> Education, socialism, papers, pigs, advertisements
> Whether fox-hunting is Christian, whether magazines do harm,
> Whether Kipling has a mission, whether Maidlow has a charm,
> Whether it is quite in order if a fluent speech and able
> Is pronounced by Mr Fordham from beneath the dining table,
> Whether Mr Langdon-Davies can be technically right

---

[48] Sams, *Old Pauline*, 46.
[49] Michael Ffinch, *G. K. Chesterton: A Biography* (London, 1986), 27.

> In addressing the debaters with a head obscured from sight
> What is our true constitution, if a club we really be
> Or a mission, or a madhouse or a chartered company.[50]

Oldershaw was the moving spirit not only behind the formation of the JDC itself, but also behind *The Debater*, of which he inevitably became editor (as well as being club secretary). Oldershaw, Chesterton remembered later, 'brought into our secrets the breath of ambition and the air of a great world'. He was the son of an actor, had travelled more than his friends, had been to other schools, knew more of 'life'. 'Above all', said Chesterton, 'there possessed him, almost feverishly, a vast, amazing and devastating idea, the idea of doing something; of doing something in the manner of grown-up people, who were the only people who could be conceived as doing things.'[51] There is about the whole enterprise an engaging combination of schoolboy lightheartedness and extreme solemnity. This was 'doing something in the manner of grown-up people': 'we wish to point out', wrote Oldershaw in his first editorial, 'that the term "junior" does not apply to the members in the positive degree, but to the club in a degree to clubs already started. For this reason, in fact, we would not call the journal the "Junior Debater," as that would certainly suggest juvenile immaturity in the individual composers.'[52]

The paper was produced, as one might expect, on a shoestring. At first, it was produced on a duplicator, though after two issues, the momentous decision was taken for it to be printed (later, when bound copies were made up, the first two issues were specially printed so that the first volume should be complete). Contributions were typed, Chesterton recorded in the *Diary*, by 'a typewriting female by name Miss Davidson, who represents herself as striving frantically to "keep" her bill "under the pound" to which sum it will, apparently, rise by some unbending natural law. First number comes out. Printing bad but matter good enough. Sale good.' Miss Davidson, however, soon proved unsatisfactory, and Chesterton himself—some form of typewriter having been acquired—undertook to replace her. The paper was managed by the paper's three prime movers:

Miss Davidson being a fraud, an autocopiist is bought, and I am hired by Oldershaw to copy out MSS. at 5s. a month, a salary which I subscribe back to the paper, having no money (except errant sixpences) to subscribe. . . . A private and unofficial

---

[50] BL MS Add. 73303B, fos. 143–4; *Collected Works*, x. 286.
[51] *Autobiography*, 61.   [52] *The Debater*, i. 2.

triumvirate of Old. Bentley & myself meet in Old's top bedroom, have uproarious larks & manage the whole thing ourselves. It is becoming quite like a secret and treasonable press & a libellous parody on Hiawatha by Bentley certainly tends to give it that character. 2nd number out. Printing better but not perfect. Sale good. I contributed essay on Spenser & 1st ch of a Jacobite story.[53]

Chesterton was, from the outset, seen by the other members as the JDC's inspiration and leading light, and presided over its proceedings as chairman. As Bentley put it, 'G.K.C. was, because we insisted on his being, the Perpetual Grand of that small lodge of Apollos; the club centred in his personality.'[54] Oldershaw told Maisie Ward that the members of this small group 'would have done anything to get the first place with Gilbert'; it was, of course, always clear who occupied this coveted position: 'our jealousy of Bentley was overwhelming.'[55]

'A literary faculty which might come to something'

Chesterton was *The Debater*'s most prolific contributor, though others—especially the other two founder members—were nearly as regular. One considerable undertaking (unusually, since most contributions were signed) was carried out anonymously, and apparently by more than one hand: a long series of essays on the English poets. According to Sams, they were all written by Oldershaw; but this cannot be true, since we also know from the Diary that Chesterton wrote the essays on Milton, Gray, and Spenser, and manuscript versions survive of the essays on Milton and Gray and of those by him on Cowper, Scott, Shelley, and Byron.[56] According to Maisie Ward,[57] Chesterton also wrote the essays on Pope, Burns, Wordsworth, and Browning. She does not, however, give her source, and may simply be assuming that only Chesterton would be capable of writing these essays. The difficulty here is that Chesterton was by no means the only one in this remarkably interesting collection of young men who had literary pretensions; and the internal evidence indicates at least two and possibly more authors. The essays we know Chesterton wrote are a good deal better than some others; this may indicate that he had his off days, or (more probably) that another author or authors were indeed involved. His piece on Milton,

---

[53] BL MS Add. 73317A, fo. 61.   [54] Bentley, *Those Days*, 49.   [55] Ward, 33.
[56] BL MS Add. 73303B, fos. 87, 88, 108–10, 116.
[57] Ward, 42; Sams, *Old Pauline*, 51–2.

for all its youthful inexperience (it was, after all, his first published effort as a literary critic), conveys a real engagement with the text of *Paradise Lost*:

when ascending 'next the seat of God' even the Muse of Milton falters and grows weak, and the same diction that is so grand and terrible in the hate and defiances of Satan seems not yet grand enough for a discussion between the persons of the Trinity. Milton's intellect could get as high as the Devil's, but no higher.... The glorious or terrible images which almost every line calls up are such as no reader can forget, but which remain within him, a cycle of mystical and eternal pictures; the uprisen Angel of Darkness reeling over the fiery lake on his spear, or flying far and solitary between heaven and earth, the blaze of the crowned and mailed angel warriors, or the sapphire brook murmuring amid the myrtle woods of Eden.[58]

His article on Gray similarly shows an appropriateness of style to subject. Of the 'Elegy in a Country Church Yard' he observes sardonically that 'Gray, like Coleridge, owes much to the fact of having written very little, but whereas in Coleridge we see the fitful productions of a restless brain subjected to a bitter self-criticism, in Gray we see only the long and laborious polish bestowed on those few works which he finally committed to the press. The result is that though he really only wrote three poems commonly read at the present day, they are each of them in their own way perfect.'[59]

Other anonymous pieces on the English poets are less interesting; some are simply crass. The fifteenth of these is about Browning, whose 'complex and abstruse style', opined the unknown author (surely *not* Chesterton), 'often made his work ugly, forgetting that the essence of art is beauty, and obscure, forgetting that the essence of art is expression. To say that his meaning is well worth finding out is an excellent reason for the reader endeavouring to discover it, but it is no reason for the author making it so obscure.'[60]

Bentley's contributions to *The Debater* were altogether more sophisticated. They were, judged Chesterton, 'the only work in the paper which might have been published by the same person fifteen years afterwards. Whatever the other relative merits of our minds, his was by far the most mature; perhaps for the very reason that it largely concerned itself to being critical or flippant.'[61] He was thinking particularly of a series of nonsensical

---

[58] *The Debater*, ii. 4.   [59] Ibid. 46.
[60] Ibid. iii. 30.   [61] *Autobiography*, 63.

parodies of Aesop's fables, the first of which, in a startling way, attracted the attention of the High Master:

A Selfish Dog one day established himself in a manger, and when the Oxen came to feed, by his constant growling and snapping prevented them from refreshing their Inner Cows. 'What a selfish hound is this,' remarked a Heifer; 'besides there is plenty in the next bin.' Saying which, she pretended to eat barley straw from the adjoining manger. The dog, disgusted at the apparent failure of his plan, soon left, when the Oxen, laughing heartily, dined with an appetite.
Moral is rather mixed, but is something about: 'Better is a dinner of herbs where the dog isn't, than to be a forestalled Ox and no food therewith.'[62]

When Mr Walker reached the phrase 'refreshing their Inner Cows', Chesterton remembered over forty years later, 'he went into unearthly convulsions of his own extraordinary laughter which, like the other movements of his extraordinary voice, began like an organ and ended like a penny whistle. "That boy looks at the world standing on his head," said the High Master of St Paul's School; and instantly we were in the full blaze of the spotlight.'[63]

The High Master's approval of the magazine was soon signalled publicly, on Apposition day, when he pronounced that it 'showed some glimmerings of talent; adding that he was not sure that he would have given it his *Imprimatur* if he had been consulted on the matter'. Chesterton commented that 'somehow . . . it would have been even more crushing if he had set his *Imprimatur*. It sounded like the thumb of a giant.'[64] The High Master had noticed particularly the promise of Chesterton's contributions, and made a point of telling him so. Years later, Bentley remembered that Walker 'did some of his best work . . . by suddenly buttonholing in a corridor, or even in the street outside, some boy who had imagined himself to be unknown to "the Old Man", and booming into his ear some shrewd piece of advice'.[65] He now buttonholed Chesterton, who recorded that 'One day, the High Master stopped me in the street and led me along, roaring in my deafened and bewildered ear that I had a literary faculty which might one day come to something if somebody could give it solidity.'[66]

But Chesterton was essentially an autodidact. It was not some unspecified 'somebody', but Chesterton himself, who determined to give solidity to his 'literary faculty', by industriously, persistently, and voluminously writing for the sake of writing. Undoubtedly, the fact that *The Debater* now existed to

---

[62] *The Debater*, ii. 47.   [63] *Autobiography*, 64.   [64] Ibid. 67.
[65] Bentley, *Those Days*, 57.   [66] *Autobiography*, 67.

publish his efforts was an incentive; nevertheless, there exists also from this period a mass of writing that never saw the light of day.

There is about his literary output, from the beginning, a certain 'star' quality. He himself may have thought that it was only Bentley whose contributions might have been published by the same person fifteen years later: but in his own first published effort, an essay on dragons, he had already found his voice. Partly this is a matter of tone, of an easy humour deriving from an almost Gilbertian (W. S.) cod pomposity designed to rescue from any suggestion of showiness what is surely, for a boy of 16, a remarkable display of literary, artistic, and historical reference. The essay created something of a sensation: Fordham and Oldershaw both recalled reading it and that they, 'rolling the words on their tongues, murmured to one another, "this is literature" '.[67] From the very first sentence, the description 'Chestertonian' is irresistible:

The dragon is certainly the most cosmopolitan of impossibilities. His eccentric figure has walked through the romances of all ages and all nations. It is a noticeable fact that many races, far separated by oceans and by ages and differing in language, customs, and surroundings, have nevertheless evolved similar creatures in the realm of the imagination. In nearly all legends, Greek, Norse, Celtic, Semetic [sic], Mediaeval, and Japanese, this scaly intruder has appeared from the earliest times, and appeared apparently with the sole object of being killed, whether by the lance of St George, the club of Herakles, the sword of Siegfried, or the arrows of Hiawatha. . . .

We will not attempt to explain the popularity of this strange conception. We will not undertake to say whether the Dragon is simply an exaggerated serpent, the Python and Hydra of Hellenic myth, or whether his widespread prominence be due to some dim, pre-historic recollection of those dragon-like ptero-dactyles and ichthiosauri, who were placid spectators of the creation of Adam.[68]

The final paragraphs of this boyish tour de force, despite their mock heroic tone, should be taken seriously; for here we see, in this first published essay, an early product of the settled cast of mind which was to determine Chesterton's vocation as an intellectual counter-revolutionary. It is almost as though he has always known that his life was to be spent doing battle with dragons. Already, he was on the lookout for them; and already he had identified them as being representatives of the prevailing culture:

Behind the scarlet coat and epaulettes, behind the ermine tippet and the counsellor's robe, behind, alas, the black coat and white tie, behind many a respectable

---

[67] Ward, 40.   [68] *The Debater*, i. 4–5.

exterior in public and in private life, we fear that the dragon's flaming eyes and grinning jaws, his tyrannous power, and his infernal cruelty, sometimes lurk.

Reader, when you or I meet him, under whatever disguise, may we face him boldly, and perhaps rescue a few captives from his black cavern; may we bear a brave lance and a spotless shield through the crushing melée of life's narrow lists, and may our wearied swords have struck fiercely on the painted crests of Imposture and Injustice when the dark Herald comes to lead us to the pavilion of the King.[69]

All his life, Chesterton was to be like the warhorse whose nostrils never cease to search for the scent of battle. 'I could be a journalist', he wrote, near the end of his life, 'because I could not help being a controversialist.' And he insisted that 'it was not the superficial or silly or jolly part of me that made me a journalist. On the contrary, it is such part as I have in what is serious or even solemn.'[70]

The emergence of a theo-philanthropist

The Debater's first issue also contained Chesterton's first published poem, and there were another eleven to come in later issues. This does not sound a prolific output over eighteen months; but the poems are sometimes of considerable length, and usually very laboured, literally so: a good deal of work has gone into them, and it shows. He was later dismissive of these examples of poetic juvenilia; nevertheless, it was his poetry rather than his prose which brought clearly to the attention of the school authorities the fact that, far from having 'a lump of fat' where his brain should be, here was a mind of some promise. 'I contributed', he wrote, 'to [the paper's] turgid poems, in which bad imitations of Swinburne were ... exactly balanced with worse imitations of the Lays of Ancient Rome.... For whatever reason, they attracted a certain amount of attention; and our experiment began to float to the surface of the school life.'[71]

These verses, in any purely literary perspective, are not great poetry, as we would expect; indeed, it is a real question whether Chesterton was ever a poet at all (in the sense that near contemporaries like Browning, or, very differently, Gerard Manley Hopkins, clearly were)—rather than an often highly effective popular versifier: T. S. Eliot, intending no disrespect, called his poetry 'first-rate journalistic balladry'.[72] 'Chesterton', argued Marshall

[69] *Autobiography*, 6.   [70] Ibid. 298.   [71] Ibid. 62.   [72] Conlon, i. 531.

McLuhan, 'was not a poet. The superstition that he was is based on the vaguely uplifting connotations of "the poetic" prevalent until recently. He was a metaphysical moralist. . . . "All my mental doors open outwards into a world I have not made", he said in a basic formulation. And this distinction must always remain between the artist who is engaged in making a world and the metaphysician who is engaged in contemplating a world.'[73]

We do not need to accept (or even consider) McLuhan's judgement that Chesterton was no poet to see that the *Debater* verses, poetry or not, are of very uncertain quality. But once we concede that McLuhan is right (as surely he is) to direct our attention away from questions of 'literary' merit—and towards the Chesterton who was a 'metaphysician who is engaged in contemplating a world'—we are liberated from the discouraging task of searching for poetic value in these early verses, and can then begin to focus our attention on their intellectual content. This is, in fact, of considerable interest, and it establishes that he had, by the age of 16, generated a clearly expressed (though not entirely coherent) philosophical view of the world, one rooted in identifiable theological perspectives—perspectives which, on the one hand, partly anticipated those of the Anglo-Catholic Chesterton who was beginning to emerge some ten years later, but which, on the other, were startlingly at odds with them. The very fact that his mind was already, even at this stage, seriously focused on what we might call the problem of God is worth knowing; and this discovery is confirmed by the recollection of his own contemporaries: as Oldershaw told Maisie Ward, 'we felt that he was looking for God'.[74] The beginnings of an attitude towards religion which is both coherent and personally engaged is generally dated a good decade later (there are reasons why this should be so, to which we will need to return). His views are nowhere systematically expounded at this time, as we might expect; but they are, nevertheless, insistently declared in these poems, as their rhetoric veers from Swinburne to Longfellow and back again.

Before addressing this small but informative body of work, we need to begin by considering in passing the poem (curiously, never published in *The Debater*) which finally expunged his reputation as an absent-minded dunce: he entered it, in 1892, in contention for the school's Milton Prize for English Verse; the subject was 'St Francis Xavier: The Apostle of the Indies'. 'Usually', recalled Sams,

---

[73] Marshall McLuhan, introduction to Hugh Kenner, *Paradox in Chesterton* (London, 1948), pp. xxi–xxii.

[74] Ward, 26.

this prize was gained by one of the 'swells' in the Classical Eighth, who would on Apposition Day recite a stanza or two apologetically, take his prize, and scurry away to live it down. Chesterton, then an obscure boy scholastically, entered for it and won it 'hands down'. On Apposition Day he mounted the dais, his copy in his hand; and, seemingly unconscious of his surroundings, dramatically recited his verses to the end. You could have heard a pin drop, even in the gallery full of small boys. Then came thunders of applause, to which the small boys contributed their full share. Chesterton, still in a dream, began to stalk off the dais, forgetful of his prize. He had to be retrieved by a master and a smiling Governor handed him the books.[75]

Years later, Bentley could 'still see him wiping the sweat from his brow as he stood, tall, gawky and untidy, reading that poem to a great audience of parents as well as boys'.[76] Shortly afterwards, a bulletin was posted on the school notice board: 'G. K. Chesterton to rank with the Eighth.—F. W. Walker, High Master.' 'The members of that body,' commented Bentley, 'who had won their way to the top of the school by hard work, did not like this very much, I gathered; few of them, if any, can have measured up the quality of G.K.C. as correctly as Walker had done.'[77] 'All this', Chesterton recalled, 'seemed like the very universe breaking up and turning topsy-turvy.'[78] Two years later (Chesterton had by then left the school) Marie Chesterton visited Walker to ask for his advice about her son's future. 'Six foot of genius', replied this remarkable man; 'cherish him, Mrs Chesterton, cherish him'.[79]

'St Francis Xavier', like most of Chesterton's schoolboy religious poetry,[80] is full of high dramatic afflatus:

> He left his dust, by all the myriad tread
> Of yon dense millions trampled to the strand,
> Or 'neath some cross forgotten lays his head
> Where dark seas whiten on a lonely land.

The message of the poem is clear enough: here was a heroic individual, who attempted ineffectually to preach a culturally inappropriate religion ('He left his name ... | That dies to silence amid older creeds, | With which he strove in vain: the fiery priest | Of faiths less fitted to their ruder needs'). The propaganda and invented myths of the Roman Church, continues the

---

[75] Sams, *Old Pauline*, 49.   [76] Bentley, *Those Days*, 59.   [77] Ibid.
[78] *Autobiography*, 68.   [79] Ward, 42.
[80] Despite the reservations of McLuhan and others, and admitting nothing either way, 'poetry' is what I shall now call it.

poem's argument, cannot hide the fact that his mission to the East was 'a dream' and 'a vanity':

> He died: and she, the Church that bade him go,
> Yon dim Enchantress with her mystic claim,
> Has ringed his forehead with her aureole glow,
> And monkish myths, and all the whispered fame
> Of miracle, has clung about his name:
> So Rome has said; but we, what answer we
> Who in grim Indian gods and rites of shame
> O'er all the East the teacher's failure see,
> His Eastern Church a dream, his toil a vanity.

Not only that, the poem continues, somewhat inconsistently: by seeking to impose Catholicism on an alien culture, he was seeking wrongly to extinguish what were in their own right valid religious traditions ('rites of shame' apparently notwithstanding). Nevertheless, Ignatius was true to his own beliefs, and in personal terms achieved heroic status:

> No child of truth, or priest of progress he,
> Yet not the less a hero of his wars
> Striving to quench the light he could not see.[81]

How seriously are we to take these views? We have seen in Chesterton's juvenile Scottish ballad (written at the age of 8 or 9) how he absorbed the anti-popery common in liberal circles; is this poem simply broadly consistent with what we might expect from an English schoolboy of Chesterton's background; or does it represent opinions which by the time he was nearly 18 had been arrived at in some more systematic—or at least more personal—way? Of 'St Francis Xavier' we might simply note, as Maisie Ward does, that in this poem Chesterton 'expresses with some power a view he was later to explode yet more powerfully',[82] and then pass on. But might not that be to underestimate the extent of the personal revolution represented by Chesterton's movement towards theological orthodoxy some ten years later?

We could (as most observers in fact do) explain the origins of Chesterton's later Christianity principally in emotional terms, as a response to the personal depression of his time at the Slade School of Art and to the 'pessimism' (his invariable description) of the *fin de siècle*, and then to his beloved young wife's

---

[81] *Collected Works*, x. 165.   [82] Ward, 42.

devoted Anglo-Catholicism. Orthodoxy, on this reading, would be for him the emergence from incoherence into clarity, the discovery—in a newly found and more systematic approach to religious belief—of a personal security hitherto impossible. But suppose that his religious impulses already had a coherent intellectual basis? And that his spiritual development is, at least in part, a matter of replacing one recognisable theological posture by another?

The *Debater* poems contain important clues. First of all, we need to register the predominance of religious themes. The JDC followed the normal rule, that there was to be no discussion of religion or politics in its debates (though this rule was later abrogated, after Chesterton argued as chairman that nobody would want to talk about these things anyway). Chesterton's theological interests emerged not in debate but in these verses. Of twelve poems, half are about openly religious themes, as their titles indicate: 'Adveniat regnum tuum',[83] 'Doubt',[84] 'Idolatry',[85] 'Worship',[86] 'St Francis of Assisi',[87] and 'Ave Maria'.[88]

The most strongly, almost lyrically, held religious posture of these poems is their repugnance for all forms of dogma; it emerges most powerfully, perhaps, in 'St Francis of Assisi' (which exhibits Chesterton in full-blown 'Hiawatha' mode):

> In the ancient Christian ages, while a dreamy faith and wonder
>> Lingered, like the mystic glamour of the star of Bethlehem,
> Dwelt a monk that loved the sea-birds as they wheeled about his chapel,
>> Loved the dog-rose and the heath-flower as they brushed his garment's hem;
> Did not claim a ruthless knowledge of the bounds of grace eternal,
>> Did not cry, 'thus far, not further, God has set the hopes of life;'
> Only knew that heaven had sent him weaker lives in earth's Communion,
>> Bade him dwell and work amongst them, not in anger nor in strife. . . .
> Dark the age and stern the dogma, yet the kind hearts are not cruel,
>> Still the true souls rise resistless to a larger world of love.[89]

We might easily explain what are not, after all, theological views of any great complexity, by repeating the simple explanation we have already touched on—that they might be expected from any late Victorian of Chesterton's social class and cultural background and that they probably

[83] *The Debater*, i. 20.   [84] Ibid., ii. 41.   [85] Ibid. 133.   [86] Ibid. 49–50.
[87] Ibid. 78–80.   [88] Ibid. 94.   [89] Ibid. 78–9.

resemble closely enough those of Chesterton's parents. Cecil Chesterton
actually tells us as much: the 'politics and religion of his parents', says Cecil,
'were emphatically Liberal'. Oldershaw, indeed, later told Maisie Ward that
'his own father, who was a Conservative in politics and had also joined the
Catholic Church, seriously warned him against the Agnosticism and Republicanism of the Chesterton household'.[90] That was certainly putting it
too strongly. The 'great Liberal [political] movement', explained Cecil, had
a faith: 'It believed, without question, in the right and power of the human
mind, if left free, to judge the world.' And liberalism of this kind had its
obvious consequences for religious belief: 'In this atmosphere of free inquiry
was developed a theology which was called undogmatic, because its dogmas
were so simple and humane that they seemed to their exponents to be self-
evident... at that time thousands found rest in a vague theo-philanthropy
such as GKC absorbed in his youth.'

But there was a more closely identifiable source for Chesterton's 'theo-
philanthropy'. 'No one in the family was ever pressed to go to church',
continues Cecil, 'but when they did go, it was to Bedford Chapel to hear the
sermons of the Rev. Stopford Brooke. There, more than fifteen years ago [in
other words, in the years leading up to 1893, when Chesterton was 18] the
young Chesterton learned from the lips of a genuine poet and orator the
whole of that system of religious thought which has been discovered by
certain Nonconformist ministers within the last eighteen months, and is now
[1908] emphatically called "The New Theology".'[91] Towards the end of his
life, Chesterton confirmed that long before he began to come under the
influence of more orthodox churchmen, he 'had sat at the feet of that large-
hearted and poetic orator, Stopford Brooke, and... long accepted the sort of
optimistic theism that he taught'; and he acknowledged that 'that was my
first faith, before anything that could really be called my first doubt'.[92]

It is not hard to see why Chesterton should have fallen under Stopford
Brooke's influence. From about 1876—when Brooke set himself up as an
independent preacher by taking out a lease on the newly opened Bedford
chapel—until his retirement in 1895, the influence of this 'genuine poet and
orator' was one of the features of London life. 'The congregation he attracted',
observes his biographer, Lawrence Pearsall Jacks, 'was composed predominantly of thoughtful men and women... men of science, doctors, barristers,
artists, actors, public singers, journalists, members of Parliament... they were a

[90] Ward, 26.   [91] Cecil, 8–9.   [92] Autobiography, 174.

great multitude.... Through them his message was touching the central currents of English life. He was preaching the religion of Love unhampered by dogma—of human love which, in its noblest form, becomes divine.'[93]

'Love unhampered by dogma': or as the youthful Chesterton put it in lines already quoted,

> Dark the age and stern the dogma, yet the kind hearts are not cruel,
> Still the true souls rise resistless to a larger world of love.

In 1880, when Brooke left the Church of England, he preached a sermon about his reasons. The years leading up to his departure had been for him a period of slow but radical development. 'The change that was taking place [in his thinking]', Professor Jacks explains, 'was more than a process of abandoning particular dogmas. It was a growing revolt against the conception of ecclesiastical dogma as a whole.'[94]

Even the most impassioned sermons of the most famous Victorian preachers do not always convey across the years why the men who preached them should have exercised such a sway over those who sat at their feet. Stopford Brooke's inverted 'Parting of Friends' sermon (the mirror-image parallel with Newman is irresistible) conveys at least part of his appeal. It comes to a climax when he explains why he has abandoned the creeds:

The truths of God in Christ are one and eternal, but they are capable of infinitely changing forms, flexible and various for every character and nation; and it is to destroy their noblest, most useful, and most divine characteristic to fix them into immoveable propositions. They are like the wind: they blow where they list.... Let them blow upon you freely, and drink their immortal freshness each of you in your own way. Then you will not be mixed up with the worst evil which the existence of creeds and confessions as tests of faith has promoted—the evil of exclusiveness and of persecution. Creeds...have been used in all ages as the weapons of spiritual tyranny, as the means whereby God has been represented to man as caring more for orthodox beliefs than for righteous life, as the terrible and angry Being who condemns those who reject theological propositions to an everlasting ruin; and thus used, they have imposed on suffering mankind the horror of religious wars, and the worse horrors of superstition.[95]

This emphasis on dogma and ecclesiastical authority as being almost synonymous with intolerance and bloodshed underlies much of Chesterton's

[93] Lawrence Pearsall Jacks, *The Life and Letters of Stopford Brooke* (London, 1917), ii. 353.
[94] Ibid. 310.
[95] Stopford Brooke, *God and Christ* (London, 1894), 357–8.

religious poetry in *The Debater*. 'I am a man, my heritage, a curse of fire and sword' | While o'er my head the purple hills in silence praise the Lord | From the old earth doth worship rise a hymn of ordered deeds, | But we have rent it into sects and coined it into creeds': man has invented (another Stopfordian theme) religious myths and creeds in order to reflect

> . . . the vision of himself, the temple of his soul,
> Within that shrine a secret lies, where nature has no share,
> Within that shrine for ever burns the mystic lamp of prayer,
> In dreaming myth and frantic creed, in flame and battle-wrath,
> In stormy flash and mystery, that secret goeth forth.[96]

It is not, Chesterton protests, in the cultic life inspired by 'frantic' dogma and concocted story that God makes himself known, but in the inner silence of the human heart. Here, we need to register a change of tone:

> There is a place of inner life where nature cannot come,
> Where all her visions are a blank and all her voices dumb.
> A deep of silent consciousness no bridge of thought can span,
> Where in the lonely places meet the souls of God and man.[97]

It is not difficult to see in these lines what Oldershaw meant when he told Maisie Ward that 'we felt that he was looking for God'; here, for the first time, we perceive the note of an authentic spiritual quest: and we realise at this point that Stopford Brooke's influence is a matter not of the adolescent Chesterton's simply adopting a ready-made polemical attitude, but of his perceiving how his own search for God might fit into a wider perspective. Brooke provided a congenial theological context, which appeared to give his own deepest instincts both internal coherence and a recognisable relationship to contemporary religious controversy (the instinctive controversialist in Chesterton responded to the same propensity in Brooke: when, a decade later, he reviewed Brooke's book on the poet Browning (1902) in *The Daily News*, he was to write that 'one of Mr Stopford Brooke's most characteristic faculties is the faculty of a certain sweeping and scornful simplicity. His power of dismissing things is beyond praise'[98]).

Literary influence is always difficult to establish; the Stopford Brooke sermon I have already quoted, for instance, was preached when Chesterton was 8. Nevertheless, it famously set the tone for Brooke's future ministry;

---

[96] *The Debater*, ii. 49.   [97] Ibid.
[98] *The Daily News*, 25 Sept. 1902. See Jacks, *Stopford Brooke*, i. 311.

and we know from Cecil's account that it was from preaching such as this 'from the lips of a genuine poet and orator' that Chesterton learned, in his teenage years, *the whole of that system of religious thought* which . . . is now emphatically called "The New Theology" '; from Chesterton himself we know that Brooke's 'optimistic theism' was 'my first faith, before anything that could really be called my first doubt'.[99] There can be little doubt as to the source of Chesterton's youthful theological liberalism; Brooke's pulpit oratory can be imagined, perhaps even more vividly than that of Newman:

Lastly, [the creeds] make religion complex, when Christ made it simple. Who is to understand the multitudinous and metaphysical distinctions of the Nicene creed? How different it is from that religion of Christ which spoke to children and unlettered men, and claimed for them the knowledge of the kingdom of God, which rested on the love of the heart, on faith, on infinite hope; which had no ceremonies and no ritual, no priesthood, and no dogma, yet which was as wide as heaven, as boundless as God, as deep as the human soul. Get rid of creeds. Be sure that in making Christianity simple, in freeing it from dogmas and legends and miracles, in restoring it to its pure and clear spirituality, you will . . . enable it to unite itself easily to all the great movements of humanity. . . . The world is weary of barren disputes about religion—it seeks a life; it is weary of complex theories—it desires an ideal—it is weary of creeds—it wants to come before its God like a little child. And in truth that is the secret of Christ—a secret which may be ours, a secret which will make creeds useless. 'Whosoever will receive the kingdom of God as a little child, he shall enter therein.'[100]

It is not enough to say that the message of this text from St Mark's Gospel had for Chesterton a profound importance, which remained solidly entrenched in his understanding as he underwent the revolutionary shift from liberal Protestantism (via near-agnosticism) to Catholic orthodoxy. For, in that shift, its meaning is transformed. To become 'as a little child' as a consequence of getting 'rid of creeds' carries with it the unavoidable implication that *any* attempt to understand the complexities of adult life will similarly impede this search for childlike simplicity; Brooke's interpretation, that is to say, arguably reflects a sentimentalised (and archetypally Victorian) view of childhood which turns Christ's words into an excuse for a Peter Pan-like withdrawal from adult life; as Brooke put it elsewhere, the 'kingdom of the child soothes our tired hearts, distressed with the burden of the present'.[101] This is in

[99] Cecil, 8–9; *Autobiography*, 174.
[100] Brooke, *God and Christ*, 357–8.
[101] Stopford Brooke, *Short Sermons* (London, 1892), 157, 152.

fundamental contrast to the way in which Chesterton came to understand being 'as a little child', which was, as we have already discussed, not an evasion of life's complexities, but a spiritual condition which is attained only when these complexities have been confronted and transcended. The contrast between the mature Chesterton and the ex-Anglican Brooke could not be more stark. McLuhan's judgement, already quoted, that 'for Chesterton the rhetoric and dimensions of childhood had also their true Christian vigour and scope' goes on to draw the contrast with other writers of the period: 'he was never tempted into the *cul-de-sac* in which the *faux-naif* of the Christopher Robin variety invariably winds up.' For Stopford Brooke, by contrast, the recovery of childlike simplicity brings not 'Christian vigour' but rest from the turmoil of a complex world: 'The world . . . is weary of complex theories—it desires an ideal—it is weary of creeds—it wants to come before its God like a little child.'[102] Brooke deeply believed that simply in 'making Christianity simple, in freeing it from dogmas and legends and miracles, in restoring it to its pure and clear spirituality, you will . . . enable it to unite itself easily to all the great movements of humanity'.

At 17 this was a view that Chesterton found entirely convincing. Within the heart of man, he believed, there is a longing for God, which unites all men; even 'the wild-eyed savage' may crouch before a 'dead stone God', but his worship 'is not dead':

> Not so; for the worshipper lives, and with him the worship grew,
> And the fear of his heart is deep and the prayer of his lips is true. . . .
> Not alone to yon ghastly idol the savage prays today,
> He prays to the presence within him that has prompted his heart to
>   pray.[103]

This liberal universalism enabled him to unite, in an uneasy and (as it was to prove) unstable synthesis, several strands of his inherited attitudes and of his teenage interests and instincts, some of which we can provisionally identify

---

[102] Brooke returned to this theme more than once over the years. In a volume of sermons published in 1892, for instance, though he goes through the motions of acknowledging, 'running through and mingling with the dream [the nostalgic dream of a regained childhood], the moral greatness of a manhood which has won much through struggle' (an equally Victorian ideal); nevertheless, the idea of the kingdom of heaven as the 'kingdom of the child', says Brooke, 'soothes our tired hearts, distressed with the burden of the present . . . and in the midst of dull decay or fatal ill, it bids a dawn of delightful hope arise, in which we see ourselves as children in the paradise of a new life, born again into a morning air, with everything, as of old, before us, everything washed in joy's most silver dew' (Brooke, *Short Sermons*, 157, 152).

[103] *The Debater*, ii. 133.

as pointing in the general direction he was to take in only a few years. Side by side with his anti-popery and anti-clericalism, we can observe the earliest literary exploration of what was to become a lifelong devotion to the Blessed Virgin Mary; together with his youthful belief in the ideals of the Reformation and in the ideology of human progress we see the clear admiration for the Middle Ages which was to lead in the end to his rejection of the Whig version of history he had taken in with his mother's milk. These juxtapositions sometimes produced curious results. 'Ave Maria', his last *Debater* poem (written in his most opaquely Swinburnian manner) begins with his customary thrust against dogma, and with the assertion (equally familiar) that men have invented religions whereby they can worship themselves ('for all faiths are as symbols, as human, and man is divine'):

> Hail Mary, thou blessed among women, generations shall rise up to greet,
> After ages of wrangle and dogma, I come with a prayer to thy feet.
> Where Gabriel's red plumes were a wind in the lanes of thy lilies at eve,
> We love, who have done with the churches, we worship who may not
>   believe.
> Shall I reck that the chiefs we revolt with, stern elders with scoff and
>   with frown,
> Have scourged from thine altar the kneelers, and reft from thy forehead
>   the crown?[104]

The expected answer is in the negative; nevertheless, although there is here a sincere belief that modern ideals of human progress ought to be the foundation of an authentic contemporary religious ethic (Stopford Brooke again[105]), the young Chesterton feels, at the same time, the tug of a powerful opposing attraction for the ages of faith which have been swept away by the 'stern elders' of the Reformation; he resolves this confusion by a bizarre suggestion that modern ideas of progress are somehow built ('the fruit of the things that have been') on the foundation of medieval religious aspirations:

> O dead worlds of valour and faith, O brave hearts that strove hard to
>   be pure,
> O wonderful longing of man, the old taint of his being to cure. . . .

---

[104] Ibid., iii. 94.

[105] Brooke gave two courses of lectures on the English poets (including even one on the atheist Shelley) designed to 'rub out the sharp lines drawn by that false distinction of sacred and profane' (Stopford A. Brooke, *Theology in the English Poets* (London, 1874), p. xii).

> Sleep, children of faith, though ye reign not, *yet men were more great in*
> *your reign,*
> More great, yet I wrong thee, O present, the fruit of the things that
> have been,
> Man's soul that was high shall be higher, man's heart that God cleansed
> shall be clean. . . .
> Therefore, breathe I a prayer for a moment, at this, the lone shrine of
> the past,
> Whose face was the sun of the ages, whose soul shall be light to the last;
> For man's hope of high things never faileth, though visions and
> worship may fail,
> O Mary, thou blessed among women, great pureness and motherhood
> hail! (my italics)[106]

It is worth reiterating that Mary is venerated here despite the fact that her most important traditional function in the economy of salvation—as Mother of God, and therefore as guarantor also of the dogma of the Incarnation—has been suppressed in Chesterton's understanding: she is venerated by him solely as an icon of motherhood and purity. But though this displays the anti-dogmatic Chesterton, it is interesting that another fundamental Christian dogma appears to be taken for granted: his acceptance of the doctrine of original sin is clearly implied by the line 'O wonderful longing of man, the old taint of his being to cure'.

Reform, revolution, and the religion of mankind

The poem's emphasis on Mary's 'pureness', and on the lofty aspiration that 'man's heart that God cleansed shall be clean', are entirely consistent with Chesterton's character and principles as they were perceived by his contemporaries at St Paul's. In an entirely unpriggish way, he appears to have been genuinely respected by these boisterous teenage boys as an exemplar of goodness and purity. One boy, a 'man about town', stopped him one day in a corridor and solemnly declared, 'Chesterton, I am an abandoned profligate,' to which Chesterton sympathetically replied, with equal seriousness, 'I'm sorry to hear it.' One of his friends later remembered that 'we watched our talk when he was with us'.[107]

---

[106] *The Debater,* iii. 95–6.   [107] Ward, 26.

This was no unreflective Puritanism, but a moral position carefully arrived at and strongly held: in one of the series of fictional letters he wrote for *The Debater*, for instance, he attacks the notion of 'Zolaism' as 'an effective moral teaching, however honestly undertaken. I am convinced, despite all that is said to the contrary, that the civilised objection to coarseness is not a mere fad or fashion, but a great protest for purity, reverence and clean imagination, against all cynical and unchivalrous buffooneries.' 'It is all very well', he went on, 'for Ouida and such dreary reactionaries to speak of decorum as the mask of an immoral age, but I never could see that Marlowe and Wycherley were personally so much better behaved than Tennyson' (as we shall see, Chesterton approved of the moral content of the poet laureate's verse).[108] The fact that, as Bentley remembered, 'laughter was never far away' saved Chesterton's youthful moral instincts from priggishness; Bentley remembered both his happiness and his capacity for reverence;[109] perhaps it was this combination of goodness and contentment that, partly at least, explains the personal magic that caused his friends to vie for the first place in his affections.

The evidence from this period of his life already shows a serious and sustained interest in the moral and authentically religious dimensions of life and literature. This drew him beyond any merely ideological impulse to curse priestcraft and ecclesiastical authority and led him towards the beginnings of an understanding—one which was to ripen into a full-hearted embrace—of the genius of the European Middle Ages. His discussion of 'Zolaism', for instance (written when he was 18), leads on to an interesting defence of medieval piety, which compares Dante and Milton to the latter's disadvantage, and which is greatly more convincing than the somewhat lame apologia for the present ('this sad but noble time') that follows it. It is a remarkable passage for its date (1892), and since it is almost unknown is worth quoting at some length:

Many Philistines and guide-book philosophers make very merry over the old Italian pictures in which ladies, bishops, martyrs and persons of the Trinity are all introduced into one canvass. They forget that this combination, however incongruous it may seem to a generation accustomed to have its fetish shut up in a cupboard and exhibited on Sundays, was the very essence of the vivid democratic mediaeval piety which felt that there was in reality a great 'communion of saints' in which they and their personal acquaintances could walk naturally with angels and

---

[108] *The Debater*, iii. 57.   [109] Bentley, *Those Days*, 59.

archangels. It was this intense reality in their religion which marks, for instance, the hell and heaven of the great mediaeval poet, filled with his own Florentine neighbours, as opposed to the vague renaissance mythology of the great poem of Milton. It was a religion dark, narrow, sometimes savagely ascetic, but it was not a sham religion: it was felt as real by those who professed it.[110]

The same issue of *The Debater* gives an account of a paper entitled 'Three Stages of Ethical Poetry in Europe' delivered to the JDC the previous month by 'The Chairman' (Chesterton), 'in which he passed from Dante, as representing the dark but vivid mediaeval religion, with its real bearing on love, hate, and friendship, to Shakespeare, in whom the human interest, freed by the Reformation and the new learning, was extended more liberally to the whole human race, and concluded with Goethe, as representing the modern ethical, sceptical, and metaphysical school'.[111] This ethical focus was repeatedly brought to bear on a variety of literary topics in Chesterton's speeches to the JDC. Two weeks later, on 22 July, in a debate on the relative poetic merits of Virgil and Horace, 'The Chairman, opening on behalf of Horace, said that much as he admired Virgil . . . he felt more sympathy with [Horace] as a moralist and teacher of his age, as opposed to a mere heroic narrator.'[112] On 26 March, he had read a paper comparing 'the thoughtful and liberal school of Tennyson, Browning, Matthew Arnold &c . . . to the new purely aesthetic school of Swinburne and Morris, in which . . . he condemned the absence of the sentiment of the moral, which he held to be the really stirring and popular element in literature'.[113] In February, 'The Chairman remarked that a fairy-tale is formed on the principles of beauty, and having a central moral idea as the basis for forming a series of vivid pictures.'[114] This location of an essential part of the literary value of a text in its moral content may be significant given the date of these speeches—at a time when the aesthetic movement, with its rallying cry of 'art for art's sake' (that is, art which expressly rejects any moral dimension), was at its high-water mark: Chesterton's moral focus, firmly established even before he has left school—(his departure was imminent; all the reports of his JDC speeches quoted above come from his final year)—can be seen to foreshadow his later emergence as a self-consciously counter-cultural figure.

For the present, the collection of assumptions he had partly inherited and partly constructed for himself seemed stable enough. Despite fleeting

---

[110] *The Debater*, iii. 57.   [111] Ibid. 53.
[112] Ibid.   [113] Ibid. 22.   [114] Ibid. 2.

glimpses of a growing sympathy for the Catholic tradition, we still have to locate Chesterton firmly in the liberal tradition he inhabited at this period, even though we can already see his theological liberalism beginning to fragment. His political liberalism was to survive the beginnings of ortho-doxy by a decade and more. His religious poetry at this date is often cloudy, confused, and rhetorically so high-flown as to be at times almost unreadable. His picturesque and distinctly non-Tory view of history, in contrast, is quite clear, and can be gauged by four poems (all written in a much more lucid poetic style) about historical figures he admired: Danton, William of Orange, Algernon Sydney, and Simon de Montfort.

Danton was available as a heroic figure for Victorians of a romantic or progressive disposition who wanted to maintain an admiration for the French Revolution without condoning its excesses, since he was seen as having died as a defender of clemency and moderation against the fanaticism of Robespierre. Danton is one of the heroes of Carlyle's *French Revolution* (then still recognised as one of the literary masterpieces of the nineteenth century); Chesterton knew Carlyle's great work well, as one of the Diary's most amusing entries indicates:

I endeavour to listen at the same time to the directions of the Maternal Voice in the event of Bentley's appearance and to the Innocent Child's [Cecil's] enquiries about Carlyle's French Revolution. The result is a fine compressed medley. Thus.
Tell Louisa—all men are equal—light the fire—with the Committee of Public Safety—Ring for Louisa and—Camille Desmoulins—ask him into the drawing room and guillotine him and if Bentley wants the Girondist Deputies they're all in the pantry.
I here find it expedient to confine my attention to the maternal mandates, and acquiescing respectfully therein, forget all about them in the course of giving my enquiring brother the requested information on the subject of Jean Paul Marat.[115]

Carlyle gives a characteristic account of the confrontation of Robespierre and Danton ('the sea-green formula looked at the monstrous colossal reality, and grew greener to behold him'[116]) and of Danton's downfall. Chesterton's poem describes Danton's execution in heroic terms:

Well may Monsieur David yonder mark me with artistic eye,
Let him tell his pale Maxmilien [*sic*], Danton did not fear to die.

[115] BL MS Add. 73317, fos. 24–5.
[116] Thomas Carlyle, *The French Revolution* (Cambridge, 1884), ii. 396.

Let him tell his cold Dictator that his time shall also come—
See his blood on yonder hatchet, hear his knell on yonder drum;
And my murdered blood shall choke him as he gasps the coward's lie
And there mobs cajoled recall me . . . [117]

This derives from Carlyle's description of Robespierre's last attempt to address the National Convention, 'his tongue dry, cleaving to the roof of his mouth. "The blood of Danton chokes him", cry they. "Accusation! Decree of Accusation!" '[118] The poem, Chesterton recorded in his last entry in the *Diary*, 'had a startling success in the school. I am seized every day by enquiring schoolfellows and made to give a complete history of the life and doings of the Revolutionaries of Arcis sur Aube.'[119]

Chesterton had a youthful penchant for historical fatalities; one of his early *Debater* articles was entitled 'Royal Death Scenes'; 'some of the royal deathbeds', he solemnly announced, 'are among the most grand, the most pathetic, or the most horrible scenes of English history'.[120] Of his four historical poems in *The Debater*, two describe executions, the third (Simon de Montfort) an impending death in battle against hopeless odds. Algernon Sydney, the subject of the other heroic execution scene, fought on Cromwell's side against the King, but defied the order to sit as one of his judges; this recalls Danton, perhaps, if we see Sydney as a revolutionary who believed nevertheless in moderation and clemency. Simon de Montfort, on Chesterton's reading, dies as a romantic and distinctly modern figure, who goes to his death believing that one day will dawn 'the promise of fulfilment for the work that I have done' and that 'never man that died for justice gave his life and blood in vain':

Through the storm of feudal battle, through the gloom of despot's reign,
'Spite of king, and priest, and baron, Freedom's fire breaks out again.[121]

The young Chesterton was excitedly opposed to any notion of authoritarian kingship. What he described as his 'Jacobite story',[122] 'The White Cockade', is actually an anti-Jacobite tract: the Jacobite white cockade, its hero declares, stands for 'authority and the upper hand', whereas those who wear the black cockade of King George are 'those who uphold the constitutional power of the subject'.[123] Chesterton's anti-Stuart feelings (which like his anti-popery we have seen emerging around his eighth year) are

---

[117] *The Debater*, i. 26.   [118] Carlyle, *French Revolution*, ii. 420.
[119] BL MS Add. 73317, fo. 62.   [120] *The Debater*, ii. 3–4.
[121] Ibid. 78–9.   [122] BL MS Add. 73317, fo. 61.   [123] *The Debater*, ii. 24–5.

expressed repeatedly at about this time; in an uncompleted fragment of a melodramatic play about James II, he depicts a tyrannical king being urged on to bloody vengeance by his confessor, Petre (royal tyranny was always more satisfying in Chesterton's teenage vision if it could be coupled with priestcraft):

King James: No man or woman shall baulk me of my justice
Petre: Truly, your majesty, you speak like a true scion of Holy Church.[124]

Another notebook of about the same period contains similarly anti-clerical and anti-Jacobite sentiments:

> Thank God we have no creed, now
> Of rule or right Divine
> To make us cringe to a villain who comes of an ancient line.[125]

These anti-Stuart sentiments may explain why he chose *Woodstock* (not one of Walter Scott's most interesting novels) to dramatise and perform with his friends: his play was entitled *The King*; the novel depicts the libidinous attempts of an unsympathetically drawn Charles II, on the run from the Parliamentary army, cynically to seduce the beautiful and virtuous Alice Lee (very much the young Chesterton's female ideal) despite the fact that she is the daughter of a cavalier knight who is putting his life and that of his family in peril by hiding him.

None of this argues a particularly sophisticated philosophy of history. History, for the schoolboy Chesterton, was a series of somewhat novelettish tableaux which allowed him to strike picturesque moral attitudes (though we should note that some of these attitudes—including his swashbuckling approval of the French Revolution—survived intact into adulthood[126]). Like his equally highly coloured (but already more complex) views on religion, these scenic glimpses present us with a partial overview of an already impressive mind at an early but crucial stage in its development: most importantly, they allow us to see how his attitude to history both mirrored and helped to form his response to the contemporary world. His feelings about the French Revolution, for instance, were echoed in his hostility to a contemporary absolute monarchy, that of the Tsar; at this time, his hostility was centred particularly on his strong feelings about Russian oppression of the Jews, which had been triggered off by reading

---

[124] BL MS Add. 7314C.   [125] BL MS Add. 7315D.
[126] See, for instance 'The Secret People', *Collected Works*, x. 408–11.

in a magazine article of the case of a 'respectable young girl of honest parents' who had been seduced by a Christian who had promised to marry her. When she reminded him of his promise, he replied that 'he would have her sent out of the city for her presumption. And he did. A cousin of his is serving in the police department, and he had no difficulty to obtain an order for her banishment "as a disorderly Jewess". "But how could you bring yourself to do such a damnable act?" [the article's author] asked. "Oh, she is only a Jewess!" he answered. "What else is she good for? Besides, everybody else does the same." '[127] Chesterton's reaction was explosive:

[Diary. Monday Jan 5, 1891]
Expect Bentley. Read in Review of Reviews. Various revelation of Jews in Russia. Brutal falsehood and cruelty to a Jewish girl. Made me feel strongly inclined to knock some-body down, but refrained.

Chesterton would not have been pacified by reading in the *Review of Reviews* the following month of the Tsar's reaction to a meeting held at the Guildhall in London to protest against Russian treatment of the Jews: 'the Tzar... declared... that he would promptly send to the devil any foreigner who ventured to interfere in the internal affairs of the Russian Empire.'[128]

Chesterton had personal reasons for feeling strongly about cruelty to the Jews in Russia. Of the twelve members of the JDC, four were Jewish: the Solomons, Lawrence and Maurice, and the D'Avigdors, Digby and Waldo. Lawrence Solomon was to be a lifelong friend, who even moved to Beaconsfield in Chesterton's wake so as to be near him: however eccentric Chesterton's later ideas on 'the Jewish question', the widely held notion that he was an anti-Semite (which he always found strange and puzzling) appears inconsistent with the evidence, which is of liking and respect for individual Jews and a persistent hatred of persecution of the Jewish people, whether under tsarist Russia or Nazi Germany.[129]

---

[127] *Review of Reviews* (Oct. 1890), ii, no. 10, 350.
[128] Ibid. (Feb. 1891), iii, no. 14, 115.
[129] Towards the end of his life he wrote that he was 'appalled by the Hitlerite atrocities' (he died in 1936 before anyone knew the full extent of what was to become the Nazi attempt at a 'final solution'): 'They have absolutely no reason or logic behind them. It is quite obviously the expedient of a man who has been driven to seeking a scapegoat, and has found with relief the most famous scapegoat in European history, the Jewish people. I am quite ready to believe now that Belloc and I will die defending the last Jew in Europe' (Ffinch, *Chesterton*, 273).

Chesterton's feelings about the persecution of Russian Jews bore somewhat melodramatic fruit in the form of a fictional letter, written as though from St Petersburg, in which Chesterton's alter ego, Guy Crawford, describes himself as joining a rebellious mob in which he recognises an obviously Jewish student called Emmanuel, and as springing to his defence, sword in hand, as the tsarist troops charge (in an earlier letter he had declared, of the persecution of the Jews in Russia, that 'It has at least done one service to orthodoxy. It has restored my belief in the devil'[130]):

I remember dealing one fellow a sabre blow that sent him reeling, and then I felt a wound and fell over Emmanuel's body. I staggered to my feet. He and I were alone under the starlight: and far tumults rose from the far end of the street. I bent over Emmanuel, 'how does it go?' he moaned. I looked hard in the distance. 'It is all dust and smoke,' I said, 'but our friends are holding the entrance to the alleys, and the soldiers cannot carry them.' Just then, borne faintly on the wind came the wild bars of the Marseillaise hurled tauntingly at the broken and repulsed soldiery. Emmanuel's lips moved to the words, and his dark eyes burnt with tears then closed, and his head fell back wearily over my arm. He was dead. I rose slowly upright in the lonely midnight street, forgetting my wound. I saw only a poor student dead on the road, with his white face to the stars, and his blood dark on the stones; unknown, unrecorded, as a champion of justice, like thousands who have fallen for it in the dark records of this dark land.[131]

Undoubtedly, the fight for liberty and justice was epitomised for Chesterton at this time in his life (and for some years to come) by those 'wild bars of the Marseillaise hurled tauntingly at the broken and repulsed soldiery'. In a JDC debate on 'Forms of Government' the previous year, he had defended the French Republic and attacked monarchy, an institution about which he expressed his feelings in an unpublished poem (probably written at around this time) entitled 'The Real Anthem'—though it should be noted that the wording indicates that the poem is not directed against the female monarch currently occupying the British throne:

> From every folly vain
> From every pride insane
> > God save the King
>
> From every lawless claim
> From every tyrant aim
> From the oppressor's shame
> > God save the King

---

[130] *The Debater*, iii. 11.   [131] Ibid. 71.

> From the red stains of blood
> From foul corruption's mud
> God save the King.[132]

Travels into an uncertain time

When Chesterton left St Paul's, in the summer of 1892, there was no presentiment that any gulf was opening up between his happy childhood and adolescence and a more emotionally insecure future. Both the JDC and *The Debater* were still going strong, and it never occurred to anyone that his connection with both would not continue. His boyhood friendships, especially that with Bentley, were firm (and were to prove durable). In some ways, leaving school was not, for Chesterton, the great final rift with boyhood and the beginning of adult life it often is; for him, that was to come rather later, in some ways traumatically. There were clouds ahead: but that summer, life was still carefree enough. He had, in the end, left school in something of a blaze of glory, the Milton Prize having at a stroke wiped out years of academic ignominy (so far only mitigated by his unaccountable form prize in French the year before). Chesterton's father, as a kind of rite of passage, decided that they would go on a journey, *à deux*, by train through northern France, ending in Paris. For Mr Ed, in a way, it was even more the end of a chapter than it was for Chesterton: it was the last time he would be the mentor of his childhood and youth, still hoping to help form his mind by delighting it, still, where he could, adding to his son's stock of knowledge. By now, though, Gilbert's mind was pretty much his own: his father could still take him to see the Cathedral of Notre Dame in Paris; but his reactions to what he saw and heard—anti-monarchist and anti-clerical as ever—were idiosyncratically his own. As he wrote to Bentley from their hotel in the Rue Saint-Honoré,

They showed us over the treasures of the Cathedral, among which, as was explained by the guide, who spoke a little English, was a cross given by Louis XIV to 'Mees' Lavallière. I thought that concession to the British system of titles was indeed touching. I also thought, when reflecting what the present was, and where it was and then to whom it was given, that this showed pretty well what the religion of the Bourbon regime was and why it has become impossible since the Revolution.[133]

---

[132] BL MS Add. 73314A; *Collected Works*, x. 408.   [133] Ward, 37.

Before they arrived in Paris, they had seen Rouen, and then had travelled through Calvados to the seaside town of Arromanches, where they stayed at the Grand Hôtel du Chemin de Fer. On the way, Gilbert's facility as a draughtsman had helped him make contact with the natives; as he commented to Bentley, 'Art is universal':

This remark is not so irrelevant . . . as it may appear. I have just had a demonstration of its truth on the coach coming down here. Two very nice little French boys of cropped hair and restless movements were just in front of us and my pater having discovered that the book they had with them was a prize at a Paris school, some slight conversation arose. Not thinking my French altogether equal to a prolonged interview, I took out a scrap of paper and began with a fine carelessness, to draw a picture of Napoleon I, hat, chin, attitude, all complete. This, of course, was gazed at rapturously by these two young inheritors of France's glory and it ended in my drawing them unlimited goblins to keep for the remainder of the interview.

He owed it to his father, Chesterton said, that he was a traveller, not a tripper; in other words, that his travels—like those with Mr Ed by train through Normandy—were journeys of discovery, untrammelled by the 'pre-arranged circuit over rails' of the Thomas Cook's tour. It was a remark that could be applied more generally to his father's entirely benign intellectual influence, from early childhood to adolescence and early manhood, over his eldest son's growing mind—an influence about which there was never anything formulaic or 'prearranged'. Chesterton owed much of his emotional stability, and the apparently natural happiness of his temperament, to both his parents; to his father, perhaps, more than to anyone else, he owed the range and originality of his mind. But all that belonged to a period in his life that was drawing to a close; how durable it would prove could not be foreseen. And now they had both returned from France, he faced a future in which, both emotionally and intellectually, he was on his own.

3

Nightmare at the Slade: Digging for the Sunrise of Wonder, 1892–4

After he left school, in the summer of 1892, Chesterton spent a year—rather in the same way that students today commonly take a 'gap' year between school and university—preparing, in theory, for a course in fine arts and other subjects at University College, London. The idea was that he would spend his time reading at home and attending art classes, and then begin his university studies in the autumn of the following year. Bentley, Oldershaw, and the other members of the JDC continued at St Paul's, working for scholarships to Oxford, a course not open to Chesterton because of his hitherto inveterate (though, as we shall see, not insuperable) lack of disciplined attention to his formal academic work. Despite Chesterton's unexpected literary success with the Milton Prize and in *The Debater*, his father supposed that he would not have the necessary application for a literary career; and in any case, he saw his son's real talents as being artistic. Gilbert drew, constantly, on any surface available, including the walls. This was a lifelong propensity (a few years later, his future mother-in-law, already unimpressed by this untidy, impecunious young man, was not won over when he absent-mindedly began to scribble a drawing of his fiancée, her daughter Frances, on the wallpaper[1]). Mr Ed himself had always regretted being unable to explore his own artistic leanings; and it was obvious that there was no point in trying to persuade Gilbert to enter the family firm of Chesterton's estate agency: so, as Cecil recalled, '[h]is father, whose leanings were far more literary and artistic than

---

[1] *Return*, 36.

commercial, and whose judgment was sane and just to a most unusual degree, wisely refrained from attempting to force him into business. During his boyhood Gilbert Chesterton had been at least as fond of scribbling drawings as of scribbling verses. Some of these were thought by good judges to show great promise, and it was decided that he should study art.'[2]

After the end of his final school term, Gilbert and his father went on their *tournée* in France. That autumn, the others returned to St Paul's, and Chesterton began his 'gap year'—though, in some respects, his former train of life, for a time at least, continued uninterrupted. The Pauline interpene-tration of school and home meant that his closest friends were still accessible (though no longer in the old easy day-to-day way of their shared school-days). The great institutional mainstays of his life, too, were still functioning. *The Debater* was still being published; and though he was, strictly speaking, now an Old Pauline, Chesterton continued attending meetings of the JDC every Friday evening during term time (its meetings, after all, took place in the members' homes rather than on school premises) and as a major contributor to its magazine. On 16 September, he was re-elected as Chair-man, and a new associated club, the Antiquarian Society, 'received its official certification', with Oldershaw, Solomon, and Vernède as founder members. Chesterton announced that one of the junior forms wanted to found a debating society, and had asked for the JDC's help; 'Mr Bentley volunteered the requisite assistance'. The weekly debates continued un-abated. On 30 September, Lawrence Solomon proposed the motion that 'illustrations are to be avoided in works of fiction': 'The Chairman said that he had often felt that an objection is to be urged against illustrations in books, but he considered that there are three cases in which they are defensible, firstly when the pictures are worth having as pictures, secondly where the artist suggests by his choice of subjects what the author cannot suggest, and thirdly in such illustrations as Doré's to Dante, which certainly popularise the poem. On the other hand, he urged the fact that a picture often conflicts with, or else, what is quite as inartistic, repeats the narrative.'[3] To the last issue of *The Debater* before Christmas, Chesterton contributed three items: a very short story, one of his series of fictional letters signed 'Guy Crawford', and his poem 'St Francis of Assisi'. On 20 September, 'a meeting was held at Mr G. K. Chesterton's house. . . . This meeting was strictly of a business nature. It was decided to purchase, for the use of

---

[2] Cecil, 16.   [3] *The Debater*, iii. 68.

the Society in particular, and the JDC in general, a Baedeker's guide to London.' A new member was proposed, and unanimously elected. On 9 December, Chesterton read a paper entitled 'Literary Composition among Boys'

He said that a creative instinct exists in [every child, who] has...a series of imaginary characters, whose proceedings he details at enormous lengths, while the desire to let off one's feelings in the form of composition, he said, comes somewhat later, and that experience of childhood shows that this is not a piece of vanity or eccentricity. He then made a few remarks on style, saying that it may almost be called a sixth sense; he said that the great danger in juvenile literature is a tendency to unmeaning grandiloquence, and that he wished that the study and practice of literary composition among the young held a higher place among educators and boys than it holds now.[4]

Chesterton was still at the centre of the club's activities; but his departure from the school had unsettled its members. On 16 December, a meeting was held to consider the club's future; Oldershaw 'remarked on the necessity for holding such a discussion, as members were already beginning to leave St Paul's School, and in a year or so more would be scattered over different parts of the world'. It was decided that with various constitutional changes the club would continue for the present, but that its magazine would have to be discontinued. In February, with due solemnity, *The Debater* announced its own demise:

With this number, *The Debater* ceases to exist. Regretful though we may be at losing our magazine, we may still claim that enthusiasm which prompted us to start it, and a belief that the idea which it was intended to embody, has been helped rather than hindered by its championship. . . . The reasons why *The Debater* is coming to an end are briefly these: primarily because we are losing financially over it; secondly because the production even of a paper like *The Debater* does not leave the mind in that repose, and takes away from that time which is required by other and more important duties, and lastly because we are dropping away from St Paul's School.[5]

In fact, only Chesterton had 'dropped away' (not that it had made any difference either to his attendance at JDC meetings or to the volume of his contributions to the magazine); more to the point were those 'other more important duties' that were beginning to concentrate the minds of such as Bentley and Oldershaw, who realised that they were well into their last two years at school, and that work for their Oxford scholarship examinations

---

[4] *The Debater*, 89.   [5] Ibid. 83.

would now have to take first place. That meant the end, not only of the magazine, but of the JDC itself. When exactly that particular blow fell is uncertain; but in June 1893 another final issue of *The Debater* appeared in order to commemorate the club's demise. It was lithographed not printed. On its final page (drawn by Chesterton) appears, in Sams's description, 'a coat of arms supported by two mourning pixies; crest, a tea-pot froide on slices of bread and butter couchants. The two first quarters are all heraldically decipherable but the last two are three tea-cups, a figure (probably Bentley) bouleversé. The motto is EHEU FUGACES.'[6] Beneath these touching armorial bearings are these lines by Bentley:

> IN MEMORIAM JDC
>
> I'll sing to you a nice little song, about the Junior Debaters;
> How they all of them came by different ends according to their different natures,
> I composed these lines on the deaths of the Members of this late lamented Society,
> And they're very much calculated to wring a sob from a bosom of the stoutest variety.

There can be little doubt that the end, first of *The Debater* and then of the JDC itself represented for Chesterton a heart-wrenching loss; it was the real end of his happy and extraordinarily creative boyhood. The daily company of the other members had come to an end the previous summer; now, the joyous weekly 'beanos', the endless talking about books, and history, and every other topic under the sun, became, after a time, things of the past. Little by little, the companionship which had nurtured his intellectual life and his happiness ebbed away. This withdrawal was not sudden, but extended over the two years after his final term at St Paul's. He left school before the others; but there were still the weekends, during which he continued to consort regularly with his St Paul's friends, particularly with Bentley. Finally, two years later, Bentley and Oldershaw went up to Oxford and other friends went elsewhere, leaving him behind in London. His old gregarious life was gone, seemingly forever; the 'Mystical City of Friends' (as Cecil called it, evoking a poem by Walt Whitman[7]) had scattered to the four winds.

---

[6] H. A. Sams, *Pauline and Old Pauline* (Cambridge, 1933), 56–7.
[7] Cecil, 25.

His first year after he left school appears, at first sight, to have been a time of increasing loneliness and inconsequent idling. Nothing in his new life seems to have left any permanent mark on him (nothing external, that is; his own thoughts are another matter). Evidence about his artistic activities, during this first year after leaving St Paul's, is sparse. According to Lawrence Solomon, Chesterton studied at an art school called 'Calderon's'. Michael Ffinch claims that this was not an art school but something called 'the St John's Wood clique', led by Philip Hermogenes Calderon, son of a 'spoiled Spanish priest';[8] actually, at this time, Calderon was Keeper of the Royal Academy (his father had been Professor of Spanish Literature at King's College). Whether Chesterton actually had anything to do with him seems extremely doubtful: at any rate, there is no evidence that he had any effect at all on his life.

Chesterton was, nevertheless, by his own account, involved in some kind of art studies, probably of a desultory kind; he attended an art college of some kind; and it was in St John's Wood. It was the only time in his life that this deeply gregarious man failed to make any durable new friendship; an unpublished poem he wrote on leaving this establishment, addressed to a fellow art student, poignantly conveys his loneliness. The poem is called 'St John's Wood March':

> I never have known of friends as you,
> Have never known, nor shall ever know,
> And you grow coldly; best then [part]
> Since God has willed, and it must be so. . . .
>
> Only the thing is a little sad
> For me who watch your eyes grow strange
> And filled with secrets I cannot know,
> The week-long treasure and exchange. . . .
>
> I move by day in a crowded world
> And know not the smiling face I scan;
> If he fell dead at my feet, my care
> Would be for the common life of—a man.[9]

Nothing seems to be known about 'Wood's', or 'Calderon's', art school; certainly, Chesterton tells us nothing, perhaps because nothing to be learned there engaged his attention. What, else then, was he doing with his time,

[8] Michael Ffinch, *G. K. Chesterton: A Biography* (London, 1986), 33.
[9] 'St John's Wood March', verses 2, 4, and 6, BL MS Add. 73321C, fos. 19v–20.

during this year, from the autumn of 1892 to the autumn of 1893 when he began his studies at University College, London? There is no hint in the *Autobiography*; in Chesterton's memory, the three years that followed his schooldays became telescoped together. It was a period of sometimes agonising mental and emotional transition. As he puts it in the *Autobiog-raphy*, 'all this time very queer things were groping and wrestling inside my own undeveloped mind. . . . I said farewell to my friends when they went up to Oxford and Cambridge; while I, who was at that time almost wholly taken up with the idea of drawing pictures, went to an Art School and brought my boyhood to an end.'[10] In fact, as we have seen, his friends went up to the university a full two years after Chesterton left St Paul's, and when they did, Chesterton's time as an art student had already come to an end. The great crisis through which he was to pass began, it seems, as his schooldays ended; but it is clear that the most intense phase of it was associated in his mind with his time at the Slade School of Art, which lasted for only the second of the three years. The state of mind he describes seems all-encompassing and overwhelming:

There is something truly menacing in the thought of how quickly I could imagine the maddest, when I had never committed the mildest crime. Something may have been due to the atmosphere of the Decadents, and their perpetual hints of the luxurious horrors of paganism; but I am not disposed to dwell much on that defence; I suspect I manufactured most of my morbidities for myself. But anyhow, it is true that there was a time when I had reached that condition of moral anarchy within, in which a man says, in the words of Wilde, that 'Atys with the blood-stained knife were better than the thing I am'. I have never indeed felt the faintest temptation to the particular madness of Wilde; but I could at this time imagine the worst and wildest disproportions and distortions of more normal passion; the point is that the whole mood was overpowered and oppressed with a sort of congestion of imagination. As Bunyan, in his morbid period, described himself as prompted to utter blasphemies, I had an overpowering impulse to record or draw horrible ideas and images; plunging in deeper and deeper as in a blind spiritual suicide. . . . Per-haps, when I eventually emerged as a sort of theorist, and was described as an Optimist, it was because I was one of the few people in that world of diabolism who really believed in devils.[11]

He began to dabble in spiritualism; years later, he told Father O'Connor (the model for Father Brown) that he had used the planchette or ouija board freely, but had been constrained to give it up because it gave him

---

[10] *Autobiography*, 76.   [11] Ibid. 90–1.

headaches.[12] His lengthy account of these dabblings in the *Autobiography* ends with the planchette bathetically (and surely implausibly) spelling out 'Orriblerevelationsinhighlife'.[13] It is all very rum.

Nevertheless, however dramatic Chesterton's memories of the period—as he recorded them over forty years later—may have been, the evidence is that his morbid state of mind was never at any point wholly debilitating, and that his struggle against the blight of what he termed 'pessimism', often seen as an external and cultural threat rather than as a personal problem, was from the beginning hard fought. The general assumption about this period of his life (fostered by Chesterton's own recollection of it) has been that there was a clearly defined period of total and paralysing neurosis, from which Chesterton escaped, partly by the recovery of some kind of religion and partly by the discovery of literary optimists like Walt Whitman and Robert Louis Stevenson. But there was probably never a time when he was wholly engulfed; he always seems to have believed firmly in the need to make the choice of optimism over pessimism; and Whitman and Stevenson were discoveries made *before* his 'whole mood', as he later claimed, 'became overpowered and oppressed' and not afterwards.[14]

What we might without exaggeration call a spiritual crisis certainly occurred, and this was a time of real mental travail; but the evidence seems to be that the recovery from it was already taking place, even as Chesterton was living through it, that any final collapse had been, as it were, pre-empted by more positive influences. It is clear, for instance, that though the Slade period was associated in his later recollection with idleness and futility as well as with a kind of actual insanity (the relevant chapter in the *Autobiography* is called 'How to be a Lunatic'), that same year also saw him making real academic progress of a wholly unbohemian kind in other departments of University College, London. At the same time, he was writing copiously, as he probably had been during the entire post-school period. In his first academic year, Chesterton read art, Latin, English, and French, and dropped Latin and art at the end of it (he took up history and political economy instead). The great Slade experiment had been an almost total failure; his drawing style at the end of it shows no sign of technical or imaginative growth or improvement; it shows, indeed, no detectable change of any kind. But the Slade was not everything; and

[12] John O'Connor, *Father Brown on Chesterton* (London, 1938), 74.
[13] *Autobiography*, 80.   [14] See pp. 101–3 below.

Chesterton's memory of this as an aimless period in which there were no real objectives and no achievements was a later reconstruction, probably unconscious, of a time in his life in which he could remember only drift and depression. 'Most of the other students', he recalled in the *Autobiography*, 'were studying for examinations; but I had not even that object in this objectless period of my life.'[15] But this is not true. He would have had, at least, to sit examinations at the end of his first year in the subjects in which he wished to continue into his second, and as it happens, we have evidence that he certainly sat the French examination; he even did well in it (his sixth-form prize in French recalls that this was a subject in which he had already excelled academically). As he cheerfully wrote to Oldershaw:

By the way, I have discovered, much to my amusement, that I did rather well in the year's French Examination at U.C. I never looked at the lists, but Morton referred to it accidentally. He declares it is because I slated Voltaire, whom [Professor] Lallemande hates; I believe myself it was the essay. I am writing a great deal, not wisely but too well. I am sending up policeman, nurse etc separately as soon as I can choose the magazines & [am] going to open fire on them with verse. I don't feel doubtful or silly: I can't imagine why. . . .

But lecture calls.

Believe me yours always

Gilbert. K. Chesterton

P.S. Are you writing anything? You never say much about that. Let me have a companion in guilt.[16]

He was undoubtedly 'writing a great deal'. His idea of 'sending up policeman, nurse etc' seems to have led to the composition—though whether any magazine published them is uncertain—not of verses but of a series of stories, the first two of which are entitled 'the prophetic policeman' and 'the nurse'; these are presented as being part of a book written by a character (possibly intended partly in self-parody) who is introduced as 'Gabriel Hope, art student, addicted to the surreptitious sonnet'. The stories are introduced by a 'prologue' consisting of a conversation represented as taking place at an anniversary meeting of 'the Human Club'. This seems to imply a possible date in the summer of 1894; his letter to Oldershaw was written after the results of his year examinations had been announced.[17] Chesterton describes the members of his own fictional Human Club as being 'simply

---

[15] *Autobiography*, 97.   [16] BL MS Add. 73197, fos. 14–15.
[17] See p. 92 below.

studious and somewhat impressionable young gentlemen, whose main characteristic next to sympathy and sincerity, was that they had too keen a sense of humour not to get it mixed up with their seriousness, and thus produce a certain sense of burlesque in everything from the name of their club downwards'.[18] The 'Anniversary meeting' to which Gabriel Hope presents his stories was probably inspired by a reunion of the JDC which took place on 16 June 1894, one year after the second 'final' edition of *The Debater* recorded the club's official demise, and two years after Chesterton himself left St Paul's School. In the autumn of that year, one of his first letters from Bentley after the latter went up to Merton seems to imply that Chesterton's fictional invention had now been brought into being: 'you will be charmed to hear', wrote Bentley, 'that the Human Club exists . . . It was decided that it would be well to discuss things, and read papers, until it got homogeneous enough to come together for the fun of the thing alone, just like the J.D.C.'[19]

Chesterton almost certainly sat an English as well as a French examination in the summer of 1894, despite the fact that the surviving forms from the beginning of the academic year apparently show, in his case, a blank where students were invited to state which examinations they had in view (Ffinch claims not only that this confirms that Chesterton did not in fact sit any examinations, but that the reason was that 'it is likely that . . . he was not considered to be up to the standard';[20] Chesterton's letter to Oldershaw disproves these assumptions). It is obvious enough, though, that success in examinations was not for him an important objective; he was 'amused' to have done well, but had not bothered to check the departmental notice board to find out. More important to his intellectual formation was his attendance at the lectures on English literature of Professor W. P. Ker, then in the early stages of a distinguished and influential career. In the 1920s, he became Professor of Poetry at Oxford; in 1893, when Chesterton became one of his students, he had been professor at University College for four years. Chesterton attended his lectures even when nobody else did, a sign that he had been gripped by an unusual and fascinating teacher; as he recalled in the *Autobiography*, 'I am able to boast myself among the many pupils who are grateful to the extraordinarily lively and stimulating learning

---

[18] G. K. Chesterton, 'An Anniversary Meeting of the Human Club', *G. K. Chesterton Quarterly*, 28–9 (Autumn and Winter 2003), 6.

[19] BL MS Add. 73191.   [20] Ffinch, *Chesterton*, 36.

of Professor W. P. Ker.... [by attending his lectures] I gained an entirely undeserved reputation for disinterested devotion to culture for its own sake; and I once had the honour of constituting the whole of Professor Ker's audience. But he gave as thorough and thoughtful a lecture as I have ever heard given, in a slightly more colloquial style; asked me some questions about my reading; and on my mentioning something from the poetry of Pope, said with great satisfaction: "Ah, I see you have been well brought up." '[21]

Ker took great pains with his lectures. They were written first, then memorised precisely and delivered without a note. In one course, on medieval poetry, he forgot how far he had reached, and delivered precisely the same lecture two weeks running. His undergraduate lectures were delivered slowly, at little above dictation speed; this was, apparently, a Scottish habit, to allow students to take down every word. His lectures were gripping, nevertheless, and clearly captured Chesterton's imagination. An assessment written years later by another former University College undergraduate, Professor B. Ifor Evans, does much to explain why Chesterton should have been fascinated by Ker's mind: with obvious adjustments, Professor Evans might, at certain points, almost be writing about Chesterton himself:

I think one must realise how vast was his memory.... The power of retention and the organising power of synthesis were formidable. The talent for comparison was the most telling element in his criticism and it often also illuminated his work in a human and moving way.... He could illuminate one author by reference to another, and often one of a different period and country. The evidence on which such comparisons were based would be the result of long reading, but the result would be expressed simply, effortlessly. The mind would be left with a fresh illumination.

Professor Evans illustrates his point with the following extract from a lecture found among Ker's University College papers:

Most great writers begin with some sort of critical opposition to the follies, pedantries, and dullness of their predecessors and contemporaries. In the case of Rabelais, as in the case of Cervantes, there has been some exaggeration by commentators: too much emphasis has been laid on their hostility to the dullness of the past; too little has been made, perhaps, of their sympathy with the things they laughed at. That Cervantes was at heart and with no small fervour a lover of

---

[21] *Autobiography*, 97.

romance, that Rabelais never escaped, nor wished to escape, out of the comfortable absurdity of the Middle Ages, will sound like paradox only to people who have taken their own opinions from the commentators.

Rabelais, Shakespeare, and Cervantes have the enormous and unfair advantage over other writers that in addition to their 'abilities'... they had the whole abandoned region of medieval thought and imagination to take over and appropriate. Of course they saw the absurdity of it, but that was only one charm the more in their inheritance. They had all the profusion and complexity, all the strength and all the wealth of the Middle Ages to draw upon. The Reformers and the common humanists rejected it all, or drove their lean and blasted cattle through the medieval fields and brought them out as poor as when they went in. The Masters have another 'more thriving and generous policy'. The middle age as reality was impossible and absurd, was restored by them in a kind of *second intention*: as a humorous or poetical world in idea. They are extractors of quintessence.[22]

Professor Evans comments of this passage that 'he has contrived to bring evidence multiple and confusing in its incidence to a single clarified idea. He has been able to exercise that synthesising power because of his memory stretched in generous and easy retention from one century to another.'[23] The relevance of all this to Chesterton's own writing is obvious enough. It is generally assumed that the wide range of reference and the capacity for imaginative comparison demonstrated by Chesterton's literary criticism is another example of his autodidact's originality, and it is certainly true that— as much of his work in *The Debater* demonstrates—this was the way his mind naturally worked (certainly, it would explain why he found in Professor Ker a kindred spirit). But it is surely inexplicable that no biographer or commentator on Chesterton has ever suggested that in W. P. Ker (who was, after all, an important influence on the whole development of the academic study of English literature) he had a model for his own future work as a literary critic.

The least it is necessary to say about his university career is that despite the debacle and accompanying traumas he always associated with his attendance at the Slade School of Art, this dark side of his undergraduate years was the obverse of an intellectually more productive and generally more cheerful aspect of the same period: Professor Ker's lectures, together with his perfectly creditable French studies, constituted an important part of his intellectual development; they were also part of a process of emotional resistance to the 'morbid' and depressive feelings he was struggling against

---

[22] B. Ifor Evans, *W. P. Ker as a Critic of Literature* (Glasgow, 1955), 12–13.
[23] Ibid. 13.

at the same time. His brother was later to record of the whole three-year period—which includes his first year of private reading and art studies, as well as his two years at university—that though his time at the Slade was a failure, 'the years during which this experiment was being made were certainly not wasted. During the whole time he was writing incessantly and publishing practically nothing. He entered it crude and unformed; he left it almost mature. These silent years were full of reading and of thinking. He was brought face to face with the modern world, the creation of that liberal philosophy in which he had been trained, and it failed to satisfy him.'[24]

Revolution and reform

This dissatisfaction with 'that liberal philosophy in which he had been trained' had, of course, already been clearly in evidence while Chesterton was still at St Paul's. He had declared himself in his writings in *The Debater* as an admirer of the French Revolution, a republican, a fierce opponent of the Russian Tsar, a true believer in progress and the brotherhood of man. His first period of reaction against bourgeois liberalism, that is to say, led him in the opposite direction from that which he was later to take: he reacted against it not by becoming a defender of orthodoxy, but by becoming an armchair revolutionary.

His political instincts at the time, however, were not wholly a matter of striking picturesque attitudes. Inseparable from his colourful 'revolutionist' sentiments were serious feelings about the condition of the poor. W. T. Stead's journal *Review of Reviews* (which, as we have seen, was one source of Chesterton's feelings about tsarist outrages against the Jews) was also a vehicle for Stead's campaigns for social reform. This reminds us that the *fin de siècle*—even in the first half of the decade—was more than what Richard Ellman in his biography of Oscar Wilde calls 'the age of Dorian'. In one respect, as I have suggested, Chesterton's strongly moralistic attitude towards literary texts, reflected in JDC speeches he made during his last year at St Paul's, can be seen as a counter-cultural reaction against 'art for art's sake' and the decadent movement; his teenage reformist instincts, however—in a way which was to have an indelible effect on the formation of his

---

[24] Cecil, 16–17.

mature social and political beliefs—were a positive response to another important strand of contemporary opinion. As Holbrook Jackson put it in his classic account of the decade, *The Eighteen Nineties* (1913), 'side by side with the poseur worked the reformer, urged on by the revolutionist. There were demands for culture and social redemption... [for] the immediate regeneration of society by the abolition of such social evils as poverty and overwork, and the meanness, ugliness, ill-health and commercial rapacity which characterised much of modern life.'[25]

For Chesterton, all this was reflected in a kind of nascent religion of humanity, which would, in his imagination, somehow take root in the debris of the old religion. In a poem probably written after he had left St Paul's in the summer of 1892, and certainly published well into his year at the art college in St John's Wood, in the first final issue of *The Debater* (February 1893), he wrote of a mystical entity he called in somewhat inflated language 'The wonder, the holy, the highest', which he envisaged as somehow 'standing among men':

> A flower growing high as a star grows, yet fed with the life of men's roots,
> A race of men nearer the spirit, men farther, not nearer to brutes.[26]

The previous year, in a poem called 'Humanity', he had described the repudiation by the poem's dramatic protagonist of the elevated mystical state he has entered, in order once more to rejoin 'the brotherhood of men':

> ... let me feel the hands of brothers in the darkness grasping mine,
> As we stumble on together from the low to the divine.
> Give me back my mortal nature, mortal death and mortal birth,
> Keep your mystic, spotless spirits; take me back again to earth.[27]

This brings us to Chesterton's first published work in the national press, a poem entitled 'The Song of Labour', which appeared in *The Speaker*, after he had left St Paul's, in December 1892. It confirms what the excitable rhetoric of much of his *Debater* poetry had begun to suggest, that Chesterton's teenage political instincts had become distinctly more exotic than those of the Victorian bourgeois liberal tradition in which he had been brought up. Holbrook Jackson's typology, in *The Eighteen Nineties*, of 'the reformer, urged on by the revolutionist' places Chesterton firmly at this point in his life with 'the revolutionist':

---

[25] Holbrooke Jackson, *The Eighteen Nineties* (London, 1913), 24.
[26] *The Debater*, iii. 96.   [27] Ibid. 18.

Stand to it silently, brothers, and watch for the hour and the day.
We have tramped and toiled for the idle, we have sorrowed and starved
for the gay;
We have hewn out the road for the passers through thicket and
mountain high—
Stand to it bravely brothers, for the day and the hour are nigh.[28]

Again, we need to register the fact that these somewhat menacing revolutionary sentiments survived intact into adulthood, being expressed most famously, perhaps, in his poem about the people of England 'The Secret People', published in 1907 (the year before *Orthodoxy*):

It may be we shall rise the last as Frenchmen rose the first,
Our wrath come after Russia's wrath and our wrath be the worst.[29]

During a certain period in Chesterton's adolescence, belief in the brotherhood of man became, for a time, a semi-mystical posture which overlaid his leanings towards the Christian tradition, even in its liberalised 'theo-philanthropic' form; it is worth emphasising, all the same, that when, after a revolution of the mind, he embraced without reservation a form of Christian orthodoxy, the mystical attractions of this religion of mankind, and of the political tradition unleashed by the French Revolution, remained undimmed. It is interesting to contrast the politically radical Anglo-Catholic Chesterton of 1907 with another famous Anglican with Catholic sympathies at a similarly early but crucial stage in his own journey towards submission to Rome. John Henry Newman, on his Mediterranean tour of 1833, had had very different feelings, both about liberalism in general and French republicanism in particular. 'I had fierce thoughts against the Liberals', he recalled in the *Apologia pro Vita Sua*; 'It was the success of the Liberal cause which fretted me inwardly. I became fierce against its instruments and its manifestations. A French vessel was at Algiers; I would not even look at the tricolour.'[30] By the time Chesterton wrote 'The Secret People', times— and politics—had changed for Anglicans of Catholic mind. It has been supposed that Chesterton's positive feelings about the French republican and revolutionary tradition derived from the influence on him of Hilaire Belloc; but on this as on much else, his views were formed well before they met; and as we shall see, the churchmen who had the greatest influence on him when he later came to embrace the dogmatic principle in religion were

---

[28] *Collected Works*, i. 413.   [29] Ibid., x. 411.
[30] John Henry Newman, *Apologia pro Vita Sua*, ed. William Oddie (London, 1993), 111.

hardly of an anti-'revolutionist' cast of mind.[31] Certainly, during his *Debater* period and after he left school he for some years saw no contradiction between Christianity and radical politics, even socialism: as he wrote to Lawrence Solomon,[32] '[t]hose early Christians were the only true socialists, with the first fresh glory of the gospel teaching around them they could not be otherwise, for democracy is an essentially spiritual idea, a contradiction of the modern materialism which would encourage the brute tendency to an aristocracy of the physically "fittest".'

The radical sentiments of the 'Song of Labour' were not specifically socialist. His friends did not necessarily think so at the time: Lawrence Solomon wrote to congratulate him 'on the poem you have got published', though he continued, 'Whether or not I can give my imprimatur to a socialistic poem must of course remain at present a matter of doubt', adding coyly '(very diplomatic, this)'.[33] The poem was not in fact 'socialistic' (except perhaps in some rhetorical sense), though Cecil, too, described it as being, 'in its general tendency at least, a socialist poem'; it is, though, open to doubt whether Chesterton, as he wrote it, had any very clear idea what socialism was. But during the year which followed its publication, Chesterton was to enter a period in his life during which he certainly came not only to understand what socialism was—though Cecil did not think that 'his grip on economic Socialism was ever very firm'—but also to see himself as a full-blown, committed socialist.

This was not, of course, how he later remembered this period of his life. His own memory, many years later, as he recalled these years in the *Autobiography*, was that he had never seriously embraced socialism at any time:

The two great movements during my youth and early manhood were Imperialism and Socialism. They were supposed to be fighting each other; and so doubtless they did, in the sense of waving Red Flags against Union Jacks. But as compared with those dim gropings in my own imagination, the two things were in union; at least as much in union as the Union Jack. Both believed in unification and centralisation on a large scale. Neither could have seen any meaning in my own fancy for having things on a smaller and smaller scale. . . . I called myself a Socialist; because the only alternative to being a Socialist was not being a Socialist. And not being a Socialist was a perfectly ghastly thing. It meant being a small-headed and sneering snob, who grumbled at the rates and the working-classes; or some hoary horrible old

---

[31] See pp. 177–81 below.   [32] Ffinch, *Chesterton*, 28.
[33] BL MS Add. 73198, fo. 155.

Darwinian who said the weakest must go to the wall. But in my heart I was a reluctant Socialist. I accepted the larger thing as the lesser evil—or even the lesser good.[34]

But this was certainly not how he reacted to socialism at the time; this passage, it has to be said, is a prime example of how, in retrospect, auto-biographies can both telescope time and rewrite personal history to conform with the predilections of later life. Chesterton's anti-imperialism, and his 'fancy for having things on a smaller and smaller scale', date from a time, a good six or seven years later, when his adult journalistic career was already under way, and when one of his first campaigns was for the pro-Boer cause; and his period as a self-confessed socialist had already come to an end well before he became an anti-imperialist.

It began at some point during 1893, when Chesterton came across one of the literary sensations of the year, a collection of articles on socialism, reprinted from *The Clarion* newspaper by the Fabian Society member who had founded it, one Robert Blatchford— with an exquisite irony, the same Robert Blatchford with whom, a decade later—as we shall see—Chesterton was to lock horns over Blatchford's campaign against Christianity (again in *The Clarion* newspaper). The book was entitled *Merrie England*: and to call it a 'best-seller' is hardly to overstate the case: it sold over two million copies (nearly a million of them in America). Before *Merrie England*'s publication, *The Clarion*'s circulation was around 34,000; afterwards, it almost doubled. Blatchford was strongly influenced by William Morris. *Merrie England* propagated a vision in which socialism (in Morris's words) would seek the 'completest physical, moral and intellectual development of every human being as the highest form of the social state, as the best and truest happiness for every individual and for every class, where, as none need overwork, so none shall be able to force others to work for their profit'.[35] Blatchford, following Morris, reacted against the inhumanities of modern society and idealised pre-industrial societies in which workers could be artists and craftsmen. All this is entirely consistent with Chesterton's later idealisation of the English Middle Ages; it may be worth asking, indeed, whether this may not be a key point in Chesterton's intellectual history for the strengthening of this particular strand in his thinking.

---

[34] *Autobiography*, 109.

[35] William Morris and H. M. Hyndman, *A Summary of the Principles of Socialism* (London, 1884), 56.

Certainly, Chesterton's reaction to the book was one of instant conversion to the cause, and of a jubilant hero-worship of Blatchford himself, as an almost chivalric figure of justice and valour. Chesterton's later claim that 'in my heart I was a reluctant Socialist' is firmly contradicted by the contemporary evidence. Chesterton declared his new enthusiasm to Oldershaw:

11 Warwick Gardens
Dear Lucien,
My cousin Jack writing from Cambridge to his sister artlessly asks if I have read 'Merrie England' and would I please say what I feel about socialism? I am writing a letter. A Blatchford! A Blatchford! St Henry George for 'Merrie England' and down with everything. I have sometimes had a curious idea (I wish it were not so cold and my letter would be legible) that I should like to have a tea-party of about six individuals: I mean real individuals. Christ, Walt Whitman, St Francis, Robert Burns, and Mr Tom Mann, round our table would be very funny. It may be noted that the first two to be mentioned have themselves undertaken to be present when required. But what I wish to draw your attention to is, that I had chosen most of these individuals before I noticed that they were none of them victors of individualism that they were all of the class which the so called individualism tends to depress & eliminate. The fact is that the dead level barrack idea of socialism is really much more true of warehouse commercialism. Under socialism people would have peace & time to be individuals instead of being clerks. The present system which tends to depress Mr Keir Hardie . . . cannot be said to be favourable to individuality, for it is quite the opposite. But it is not you that have asked for my views on socialism. Suffice it to say that I believe that this [is] what the Old Churches felt instinctively to be the essential conflict between riches and the soul.[36]

His later belief that socialism was about 'unification and centralisation on a large scale' is implicitly rejected here: individuality is seen as being most threatened by laissez-faire individualism, whereas 'Under socialism people would have peace & time to be individuals instead of being clerks'.

Tom Mann, whom Chesterton mentions here with Christ, St Francis, and others (characteristically, imagined as being gathered around a tea table, presumably well furnished with sticky buns), was an openly declared Marxist, having been converted by reading the *Communist Manifesto* in 1886. He subsequently became campaign manager of Keir Hardie's successful attempt to enter Parliament, and in 1889 became one of the organisers of the London dock strike. 'St Henry George' was Henry George, an American socialist journalist, author of the hugely successful *Progress and*

[36] BL MS Add. 73197, fo. 6.

Poverty (1879), in which he invented the concept of wage slavery. These, in socialist circles, were the iconic names of the day; Chesterton may simply be bandying them round here, or he may have gone deeper into his subject than, without further evidence, we can tell. What seems unmistakable, however, is Chesterton's youthful enthusiasm for this new political cause, which gave him, for a time, a perspective within which he could locate the question of religion. His last *Debater* poem, 'Ave Maria', was written towards the end of 1892 or in early 1893; as we have seen,[37] it is based on the idiosyncratic notion that modern ideas of progress are somehow built on the foundation of medieval religious aspirations. Chesterton's 'view of socialism' now was that 'I believe that this [is] what the Old Churches felt instinctively to be the essential conflict between riches and the soul.' Religion, he thought, was not dead, but in a process of transition. 'The Old Churches' belonged to the past: their structures lay in ruins, but their foundations were being built on by others, who represented more fundamental and unshakeable human verities. As he had expressed it in 'The Song of Labour',

> God has struck all into chaos, princes and priests down-hurled,
> But he leaves the place of the toiler, the old estate of the world.
> In a season of doubt and wrangle, in the thick of a world's uproar,
> With the new life dark in wrestle, with the ghost of a life that is o'er,
> When the old Priest fades to a phantom, when the old King nods on his
>   throne,
> The old, old hand of Labour is mighty and holdeth its own.[38]

We have touched on the great upheaval which during this year was raging in Chesterton's mind and feelings, and we can see it reflected, perhaps, in his confused ideas about the Christian religion (which he began to see as being on the edge of some great spiritual revolution); we can see it, too, in a theme which begins to recur in his thinking, the problem (both cultural and personal) of 'pessimism'. This became for him, almost obsessively (and for the rest of his life), one distinguishing mark of the great intellectual enemy of the times, the dragon that had to be slain; at this period, it represents also, perhaps, the depressive tendency within himself, which over the next two years was nearly to overwhelm him before it was exorcized for ever. Socialism for the 18-year-old Chesterton is on the side of optimism—it performs for him the role of a kind of political

---

[37] See p. 73 above.   [38] *Collected Works*, x. 412–13.

anti-depressant. The concurrent influence of Whitman is crucial here, for, as Cecil pointed out, 'though Whitman himself was an Anarchist rather than a Socialist, his influence on the Socialist movement was immense, and young Socialists talked continually the language of Whitmanism, preaching comradeship, equality, and good will among men—in a word, the very things which G. K. Chesterton was then intent on proclaiming'.[39] Optimism is the great test: Chesterton's great heroes, his list of 'real individuals' gathered around his imaginary tea table, are those who inspire it: Christ (whom, as we shall see, he describes at about this time as 'the great optimist of history'[40]), Walt Whitman, St Francis, Robert Burns, Tom Mann.

All these themes are fascinatingly touched on in a long letter to Bentley, written during the 1893 long vacation. The letter's relevance to Chesterton's own personal situation is very clear; the phrase 'morbid young men who might lie under the cloud' could even be taken as referring directly to his own current frame of mind:

Fernbank, North Berwick

... I have, as you remarked in a previous letter, followed the suicide controversy in the incomparable Chronicle with interest, read especially the letter of Morison Davidson (Socialist and Christian) and the leading article. The latter stirred me very much because it was evidently directed, with a personal earnestness, which the prosy, bewigged old Times would frown on, at morbid young men who might lie under the cloud, and the whole of its manly peroration was a direct appeal to them. 'As for the pessimists,' it said in conclusion 'we are convinced that though they may from time to time draw away one or two weak natures, they will never permanently depress the unconquerable soul of man.' That is what I think of when I say that it is 'all very well' to abuse journalism. My advice about Ernest and his like is this. Face for a moment the conception of the world being a sham, of the sum of all things being barren, and you will feel it is impossible. Whatever the secret of the world may be, it must in the face of feelings that are in me, be something intelligible and satisfying. This instinct of the hidden meaning is the eternal ground of all religions: every deity and heaven ever conceived was only an embodiment of the ultimate or central victory of right. From the lowest savage who thought the world would be more sensible if there were a spirit in that cocoa-nut, up to the great optimist of history who taught that God fed the ravens and arrayed the lilies, religion has always been, relatively to the time, good news. If we cannot, in this transition stage, on the eve I fancy of a new spiritual movement, say our shibboleth to any distinct sect or dogma of existing religion, we can at least rest on the eternal natural ground of belief in the world from which all religions spring. That is my

---

[39] Cecil, 27.   [40] BL MS Add. 73191.

view of pessimism in its abstract light, but of course the real remedy for such faddists is, as you said, genuine friendship: together with a little touch of the real hardship which Morison Davidson mentions as a thing that the unhappy masses, with no grasp of the aesthetic have to stoically endure.[41]

'Morison Davidson' was John Morrison Davidson, a barrister of the Middle Temple, and an eccentrically radical Christian socialist. In one of his letters to the *Daily Chronicle*, published on 24 January 1893, he describes Christ and his followers as communists, and insists that though 'Karl Marx was an utter pagan', 'there is not an essential proposition in *Das Kapital* that Jesus of Nazareth did not inculcate'. His letter to the *Daily Chronicle* on suicide, written on 22 August, not only insists that the teachings of Jesus were intrinsically hostile to private property, but strongly implies that capitalism is the root cause of suicide:

Within a comparatively brief period ten men of good culture, with whom I was more or less intimately acquainted have committed suicide . . . all of them succumbed directly or indirectly to the fierce strain put upon them by the cruel Moloch of competition. 'Disgust and secret loathing fell' upon them they hardly knew why; but alas! They fell. They were wearied with *competition* which means *war*, and they were unable to embrace *co-operation* which means *peace*.
Six of them were Christians but not one of the six . . . could be made to comprehend Christ's cardinal mission on earth, or their end would have been otherwise. That mission was to dethrone the brute god of this world, 'Mammon', otherwise to uproot the baleful institution of 'private property'.[42]

'A sick cloud upon the soul'

The academic year 1892–3 was the year when Chesterton became a socialist; the next academic year, 1893–4, he began his studies at University College, London, in whose buildings the Slade School of Art (though an independent entity) was housed. Some biographies skate over the fact that Chesterton studied other subjects apart from art, and it is understandable why they should. For, though his formal artistic studies did little to turn him into a real artist, it was at the Slade that he came into contact with current trends in art—particularly as they embodied the principles and intellectual implications of Impressionism (which he seems to have understood as

---

[41] Ibid.
[42] Reprinted in J. Morrison Davidson, *The Gospel of the Poor* (London, 1896), 153 and 161–2.

one manifestation of the philosophy of the aesthetic or decadent movement, of 'art for art's sake'). The intellectual atmosphere of the Slade affected him profoundly, in a way which he was always to associate with the 'morbid' state of mind into which, intermittently, he fell most intensely during that year.

In the *Autobiography*, he identifies contemporary aesthetic theory as epitomising the way in which one particular intellectual error was inseparable from the 'morbidities' into which he found himself falling:

Mine was the time of Impressionism. . . . The very latest thing was to keep abreast of Whistler and take him by the white forelock, as if he were Time himself. Since then that conspicuous white forelock has rather faded into a harmony of white and grey and what was once so young has in its turn grown hoary. But I think there was a spiritual significance in Impressionism, in connection with this age as the age of scepticism. I mean that it illustrated scepticism in the sense of subjectivism. Its principle was that if all that could be seen of a cow was a white line and a purple shadow, we should only render the line and the shadow; in a sense we should only believe in the line and the shadow, rather than in the cow. . . . Whatever may be the merits of this as a method of art, there is obviously something highly subjective and sceptical about it as a method of thought. It naturally lends itself to the metaphysical suggestion that things only exist as we perceive them, or that things do not exist at all. The philosophy of Impressionism is necessarily close to the philosophy of Illusion. And this atmosphere also tended to contribute, however indirectly, to a certain mood of unreality and sterile isolation that settled at this time upon me; and I think upon many others.[43]

This particular critique of Impressionism seems remote to us now: but it was very much to the point at the time; the reaction against 'scepticism in the sense of subjectivism'—that 'we should only believe in the line and the shadow' rather than in the object represented—was, for instance, essentially the issue that had famously emerged when Whistler sued Ruskin for libel for describing one of his paintings as 'flinging a pot of paint in the public's face'. When Ruskin's counsel asked Whistler what a nocturne was, he replied that it was a word he applied to his night pieces, which were primarily arrangements of line, form, and colour, to be looked on as such and not because of any outside interest; when the judge asked whether *Nocturne in Blue and Silver* represented Battersea bridge, and whether the figures on top were intended for people, Whistler replied, 'They are just

[43] *Autobiography*, 88–9.

what you like.'[44] In his influential best-seller *Modern Painting* (published in 1893, the year Chesterton began his time at the Slade) George Moore—who reputedly introduced the British public to Impressionism and was a major influence over the Slade's principal, Fred Brown—wrote (interestingly, with Ruskin's attack specifically in mind) that '[m]ore than any other man, Mr. Whistler has helped to purge art of the vice of subject and belief that the mission of the artist is to copy nature'.[45] Moore was an influence, too, over Brown's colleagues at the Slade, Henry Tonks and P. Wilson Steer.[46]

But it was not Impressionism, or even subjectivism, that brought Chesterton to the edge of mental and emotional breakdown, to the period in his life he was to look back on later with such horror. His revulsion was against one particular aspect of contemporary culture, and is not to be dismissed as reflecting simply his own morbid frame of mind at the time. It had already begun in his time at St Paul's; as he recalled in his dedication to Bentley of *The Man who was Thursday* (referred to hereafter as 'the Bentley dedication'):

> A cloud was on the mind of men
> And wailing went the weather,
> Yea, a sick cloud upon the soul
> When we were boys together

Cecil refers to his disappointment in the liberalism in which Chesterton had grown up having been 'aggravated by his loathing for the decadent school which then dominated "advanced" literature', and records that 'it...set him thinking'.[47] The Bentley dedication recalls (in a context that makes the reference to the decadents clear) that the two boys talked, on their long walks together, of

> The doubts that drove us through the night
> As we two talked amain,
> And day had broken on the streets
> Ere it broke upon the brain

---

[44] William Gaunt, *The Aesthetic Adventure* (London, 1957), 109, 112.

[45] George Moore, *Modern Painting* (London, 1893), 23–4.

[46] John D. Coates, *Chesterton and the Edwardian Cultural Crisis* (Hull, 1984), 196–7.

[47] Cecil, 17. This actually reads '*must have* set him thinking': I have omitted the words 'must have' , since their purpose is clearly to preserve Cecil's anonymity. His meaning is that these things *did* set him thinking. Cecil, of course, was in his early teenage years at the time; his knowledge of his brother's frame of mind at this period of his life probably derived from later discussion.

Oldershaw, too, joined in what was probably a general disapproval of the decadent school among members of the JDC, though it was never formally debated, and except for occasional references to Swinburne as representing a school of poetry deficient in the moral sense, was studiously ignored in *The Debater*. We know, however, from the Diary that Oldershaw disapproved of the aesthetic movement as much as Chesterton and Bentley did:

Drawing room of 7 Talgarth Road. Old's sister discovered.
To her enter Oldershaw and Y[our] H[umble] S[ervant]
Old (to sister) What are you reading?
(Volume displayed, 'yellow-backed to the core' as Bentley would say).
Old (with some asperity) Reading that again
Sister (defiantly) Yes.[48]

The intensely controversial nature of the decadent movement (and everything it implied in terms of moral—particularly sexual—principles and behaviour) had already been forgotten a generation later. In a review of the *Autobiography*, published after Chesterton's death in 1936, Sidney Dark, editor of the *Church Times*, quoted the Bentley dedication:

> Life was a fly that faded, and death a drone that stung:
> The world was very old indeed when you and I were young.
> They twisted even decent sin to shapes not to be named:
> Men were ashamed of honour; but we were not ashamed.

'The assumption is', commented Dark, 'that the nineties really were the extremely naughty nineties. The truth is that the nineties were no more naughty than the eighties or the seventies.'[49] This, if it means that the intellectual undercurrents of the time, as the turn of the century approached, displayed no observable shift in sexual ethics or mores, is simply wrong. The 'decadent' movement was at the height of its influence; its 'decadence' was self-declared, and it declared itself, *inter alia*, in terms of sexual behaviour, notably homoerotic sexual behaviour—what Chesterton calls here 'twisting even decent sin to shapes not to be named'. And 'aesthetes' apart, there was in the 1890s a more general sense that the moral atmosphere of the period had changed, that the Victorian age was in the process of coming—or had in some sense already come—to an end,

---

[48] BL MS Add. 73317A, fo. 55. This is not a reference to Aubrey Beardsley's *Yellow Book*, which did not appear until 1894, but to the decadent 'yellow-back' French novels to which the title of Beardsley's journal itself referred. 'Yellow-backed to the core' means 'decadent'.

[49] Sidney Darke, signed review, *Church Times* (6 Nov. 1936); Conlon, 538.

in short that a *fin de siècle* had arrived in some more than merely literal sense. Chesterton's perception, in 'The Song of Labour' (1892), was that this was 'a season of doubt and wrangle...With the new life dark in wrestle, with the ghost of a life that is o'er'. Literature and art were seen as having moved into a new and distinctive period; the unchallenged certainties of Victorian England (those few certainties, at any rate, that actually *were* unchallenged) had already passed away. One has to add that *making* them pass away had been for some of the most publicly noticeable artists and writers their principal aspiration.

For such as these, the first and most obvious target had to be the notion that art had a moral purpose, a notion which was one of the central maxims of Victorian aesthetic theory. The declaration that the purpose of art was art itself was in the first place a declaration of autonomy from ethical meaning: this was the issue underlying the controversy between Ruskin and Whistler, and more obviously in Oxford between Ruskin and Walter Pater. As Wilde puts it, almost insolently, in his preface to *The Picture of Dorian Gray*, 'There is no such thing as a moral or an immoral book. Books are well written or badly written. That is all.... No artist has ethical sympathies. An ethical sympathy is an unpardonable mannerism of style.'[50]

It is also true, of course, that the cultural roots of the 1890s were to be found in the 1880s and the 1870s, just as the roots of any decade are in the decades that precede it. These are the necessary platitudes of cultural history. Thus, in speaking of the aesthetic movement, whose popular apogee certainly arrived in the 1890s, of course we have to remember that the English movement was well under way by the beginning of the 1880s. It was in 1881—when little Gilbert Chesterton was 7—that Oscar Wilde had been caricatured in Gilbert and Sullivan's *Patience*; and the real origins of the aesthetic movement in England are to be found even earlier.[51] In *De Profundis*, Wilde refers to the influence on him of Walter Pater's *Studies in the History of the Renaissance* (1873), describing it as 'that book which has had such a strange influence over my life'; here if anywhere is the English movement's most seminal text, if not its *fons et origo*. Pater's influence on Wilde was personal as well as literary, of course; they were friends in Oxford when Wilde was an undergraduate at Magdalen and Pater a fellow of Brasenose; Pater lent him subversive books (such as Flaubert's

---

[50] Oscar Wilde, *The Picture of Dorian Gray*, *Collected Works* (London: Collins Classics, 1994), 17.
[51] William Gaunt, *The Aesthetic Adventure* (London, 1957), 61 ff.

Trois Contes, a source for *Salomé*) and they often went for walks and took tea together.[52]

Pater had a 'strange influence' on many more than Wilde. We need to ask why this was. The first explanation, perhaps, was Pater's emphasis on the subjective experience of the moment as the overwhelming priority for the way life was to be lived: this is always dangerously seductive to the young, and actually to the middle-aged, too. It was to be a dangerous belief for the twentieth century: and it was held passionately by Pater and his followers. Here it is in the most famous (and influential) passage in Pater's *History of the Renaissance*:

Every moment some form grows perfect in hand or face; some tone on the hill or sea is choicer than the rest; some mood or passion or insight or intellectual excitement is irresistibly real and attractive to us—for that moment only. Not the fruit of experience but experience itself, is the end. . . . How shall we pass from point to point, and be present always at the focus where the greatest number of vital forces unite in their purest energy?

To burn always with this hard, gem-like flame, to maintain this ecstasy is success in life. In a sense it might even be said that our failure is to form habits. . . . While all melts under our feet, we may as well grasp at any exquisite passion, or any contribution to knowledge that seems by a lifted horizon to set the spirit free for a moment, or any stirring of the senses, strange dyes, strange colours, and curious odours, or work of the artist's hands, or the face of one's friend. Not to discriminate every moment some passionate attitude in those about us, and in the very brilliancy of their gifts some tragic dividing of forces on their ways is, on this short day of frost and sun, to sleep before evening. . . . Great passions may give us this quickened sense of life, ecstasy and sorrow of love. . . . Of such wisdom, the poetic passion, the desire of beauty, the love of art for its own sake, has most. For art comes to you proposing frankly to give nothing but the highest quality to your moments as they pass, and simply for those moments' sake.[53]

It is not hard to see, coming when it did—in the early 1870s—why writing like this was so influential on the young. And its influence, of course, was not only aesthetic but moral: for this passionate and, one has to say, intrinsically egotistical obsession with the spirit set free to experience anything and everything was, inevitably, accompanied by a deeply held moral relativism which confronted all moral principles and religious creeds, and any social institution—most obviously, for instance, marriage—which might stand in the way of burning with a 'hard, gem-like flame'. Thus, Pater

[52] Richard Ellman, *Oscar Wilde* (London, 1987), 80–1.
[53] Walter Pater, *Studies in the History of the Renaissance* (London, 1873), 373.

rejects any 'theory or idea or system which requires of us the sacrifice of any part of this experience'.

We have seen Chesterton's strong inclination, in JDC debates held during his final year in school (1891–2), to judge art and literature by its moral content before all else, and it seems clear that he was, even then, already reacting against the currently fashionable mantra 'art for art's sake'— a slogan given currency in England at least partly by Pater's general notion, as he expresses it in the famous concluding passage from his *Renaissance* quoted above, that art 'comes to you proposing frankly to give nothing but the highest quality to your moments as they pass, and simply *for those moments' sake*'.[54] At no time did Chesterton's views on the essentially moral character of art and literature waver. In a notebook which appears to date from around his time (1893–4) at the Slade School of Art[55] (it will be convenient to refer to this hereafter as 'the Slade notebook') Chesterton recorded his reactions to this passage (which he dismisses at the outset with the words 'Walter Pater is all beautiful bosh'). He comments first that

You cannot have glorious moments and enjoy them 'simply for those moments' sake'. For suppose a man has a truly glorious moment, not something about a bit of enamel, I mean, but something violently and painfully happy. A moment of ecstasy in first love, for instance, or a moment of victory in battle. The lover enjoys the moment, but not for the moment's sake. He enjoys it for the woman's sake. The warrior enjoys the moment but not for the moment. He enjoys it for the sake of the flag. The cause of the flag may be foolish. The love may be calf-love and last a week. But the patriotic soldier thinks the flag immortal: the lover thinks his love will never die. These moments are full of eternity: these moments are splendid

---

[54] My emphasis. Pater was one of two writers who first used the English phrase 'Art for Art's sake' (the other was Swinburne) in 1868; it is a translation of 'L'Art pour l'Art', a slogan attributed to Théophile Gautier, and Pater used it in a review of William Morris's poetry in the *Westminster Review*, a modified version of which appeared in his *Studies in the History of the Renaissance* five years later.

[55] The original notebook appears to have been lost, but extracts from it were transcribed by Chesterton's secretary, Dorothy Collins, and published by *The Tablet* (4 Apr. 1953). Her typescript is headed 'EXTRACTS FROM NOTE-BOOK (About 1893. G.K.C. aged 19)'. There is no firm internal evidence for this date, but the notebook's contents are consistent with a dating around 1893 to the first half of 1894—after the summer of 1894 Chesterton's preoccupations, recorded copiously in the well-known notebook (see pp. 144–56 below) which we can date firmly as beginning in the autumn of 1894, changed radically. The concerns of the 'Slade notebook' reflect what I have called his 'struggle against the blight of…"pessimism"' and his hatred of decadence and the aesthetic movement: his preoccupations in this earlier notebook include Walter Pater, the nature of optimism (see p. 115), and the need to believe in a devil and engage in spiritual warfare against him (see pp. 115 and 118 ff).

because they do <u>not</u> seem momentary. Man cannot love mortal things: he can only love immortal things for an instant.[56]

Chesterton now proceeds to record a *pensée* on Pater's essentially amoral axiom that 'Great passions may give us [the] quickened sense of life' which is for him the test of 'success in life'; his reaction is characteristically a moral one: 'Purity and simplicity are essential to passions—yes, even to vile passions. Even vice demands virgins.' In another entry he addresses what he sees as 'Pater's root mistake', 'revealed in his most famous phrase. He asks us to "burn with a hard, gemlike flame". You cannot handle flames. You cannot handle passions. His error is precisely that he wishes us to treat flames as one treats gems. He will burn his fingers'[57]—an analysis which exemplifies a feature of Chesterton's imagination which was to become more and more characteristic: his distaste for the abstract and high-flown, and his love of the actual and tangible, for what can be touched and 'handled'.

Pater's *Renaissance* appeared in the year before Chesterton was born in 1874: thus, we can say that the English aesthetic movement's single greatest influence appeared just before Chesterton's birth, that the movement came to its years of greatest notoriety in the five years beginning in 1890, when Chesterton was 16, and then disappeared virtually overnight with Oscar Wilde's conviction for sodomy in 1895—that is, when Chesterton was 21. So English aestheticism grew to its full maturity as Chesterton did, and came to a sensational end as Chesterton came of age.

Within a decade of Wilde's death, Chesterton himself perceptively wrote that 'the very cloud of tragedy that rested on his career makes it easier to treat him as a mere artist now': 'the healthy horror of the evil', said Chesterton, had been neutralised by a 'healthy horror of the punishment'.[58] It is worth asking, though, *what was the evil that Chesterton had in mind?* There can be little doubt that (as he expressed it in the dedication to *The Man who was Thursday*) this 'sick cloud upon the soul' affected him deeply, despite his apparent dismissal of its effect in the *Autobiography*. 'Something may have been due', he wrote forty years later—in explanation of the 'mood of unreality and sterile isolation that settled at this time upon [him]'—'to the atmosphere of the Decadents, and their perpetual hints of the luxurious horrors of paganism; *but I am not disposed to dwell much on that*

---

[56] G. K. Chesterton, 'From the Note-books of G.K.C.', *The Tablet* (4 Apr. 1953).
[57] Ibid.
[58] G. K. Chesterton, *A Handful of Authors*, ed. Dorothy Collins (London, 1953), 143.

defence'. By the 1930s, the memory of his revulsion at the implications of 'the green carnation' had dimmed, perhaps: but as we shall see, references to the decadents made by him during the first decade of the new century reflect a still raw and passionate loathing.

It is important to be clear, when seeking to understand what Chesterton meant by his 'healthy horror of the evil', that we are *not* discussing the simple question of Wilde's personal 'sexual preference'. It was Wilde's symbolic position as the centre and figurehead of an artistic and literary subculture that was not only pervasively homoerotic but also expressly subversive that so alarmed many of his contemporaries, including the youthful Chesterton. And in this undermining of moral stability, art was apparently encouraged by science in the sweeping away of all existing creeds and social institutions. To return to the opening of the Bentley dedication,

> Science announced nonentity
> And art admired decay:
> The world was old and ended
> But you and I were gay.

What Cecil Chesterton describes as 'the decadent school, which then dominated "advanced literature"'' had, I am certain, a more powerful effect on the development of Chesterton's thought than we have yet fully recognised. The decadents, of course, were far from monopolising social and moral thinking in the 1890s. I have quoted Holbrook Jackson's formulation,[59] that 'side by side with the poseur worked the reformer, urged on by the revolutionist'; it would be more true to say that the reformer was working against or in denial of the poseur as much as side by side with him (despite Wilde's *The Soul of Man under Socialism* (1891), a perhaps unique attempt to establish an intellectual compatibility). It was what he believed to be an ultimate incompatibility of poseur and reformer which later impelled Chesterton, even as he argued against Shaw and the Fabians, to give them the honour due to those who had at least gone against the grain of what he undoubtedly perceived as the dominant culture of the early 1890s. The 'clean appetite for order and equity', he wrote in *George Bernard Shaw* (1909), 'had fallen to a lower ebb, had more nearly disappeared altogether, during Shaw's earlier epoch than at any other time. . . . The decay of society was praised by artists as the decay of a corpse is praised by

---

[59] Jackson, *The Eighteen Nineties*, 24.

worms. The aesthete was all receptiveness, like the flea. His only affair in this world was to feed on its facts and colours, like a parasite on blood.' This image of the decadents as parasites is even more vividly expressed in *Robert Browning* (1903), in which he describes the responsibility of Elizabeth Barrett's father for her ill health by declaring that 'The truth was that Edward Barrett was living emotionally and aesthetically, like some detestable decadent poet, upon his daughter's decline.'[60] Chesterton's expressions of revulsion for Wilde and his milieu, in books written a decade and more after the decadent movement had crashed into ruins, reflect in their raw passion how closely he had been affected by it at a crucial stage in his own intellectual development:

I have in my time had my fling at the Fabian society, at the pedantry of schemes, the arrogance of experts; nor do I regret it now. But when I remember that other world against which it reared its bourgeois banner of cleanliness and commonsense, I will not end this chapter without doing it decent honour. Give me the drain-pipes of the Fabians rather than the pan-pipes of the later poets; the drain-pipes have a nicer smell. Give me even that business-like benevolence that herded men like beasts rather than that exquisite art which isolated them like devils; give me even the suppression of *Zaeo*[61] rather than the triumph of *Salome*.[62]

One effect of the decadent school for Chesterton was profoundly to depress him, or at least to mirror the state of morbid depression into which he fell, intermittently, during his year at the Slade. 'In that period', he wrote of the early 1890s in *Robert Louis Stevenson* (1927), 'we might almost say that pessimism was another name for culture. Cheerfulness was associated with the Philistine, like the broad grin with the bumpkin. . . . Oscar Wilde, who perhaps filled up more room . . . than anybody else on that stage at that moment, expressed his philosophy in that bitter parable in which Christ seeks to comfort a man weeping and is answered, "Lord, I was dead and you raised me to life; what else can I do but weep?" '[63]

Here, we have to note a great irony: all that aesthetic grasping—to quote Pater—'at any exquisite passion, or any contribution to knowledge that seems by a lifted horizon to set the spirit free for a moment' had led, by the decadent movement's heyday in the early 1890s, not to the passionate

[60] G. K. Chesterton, *Robert Browning* (London, 1903), 60.

[61] Miss Zaeo was a dancer notorious for her skimpy costume; a charming poster (of which Chesterton obviously did not disapprove) showing her thus attired was suppressed by the London County Council.

[62] *Collected Works*, xi. 401.   [63] Ibid., xviii. 74–5.

intensity that Pater longed for, but to the reverse—to a state of mind characterised by a uniform tone of languor and disillusionment. If to burn with a 'hard gem-like flame' and 'to maintain this ecstasy' was indeed 'success in life', then the movement had utterly failed. Consider this informative exchange (which shows Wilde as being as much a detached commentator on the decadent movement as an exemplar of it) from *The Picture of Dorian Gray*:

'Fin de siècle', murmured Lord Henry.
'Fin du globe', answered his hostess.
'I wish it were fin du globe', said Dorian with a sigh. 'Life is a great disappointment.'[64]

'A cloud was on the mind of men', wrote Chesterton looking back from a safe distance; 'a sick cloud on the soul'.

This brings us back to the Bentley dedication, the middle stanza of which, I suggest, contains vital clues about Chesterton's spiritual crisis and his struggle against it. We begin with Whitman, then proceed to Stevenson, then end, rather unexpectedly, perhaps, with John Bunyan. The antithesis for all of them is Oscar Wilde, here evoked by his symbol, the green carnation:

> I find again the book we found,
>   I feel the hour that flings
> Far out of fish-shaped Paumanok
>   Some cry of cleaner things;
> And the Green Carnation withered.
>   As in forest fires that pass,
> Roared in the wind of all the world,
>   Ten million leaves of grass.

Whitman's *Leaves of Grass*, of course, is 'the book we found'; 'fish-shaped Paumanok' is Long Island, Whitman's home. Chesterton now moves on to Stevenson:

> Or sane and sweet and sudden as
>   A bird sings in the rain—
> Truth out of Tusitala spoke
>   And pleasure out of pain.
> Yes, cool and clear and sudden as

---

[64] Wilde, *Collected Works*, 130.

> A bird sings in the grey,
> Dunedin to Samoa spoke,
> And darkness unto day

Tusitala is the name of the Samoan natives for Stevenson (it means 'story teller'); Dunedin is the Gaelic form for Edinburgh, Stevenson's birthplace; Samoa, of course, is where Stevenson settled and finally died. Stevenson, according to Cecil, 'was the only writer who could be said to compete' with Whitman as an influence on the young Gilbert. His explanation was that his was a philosophy in which 'It was a fine thing that the weak should take the sword and conquer the strong'.[65]

This brings us naturally to Bunyan. And here we note a new dimension.

> But we were young; we lived to see
> God break their bitter charms,
> God and the good republic
> Come riding back in arms:
> We have seen the City of Mansoul,
> Even as it rocked, relieved—

This is a reference to *The Holy War* (1682), Bunyan's second spiritual allegory. By general consent it lacks the force of *Pilgrim's Progress*: but what appears to have interested Chesterton was that it is about the struggle for the salvation of a whole culture as much as for the salvation of individual souls. In Bunyan's story, the City of Mansoul is besieged by the hosts of Satan. The City is relieved by the army of Emanuel, and is later undermined by further diabolic attacks and plots against his rule.

Now, we have moved on in no uncertain way. And it is at this point, it seems to me, that we find an important key to Chesterton's own feelings about those years in which he was coming to literary maturity. It is not simply that the *fin de siècle* was a period in which men had gone mad: it was a time when they were possessed by a great evil, in which the city, like Mansoul, was besieged by the hosts of the devil. As he goes on to put it in the Bentley dedication—in dramatic and almost allegorical language which really does make one think of Bunyan—men were 'cowed' by 'colossal gods of shame'. They were filled with doubts 'dreadful to withstand'; it was a time in which 'huge devils hid the stars'.

This is a language very different from that of the humorous argumentation with which Chesterton was, in the early years of the new century,

---

[65] Cecil, 40.

already fighting the culture wars of later decades. And yet it is here, I think, that we must look for the real origins of Chesterton's mature philosophy of life. Chestertonian orthodoxy begins not simply with a perception of unorthodoxy, of intellectual incoherence or aberration, but with a vision of positive evil. As he puts it in the *Autobiography*, 'I dug quite low enough to discover the devil; and even in some dim way to recognise the devil. At least I never, even in this first vague and sceptical stage, indulged very much in the current arguments about the relativity of evil or the unreality of sin. Perhaps, when I eventually emerged as a sort of theorist, and was described as an Optimist, it was because I was one of the few people in that world of diabolism who really believed in devils.'[66] This was a nightmare which faded with the light of day, but which remained with Chesterton to the end of his days, hidden but always there as an imaginative and intellectual force.

The nightmare had for Chesterton an emblem of horror: the green carnation. So it was that forty years later he remembered in the *Autobiography* that when the time came for his career as a writer to begin he was 'full of a new and fiery resolution to write against the Decadents and Pessimists who ruled the culture of the age'. He had become what Walter de la Mare was to call him later: a 'Knight of the Holy Ghost', the mills of Satan keeping his lance always in play. The sequence is this: the perception of evil leads to the perception that it is heresy that has led to the evil and that it is only the sanity of orthodoxy that will overcome the madness of evil. Life for Chesterton has now become, to evoke Bunyan again, a Holy War.

All this leaves us, however, with a problem. For that is not how we tend to look back on the 1890s now. We go to a performance of *The Importance of Being Earnest* and it all seems rather attractive—certainly Wilde himself seems attractive. It is necessary to insist, nevertheless, that there was about one aspect of the literary culture of the early years of the final decade of the nineteenth century something widely perceived as dangerous, even sinister. This was not principally because of its homoerotic element. Richard Ellman, Wilde's biographer, calls the period 'The Age of Dorian',[67] after *The Picture of Dorian Gray*, a book which was in many ways the defining Vade Mecum of the decadent movement. An atmosphere of scandal surrounded the book at the time, particularly in its first and most explicitly homoerotic version, which was published in March 1891. Even the bowdlerised version, which appeared a month later, was too shocking for

---

[66] *Autobiography*, 90–1.   [67] Ellman, *Oscar Wilde*, 288 ff.

W. H. Smith, who refused to carry it, on the grounds that it was 'filthy'.[68] Pater refused to review the first edition, on the grounds that it was 'too dangerous', but praised the revised version in *The Bookman*. There can be little doubt that, as Ellman puts it, 'Many young men and women learned of the existence of uncelebrated forms of love' through the hints contained in the book. One of them was Lord Alfred Douglas, then an undergraduate at Magdalen: Lord Alfred by his own account read it 'fourteen times running'. At the first opportunity he went to meet Wilde, who was greatly smitten by his good looks, and duly seduced him. They were introduced by the poet Lionel Johnson, who had written a flowery Latin poem about *Dorian Gray*, which included the lines 'Hic sunt poma Sodomorum | Hic sunt corda vitiorum; | Et peccata dulcis' (Here are apples of Sodom, here are the very hearts of vices, and tender sins).[69]

Here was much of what Chesterton meant when he wrote in the Bentley dedication: 'They twisted even decent sin to shapes not to be named.' We do not need to be Sherlock Holmes or Father Brown to understand that this is a clear reference to the literary subculture of which Wilde was such a central part: but there was more to it than that. It was the active subversion not simply of sexual morality but of all morality that was seen at the time as one of the decadent movement's most frightening ambitions. And there was, indeed, a real sense of danger abroad. The decadents were seen as being not simply unacceptably unconventional, but as embodying a threat to social and even personal moral stability.

Nor, it has to be said, was this perception wholly misjudged. We look on Wilde now as a victim and so he was. He was also lovable and endlessly entertaining. These are the things we remember about him now: to repeat Chesterton's own assessment, 'the healthy horror of the evil' has been neutralised by a 'healthy horror of the punishment'. To understand Chesterton's very strong revulsion for 'the evil', we have to return if we can to the way Wilde was seen before his trial, at the height of his public reputation: for there was also a more shadowy reputation, conveyed through the city by anecdote and rumour. And we have to say that despite his brilliance and personal attractiveness, there was about Wilde's personality, nevertheless, something distinctly sinister. Chesterton's 'healthy horror' was very far from being a mere petty bourgeois moralism. We have to remember that the decadent movement of the Age of Dorian really did believe, not only in

---

[68] Ellman, *Oscar Wilde*, 305.   [69] Ibid. 305–6.

the irrelevance of morality but in the corruption of virtue. Here, the greatest transgression was self-control and self-denial. Wilde's celebrated quip to the effect that 'the only way of resisting temptation is to give in to it' was actually a fundamental axiom (it was also an excellent example of the way in which Wilde used his wit to disarm potential hostility). It was a joke, but the point is that he meant it. As Wilde expresses it in 'The Critic as Artist': 'Self-denial is simply a method by which man arrests his progress, and self-sacrifice a survival of the mutilation of the savage, part of that old worship of pain which is so terrible a factor in the history of the world, and which even now makes its victims day by day, and has its altars in the land.'[70] The corruption of sexual virtue was thus almost a moral imperative. It is as though there were at play here a deliberate reversal of categories, in which virtues became sins and sins virtues.

Nor was this mere talk. The most striking example, perhaps, was Wilde's deliberate seduction of the young writer André Gide. Gide had been brought up within a strict Protestant moral code. In Algeria, he had come across Wilde and Lord Alfred Douglas. Earlier acquaintance with Wilde had left him feeling as though he had undergone a kind of intellectual seduction: he wrote in his journal (1 January 1892), 'Wilde, I believe, did me nothing but harm. In his company I lost the habit of thinking. I had more varied emotions, but had forgotten how to bring order into them.'[71]

Three years later, in Algiers, Wilde went one stage further. Douglas had gone off on his own leaving Gide alone with Wilde. Gide records that he said at one point, 'I have a duty to myself to amuse myself most frightfully'—the use of the word duty here epitomising the deliberate subversion of language which explains why it was that in his company Gide had 'lost the habit' (or even the possibility perhaps) 'of thinking'. Then, Wilde specified, having spoken of the duty of amusing himself, 'frightfully'—'not happiness. Above all not happiness. Pleasure! You must always aim at the most tragic.' Then they went to a café, where Gide was captivated by a young Arab boy playing the flute. Outside the café, Wilde asked Gide, 'Dear, vous voulez le petit musicien'—do you want the little musician?' Gide said 'yes', as he remembered later, 'in the most choked of voices'. Wilde's response, as Gide described it, was to break into 'Satanic laughter'. Then, Wilde went into the café to make the arrangements.[72]

---

[70] Wilde, *Collected Works*, 1122.   [71] Ellman, *Oscar Wilde*, 335.   [72] Ibid. 405.

It is as though Wilde had wanted to draw Gide into the ambit of his own instinct for self-destruction (only two months later, he was to launch the insanely risky legal proceedings against the Marquess of Queensberry which were to bring about his final ruin). Wilde, comments Professor Ellman, had 'what Henry James calls "the imagination of disaster". Nothing less than total ruin would do.'[73] We might add that this is not simply true of Wilde himself but of the whole underlying psychology of aestheticism and the decadent movement. Wilde, of course, was aware of this: this is why there is about *The Picture of Dorian Gray*—as there is indeed about the whole decadent mentality—such a clear ambivalence. Wilde asserts in the book's preface that 'All art is at once surface and symbol. Those who go beneath the surface do so at their peril.' But, of course, it is the purpose of a symbol precisely to draw us beneath the surface; and beneath the Wildean surface there lurk perils indeed. Thus, in *Dorian Gray*, as Ellman puts it, 'Wilde was to write the tragedy of aestheticism. . . . The life of mere sensation is uncovered as anarchic and self-destructive. Dorian Gray is a test case. He fails. Life cannot be lived on such terms. Self-indulgence leads him to vandalise his own portrait, but this act is a reversal of what he intends . . . By unintentional suicide, Dorian becomes aestheticism's first martyr.'[74]

All this brings us irresistibly to that strange incident which Chesterton was to describe, in 1907, the year before *Orthodoxy*, in a *Daily News* article entitled 'The Diabolist' (it is worth recalling that Chesterton was to refer to the decadent milieu as 'that world of diabolism'[75]). The incident dates from Chesterton's time at the Slade, that is, the academic year 1893–4, about a year after the publication of *The Picture of Dorian Gray*. It concerns a young man clearly identifiable as a product of the aesthetic movement. The influence on his thinking either of Walter Pater himself or of some disciple of Pater's, perhaps Wilde—or simply of the broad aesthetic/decadent/*fin de siècle* ethos of the time—is quite clear. He believes with Pater that experience, not the fruit of experience, is the first priority. He is wholly opposed to any objective ethical notions of right and wrong, and vehemently argues for a particular course of action because after it he will no longer know the difference between them. His beliefs are destructive first of others and then of himself: Like Dorian Gray, he epitomises the tragedy of aestheticism by effectively committing suicide. And finally (and for our purpose most importantly) he—or at any rate Chesterton's reaction to him—clearly

    [73] Ellman, *Oscar Wilde*, 406.   [74] Ibid. 297.   [75] *Autobiography*, 91.

establishes the link between the decadent movement and Chesterton's intellectual response to it, that is, the identification of the struggle against heresy as being the battleground on which evil must be fought. It is a famous passage, often quoted: but I do not believe we have yet perceived its full significance, partly because it is not normally quoted at sufficient length.

'He was', says Chesterton of 'the Diabolist', 'a man with a long ironical face, and close and red hair. He was by class a gentleman, and could walk like one, but preferred to walk like a groom carrying two pails. . . . And I shall never forget the half-hour in which he and I argued about real things for the first and the last time.' There now follows a passage which seems to me central to any adequate understanding of Chesterton's intellectual history (it is omitted from Cecil's quotation from the article, and hence from Maisie Ward's, since she quotes Cecil rather than the article itself; other books on Chesterton follow her in this as in nearly all else):

The man asked me suddenly why I was becoming orthodox. Until he said it, I really had not known that I was; but the moment he said it I knew it to be true. And the process was so long and full that I answered him at once, out of existing stores of explanation.

'I am becoming orthodox', I said, 'because I have come, rightly or wrongly, after stretching my brain till it bursts, to the old belief that heresy is worse than sin. An error is worse than a crime, for an error begets crimes. . . . I hate modern doubt because it is dangerous.'

'You mean dangerous to morality', he said in a voice of wonderful gentleness. 'I expect you are right. But why do you care about morality?'

. . . I had an unmeaning sense of being tempted in a wilderness; and even as I paused a burst of red sparks burst past.

'Aren't those sparks splendid?' I said.

'Yes,' he replied.

'That is all that I ask you to admit', said I. 'Give me those few red specks and I will deduce Christian morality. Once, I thought like you that one's pleasure in a spark was a thing that could come and go like that spark. Once I thought that the delight was as free as the fire. Once I thought that red star we see was alone in space. But now I know that the red star is only on the apex of an invisible pyramid of virtues. That red fire is only the flower on a stalk of living habits which you cannot see. . . . That flame flowered out of virtues, and it will fade with virtues. Seduce a woman, and that spark will be less bright. Shed blood, and that spark will be less red. Be really bad, and they will be to you like the spots on a wall-paper.'

He had a horrible fairness of the intellect that made me despair of his soul. A common, harmless atheist would have denied that religion produced humility or humility a simple joy. But he admitted both. He only said, 'But shall I not find in evil a life of its own? Granted that for every woman I ruin one of those red sparks will go out: will not the expanding pleasure of ruin...'

'Do you see that fire?' I asked. 'If we had a real fighting democracy, someone would burn you in it; like the devil-worshipper you are.'

'Perhaps', he said, in his tired, fair way. 'Only what you call evil I call good.'

He went down the great steps alone, and I felt as if I wanted the steps swept and cleaned. I followed later...and as I went to find my hat...I suddenly heard his voice again...then I heard the voice of one of the vilest of his associates saying, 'nobody can possibly know'. And then I heard the Diabolist say, 'I tell you, I have done everything else. If I do that I shan't know the difference between right and wrong.' I rushed out without daring to pause; and as I passed the fire I did not know whether it was hell or the furious love of God.

I have since heard that he died: it may be said, I think, that he committed suicide with tools of pleasure, not with tools of pain. God help him, I know the road he went.[76]

The parallels with the story of Dorian Gray are strikingly close; and we surely have here all the explanation we need of Chesterton's loathing for the Wildean *fin de siècle*, which came to such an abrupt end with Wilde's own ruin halfway through the decade. Another possible resonance—at the least, an illuminating parallel—with the diabolists' views on the aesthetic pleasures of seduction and moral ruin is to be found in *Confessions of a Young Man* (1888) by George Moore (both an admirer of Pater and an influence over the Slade's teaching staff and—who knows?—perhaps over one of its students, the 'diabolist', too). Writing of Ingres's painting *La Source*, for which the 'price' was the seduction and death of the model through drink, he languidly observes that 'the knowledge that a wrong was done...that a girl or a thousand girls, died in the hospital for that one virginal thing, *is an added pleasure which I could not afford to spare*'.[77] Was it to this passage that Chesterton was referring in his Slade notebook when he wrote that 'even vice demands virgins'?[78] Whatever the answer, it is not surprising that in *Heretics*, Chesterton was, uncharacteristically, to write of George Moore with such absolute personal contempt.

Of 'The Diabolist', Michael Coren asks the question: 'How much is a real encounter, how much an artificial construction?'[79] Chesterton certainly presented it as a real encounter, and intended that it should be taken seriously

[76] G. K. Chesterton, 'The Diabolist', *The Daily News* (9 Nov. 1907).

[77] George Moore, *Confessions of a Young Man* (London, 1888), 118. My emphasis.

[78] Chesterton, 'From the Note-books of G.K.C.'

[79] Michael Coren, *Gilbert: The Man who was Chesterton* (London, 1989), 52.

as such. 'What I have now to relate', he wrote, 'really happened. ... It was simply a quiet conversation which I had with another man. But that quiet conversation was by far the most terrible thing that has ever happened to me in my life. It happened so long ago that I cannot be certain of the exact words of the dialogue, only of its main questions and answers; but there is one sentence in it for which I can answer absolutely and word for word. It was a sentence so awful that I could not forget it if I would. It was the last sentence spoken; and it was not spoken to me.' We can, surely, be confident that this was indeed 'a real encounter'.

A 'mystical minimum of gratitude'

'The Diabolist' appeared in *The Daily News* in 1907, probably during the period of gestation of *Orthodoxy* (1908), which Chesterton described as 'a kind of slovenly autobiography'; so it has to be seen as part of the process of reminiscence and self-assessment through which Chesterton was going at this time, a process in which the Bentley dedication is another key document. This prompts the question: what does Chesterton mean when he reports himself in 1907 as declaring, some fifteen years before, that 'I am becoming orthodox'? 'Heresy' and 'orthodoxy' had during the first decade of the twentieth century become key words for Chesterton in his career as a public controversialist (*Heretics* appeared in 1904): has he, in 'The Diabolist', distorted his account of an earlier period in his life by importing into his reminiscence of it a personally anachronistic vocabulary? Whatever 'orthodoxy' had meant for him in the early 1890s, it could scarcely be the same as it came to mean by the time he used the word, over a decade and a half later, as the title for one of his key works. In 1894 he was still—after an adolescence in which his religious beliefs had been aggressively anti-dogmatic, followed by a period in which religious belief had collapsed almost entirely—'engaged ... in discovering, to my own extreme and lasting astonishment, that I was not an atheist' (though this implied claim to have been, however briefly, a total unbeliever is probably as doubtful as his claim, also made in the *Autobiography*, that he was never really a socialist). At the time of the incident itself, he says that he cannot remember the exact words of the exchange with the 'Diabolist', 'only ... its main questions and answers'. But when his interlocutor asks why he was becoming orthodox, he comments that 'Until he said it, I really had not known that I was; but the moment he said it I knew it to be true. And the process was so long and full that I answered him at once, out of existing stores of explanation.' This seems to imply not only that the key word 'orthodox' was indeed used on this occasion, but also that the idea of orthodoxy itself was something that had been growing in importance in his mind (even though, as we shall see, when he finally emerged from the spiritual crisis of these years, his theological presuppositions were still firmly under the influence of the anti-dogmatic Stopford Brooke). But even during the Slade period, he almost certainly saw himself as being in some way within the Christian tradition, and understood that tradition as being part of what defined his growing notions of 'orthodoxy' as against the 'heresy' of views (not only unambiguously anti-religious views like Pater's, but also more undeniably religious deviations from the mainstream Christian norm) which were inconsistent with it. His Slade notebook contains the following *pensée*:

I do not mind a man of some other creed hating mine, but I do object to his patronizing it. If a Theosophist [one who believes that a knowledge of God may be achieved through spiritual ecstasy or direct intuition] excludes Christianity he is acting within his rights. It is when he 'includes' Christianity that I black his eyes.[80]

The use of the word 'creed' here does not imply that Chesterton at this period accepted any systematic body of theological belief; but it does imply a certain partisan self-inclusion within a broad tradition, probably that in which he grew up, and it does mean that he believed that there was an objective difference—which needed imperatively to be identified—between truth and error. His response to the diabolist's question, 'why [he] was becoming orthodox', is worth considering here in full:

'I am becoming orthodox,' I said, 'because I have come, rightly or wrongly, after stretching my brain till it bursts, to the old belief that heresy is worse even than sin. An error is more menacing than a crime, for an error begets crimes. An Imperialist is worse than a pirate. For an Imperialist keeps a school for pirates; he teaches piracy disinterestedly and without an adequate salary. A Free Lover is worse than a profligate. For a profligate is serious and reckless even in his shortest love; while a Free Lover is cautious and irresponsible even in his longest devotion.

The paradoxical style here ('serious and reckless'; 'cautious and irresponsible') has the smack of Chesterton's early maturity about it. What follows, however, seems consistent with what we know from other sources about

---

[80] Chesterton, 'From the Note-books of G.K.C.'

Chesterton's emergence from doubt to faith, or at least from pessimism to optimism, at this earlier period in his life: and it confirms that the Christian tradition was in some way part of how he understood what was orthodox and what heretical:

Give me those few red specks and I will deduce Christian morality.... now I know that the red star is only on the apex of an invisible pyramid of virtues.... Only because your mother made you say 'Thank you' for a bun are you now able to thank Nature or chaos for those red stars of an instant or for the white stars of all time. Only because you were humble before fireworks on the fifth of November do you now enjoy any fireworks that you chance to see.... That flame flowered out of virtues, and it will fade with virtues.

The particular virtue that lay behind Chesterton's recovery of optimism was the virtue of gratitude: and if we seek for a corresponding doctrinal element in his recovery of some kind of religious belief, it was his discovery of the fundamental necessity of the doctrine of creation. As he explained in the *Autobiography* in a key passage for our understanding of the mind of Chesterton:

I had wandered to a position not very far from the phrase of my Puritan grandfather, when he said that he would thank God for his creation if he were a lost soul. I hung on to religion by one thin thread of thanks. I thanked whatever gods might be, not like Swinburne, because no life lived for ever, but because any life lived at all; not, like Henley, for my unconquerable soul ... but for my own soul and my own body, even if they could be conquered. This way of looking at things, with a sort of mystical minimum of gratitude, was ... assisted by those few of the fashionable writers who were not pessimists; especially by Walt Whitman, by Browning and by Stevenson; Browning's 'God must be glad one loves his world so much,' or Stevenson's, 'belief in the ultimate decency of things'.... What I meant ... was this; that no man knows how much he is an optimist, even when he calls himself a pessimist, because he has not really measured the depths of his debt to whatever created him and enabled him to call himself anything. At the back of our brains, so to speak, there was a forgotten blaze or burst of astonishment at our own existence. The object of the artistic and spiritual life was to dig for this submerged sunrise of wonder; so that a man might suddenly understand that he was alive, and be happy.[81]

This later recollection is confirmed by a letter to Bentley written during the summer of 1894, a few weeks after the trauma of his time at the Slade had come to an end:

[81] *Autobiography*, 91–2.

Inwardly speaking I have had a funny time. A meaningless fit of depression, taking the form of certain absurd psychological worries, came upon me, and instead of dismissing it and talking to people, I had it out and went very far into the abysses indeed. The result was that I found that things, when examined, necessarily spelt such a mystically satisfactory state of things, that without getting back to earth, I saw lots that made me certain it is all right. The vision is fading into common day now, and I am glad. It is embarrassing talking to God face to face, as a man speaketh to a friend.[82]

Such was the nightmare through which Gilbert Chesterton had travelled, 'very far into the abysses'; and such was the rediscovery of the 'submerged sunrise of wonder' that ended it forever, which made Chesterton certain once more, as he was now always to be, 'that it is all right'. This nightmare and this sunrise it was that Chesterton recalled when he came to write *The Man who was Thursday*, with its dedication to the companion who had been with him as he had entered his solitary ordeal:

> Between us, by the peace of God,
> such truths can now be told...
> And I may safely write it now,
> And you may safely read.

There is a kind of epilogue to this story. Chesterton was not the only survivor of the *fin de siècle* to find salvation in a rediscovery of orthodoxy: so, too, did many of the aesthetes, most famously, of course, Wilde himself. Long before his death he had said that 'Catholicism is the only religion to die in'; he also said that 'The Catholic Church is for saints and sinners alone. For respectable people the Anglican Church will do.' Three weeks before he died he said to a correspondent for the *Daily Chronicle*, 'much of my moral obliquity is due to the fact that my father would not allow me to become a Catholic. The artistic side of the Church and the fragrance of its teaching would have cured my degeneracies. I intend to be received before long.'[83] And so he was, on the very edge of death—over two decades before Chesterton himself submitted to Rome.[84] Was this the reason that Chesterton did not persist in his angry denunciations of the 'green carnation'? Perhaps it was of this deathbed reception that he was thinking when he wrote (in 1909, two years after he composed the Bentley dedication) that Wilde 'was so fond of being many-sided that among his sides he even

---

[82] Ffinch, *Chesterton*, 41. BL MS Add. 73191.
[83] Ellman, *Oscar Wilde*, 548.   [84] Ibid. 548–9.

admitted the right side. He loved so much to multiply his souls that he had among them one soul at least that was saved. He desired all beautiful things—even God.'[85]

If he did, he was not alone. Other refugees from the Age of Dorian were Wilde's lover, the poet John Gray, who provided Dorian Gray with his surname, and who became a much-loved parish priest in Edinburgh. Other Catholic converts included Aubrey Beardsley, and the poet Lionel Johnson (who introduced Wilde and Alfred Douglas). Becoming a Catholic, indeed, became almost a recognised feature of the *fin de siècle*. With the end of the century, the *fin de siècle* really did come to an end. W. B. Yeats wrote a kind of epitaph:

Then, in 1900, everybody got down off his stilts; henceforth nobody drank absinthe with his black coffee; nobody went mad; nobody committed suicide; nobody joined the Catholic Church ... [86]

He was wrong about the Catholic Church of course; but that is another story: and Chesterton had a good deal to do with that one, too.

[85] G. K. Chesterton, 'Oscar Wilde', *A Handful of Authors*, ed. Dorothy Collins (London, 1953), 146.
[86] Introduction to *The Oxford Book of Modern Verse* (Oxford, 1936), p. xx.

4

Beginning the Journey around the World, 1894–9

Chesterton finally emerged from his periodic depressions two years after he left St Paul's School. They had, in fact, already begun while he was still there: in the *Autobiography* he describes his feelings as 'very queer things' which 'were groping and wrestling inside my own undeveloped mind'; and he claims that 'it was the sustained and successful effort of most of my school life to keep them to myself'.[1] Once he had left school he was more and more alone, and at the mercy of his moods, though, as we have seen, even during this dark time in his life there were periods of cheerfulness and optimism, and of real achievement. Literary psychoanalysis at such a distance of time and without adequate evidence is always a dubious business. But we can certainly say that there *is* enough evidence to warrant an assertion that at no time did Chesterton sink into a state of what today would be termed clinical depression, and that the cloudless happiness in which, 'queer things' notwithstanding, he had for the most part grown up never became wholly remote, was always, indeed, prone for a time to break through even the most overcast skies. One distressing period for him seems to have been the summer term of 1894, which was to be his last at the Slade School of Art. But during the Easter vacation of the same year, he had written to Bentley from Italy in a distinctly optimistic frame of mind. From Florence, he wrote, among other topics, of a conversation with an elderly American about Walt Whitman and about a guided tour of Santa Maria Novella:

Particularly noticeable was the great fresco expressive of the grandest mediaeval conception of the Communion of Saints, a figure of Christ surmounting a crowd of

[1] *Autobiography*, 76.

all ages and stations, among whom were not only Dante, Petrarca, Giotto, etc., etc., but Plato, Cicero, and best of all, Arius. I said to the guide, in a tone of expostulation, 'Heretico!' (a word of impromptu manufacture). Whereupon he nodded, smiled and was positively radiant with the latitudinarianism of the old Italian painter. It was interesting, for it was a fresh proof that even the early Church united had a period of thought and tolerance before the dark ages closed around it.[2]

Maisie Ward comments that '[n]o one would have enjoyed more than Gilbert re-reading this letter in after years and noting the suggestion that the fifteenth century belonged to the early Church and preceded the Dark Ages';[3] one could add that he might also have been interested by the fact that he was still equating 'thought and tolerance' and regarding 'latitudinarianism' as a positive virtue so soon before making his great declaration to the 'diabolist' that he was becoming 'orthodox' because he had come 'to the old belief that heresy is worse even than sin'.[4] But his emergence from 'the abysses' at the age of 20 led him at first more to the recovery of his boyhood's deeply felt theological liberalism[5] than to the discovery he was to make fully only as he approached his thirties of the historic Christian tradition, believed *ubique, semper et ab omnibus.*

His mood in the springtime of 1894 was one of determined optimism about the future. From Milan he wrote cheerfully, with an engaging jumble of thoughts about Italian art and architecture, Professor Huxley (against whom, Chesterton told Bentley, he denied being prejudiced 'with indignation and scorn'), St Francis, Walt Whitman (again), and 'a nice letter' he had received from Lawrence Solomon. Chesterton's letter concluded that all this made him think that 'it is all going to be the fair beginning of a time'.[6] His optimism was premature; there was one more time of trial, perhaps the most formidable of all, yet to endure. The letter to Bentley, already quoted,[7] in which Chesterton speaks of '[a] meaningless fit of depression, taking the form of certain absurd psychological worries' and of having gone 'far into the abysses indeed', clearly refers to something that has taken place after his return from Italy, during the summer term, since the sequel—'that I found that things, when examined, necessarily spelt such a mystically satisfactory state of things, that . . . I saw

---

[2] Ward, 50–1. Chesterton's letter is undated, but we can date his Italian journey by a letter from Oldershaw (BL MS Add. 73197) dated 29 March 1894, referring to 'the masterpieces of Michelangelo or whatever other products of the unfortunate country you are exploring'.

[3] Ward, 52.   [4] See p. 119 above.

[5] See pp. 63–74.   [6] BL MS Add. 73191.   [7] See pp. 145–50 below.

lots that made me certain it is all right'—can be dated at some point in or just after the same term, that is, around July or August of the same year. It is worth recalling that it was towards the end of the same term that he sat the French examination whose satisfactory results we have noted. We appear to be observing a kind of emotional see-saw, in which deep depression and 'morbid' feelings alternate with more constructive and optimistic moods. It may have been this emotional instability, as much as the depth of 'the abysses' into which he periodically fell, that so distressed him as the two academic years that followed his departure from St Paul's School ran their course. When he finally realised definitively that 'it is all right' he never sank into the abysses again.

His emergence into this new sunrise was followed by a major decision. After only one year at the Slade School of Art, Chesterton brought his studies there abruptly to an end, thus changing the direction, not only of his university years, but of his whole life. His ambition had been to become an artist. The main reason for his attending University College, London, had almost certainly been its association with the Slade; Chesterton's other studies (in Latin, English, and French) were of secondary importance. By the end of the academic year 1893–4, his artistic aspirations had been laid to rest with what seems at first a curious lack of persistence; one is tempted to wonder, indeed, how seriously his ambition had been originally conceived. Was the notion of becoming an artist, in fact, entirely Chesterton's idea in the first place; or was it, in part at least, a matter of his having been encouraged (unconsciously) by his father to act out his own frustrated ambition?

Perhaps. But whatever the truth of such speculations, it seems to have become clear that he was learning nothing at the Slade. That, at any rate, was the explanation generally given in later years not only by Chesterton, but by his brother, too: quite simply, that he was not temperamentally given to the kind of discipline then still thought to be inseparable from the academic study of art. As Cecil put it, 'he shrank from the technical toils of art as he has never shrunk from the technical toils of writing'.[8] One of his professors later remarked that when Chesterton was at the Slade he always seemed to be writing and when he was listening to lectures on other subjects he was always drawing; according to Maisie Ward, who consulted one of them, none of his teachers at the Slade regarded him as a serious student of

[8] Cecil, 16.

art, and later pointed to the illustrations to Bentley's book of clerihews, *Biography for Beginners*, as proof that he had never learnt to draw.[9] The simple fact was that Chesterton's style of draughtsmanship, at its most successful, was essentially spontaneous; it could only have been destroyed by scholarly restraint.

As an explanation of why Chesterton brought to an end his formal study of art, all this seems at first convincing enough (at this point, it should perhaps be mentioned in passing that there is no evidence of any kind for Michael Coren's curious claim that '[a]fter one year of study Gilbert was asked to leave'[10]). But there is something missing in the generally accepted view of why he decided to end the 'experiment', as Cecil called it. One can understand some such justification being suggested if the experiment had been given a fair chance of success by being allowed to run its full course of two years. But to cut and run after only twelve months surely implies that there was, as well, some other cause for this premature abandonment of his artistic career. And there was indeed another probable basis, perhaps more fundamental, for Chesterton's decision to bring his time at the Slade so abruptly to an end: that he was making good his escape from the prevailing intellectual atmosphere there, and particularly from current theories of art—particularly those surrounding Impressionism—which, as we have seen, he thought led 'to the metaphysical suggestion that things only exist as we perceive them, or that things do not exist at all'; this was a notion which he unquestionably saw as contributing to the 'mood of unreality and sterile isolation that settled at this time upon [him]'.[11] At the Slade, the dominant teachers in Chesterton's time were the Professor of Art, Fred Brown, and the painters Henry Tonks and P. Wilson Steer, all of whom had been to a greater or lesser extent influenced by the Impressionists (Steer had studied in Paris, and was a founder member of the New English Art Club, the aim of which was to challenge the conservative attitudes of the Royal Academy). It was a matter of weeks after he had left the Slade that Chesterton told Bentley that he had been 'very far into the abysses indeed'; it is surely not unlikely that he abandoned the Slade, along with the abysses, as being part of what had exacerbated his 'mood of unreality' in the first place.

[9] Ward, 49.

[10] Michael Coren, *Gilbert: The Man who was Chesterton* (London, 1989), 53.

[11] *Autobiography*, 88–9.

In his second year at University College, Chesterton also discontinued the study of Latin. We know nothing of why he did this. His Professor of Latin was the poet A. E. Housman, who had been appointed to his chair the year before Chesterton became an undergraduate. Did he attend Housman's lectures? We do not know. If he did, they seem to have made little impression on him, unlike those of his English professor, W. P. Ker: his only mention of Housman in the *Autobiography* was as one of a number of poets (the others he names are Hardy, Henley, and Swinburne) who produced on his mind 'a curious cloudy impression of being all one background of pagan pessimism'.[12] But though Chesterton was reacting strongly against 'pessimism' at the time, it cannot have had any influence on his decision to sever his apparently tenuous academic connection with Professor Housman: *A Shropshire Lad* was not published until 1896, and until then nobody had any idea that Housman was anything other than a distinguished authority on Ovid and Propertius. Instead of Latin and art, for his last year at University College Chesterton took up the study of history and political economy. These decisions are easy enough to understand: he had always been (and was always to be) fascinated by history, and his recent (and passionate) conversion to socialism under the influence of Robert Blatchford's *Merrie England* may explain why he opted to read so dry a subject as political economy.

Some of his undergraduate notes from his second year at University College have survived: they confirm that Chesterton often drew when listening to lectures about subjects other than art. One notebook has sketches of his Professor of Political Economy, followed by notes on Adam Smith and Utilitarianism: 'Bentham's position was new. But vague after all. What happiness and what number: x=happiness, x=number. Benthamism a most important lever of reform. James Mill. Ricardo. First philosophic anarchist. Godwin'. This is followed by a drawing of Christ wearing a crown of thorns and holding a bulrush sceptre; then, a return to political economy: 'Malthus an anticipation of Darwin'.[13] His notes on history are prefaced by a graphic description of his first meeting with the subject's professor, in the manner of his old 'dramatic diary': 'Professor Montague a round-headed bland short man with tight grey whiskers & moustache & a huge nose and spectacles at the very tip of it, discovered. To him enter myself. "I believe I am right in supposing that this is the history

---

[12] *Autobiography* 292.   [13] BL MS Add. 73330D.

class". Professor Montague's smile well behind. "Yes. Yes.——yes. This is
the history class". Enter others. Professor leans over the back of his chair and
bangs to & fro. Professor lectures.'[14] Even Professor Ker, on whose lectures
Chesterton was to look back with considerable respect, was not now exempt
from his second year undergraduate's lofty iconoclasm: 'Enter Ker.... In
Pope's time large audience ready for any amount of talk about literary
principles just as they crowd now to hear a man talking rhetorically about
evolution (ha! ha! ha! loud cheers and uproar)';[15] In another lecture, Ker
spoke about the first references to scenery in English literature, in the letters
of Horace Walpole: 'Walpole descriptions of wild places not like Wordsworth or Ruskin (loud cheers. The audience singing "for he's a jolly good
fellow")'; later in the same notebook, Chesterton adds to his notes recording
Ker's description of the recent development of studies on early English
literature—on which Ker was himself a considerable authority—as being 'a
fact of some significance' the sarcastic parenthesis '(ha! solemn and significant! What fact could be more sacred. Let us adore the event)'. On the
opposite page is the isolated sentence 'Montague, still as round as ever'.[16]

His friends had now finally left school. Bentley and Oldershaw had gone
up to Oxford with scholarships—Oldershaw to Christ Church and Bentley
to read history at Merton—at the beginning of the new academic year
(1894–5). It was their first year at university, and Chesterton's last. There is
no doubt that Chesterton missed their company, especially Bentley's. He
described his solitary feeling in a poem called 'The Idyll':

> Tea is made; the red fogs shut round the house but the gas burns
> I wish I had at this moment round the table
> A company of fine people.
> Two of them are at Oxford and one in Scotland and two at other
>   places.
> But I wish they would all walk in now, for the tea is made.[17]

Many writers on Chesterton have at best a confused idea of the chronology
of this part of Chesterton's life, a confusion which has led to serious
misjudgements. According to Mark Knight, 'the departure of his closest
friends from the JDC to Oxford University helps to explain the introspection that Chesterton struggled with at [his time at the Slade]'.[18] This is a

---

[14] BL MS Add. 73328B.   [15] BL MS Add. 73330D.
[16] BL MS Add. 73328B.   [17] Ward, 47.
[18] Mark Knight, *Chesterton and Evil* (New York, 2004), 13.

fundamental error based on an incorrect premiss, widely shared. Alzina Stone Dale perpetuates the same easily avoidable blunder: '[i]t was during Chesterton's last year at the Slade in 1895', she asserts, 'that the crucial break occurred—when his J.D.C. friends, having finished at St. Paul's School, went up to Oxford.'[19] But Chesterton *had already left the Slade* when his friends went up to various universities (in 1894 not 1895) and his 'period of introspection' (meaning his period of depressive feelings) *was already over*. Similarly, attempts to suggest that feelings of exclusion from Oldershaw's and Bentley's new life at Oxford brought about a continuation or renewal of his morbidly depressive feelings *after* his experience of a 'sunrise of wonder' and his realisation that 'it is all right' (an event which can *only* be dated at some point in the summer of 1894) are wide of the mark. Michael Ffinch states baldly that '[t]he autumn of 1894 was a difficult time' for him, and that when a friend wrote from Oxford to tell him that a group of Old Paulines had started a kind of Oxford version of the JDC called the Human Club and that Bentley had read a paper on Chaucer to an audience of twenty-two, '[i]t was hardly bearable'.[20] All the evidence we have suggests, on the contrary, that having emerged from his period of crisis, his final year at University College was a time of self-orientation and discovery which was spent in a consistently optimistic frame of mind. 'The Idyll' has been seen as evidence that his friends' various departures induced feelings of loneliness and depression. But on the same page in his notebook we read the following:

> Who said angel's tears?
> I say angels roaring with laughter
> For angels love and know say the Rabbis
> And laughter is the juncture of love & knowledge.[21]

On the same page, too, he wrote a series of *pensées*, which show a new flourishing of his old religious interests (as undogmatic as ever) together with his newly rediscovered optimism, his gratitude for his own existence and that of his fellow men, and his rejection of his former depressive self; there is a clear sense, here and in other writings from this period, that a corner has been turned and that a new life is now beginning:

---

[19] Alzina Stone Dale, *The Outline of Sanity* (Grand Rapids, Mich., 1982), 43.
[20] Michael Ffinch, *G. K. Chesterton: A Biography* (London, 1986), 42.
[21] BL MS Add. 73334, fo. 7.

It matters less what a man's religion is
As long as it keeps ahead of him

Charity to one's stupid old selves
It is the only hard charity

Existence is the deepest fact we can think of
And it is such a nice fact

If I could sing the most poetical poem of my vision
I would sing the poem of Charing Cross Station.[22]

Immediately following this is a poem called 'A Tea-Party', at which he imagined the company of a group of personalities, the first three of whom we have already seen identified in similar imaginary circumstances as constitutional optimists and therefore suitable teatime companions:[23]

How I should love to have at one end
Of the table Browning and at the other Whitman
& St Francis of Assisi, along with St James the Apostle . . .

'A faith to hold to and a gospel to preach'

The influence of Walt Whitman seems to have been as important at this point in his life as it had been both in his emergence from pessimism and also, as I have suggested, in a process of continuing resistance to his depressive feelings which went on even during Chesterton's darkest hours. He had first discovered Whitman with Oldershaw, some two years previously. Cecil Chesterton's recollection is very clear:

just about the time that he was leaving school he met with a book which had a profound and decisive influence on the growth of his mind. That book was Walt Whitman's 'Leaves of Grass.' The effect which Whitman's poems produced on him was electric. They seemed to sum up the aspirations of his own youth. They gave him a faith to hold to, and a gospel to preach. He set himself to proclaim 'the whole divine democracy of things,' as he calls it in the 'Wild Knight.' He idealized the remnant of the J.D.C. into the Mystical City of Friends.[24]

The 'Mystical City of Friends' is a reference to Whitman's short poem 'I dream'd in a dream':

> I dream'd in a dream I saw a city invincible to the attacks of the whole of
>   the rest of the earth,
> I dream'd that was the new city of Friends,
> Nothing was greater there than the quality of robust love, it led the rest,
> It was seen every hour in the actions of the men of that city,
> And in all their looks and words.[25]

The notebook from which I have just quoted Chesterton's brief poem 'The Idyll' is full of reflections about his own friends. Chesterton's belief in the importance—almost in the mystical power—of friendship was not new: 'genuine friendship', he had written to Bentley in the long vacation of 1893, was 'the real remedy' against the profound evil of 'pessimism',[26] a word which as we have seen summed up for Chesterton not only his own intermittent mood but also all the cultural and social evils of the time. This deep belief in the spiritual power of friendship was held by all his friends, certainly by the inner triumvirate of Chesterton, Bentley, and Oldershaw. An interesting fragment of evidence survives: as Lucian Old-ershaw came to the end of his time at St Paul's (and as Chesterton ended his first year at University College) he presented Chesterton with a copy of Whitman's *Democratic Vistas* (1888), which he inscribed 'G. K. Chesterton, from his very sincere friend and fellow 'humanist'—Lucian R. F. Old-ershaw'. Below this, he added: 'Friendship, like the immortality of the soul, is too good to be believed. May 29. 1894.'[27] One poem in the notebook Chesterton was keeping later in the same year is called 'A List': the final 'Amen' seems to confirm that friendship had, for Chesterton too, an almost religious significance:

> I have a friend, very strong and good. He is the best friend in the world.
> I know another friend, subtle and sensitive. He is certainly the best
>   friend on earth.
> I know another friend: very quiet and shrewd, there is no friend so
>   good as he.
> I know another friend, who is enigmatical and reluctant, he is the best
>   of all.
> I know yet another: who is polished and eager, he is far better than the
>   rest.

[25] Walt Whitman, *Leaves of Grass*, ed. Ernest Rhys, 'Canterbury' Edition (London, 1886), 40.
[26] BL MS Add. 73191.
[27] Aidan Mackey, 'Books from G. K. Chesterton's Library' (unpublished), no. 38.

I know another, who is young and very quick, he is the most beloved
 of all friends.
I know a lot more and they are all like that.
 Amen.[28]

These religious overtones are to be taken seriously, as another poem in
the same notebook confirms:

A talk in front of the fire
Two friends and I in front of the fire
But I come away from it as from a divine vision.[29]

Gilbert, wrote Cecil, 'embraced passionately the three great articles of
Whitman's faith, the ultimate goodness of all things implying the acceptance
of the basest and meanest no less than the noblest in life, the equality and
solidarity of men, and *the redemption of the world* by comradeship'.[30] Certainly, not only Whitman's emphasis on comradeship but also his boisterous
American love of democracy and his contempt for the crumbling thrones of
old Europe were absolutely to Chesterton's taste at this period of his life; his
genuine love for the common man remained always with him and may well
have been born—at the very least it must have been greatly strengthened—
in the real excitement he and Oldershaw had felt on their discovery of
Leaves of Grass. Looking back, over three decades later, the excitement of
that first discovery was still a vivid memory for Chesterton: 'My whole
youth,' he remembered, 'was filled, as with a sunrise, with the sanguine
glow of Walt Whitman. He seemed to me something like a crowd turned to
a giant. . . . It thrilled me to hear of somebody who had heard of somebody,
who saw him in the street; it was as if Christ were still alive. . . . What
I saluted was a new equality, which was not a dull levelling but an enthusiastic lifting. . . . Real men were greater than unreal gods; and each remained
as mystic and majestic as a god. . . . A glory was to cling about men . . . the
least and lowest of men. . . . Whitman was brotherhood in broad daylight,
showing endless varieties of radiant and wonderful creatures, all the more
sacred for being solid.'[31] In the notebook he was keeping he wondered
'whether there will ever come a time when I shall be tired of any one
person'. In the same notebook, overleaf from 'The List', Chesterton wrote

---

[28] BL MS Add. 73334, fo. 6.   [29] Ibid., fo. 39.
[30] Cecil, 25. My emphasis.
[31] G. K. Chesterton, *The Thing: Why I am a Catholic*, *Collected Works*, iii. 147–8.

a poem called 'The Average Man'—a Whitmanesque title which, as we shall see, could well have been a quotation:

> I passed a plain man in the street
> And I knew that if I broke with prophecies like Isaiah
> Or with epics like Homer or dramas like Shakespeare
> That man would remain my judge
> And his glory my aim.[32]

It is pure Whitman. Years later, Oldershaw wrote to Maisie Ward: 'I shall never forget reading to [Gilbert] from the Canterbury Walt Whitman in my bedroom at West Kensington. The séance lasted from two to three hours, and we were intoxicated with the excitement of the discovery.'[33] It is not difficult to see why Chesterton in his youthful 'revolutionist' mode —it was at about this time that he wrote 'The Song of Labour', and he was soon to be enthusiastically convinced by the full-blown socialism of Robert Blatchford's *Merrie England*—should have been be so 'intoxicated' by such heady sentiments as these:

> What historic denouements are these we so rapidly approach?
> I see men marching and countermarching by swift millions,
> I see the frontiers and boundaries of the old aristocracies broken,
> I see the landmarks of European kings removed,
> I see this day the People beginning their landmarks, (all others give
>   way;)
> Never were such sharp questions ask'd as this day,
> Never was average man, his soul, more energetic, more like a God,
> Lo, how he urges and urges, leaving the masses no rest.[34]

Oldershaw and Chesterton were far from alone in their inebriated response to Whitman. 'Whitman's championing of the common man', wrote H. W. Blodgett in *Walt Whitman in England* (1934), 'and his celebration of the mystic doctrine of inspired comradeship were profoundly exciting to those whom William James called the tender-minded': this category included the young socialist writer Ernest Rhys, who, on learning that Whitman was to be represented in the popularly priced Canterbury Poets series, asked for the assignment of editing *Leaves of Grass*, and having obtained it, wrote excitedly to Whitman to ask for his permission to proceed. His letter reveals his motives: 'You know what a fervid stir and

---

[32] BL MS Add. 73334, fo. 6.   [33] Ward, 49.
[34] Walt Whitman, 'Years of the Modern', *Leaves of Grass*.

impulse forward of humanity there is today in certain quarters!' he told Whitman; 'and I am sure you will be glad to help us *here*, in the very camp of the enemy, the stronghold of caste and aristocracy and all selfishness between rich and poor.'[35] Whitman gave his sanction to the new edition, and it appeared in 1886; it was this edition that so excited Chesterton and Oldershaw when they discovered it, at about the time Chesterton was leaving school, in the summer of 1892. Rhys's edition of *Leaves of Grass* is far from complete (it omits over 100 poems) and we can infer from it two principles of selection which are germane to Chesterton's reading of Whitman. First, Rhys removed all the more obviously carnal expressions of Whitman's homosexuality. 'Give me now libidinous joys only, | Give me the drench of my passions, give me life coarse and rank, | . . . I am for those who believe in loose delights, I share the midnight orgies of young men.'[36] would undoubtedly have shocked Chesterton, with his strongly held views on sexual purity, and his distaste for homosexuality, sufficiently to have brought his appreciation of *Leaves of Grass* to an abrupt and final end. Secondly, this is an edition intended for the working man, and Rhys selects poems which he saw as helpful to his own socialist political purposes. Nevertheless, if Rhys was a socialist, he was (in contrast, say, to Robert Blatchford) a distinctly Christian socialist. '[T]he Golden Rule', wrote Rhys in his introduction, 'though always potent for love and human fellowship, has in the perfect meaning the Christ gave to it been often sorrowfully lost to us. . . . To restore this spirit to heroic and active influence among men were a poet's work worthy of the highest, and it is this which is the most immediate significance of the "task eternal, and the burden and the lesson," which Walt Whitman has taken up.'[37] This is a reference to Whitman's poem 'Pioneers! O Pioneers!', a celebration of the spirit of America, as it turned its back on the old world to create a more vigorous and egalitarian culture:

> Have the elder races halted?
> Do they droop and end their lesson, wearied over there beyond the
>   seas?
> We take up the task eternal, and the burden and the lesson,
> Pioneers! O pioneers!
> All the past we leave behind,

[35] H. W. Blodgett, *Walt Whitman in England* (London, 1934), 192–3.
[36] 'Native Moments', *Leaves of Grass* (New York, 1892), 194.
[37] Whitman, *Leaves of Grass* ('Canterbury' Edition, 1886), p. x.

> We debouch upon a newer mightier world, varied world,
> Fresh and strong the world we seize, world of labour and the march.[38]

This is not quite the 'golden rule'; nevertheless, Chesterton's own school-boy perception that modern ideas of progress are somehow built ('the fruit of the things that have been'[39]) on the foundation of traditional Christian aspirations, and his slightly more developed view that socialism itself was what Christianity had been aspiring to in its perception of an essential conflict between the possession of riches and the soul's salvation[40]—together with his lifelong hostility to aristocracy and the crumbling mon-archies of Europe—made him peculiarly receptive to Whitman's poetry as it was mediated by Rhys. In this, Chesterton was part of a wider current of opinion; as Blodgett concludes, 'in the main Whitman challenged English attention as a crusader, a rebel against the *status quo*, who furnished to a few ardent minds a means for both social and personal improvement. It was as a moralist and a prophet rather than as an artist that he threw the gauntlet to the English.'[41]

Whitman appealed to Chesterton, too, as an antidote to the aesthetic movement, with its almost ideological insistence on the suppression of moral content in art and literature and its apparent withdrawal from the lives of 'Real men'. In a novel (unpublished during his lifetime[42]) probably written in late 1893 or early 1894,[43] while Chesterton was at the Slade, he has his hero, Basil Howe, defend the egalitarian vigour of the modern world against the aesthetic distaste of a young poet:

> ... When our fancies are blurred with those fin de siècle phantoms, old Chaucer blows through one like an April wind. In Chaucer he and his age appear as what they were and ought to have been, more or less, a strong, varied, hopeful, vigorous, coarse society.... Chaucer had faith in his society, and you poets will not allow us to have faith in ours.... It is all very well for you to talk about ugliness, but your talk is the merest aestheticism, it doesn't touch the moral wants of the people at all.... Why don't you write the epic of the Steam-engine as Homer wrote the epic of the chariot? ... It was only the seeing eye that saw its beauty in its use. For my

---

[38] Whitman, *Leaves of Grass* ('Canterbury' Edition, 1886), 102–3.
[39] 'Ave Maria', *The Debater*, iii. 95–6. My emphasis.
[40] BL MS Add. 73197.
[41] Blodgett, *Whitman*, 217.
[42] It was published under the title *Basil Howe: A Story of Young Love* only in 2001, having been discovered, transcribed, and edited by Professor D. J. Conlon.
[43] D. J. Conlon, introduction to G. K. Chesterton, *Basil Howe* (London, 2001), 12–13.

part Whitman's 'Song of the Broad Axe' seems to me a long way the most heroic poem of this time.[44]

'Song of the Broad-Axe', like many if not most of Whitman's poems, is a song of praise for the myriad activities of 'the average man' and (to borrow Chesterton's characterisation of the age of Chaucer) for the 'strong, varied, hopeful, vigorous, coarse society' these activities make possible:

> The butcher in the slaughter-house, the hands aboard schooners and
>   sloops, the raftsman, the pioneer, daybreak in the woods, stripes of
>   snow on the limbs of trees, the occasional snapping,
> The glad clear sound of one's own voice, the merry song, the natural life
>   of the woods, the strong day's work,
> The blazing fire at night, the sweet taste of supper, the talk, the bed of
>   hemlock-boughs and the bear-skin;
> The house-builder at work in cities or anywhere . . .[45]

It is not difficult to understand why, when he later came to write the dedication of *The Man who was Thursday*, Chesterton should have evoked Whitman's 'cry of cleaner things' as an antidote to the languor and disillusion of the 'green carnation'. In *Basil Howe*, we see Chesterton appealing to Whitman not retrospectively but at a time when we know he was reacting against the 'beautiful bosh' of Walter Pater and felt oppressed by a related contemporary aesthetic theory, particularly prevalent at the Slade (possibly because of the influence over the School's teaching staff of the writer and art critic George Moore[46]) in a form which Chesterton later felt contributed to the 'mood of unreality and sterile isolation that settled at this time upon [him]': Impressionism seen as a means of dissociating art from its own subject matter and from any moral content that subject matter might contain.

A penny plain and twopence coloured: the return to Skelt

Whitman's 'cry of cleaner things' was paralleled by the impact of another writer whose writings Chesterton also later believed had helped him to emerge from 'the abysses': Robert Louis Stevenson, who had himself,

---

[44] Chesterton, *Basil Howe*, 166, 168.   [45] Whitman, *Leaves of Grass* (1886), 80.
[46] See John D. Coates, *Chesterton and the Edwardian Cultural Crisis* (Hull, 1984), 196 ff.

a generation before Chesterton, been helped by Whitman to come through
his own youthful crisis of identity. 'I date my new departure', Stevenson
wrote, 'from three circumstances: natural growth, the coming of friends,
and the study of Walt Whitman'.[47] In *Essays in the Art of Writing* he
described Whitman's attraction for him in a way which explains why
both writers appealed so strongly to the young Chesterton: *Leaves of
Grass*, wrote Stevenson, 'tumbled the world upside down for me, blew
into space a thousand cobwebs of genteel and ethical illusion, and having
thus shaken my tabernacle of lies, set me back again upon a strong foundation of all the original and manly virtues'.[48] Chesterton was to write, in
Robert Louis Stevenson (1928), that 'an Essay on Optimism might couple
the names of Pope and Whitman. It might also include the name of
Stevenson';[49] and for Chesterton, the idea of 'Optimism' undoubtedly
included Stevenson's notion of 'manly virtues' as an essential part of what
was needed to overcome the dragon of 'pessimism': dragons, Chesterton
believed, had to be confronted, sword in hand, not pusillanimously evaded.
Stevenson strengthened all Chesterton's natural swashbuckling pugnacity.
As Cecil noted (pointing out that 'Stevenson was the only writer who could
be said to compete with Whitman in forming the philosophy of his adolescence'), Chesterton 'interpreted the Stevensonian gospel of fighting in a
manner altogether different from that of Mr. Henley and his [imperialist]
school. Fighting was noble and romantic, but only if you fought against
odds. Alan Breck at the round-house door was a figure to be admired,
because he was one man against a ship's crew.'[50]

To understand Stevenson's hold over Chesterton's imagination, both
throughout his boyhood and then, undimmed, into his maturity, we need
to remember Chesterton's own love of toy theatres, a passion he shared with
Stevenson himself. Chesterton's scenery and cut-out characters were
designed and painted, of course, by Chesterton's father, who had also
devised the plays and built the huge toy theatre in which they were
performed. But Mr Ed was working within a much loved and highly
sophisticated contemporary form. From the early years of the nineteenth
century, print sellers were purveying sheets ('a penny plain and twopence

[47] Blodgett, *Whitman*, 172.
[48] R. L. Stevenson, *Essays in the Art of Writing* (London, 1905), 80.
[49] *Collected Works*, xviii. 52.
[50] Cecil, 39–40.

coloured') which featured the characters and scenery of the latest popular plays: these would be pasted onto card and cut out, then, on the end of long strips of card, the pasteboard tragedians would be pushed on to the stage of toy theatres, which could themselves be purchased at the print shops for assembly at home, as could condensed versions of the plays' texts. Stevenson never forgot his visits to a shop in Edinburgh which sold characters and scenery produced by a print seller called Skelt, where he was sometimes 'suffered to...breathlessly devour those pages of gesticulating villains, epileptic combats, bosky forests, palaces and war-ships, frowning fortresses and prison vaults—it was a giddy joy....Every sheet we fingered was another lightning glance into obscure, delicious story; it was like wallowing in the raw stuff of story-books.'[51]

Chesterton was in no doubt as to the influence of what he called 'Skeltery' over Stevenson's writings, or of the way in which this made Stevenson irresistible to him personally: we are reminded, perhaps, of the way Mr Ed's theatrical creations could transform Gilbert's home into 'a glimpse of some incredible paradise', and of the way his own toy theatre came to symbolise 'all that I happen to like in imagery and ideas', especially his love for 'edges; and the boundary-line that brings one thing sharply against another' (a clear aesthetic contrast, incidentally, with the Impressionists' mistier images).[52] 'All his images', Chesterton wrote of Stevenson, 'stand out in very sharp outline; and are, as it were, all edge.... If we ask, "Where does the story of Stevenson really start; where does his special style or spirit begin ... " I have no doubt about the answer. He got them from the mysterious Mr. Skelt of the Juvenile Drama, otherwise the toy theatre, which of all toys has most of the effect of magic on the mind'; he had already suggested that 'the story of Stevenson ... began with cutting figures out of cardboard'.[53]

This is not to say that Chesterton saw Stevenson's characters, or the dramas they acted out, as being in any sense two dimensional or artistically insubstantial. In the long vacation of 1893, when Chesterton was 19, he wrote to Bentley:

I have been reading 'Treasure Island' again and inferior as it is to many of his books, I cannot help feeling that it is a work of considerable power. The suggestive way in which the old buccaneer plan and mystery gathers slowly round the little west

---

[51] Robert Louis Stevenson, *Memories and Portraits* (Glasgow, 1990), 150–1.
[52] *Autobiography*, 28–9.   [53] *Collected Works*, xviii. 58.

country inn, the vivid variety of ruffians and horror in the different pirates, the vaguely terrible way in which Captain Flint, the supreme devil, is kept in the background, the grim idea of the parrot catching and repeating the echoes of old forgotten crime; all these points mark out the book as no mere vulgar horror, but a really artistic and dramatic work of that vividly and realistically romantic type peculiar to Stevenson.[54]

It was a genre Chesterton came to see as having a profound personal resonance for himself. Stevenson's stories for boys, he believed, enacted two different battles, not merely a personal battle but a cultural one, too. He saw Stevenson's 'Optimism' as essentially paradoxical: as Chesterton wrote in an essay published in 1902, referring to Stevenson's struggles against ill health, '[o]ther men have justified existence because it was a harmony. He justified it because it was a battle, because it was an inspiring and melodious discord.'[55] He perceived Stevenson's personal battle as being close to the source of his fiction: '[i]t is one thing to be the kind of optimist who can divert his kind from personal suffering by dreaming of the face of an angel, and quite another thing to be the kind of optimist who can divert it by dreaming of the foul fat face of Long John Silver.'[56]

But Chesterton understood Stevensonian Optimism—imaginatively conveyed by the bright magic-lantern colours and sharply delineated characters of his boys' stories—not only as a private battle against personal adversity but also as a kind of pre-emptive strike against the nihilism of the *fin de siècle*. As he put it in his book on Stevenson, 'the time was to come when he was truly, like Jim Hawkins, to be rescued by a leering criminal with crutch and cutlass from destiny worse than death and men worse than Long John Silver—from the last phase of the enlightened nineteenth century and the leading thinkers of the age'.[57] Given the dates of the various works in question—most of Stevenson's adventure novels were published in the 1880s and his experience of artistic circles in France was gathered during the 1870s—this perception may tell us more about Chesterton's reading of them than about Stevenson himself (we can assume that by 'the last phase of the enlightened nineteenth century' Chesterton means particularly the first five years of the 1890s). Certainly, it explains convincingly why Stevenson was so central to Chesterton's own emergence in 1894

[54] BL MS Add. 73191.
[55] W. Robertson Nicoll and G. K. Chesterton, *Robert Louis Stevenson* (London, 1902), 23.
[56] Ibid. 21–3.   [57] *Collected Works*, xviii. 61.

from 'the abysses' into which he believed he had been drawn, *inter alia*, by the ideology of 'art for art's sake' and by the 'scepticism in the sense of subject-ivism' which after his time at the Slade he perceived to be the philosophy underlying Impressionism:

Stevenson seemed to say to the semi-suicides drooping round him at the café tables; drinking absinthe and discussing atheism: 'Hang it all, the hero of a penny-dreadful play was a better man than you are! A Penny Plain and Twopence Coloured was an art more worthy of living men than the art that you are all professing. Painting pasteboard figures of pirates and admirals was better worth doing than all this, it was fun; it was fighting; it was a life and a lark; and if I can't do anything else, dang me but I will try to do that again!' . . . Of all that intellec-tualism in Bohemia the result was the return to Skelt. Of all that wallowing in Balzac the remarkable outcome was—Treasure Island. But it is no exaggeration to say that it had still more to do with toys than treasures. Stevenson was not really looking forward or outward to a world of larger things, but backward and inward into a world of smaller ones: in the peepshow of Skelt, which was still the true window of the world.[58]

For the mature Chesterton—the passage I have just quoted is, of course, from *Robert Louis Stevenson* (1927)—Stevenson represented (as well as hav-ing partly enabled) his own return to clarity and vitality from a nightmare world of lassitude and illusion; and this return was to become not only a chapter in his own personal history but also an ultimate goal: that of victory over the dragon of 'pessimism' in the battle to restore sanity to modern culture.

'The tremendous Everything that is anywhere'

Nearly three and a half decades earlier, in the autumn of 1894, Chesterton had newly emerged from his personal nightmare and was in no mood for introspective enquiries as to how, intellectually and emotionally, he had come through them and emerged safely on the other side. That would come in its own due season; for the moment, it was enough to look around and to ruminate on where he was now and where he was to go next. This year in his life is generally either—as we have seen—lumped in with the rest of the three-year period between school and the beginning of his working life

[58] *Collected Works*, xviii. 76.

(as he did himself in the *Autobiography*) or simply excised from the record: Maisie Ward refers to 'the year 1895, in which G.K. left art for publishing';[59] similarly, Cecil says that 'having abandoned art, he passed through the offices of two publishers'.[60] Joseph Pearce tells us that Chesterton left the Slade School of Art at the end of the summer term, 1895; Alzina Stone Dale that 'it was during Gilbert's last year at the Slade in 1895 that the crucial break occurred', that is, when his JDC friends left school for university.[61] The chronology here is important. As we have seen, his friends went up to Oxford, Cambridge, and elsewhere in the autumn of 1894, and Chesterton himself left the Slade in the summer of 1894, not for publishing, but for his last year at University College. It was a year in which, having sailed emotionally into more tranquil waters, he could take time to find himself, in a spirit of considerable relief at his re-emergence. His prevailing mood was of a growing sense of gratitude for his own existence and for that of all creation. The most important document for understanding Chesterton's mood at this point in his life is perhaps the only one of his notebooks which not only covers an easily identifiable period, but which seems to have been kept as a record of his thoughts and feelings at what he clearly understood *at the time* to be a pivotal epoch in his own life. Dudley Barker describes it as 'a writer's notebook, full of thoughts, phrases, philosophical ideas, rudimentary verses, to be developed later as he needed them'.[62] Maisie Ward singles this document out from all the other notebooks that have survived (some two hundred of them) as 'The Notebook' and devotes to it an entire chapter of her biography, quoting copiously. We will need to return to The Notebook; but first, it is important to give some attention to another, thinner, notebook (previously ignored), which though it contains less is in some ways just as revealing, particularly about the development of Chesterton's religious sensibility at this time. It shows a clear fascination with the person of Christ; and since it appears to be contemporary with, or maybe to pre-date, the earliest pages of The Notebook itself,[63] it is a useful

---

[59] Ward, 54.   [60] Cecil, 23.

[61] Joseph Pearce, *Wisdom & Innocence: A Life of G. K. Chesterton* (London, 1996), 35; Dale, *The Outline of Sanity*, 43.

[62] Dudley Barker, *G. K. Chesterton: A Biography* (London, 1973), 64.

[63] The evidence for this dating is in this notebook's content: The crossed-out title for one (unwritten) item, for instance, is 'The human circulating library. This idea was later realised in an item in The Notebook, entitled 'THE HUMAN CIRCULATING LIBRARY NOTES', and beginning 'Get out a gentleman for a fortnight, then change him for a lady, or your ticket. No person to be kept out after a fortnight, except with the payment of a penny a day' (Ward, 58).

corrective, perhaps, to Ward's implied judgement that Chesterton's attention only became focused on him towards the end of the period it covers—
the autumn of 1894 to late 1896—since, as she (inaccurately) puts it, 'most of
the quotations about Our Lord come in the later part of the book'.[64]

What is important to note is *how*, at the beginning of this period, he
sees Christ: not as the divine Son of God, but as the perfection and epitome
of Mankind. In the probably earlier notebook (hereafter called the pre-
Notebook) are three 'Fragments for a life of Christ', the first of which makes
the point clearly enough:

Once there was a man who, instead of any more special title called himself Man, the
son of Man. He spoke words that overthrew Empires, founded churches, and
changed the history of the globe on which he walked. But if he had spoken no
other word but that strange symbolic title, we might well [have] reckoned him the
spiritual colossus of humanity.[65]

It is on Christ's love of humanity, and especially on what Chesterton
perceived as his revolutionary love of the poor, that this second-year
undergraduate's attention is focused, as his third 'fragment' confirms:

The beaches were covered with poor folk, buying, selling, bickering, haggling,
toiling the sordid, yet wholesome round of humble life, broken up into ragged
groups, some crying their wares, some hurrying home with their purchases, and the
light of sunset lit up the side of the hill and the young carpenter that walked there
and looked across the crowded shore, with thoughts that were new in history.
Suddenly his voice rang like a trumpet.
    'Blessed are ye poor, for yours is the Kingdom of Heaven'.
    If the dead heard but one voice, it might have been that.[66]

The young Chesterton saw Christ as a radical and forceful figure, very
different from the 'gentle Jesus, meek and mild' of Charles Wesley's hymn.
A verse entitled 'Jesus of Nazareth' occurs a few pages before the 'Fragments':

> He was the friend of the meek and lowly
>   But he was not of the meek
> The friend of the meek and lowly cannot be meek
> He would be a coward and a traitor if he were meek.[67]

---

[64] Ibid. 64. In fact, the last third of The Notebook contains only one such reference.
[65] BL MS Add. 73332B, fo. 14.
[66] Ibid., fo. 15.   [67] Ibid., fo. 8.

In all this there is under way what we can see as part of a typically
Chestertonian imaginative project: the attempted recovery of a tradition
that he perceived as having become petrified by intellectual and aesthetic
agendas whose purpose was to control (by emasculation) what they had
reinterpreted. In a manuscript fragment dating from perhaps two or three
years later, he attempted another imaginative liberation of the 'real' Jesus
from centuries of what he saw as compromised artistic and institutional
accretions:

> More than a thousand years ago a young man stood among the patches of
> cornfield and brier that dapple the slopes about an Eastern village, and thought
> of many things, not without effect on ourselves. In pictures of this or similar
> scenes He is generally represented in a formal-looking white or blue robe with a
> gold halo round His head. Here, however I should like you to imagine Him
> as He probably was, a lithe sunburnt child of those God-fearing hill-folk, with
> their old starry enigma in his eyes. The same accumulated fallacy that has draped
> the fiery, ragged figure of the young Syrian artisan with the formal lines
> of decorating arts, has toned down the lightning imagination, the defiant com-
> panion, the many-sided and burning personality of the man into a scheme of
> decorative virtues, mildness, patience, self-restraint, an effeminate stoicism. This
> mistake was of course a necessary one, a temporary petrifaction needed to
> preserve Christianity.[68]

This removal of the 'gold halo round His head', and the emphasis on the fact
that Jesus 'called himself Man, the son of Man', was consistent theologically
with the teachings of Stopford Brooke, still clearly at this date, and probably
for some time to come, a powerful influence on Chesterton's religious ideas
(though, as we shall see, there were already signs of disengagement). In one
discourse, entitled 'The Humanity of Jesus' and published in 1894, Brooke
confronted the basic Christian doctrine of the Incarnation: 'Of the two
doctrines, one of which maintains that Jesus Christ is God, and that he was a
man like to ourselves, we hold here the latter. The first predicates the
miraculous. It is not according to reason that the absolute God and a man
who lived and died as we live and die, should form one person, and when
we hear of it we say—"if this be true, it is unique in experience; it never
occurred before in Man's history".'[69] Brooke, like other theological liberals,
believed in the deconstruction of the Gospel stories by filtering out from

---

[68] BL MS Add. 73307, fos. 177–8. G. K. *Chesterton Quarterly*, 30–1 (Spring and Summer 2004), 21.

[69] Stopford A. Brooke, *Jesus and Modern Thought* (London, 1894), 1.

them all miracles and other supernatural elements; this had been the basis, since Strauss's *Leben Jesu* (1835), of the 'quest for the historical Jesus' which we can see as the general context in which we have to understand Chesterton's increasing interest, during the post-Slade period, in the person of Christ. In the fragment just quoted, Chesterton goes on to say that 'it is one of the most hopeful signs of this most hopeful age of Christianity's comprehension that the Christ of real history is being understood, a man who was as manifestly a character as can be drawn by words, generous and pitiful because keen and impulsive by nature, a man living in the full circle of all the emotions'. Christ, in other words, was 'a man who lived and died as we live and die': the consistent sense of all Chesterton's juvenile and undergraduate writings, from the religious poetry published in *The Debater* (1892–3) and—so far as I can discover—his unpublished writings from that time until around the end of 1896, was that Jesus was human and not divine. But this did not, in this Unitarian view, diminish his appeal: 'this view of him', in Brooke's words, 'is not only the highest, but also the most spiritual, and the most full of consolation to mankind'; once the Trinitarian view was 'really gone',

... men will at last perceive that it was a fond thing vainly invented, and cast about for the truth. And there the truth will stand, lovely and ready for their embrace— the truth as it is in Jesus—That every man is a Son of God and Son of Man, and that he may become on earth, and of his own nature, filled and inspired with his Father's Spirit, and as full of love as Jesus.[70]

Could Chesterton have heard Brooke deliver this discourse in the Bedford chapel? Perhaps; certainly, as Cecil recalled, if any member of the Chesterton family ever went to church, it was to the Bedford chapel that they went.[71] The Notebook contains a brief verse, entitled 'In Church', which seems entirely consistent with the dominant theme of 'The Humanity of Jesus':

> Out of a hundred people in the place,
> There is hardly one who is not to someone,
> A glory and an incarnation of good.[72]

Not only Jesus but every man, Brooke taught, is 'Son of God and Son of Man'. The only thing against the general knowledge of this truth, he preached, was

---

[70] Ibid. 19.
[71] Cecil, 8. [72] BL MS Add. 73334, fo. 38.

not only the 'long traditions of 1800 years, since the teaching of Jesus was first perverted by the intellect for the sake of selfishness in the world',

... but the vast organisations of the Roman, the Greek, and the English Churches, and the vast array of almost every sect of Protestant believers, all of whom, with diverse differences, maintain the main outlines of the scheme of doctrine which is founded on that vital separation between man and God which necessitated that any Saviour should be of a different nature from ours.[73]

Stopford Brooke's thinking was reflected by Chesterton's. The young Chesterton's growing fascination with the figure of Christ was paralleled by a persistent distaste for the institutional Churches, which he saw not only as the most reprehensible of all the accumulated obstacles to the knowledge of 'the Christ of real history' but also as being in any case in the last stages of decay and irrelevance. As Brooke put it, 'huge as the army of opposition is, it is now disbanding, and its doctrine is thinning out with it. Every ten years sees something of it dissolved away.'[74] In the early pages of The Notebook, Chesterton asserts that 'to this age it is given to write the great new song, and to compile the new Bible, and to found the new Church, and to preach the new religion'.[75] He had recovered his boyhood's religious quest; in The Notebook, he wrote a brief poem called 'A Walk':

> Have you ever known what it is to walk
> Along a road in such a frame of mind
> That you thought you might meet God at any turn of the path?[76]

Later in the same Notebook, God's presence has become more insistent:

> The axe falls on the wood in thuds, 'God, God.'
> The cry of the rook, 'God' answers it,
> The crack of the fire on the hearth, the voice of
>   the brook, say the same name;
> All things, dog, cat, fiddle, baby,
> Wind, breaker, sea, thunderclap
> Repeat in a thousand languages—
>   God.[77]

---

[73] Brooke, *Jesus*, 18–19.   [74] Ibid. 19.
[75] Ward, 64.   [76] BL MS Add. 73334, fo. 13.
[77] Ibid., fo. 54^{v}; Ward, 61.

He was once more, as Oldershaw remembered him at St Paul's, 'searching for God', but now for a knowledge of God which would be valid not simply for himself but for the common man; the influence of Whitman is probably important here. In religion, as in all else, the test now had to be authenticity and personal meaning:

> What is the good of all songs, poems, denunciations, schools, ideals
> What is the use of any genius, prophet, poet, of any Bible or Church
> If not as something entering into the plain story of a man's life?[78]

The enemy was no longer—for the present at least—Impressionism or 'the green carnation': it was those who, as he saw it, had seized the idea of God and emasculated it for their own ends:

> There is one kind of infidelity blacker than all infidelities
> Worse than any blow of secularist, pessimist, atheist,
> It is that of those persons
> Who regard God as an old institution.[79]

The angry vigour of Chesterton's anti-clericalism in the mid-1890s should not be underestimated; it was perhaps most strikingly expressed in his poem 'Easter Sunday', published, interestingly enough, in Blatchford's *Clarion* in 1895; this was developed from a rudimentary version of it in the pre-Notebook, probably written the year before, and entitled simply 'Easter':

> He is risen?
>   If ever a man rose, he might rise today
> God's guard around the tomb is stern
>   He has not heard the cry of the weak or the lost whom he loved,
>   But here are his priests, bishops, pageants,
> Good God! He might rise surely
>   If it were but to smite these liars on the lips.[80]

His anti-clericalism was graphically illustrated in an unfinished short story called 'The Black Friar', probably written at about this time. The eponymous 'Black Friar' turns out to be the devil, to whom 'His Grace the Right Reverend the Lord Archbishop of Brixanmorta', a figure of the most luridly melodramatic anti-papist fantasy, sells his soul (dressed 'in full pontificals')

[78] BL MS Add. 73334, fo. 13ᵛ.   [79] Ibid., fo. 43; Ward, 61.
[80] BL MS Add. 73332B, fo. 10.

in order to stop the wedding of 'the most beautiful of the maidens of the village':

The scheming Archbishop regarded this [wedding] as a double evil, both as an expenditure of the funds he had hoped for, and as a loss to the 'higher life' of religious celibacy to which the bride had been originally intended until the appearance of the brave and ardent lover, who had saved her from a wolf and wore her colours in the tournament, raised in the young lady's mind a considerable alteration in her views of monastic virginity.[81]

It is probably true to say, nevertheless, that at this time Chesterton's anti-clericalism, though clear and strongly felt, was not obsessive; to some extent, it was an obvious component of his theological liberalism, but equally pertinently of his continuing admiration for the French republican tradition and also of his more recent socialist enthusiasm. The Notebook certainly reflects it briefly, in a short passage entitled 'Extracts from a Prose Drama':

Gabriel is hammering up a little theatre and the child looks at his hands and finds them torn with nails
Clergyman. The Church should stand by the powers that be.
Gabriel. Yes? . . . That is a handsome crucifix you have there at your chain.[82]

But The Notebook's most powerful theme, insistently returned to again and again, is his gratitude for everything in his life:

> You say grace before meals,
>   All right
> But I say grace before the play and the opera,
> And grace before the concert and the pantomime,
> And grace before I open a book,
> And grace before sketching, painting,
> Swimming, fencing, boxing, walking, playing, dancing;
> And grace before I dip the pen in the ink.[83]

On the same page, there follows a brief couplet entitled 'A Pessimist':

> So you criticise the cosmos
> And borrow a skull and a tongue to do it with.

[81] BL MS Add. 73316; G. K. Chesterton, 'The Black Abbot', *G. K. Chesterton Quarterly*, 30–1 (Spring and Summer 2004), 16.
[82] BL MS Add. 73334, fo. 69ᵛ.
[83] Ibid., fo. 5; Ward 59.

In a letter to Bentley written at about this time he developed the idea: 'A cosmos one day being reviled by a pessimist, replied, "How can you, who revile me, consent to speak by my machinery. Permit me to reduce you to nothingness and then we shall discuss the matter." Moral. You should not look a gift universe in the mouth.'[84] In The Notebook, the idea of 'criticising the cosmos' is developed overleaf in an untitled verse:

> If I set the sun beside the moon,
> And if I set the land beside the sea,
> And if I set the flower beside the fruit
> And if I set the town beside the country
> And if I set the man beside the woman
> I suppose some fool would talk
>   About one being better[85]

This is followed by the poem, already quoted, entitled 'A List', in which he gives thanks for all his friends, one by one, ending with the word 'Amen', and on the next page a short poem:

> Give me a little time
> I shall not be able to appreciate them all
> If you open so many doors
> And give me so many presents
>   O Lord God.[86]

He seems almost dazed by the new world into which he has emerged:

> Have you taken in the conception
> Of the tremendous Everything which is anywhere
> And dreamed that it could fail to satisfy anything in you?[87]

Underlying this new gratitude for the gifts of creation is a feature of the Chestertonian imagination which originates in his childhood: he has recovered the 'permanent anticipation of surprise' that was the gift of his father, the expectation that the everyday is the gateway to the unforeseen and the marvellous which had been nurtured by George MacDonald's 'real sense that every one had the end of an elfin thread that must at last lead them to paradise'.[88] All this was to be evoked by Chesterton forty years later, as he recalled his re-emergence from the spiritual 'abysses' of his youth. The

[84] BL MS Add. 73191, fo. 145.   [85] BL MS Add. 73334, fo. 5[v].
[86] Ibid., fo. 6; Ward, 57.   [87] BL MS Add. 73334, fo. 20.
[88] G. K. Chesterton, The Victorian Age in Literature, Collected Works, xv. 487.

Notebook provides comprehensive evidence that this part of Chesterton's reminiscences, whatever the distortions and readjustments we have noted elsewhere in the *Autobiography*, is based on a vivid and truthful memory of this crucially formative epoch in his life: he understood clearly what was happening to him at the time, and he never in later years lost touch with it. His later memory of this new vision—that it was '[t]he object of the artistic and spiritual life . . . to dig for this submerged sunrise of wonder; so that a man might suddenly understand that he was alive, and be happy'[89]—is substantially confirmed by the contemporary record. Halfway through The Notebook appears this telling enunciation of what was throughout his writing career to be a primary Chestertonian principle:

> There is one secret for life
> The secret of constant astonishment.[90]

I have quoted the conclusion of the *TLS* reviewer of the *Autobiography* that '[t]he other articles of the Chestertonian creed fall into place once this ruling principle of 'wonder in all things' . . . is firmly grasped'.[91] That was a verdict arrived at in the immediate aftermath of Chesterton's death, on the basis of his mountainous life's work; and there is a sense in which we can see that massive oeuvre as a continuing and lifelong endeavour to articulate the dazed vision of his early manhood; turning the pages of The Notebook, one has the strong feeling that at times he is struggling for words, that the 'sunrise of wonder' is beyond his powers of utterance to describe; at one point he expresses his frustration:

> . . . I pause between two dark houses,
>   For there is a song in my heart,
> If I could sing at this moment what I wish to sing,
> The nations would crown me,
>   If I were dumb ever afterwards,
> For I am sure it would be the greatest song in the world . . .
>   But it will not come out.[92]

The dominant theme of The Notebook is one of thanksgiving: explicitly for the wonder of creation, but also, implicitly, for his own deliverance. Both style and content are personal; Maisie Ward's suggestion that at this period he was writing 'in the Whitman style' is simply not borne out by the texts,

---

[89] *Autobiography*, 91–2.   [90] BL MS Add. 73334, fo. 40ᵛ.
[91] Conlon, 542.   [92] BL MS Add. 73334, fo. 4.

though Whitman's influence at this time is clear enough. But Mrs Ward's assessment of the limits of Whitman's influence is well judged, though possibly unfair to Whitman himself: 'Whitman', she continues, 'is content with a shouting, roaring optimism about life and humanity. Chesterton had to find for it a philosophical basis.'[93] She is right, too, to say that 'even in this early Notebook, he goes far beyond Whitman', though it is perhaps strange that despite the fact that she quotes copiously from The Notebook she does not quote the one poem in it which really is written very conspicuously 'in the Whitman style', and which, in its last three lines, shows Chesterton in the process of moving beyond Whitman's 'roaring optimism' into a new dimension:

> I am he who has known many joys
> Joys of the stride up the bright noisy street
> Joys of the odd fancy, of the passionate apocalypse of thought
> But of the one great joy among joys I would sing
>
> That when the heart and brain are dark
> When the thoughts grow slow and ache,
> And the earth and sky seem empty:
> When all joys grow tasteless for an hour,
> When we have no more to say or think:
> Then to rise, like a giant in darkness
> Then to say 'I lonely and confounded
> I will go and serve my brothers and sisters
> I will make their faces happy, I will bend
> Over them, labouring for them.
> I will be unmeasureably diligent and unselfish, I know not why'
> Then among the tasks and assistances,
> Comes a far off note, silvery and unspeakably sweet,
> Which is beyond the world.[94]

It is at this point that we need to return to the fascination with the figure of Christ that is evident in what I have called the pre-Notebook and is continued throughout The Notebook itself. On another page, in very faint pencil, he writes that

> It is a good thing to be a Christian
> It is still better to be a Christist
> But it is best of all to be a Christ[95]

---

[93] Ward, 49.   [94] BL MS Add. 73334, fo. 21.   [95] Ibid., fo. 40.

In another brief verse, he reflects, of the Meditations of Marcus Aurelius, that for all the virtues of this 'large-minded, delicate-witted, strong man', 'one thing is wanting in him. He does not command me to perform the impossible.'[96] I have suggested that he sees Christ at this time pre-eminently as an epitome of Mankind rather than as the divine Son of God. But there is, at the same time, a clear movement towards a more fully Christian understanding. It begins hesitantly. Nearly halfway through The Notebook, he wrote a brief verse entitled 'Xmas Day':

> Good news: but if you ask me what it is, I know not;
> It is a track of feet in the snow,
> It is a lantern showing a path,
> It is a door set open.[97]

On the same page is another brief verse, less hesitant, entitled 'Julian':

> 'Vicisti Galilaee,' he said, and sank conquered
> After wrestling with the most gigantic of powers
> A dead man.

Two pages later, his quest, though still uncertain, has found a more personal focus:

> I live in an age of varied powers and knowledge,
> Of steam, science, democracy, journalism, art;
> But when my love rises like a sea, I have to go back to an obscure tribe
> and a slain man
> To formulate a blessing.[98]

That poem is entitled 'The Grace of Our Lord Jesus Christ'; a few pages later, however, there is a relapse from Grace to a distinctly Pelagian, not to say positively pagan, posture:

> What is a Christian?
> Shall we attempt an answer?
> He who, if the universe were black and dead
> If there were no answer to his cry for good
> In all the worlds and stars;
> If there were no God, no Christ, no immortality
> Could declare that he loved & would love
> Defying all things, standing on his own feet
> Love sufficing him.

---

[96] BL MS Add. 73334, fo. 44.   [97] Ibid. fo. 36; Ward, 62.
[98] BL MS Add. 73334, fo. 37^v; Ward, 62.

There is peace for weary souls, doubtless
But it is such giants as these
    That form the body guard of the Lord.[99]

Three pages later, he returns to the person of Christ, with a poem called 'The Carpenter':

The meditations of Marcus Aurelius.
Yes: he was soliloquising, not making something.
Do not the words of Jesus ring
Like nails knocked into a board
    In his father's workshop?[100]

On the following page, we have a new profession of faith, vague but loftily expressed, in a distinctly Unitarian 'religion of humanity', one in which, to use words of Stopford Brooke already quoted, 'every man is a Son of God and Son of Man':

Man is a spark flying upwards. God is everlasting. Who are we, to whom this cup of human life has been given, to ask for more? Let us love mercy and walk humbly. What is man, that thou regardest him?

Man is a star unquenchable. God is in him incarnate.

His life is planned upon a scale colossal, of which he sees glimpses. Let him dare all things, claim all things: he is the son of Man, who shall come in the clouds of glory.

I saw these two strands mingling to make the religion of man.[101]

For the next thirty pages there is no reference, even oblique, to Christ or to any kind of religion; it seems almost as though he had nothing further to say on the matter. But then, very near the end of the 160-page Notebook, occurs what looks very like a turning point, a new stage in the young Chesterton's pilgrimage: an affirmation that this Son of Man, though indeed the greatest of all Mankind, was also something very much more. This is almost certainly unprecedented: there is throughout The Notebook and in other manuscript material (some of which we have considered here) clear and growing evidence of an often powerfully expressed theism, and at the same time of a fascination with the 'real' personality and the historical influence of Jesus Christ, the two of these 'strands' mingling to make a personal 'religion of man'. But this appears to be the first occasion on which he moved beyond the Unitarian view by which he had thus far been

[99] BL MS Add. 73334, fo. 41ᵛ.   [100] Ibid. fo. 44ᵛ; Ward, 62.
[101] BL MS Add. 73334, fo. 45; Ward, 61.

so heavily influenced, to express something very close to mainstream Christian belief. Like most of the verses in The Notebook, this one, entitled 'Parables', is brief; but it is as powerful as any he ever wrote:

> There was a man who dwelt in the east centuries ago,
> And now I cannot look at a sheep or a sparrow,
> A lily or a cornfield, a raven or a sunset,
> A vineyard or a mountain, without thinking of him;
> If this be not to be divine, what is it?[102]

For Stopford Brooke, the divinity of Christ was a major strategic polemical target. The last line of 'Parables' thus represents for Chesterton a real departure from a way of thinking that in one way or another had formed the background of his life for much of his childhood and had become central to his religious presuppositions during his adolescence and then his early manhood. It is excessive to claim, as Maisie Ward does, that 'without a single Catholic friend' he had discovered what she describes (writing of all the religious or quasi-religious verses and aphorisms in The Notebook) as 'this wealth of Catholic truth': Chesterton was still a long way from 'Catholic truth'. But he had taken the essential first step towards mainstream Christian belief: and as Ward rightly concludes, 'he was still travelling'.[103]

Moving on

We can date 'Parables' at around the end of 1896. Much had happened in his personal life since he had begun The Notebook more than two years before, in the autumn of 1894. He had celebrated his twenty-first birthday; he had left University College and begun work; and he had met Frances Blogg, the woman who was to be his wife. He had also begun his journalistic career with two reviews in The Academy, a weekly literary review. He described his first interview with The Academy's editor in a letter to Bentley written in May 1895:

Mr Cotton is a little bristly, bohemian man, as fidgety as a kitten, who runs round the table while he talks to you. When he means anything seriously he ends up with a loud nervous laugh. He talks incessantly and is mad on the history of Oxford.

[102] BL MS Add. 73334, fo. 78.   [103] Ward, 64.

I sent him my review of Ruskin and he read it before me (Note, Hell) and delivered himself with astonishing rapidity to the following effect: 'This is very good: you've got something to say: Oh, yes, this is worth saying ... this is good: you've got no idea: if you saw some stuff ... I've got another book for you to review: you know Robert Bridges? Oh, very good, very good: here it is.[104]

Maisie Ward says that these reviews were never published, on the ground that '[n]owhere in the *Academy* columns for 1895 or 1896 are to be seen the initials G.K.C., yet at that date all the reviews are signed'.[105] But this is simply not the case. Full-length essays, by such established writers as George Saintsbury, a regular contributor to *The Academy*, were indeed signed with their authors' full names (there were no initials); but each issue also contained a page of shorter, unsigned reviews, under the heading 'Current Literature'. It was on this page that both the reviews commissioned by Mr Cotton appeared, the first, of a selection of passages from the works of John Ruskin, in June (the month after his letter to Bentley), the second, the following October. The Ruskin review demonstrates a good working knowledge of Ruskin's writings; not its least interesting feature is that it shows Chesterton already moving away from his socialist enthusiasm of only two years before.[106] Both reviews, particularly that of *The Ruskin Reader*, were cutting; in this first foray into adult journalism, Chesterton's natural pugnacity was well to the fore:

Poor Mr Ruskin has been trotted out again, to do duty this time as a school 'Reader.' To this end, passages have been selected from his three great works on Art. The editor is Mr W. G. Collingwood, who in his somewhat premature Life of Mr. Ruskin, proved he had not to the full that understanding sympathy with his subject which every biographer should possess. The present work suffers from the same deficiency. It is inconceivable that either Mr Ruskin or anyone appreciating him rightly could have 'attempted to give the main lines of Mr Ruskin's teaching ... in a series of extracts from his great early works.' The 'main lines' of his teaching are to be found, not in his early works, but concentrated in *Unto this Last*, and more diffused in *Time and Tide* and *Fors Clavigera*; and this is a truth so strongly insisted on by Mr Ruskin himself that the disregard of it by editors, or others who undertake to expound him, is without justification. Truly, it is pathetic that a man of Mr Ruskin's calibre and achievements, after giving his fortune and his life to the service

---

[104] BL MS Add. 73191; Ward, 65.   [105] Ward, 66.

[106] As late as February 1901, however, we find him (though perhaps not entirely seriously) describing himself as a socialist in a letter to Frances about his financial affairs: 'I am a Socialist, but I love this fierce old world and am beginning to find a beauty in making money (in moderation) as in making statues' (Ward, 128).

of others, should in his old age be 'exploited' . . . for any purpose whatever, by persons who can give him at best only a hesitating, condescending and qualified approval; doubting, it would seem, whether his teachings, as a whole, if given to the multitude without their manipulation, would not be baneful. To see him seized and claimed, when he could no longer defend himself, by the Socialists, was sad enough; but the spectacle of Mr Ruskin modified for the million, and sanctioned by his secretary and his publisher, is shocking.[107]

His review of the latest publication of Robert Bridges was not of his *Shorter Poems*, probably the work by which he is principally known today, the final volume of which had appeared the previous year, but a book of miscellaneous prose which has sunk without trace. Chesterton was scornful: 'except that a man is entitled to his own name', he wrote, 'the new Robert Bridges might reasonably be asked to choose a well-sounding pseudonym. Seriously, we should have felt a grievance had we bought this book believing it to be the work of the poet. It is an altogether unnecessary book, and as the work of a clever man, there is no excuse for its publication. . . . Certainly, they ought not to be served up in the elegant binding and printing that are so creditable to Mr Lane. Mr Bridges can do better work, and should set about it at once.'[108]

His twenty-first birthday found him in Oxford, visiting Bentley and Oldershaw, who were now nearing the end of their first year there. His mother wrote a touching letter on the occasion:

My dear Gilbert,
My heart is full of thanks to God for the day that you were born and for the day on which you attain to manhood. Words will not express my pride and joy in your boyhood which has been without stains and a source of pleasure and good to so many. I wish for a long happy useful life. May God grant it. Nothing I can say or give would express my love and pleasure in having such a son. The enclosed is for Oxford expenses or books. Your loving
Mother[109]

Back in London again, he wrote to Bentley that '[b]eing twenty-one years old is really rather good fun. It is one of those occasions when you remember the existence of all sorts of miscellaneous people. . . . My mother has received a most amusing letter from an old nurse of mine, an exceptionally nice and intelligent nurse, who writes on hearing that it is

[107] 'The Ruskin Reader', *The Academy*, 47 (22 June 1895), no. 1207, 523.
[108] 'Robert Bridges', *The Academy*, 48 (19 Oct. 1895), no. 1224, 315.
[109] BL MS Add. 73193.

my twenty-first birthday . . . Yes, it is not bad being twenty-one, in a world so full of kind people.'[110]

At the end of the summer term of 1895, he left University College; it is usual in his biographies to add 'without a degree', as though that indicated academic failure: but leaving university without a degree was not uncommon at the time, and was probably Chesterton's original intention: his first plan, after all, had been to study art with an eye to becoming a professional artist: his study of other subjects had been less important at that stage. Not having a degree was not the barrier to certain professions that it has become: it would not even have been a bar to further academic work (no enquiries were made about whether or not he had a degree when as a result of his Browning biography (1903) he was invited to apply for the chair of English at Birmingham University). Certainly, it was not a bar to a career in publishing; and at the end of September, having spent his summer first with the family of his friends the Solomon brothers in Broadstairs, and then with his parents in Southwold, he began work at Redway's, a small and rather strange firm specialising in, of all things, books on spiritualism and the occult. From the outset, this seems to have been an experience rich in the most splendid absurdities, certainly to a young man of Chesterton's temperament:

On my first day in the office I had my first insight into the occult; for I was very vague about the business, as about most other businesses. I knew we had just published a big and vigorously boomed book of the Life and Letters of the late Dr. Anna Kingsford, of whom I had never heard, though many of our customers seemed to have heard of hardly anybody else. My full enlightenment came when a distraught lady darted into the office and began to describe her most complex spiritual symptoms and to demand the books most suited to her complaint, which I was quite incompetent to select. I timidly offered the monumental Life and Letters; but she shrank away with something like a faint shriek. 'No, no,' she cried, 'I mustn't! Anna Kingsford says I mustn't.' Then, with more control, 'Anna Kingsford told me this morning that I must not read her Life; it would be very bad for me, she said, to read her Life.' I ventured to say, or stammer, with all the crudity of common speech, 'But Anna Kingsford is dead.' 'She told me this morning,' repeated the lady, 'that I must not read the book.' 'Well,' I said, 'I hope Dr. Kingsford hasn't been giving that advice to many people; it would be rather bad for the business. It seems rather malicious of Dr. Kingsford.'[111]

---

[110] BL MS Add. 73191.   [111] *Autobiography*, 84.

His work for Redway's was no sinecure. He had to go, he told Bentley, 'through a room full of MSS, criticising deuced conscientiously, with the result that I post back some years of MSS to addresses, which I should imagine, must be private asylums'. He had also to take charge of the press department, sending out review copies; this involved keeping records and deciding which magazines would be most likely to be interested in a particular title. After a full day's employment he spent the evenings writing, not as a hobby, but as the serious part of his long day's work. This was the most demanding part of the day. He 'positively enjoyed' the responsibility of his work for Redway's; 'but, now that I have tried other kinds of hurry and bustle, I solemnly pledge myself to the opinion that there is no other work so tiring as writing, that is, not for fun, but for publication. Other work has a repetition, a machinery, a reflex action about it somewhere, but to be on the stretch inventing things, making them out of nothing, making them as good as you can for a matter of four hours leaves me more inclined to lie down and read Dickens than I ever feel after nine hours ramp at Redway's. The worst of it is that you always think the thing so bad, too, when you're in that state.'[112] He had just published his Robert Bridges review in *The Academy*; he was currently working on a story (which was published in 1896) called 'A Picture of Tuesday', for *The Quarto*, the organ of the Slade School of Art.

This is worth some attention in passing, first because it contains the germ of an idea which was later developed more fully in *The Man who was Thursday*. The story concerns a sketching club, the members of which are asked to produce sketches entitled 'Tuesday'. One member produces a large picture, 'dark with an intricate density of profound colours, a complex scheme of sombre and subtle harmonies':

The whole was a huge human figure. Grey and gigantic, it rose with its back to the spectator. As far as the vast outline could be traced, he had one hand heaved above his head, driving up a load of waters, while below, his feet moved like a solemn, infinite sea. It was a dark picture, but when grasped, it blinded like a sun.

Above it was written 'Tuesday', and below, 'And God divided the waters that were under the firmament from the waters that were above the firmament: and the evening and the morning were the second day.[113]

---

[112] BL MS Add. 73191; Ward, 67.   [113] 'A Picture of Tuesday', *Collected Works*, xiv. 62.

This is clearly identifiable as the prototypical germ of the character of Sunday in *The Man who was Thursday*, and as we shall see,[114] there is other evidence that during this period he was already at work on one or more early versions of the novel. This early story is worth quoting further, for its confirmation of the predominating theme of this period of his life (he was still working on The Notebook), that is, his gratitude for creation itself. This short story contains an excitedly lyrical treatment of this theme:

'It is certainly very good,' he said, 'like creation. But why did you reckon Tuesday the second instead of the third day of the Jewish week?'

'I had to reckon from my own seventh day: the day of praise, the day of saying "it is good," or I could not have felt it a reality.'

'Do you seriously mean that you, yourself, look at the days of the week in that way?'

'The week is the colossal epic of creation,' cried Starwood excitedly. 'Why are there not rituals for every day? The day of the creation of Light, why is it not honoured with mystic illuminations? The Day of the Waters, why is it not the day of awful cleansings and sacred immersions? . . . The Day of the Earth— what a fire of flowers and fruit; the Day of birds, what a day of decorative plumage . . . '[115]

Of Sunday, 'the day of praise', he was writing at about this time in The Notebook that 'This day is the most tremendous thought ever thought by Man | It is the rest of God'.[116]

'Writing . . . for publication' did not mean that when he wrote he necessarily had any particular means of publication in mind. During the whole period from leaving school in 1893 until his final emergence from obscurity at the turn of the century, during the years at University College and the Slade, his time at Redway's and then at Fisher Unwin's—the publishers who employed him after he left his rather strange first job—his productivity was immense. Those four hours after work produced a huge amount of manuscript material, much of it worked up later—in some cases as much as a decade later—for publication. In some cases, we have intimations of important ideas on which he was later to build extensive intellectual structures: one of these—to which it will be necessary to return when in due course we enquire into the development of the ideas which come to their finally developed state in *Orthodoxy*, was a story entitled 'Homesick at Home', in

---

[114] See pp. 329–330 below.
[115] 'A Picture of Tuesday', 62–3.
[116] BL MS Add. 73334, fo. 8^v.

which the central character discovers that 'the shortest journey from one place to the same place is round the world'; a traveller leaves his own home, of which he has grown weary, in search of an ideal of what home should be: he comes, at the end of the world, to a White Farmhouse by a river; and '[s]uddenly a strange feeling came over him. . . . He felt like one who has just crossed the border of elfland.' The farmhouse was his own home: 'But it could not be his home till he had gone out from it and returned to it. Now he was the Prodigal Son.' Chesterton had written what can be seen as a parable about his own return—after a period of exile—to the Christian tradition, a parable which was later to provide an important contribution to a new Christian apologetic. It would be difficult to exaggerate the importance of this development. It seems fairly clear that Chesterton himself was well aware of it; he extensively worked and reworked this story in his notebooks (as he did other works which later saw the light of day), and though it was never published in his own lifetime—perhaps because its real literary outcome was the first chapter of *Orthodoxy*—four versions of it in various stages of development have survived.[117]

Chesterton remained at Redway's for just over twelve months, from September 1895 to the end of October 1896; he moved to the more substantial premises of Fisher Unwin in Paternoster Buildings in the City the following month. He was to remain there for the next five years. Among his duties was that of reading unsolicited manuscripts. Ffinch speculates that it may have been Chesterton who recommended Somerset Maugham's *Lisa of Lambeth*, thus launching his career;[118] but the evidence of what he read has for the most part long since been lost, and we cannot know. It was work he clearly took seriously. Many years later, his wife Frances, to illustrate Chesterton's phenomenal memory, told Father John O'Connor—perhaps exaggerating a little—that 'he must have read ten thousand novels for Fisher Unwin before he was twenty-two, and I guess he knows all the plots and most of the characters yet'. Father O'Connor decided to put Chesterton to the test:

ME. 'Do you recollect passing for publication a novel by Dr. William Barry, called *The Two Standards*?'
G.K.C. 'Let me see . . . Oh Yes! That's where the Rector's daughter goes atheist through reading the book of Job, isn't it?' Yes it is.[119]

---

[117] BL MSS Add. 73307; 73337A; 73338B, D.   [118] Ffinch, *Chesterton*, 48.
[119] John O'Connor, *Father Brown on Chesterton* (London, 1938), 36–7.

Cecil Chesterton later wrote that his employers 'probably found [Gilbert] something lacking on the commercial side of his duties';[120] but his own account of his duties, recorded at the time, leaves no doubt about his usefulness in a variety of activities; his work was by no means confined to the perusal of many novels. He was involved, too, in editorial and production work. One book on which he worked was 'Rome and the Empire', which was 'a kind of realistic modern account of the life of the ancient world. I have got to fix it up, choose illustrations, introductions, notes, etc.';[121] this task devolved on to him as a result of having read 'a treatise by Dean Stubbs on "The Ideal Woman in the Poets" in which the Dean remarked that "all the women admired by Horace were wantons." This struck me as a downright slander, slight as is my classical knowledge, and in my report I asked loftily what Dean Stubbs made of those noble lines on the wife who hid her husband from his foes.

Splendide mendax et in omne virgo
Nobilis aevum

One of the purest and stateliest tributes ever made to a woman. (The lines might be roughly rendered "a magnificent liar and a noble lady for all eternity"...). In consequence of my taking up the cudgels against a live Dean...the office became impressed by the idea that I know something about Latin literature.'[122] Other tasks were the composition of a text to accompany a selection of illustrations for the history of China (this despite the fact that 'I know no more of China than the Man in the Moon'), and a report on a translation from the Norwegian: 'a History of the Kiss, Ceremonial, Amicable, Amatory etc.—in the worst French sentimental style, God alone knows how angry I am with the author of that book. I am not sure that I shall not send up the brief report "a snivelling hound".'[123]

' ... who brought the Cross to me'

'The Notebook' covers the period of his last year at University College, his time at Redway's, and his first months at Fisher Unwin's. It was filled up sometime near the end of 1896, and there seems to have been no sequel to it. There survive many notebooks dating from this time until his emergence

---

[120] Cecil, 23.   [121] Ward, 68.   [122] Ibid. 69.   [123] Ibid. 70.

from obscurity in 1900; these contain a wide variety of literary projects—stories, essays, poetry, and rudimentary versions, already mentioned, of what was to develop into *The Man who was Thursday*, which he describes in a letter to Frances as 'The Novel—which though I have put it aside for the present—yet it has become too much a part of me not to be constantly having chapters written—or rather growing out of the others'.[124] Some of these projects were completed, others left unfinished, but none were like The Notebook, which was a kind of diary of his thoughts and aspirations, especially, as we have seen, of his gratitude for his deliverance from despair and of his newly rediscovered quest for God. But these were not his only preoccupations at this time, as one of the poems which appears quite early in The Notebook (a poem no biographer has failed to notice) poignantly illustrates:

> About Her whom I have not yet met.
> > I wonder what she is doing
> > Now, at this sunset hour,
> Working perhaps, or playing, worrying or laughing,
> Is she making tea, or singing a song, or writing, or praying, or reading?
> Is she thoughtful as I am thoughtful?
> > Is she looking now out of the window
> > As I am looking out of the window?[125]

But then, quite near the end of The Notebook, he wrote the following almost lapidary couplet:

> > You are a very stupid person.
> > I don't believe you have the least idea how nice you are.[126]

This appears under the heading 'F.B.',[127] the initials of Frances Blogg, whom Chesterton had met at her family home in Bedford Park in the autumn of 1896. She was one of three daughters of a diamond merchant who had died some years previously, leaving the family in circumstances which were reduced enough for all three sisters to have to work: Gertrude was Rudyard Kipling's secretary; Ethel worked as secretary to a group of

---

[124] Ward, 70.   [125] BL MS Add. 73334, fo. 23; Ward, 77.

[126] BL MS Add. 73334, fo. 65; Ward, 77

[127] Though Dr R. A. Christophers, in his magisterial catalogue of the Chesterton Papers (*The British Library Catalogue of Additions to the Manuscripts: The G. K. Chesterton Papers* (London, 2001), 110), adds the caveat that the initials F.B. are 'possibly amended by Chesterton from other initials to those of Frances Blogg' afterwards.

women doctors at the Royal Free Hospital; and Frances was secretary of an 'advanced' organisation called the Parents' National Educational Union (PNEU). The family was of Huguenot descent, and at some stage had infelicitously changed its name from de Blogue to Blogg. Chesterton had been taken, by Oldershaw (who was at the time paying court to his future wife, Frances's sister Ethel Blogg), to a meeting of a debating club in Bedford Park. 'It was', recalled Chesterton, 'frightful fun. It was called the "I.D.K."; and an awful seal of secrecy was supposed to attach to the true meaning of the initials. . . . it was a strict rule of the club that its members should profess ignorance of the meaning of its name. . . . The stranger, the mere intruder into the sacred village, would ask, "But what does I.D.K. mean?"; and the initiate was expected to shrug his shoulders and say, "I don't know,' in an offhand manner; in the hope that it would not be realised that, in a seeming refusal to reply, he had in fact replied.'[128] The IDK met in the Bloggs' house in Bedford Park. On Chesterton's first visit, Frances was not there, but he met her mother and sisters. On his second visit, Frances was present. We have two accounts of their first meeting composed by Chesterton himself, one (despite Frances's request that he keep her out of his writings) written four decades later in the *Autobiography*. He was, he remembered, impressed by her intellectual independence: 'She never knew what was meant by being "under the influence" of Yeats or Shaw or Tolstoy or anybody else. She was intelligent, with a great love of literature, and especially of Stevenson. But if Stevenson had walked into the room and explained his personal doubts about personal immortality, she would have regretted that he should be wrong upon the point; but would otherwise have been utterly unaffected.' He was also struck by her practicality, and even more by the way in which this extended to her religious beliefs. For much of his life, he had in one way or another been fascinated by religion: but he had never known anyone for whom religion was naturally an incontestable functional part of their everyday life. As he put it, '[s]he practised gardening; in that curious Cockney culture she would have been quite ready to practise farming; and on the same perverse principle, she actually practised a religion. This was something utterly unaccountable both to me and to the whole fussy culture in which she lived. Any number of people proclaimed religions, chiefly oriental religions, analysed or argued about them; but that anybody could regard religion as a practical thing like

---

[128] *Autobiography*, 151–2.

gardening was something quite new to me and, to her neighbours, new and incomprehensible. She had been, by an accident, brought up in the school of an Anglo-Catholic convent; and to all that agnostic or mystic world, practising a religion was much more puzzling than professing it.'[129]

A more immediate account was composed not long after the event as the culmination of an epistolary autobiography Chesterton sent to Frances sometime in 1898, after they were engaged; it very powerfully situates his love for Frances in the context of his whole moral and spiritual development until that time. Chesterton's letter is worth quoting at some length:

The second time he went [to the Bloggs'] he was plumped down on a sofa beside a being of whom he had a vague impression that brown hair grew at intervals all down her like a caterpillar. Once in the course of conversation she looked straight at him and he said to himself as plainly as if he had read it in a book: 'If I had anything to do with this girl I should go down on my knees to her: if I spoke with her she would never deceive me: if I depended on her she would never deny me: if I loved her she would never play with me; if I trusted her she would never go back on me; if I remembered her she would never forget me. I may never see her again. Goodbye.' It was all said in a flash: but it was all said. . . .

Two years, as they say in the playbills, is supposed to elapse. And here is the subject of this memoir sitting on a balcony above the sea. The time, evening. He is thinking of the whole bewildering record of which the foregoing is a brief outline: he sees how far he has gone wrong and how idle and wasteful and wicked he has often been: how miserably unfitted he is for what he is called upon to be. Let him now declare it and hereafter for ever hold his peace.

But there are four lamps of thanksgiving always before him. The first is for his creation out of the same earth with such a woman as you. The second is that he has not, with all his faults, 'gone after strange women.' You cannot think how a man's self-restraint is rewarded in this. Then third is that he has tried to love everything alive: a dim preparation for loving you. And the fourth is—but no words can express that. Here ends my previous existence. Take it: it led me to you.[130]

Years later, Chesterton was more than once to attribute to Frances his commitment to the Christian religion. In 1912, he told Father John O'Connor that he had 'made up his mind to be received into the [Catholic] Church' (an event which was not to take place for another decade) 'and was only waiting for Frances to come with him, as she had led him into the Anglican Church out of Unitarianism'.[131] The previous year, in the

[129] *Autobiography*, 152–3.   [130] BL MS Add. 731193; Ward, 93–4.
[131] O'Connor, *Father Brown on Chesterton*, 85.

dedication to her of *The Ballad of the White Horse* he publicly proclaimed what he must already have declared in private:

> Lady, by one light only
> We look from Alfred's eyes,
> We know he saw athwart the wreck
> The sign that hangs about your neck,
> Where One more than Melchizedek
> Is dead and never dies.
>
> Therefore I bring these rhymes to you
> Who brought the Cross to me.[132]

Are these examples of memory modified by hindsight? We have seen something of the substantial body of evidence for Chesterton's increasing fascination by the person of Christ during the post-Slade period, beginning a good two years before he met Frances: but fascination, even when it is intense, is not commitment. What does seem to have happened, whether coincidentally or not, at about the same time as the first meeting with Frances in late 1896, is the shift in Chesterton's view of Christ from a Unitarian view of him as being perhaps the most inspirational human being who ever lived to something nearer a more mainstream Christian view—near enough, certainly, to amount to a belief that he was One about whom the possibility of his divinity must at least be entertained. 'Parables', with its question 'If this be not to be divine, what is it?', appears in The Notebook ten pages after the couplet entitled 'F.B.'; this inevitably prompts questions as to whether *post hoc* may be a matter, in this case, of *ergo propter hoc*.

These questions, of course, can never be answered. But his declaration to Frances 'Here ends my previous existence. Take it: it led me to you' must be taken at face value. His previous existence, including its intellectual and religious explorations, now moved into new territory, for which there were new charts, even a new compass; there was in his life now, inevitably, a new perspective on matters which had seemed until then quite settled. Chesterton's intellectual and religious assumptions were already developing rapidly; the influence of Frances now became a catalyst, which perhaps enabled him to shed some of his unexamined assumptions sooner than he might otherwise have done.

One of these was his crude anti-clericalism: as we shall see, the experience of meeting, and strongly approving of, actual clergymen was fatal to this

---

[132] G. K. Chesterton, *The Ballad of the White Horse* (London, 1911), p. xvi.

colourful and satisfying polemical stance; but that came some years after he met Frances. An earlier example of how, in the final years of the century, his new perspective on Christianity was becoming central to his view of the world is to be found in his changing attitude to socialism. His enthusiastic embrace of the socialism of Robert Blatchford's *Merrie England* in 1893 had led him to the view, not only that socialism would lead to personal fulfilment, but that its message was essentially that of the Christian tradition: 'Under socialism', he had written to Oldershaw, 'people would have peace & time to be individuals instead of being clerks. . . . I believe that [Socialism is] what the Old Churches felt instinctively to be the essential conflict between riches and the soul.'[133] Now, some five years later, he wrote a long essay on socialism and Christianity, arguing that there was between the two traditions an essential divergence: and that it was precisely socialism's lack of an individual dimension that he perceived as making it less persuasive than Christianity as an account of human nature and as a prescription for social progress:

Let us take the 'rich young man' of the Gospels and place beside him the rich young man of the present day, on the threshold of Socialism. If we were to follow the difficulties, theories, doubts, resolves, and conclusions of these characters, we should find two very distinct threads of self-examination running through the two lives. And the essence of the difference was this: the modern socialist is saying, 'What will society do?' while his prototype, as we read, said, 'What shall I do?' Properly considered, this latter sentence contains the whole essence of the older Communism. The modern socialist regards his theory of regeneration as a duty which society owes to him; the early Christian regarded it as a duty which he owed to society; the modern socialist is busy framing schemes for its fulfilment, the early Christian was busy considering whether he would himself fulfil it there and then; the ideal of modern socialism is an elaborate Utopia to which he hopes the world may be tending, the ideal of the early Christian was an actual nucleus 'living the new life' to whom he might join himself if he liked. Hence the constant note running through the whole gospel, of the importance, difficulty and excitement of the 'call,' the individual and practical request made by Christ to every rich man, 'Sell all thou hast and give to the poor.'[134]

This was unpublished during Chesterton's lifetime, and it is likely that, at the time he wrote it, he entertained little hope that it might see the light of day in any foreseeable future. But his ambitions to be a published writer were gathering momentum. From about 1898, he was working hard at

[133] BL MS Add. 73197.   [134] BL MS Add. 73308A, fos. 38–52; Ward, 72–3.

various projects aimed at getting himself into print, both in the press and between hard covers. He was writing a lengthy dramatic poem called *The Wild Knight*; at the same time, he was working on a number of shorter poems which were eventually to appear with it in The *Wild Knight and Other Poems* (1900); many of these went through several drafts, which are to be found scattered through a number of different notebooks.[135] At the same time he was writing comic verses and drawing the illustrations for the collection *Greybeards at Play*, which was to appear in the same year; this collection, too, was being assiduously worked at.[136] But when, in the summer of 1898, about eighteen months after he met her, he finally proposed to Frances (she had begun to wonder if he would ever come to the point) there was no clear sign that he would ever succeed in becoming an established writer, or even a professional journalist. Since his unsigned reviews in *The Academy* in 1896, and two stories in the Slade magazine *The Quarto* in the same year, he had published nothing. There were to come, certainly, one or two early green shoots, which with hindsight we can see as harbingers of the springtime of his literary fame early in the decade to come. In October 1899, he wrote to Frances (who was abroad at the time) to tell her that she would 'come back next week probably just in time to see my first experiment in art criticism in *The Bookman*'(Hodder's literary review).[137] This appeared, in fact (still anonymously), in the December issue. In October, there had been unfulfilled hopes of a book review in *The Speaker*. But there was no realistic sign that Chesterton's ambitions were close to realisation. He was in the following year to become a regular book reviewer in *The Speaker*; his reviews were to lead to articles on miscellaneous subjects some of which were to be collected in book form in 1901; even more importantly, he was, early in the new decade, to begin writing on the books page of *The Daily News*, a prelude to acquiring, in 1903, a fortnightly column which was to become the weekly column which finally established his journalistic pre-eminence. He was soon finally to leave Fisher Unwin's offices in the City for the altogether more congenial life of Fleet Street. But none of this was predictable. As the 1800s finally came to an end, Chesterton was still an obscure young publisher's assistant, struggling to earn enough money to get married; and the future was as yet obscure.

---

[135] BL MSS Add. 7321A; 73236; 73243A, B; 73308A; 73343A, C; 73345A; 73346E; 73385.
[136] BL MSS Add. 73231A; 73242A, B; 73304A; 73395A; 73306; 73347B; 73385.
[137] BL MS Add. 73193.

PART II

5

Who is GKC? 1900–2

When Chesterton began his journalistic career, in December 1899, with an article in *The Bookman*, it was, he wrote to Frances, 'as a sort of art critic', a description which derived, he said, from a 'persistent delusion' which possessed the paper's editor.[1] It was not, of course, his first article on artists or art historians (his first published review, in *The Academy*, had been of a collection of extracts from the works of John Ruskin), and it was not his last: during the following year, jointly with Ernest Hodder Williams (whom he had known as a fellow undergraduate at University College, London), he was to write, for *The Bookman*, a lengthy three-part survey of the contemporary artistic scene; and in December 1900 he contributed an important article on G. F. Watts, which we can see as a precursor to his full-length study of the artist, published in 1904.

His first *Bookman* article is as striking—not merely in the fluency of its style, but in its intellectual boldness—as anything he was to write in his maturity. It already exhibits some of the qualities which were to make him one of the great critics of his age: the capacity for striking analogy; the understanding of the medium in which the object of criticism is operating; the forensic analytical facility he could deploy in order to cut away a false perception; the way in which he always, at his best, used humour as a means of serious discernment rather than merely of light entertainment. The first half of his review was of *Velasquez*, by R. A. M. Stevenson. Stevenson's argument might almost have been calculated to draw Chesterton's fire:

That Velasquez was an Impressionist may be called the main thesis of the book, and in one sense, doubtless, it is true enough. But we must beg leave to draw a strong distinction between Impressionism as understood by Velasquez and Impressionism as understood by some young gentlemen we know. Velasquez subjects all detail to effect. There is something magnificent in the breadth, the courage, we had almost

---

[1] Michael Ffinch, *G. K. Chesterton: A Biography* (London, 1986), 67.

said the scorn, with which he splashes in his great backgrounds, as blank and grey as Mr Whistler's. He is never a realist in the sense that a realist is another name for a snob, a painter of fur that might be stroked, of satin that might be meant for sale. In his wonderful picture of the Dwarf Antonio, for example, there are no properties round the actor. No carpet peers like an ill-mannered dog between his legs; no bedstead or Dutch clock rears itself behind, as insolently truthful as a candid friend. Not that this painter of dwarfs or idiots thinks anything below him. He would paint a turnip seriously; but never with that blatant materialism that seems to say in every line, 'this is a turnip; you have often seen one before.' His picture would say, the one lesson of all art, all philosophy, all religion, 'this is a turnip. You have never seen one before.'[2]

This is more, it needs to be said, than merely an amusingly written perception of the foibles of a particular artist or a particular book: like all substantial criticism, it exemplifies criticism's fundamental purpose, which is to seek to come to a judgement on the capacity of a particular work of art or literature to fulfil the purpose of 'all art, all philosophy, all religion'—that is, to understand some aspect of reality in a new way. It is an early example of one of Chesterton's implicit (and probably unconscious) intellectual principles: that all analysis should be in the defence of some higher idea. Thus, Chesterton's destruction of Stevenson's ill-advised and ideological attempt to recruit Velázquez as an Impressionist has been encompassed only as a secondary consequence of identifying what it is about the artist's genius which makes Stevenson's theory so futile: the piece, that is, is more about Velázquez than about Stevenson.

Successfully to criticise a work of criticism is necessarily to write, to some extent effectively, about both the critic and their subject. Chesterton's article on 'The Literary Portraits of G. F. Watts', which argues Watts's understanding of the literary achievements of his sitters, is, in a similar way, a successful example of both literary critical writing and art criticism. Like his first piece, and like the three pieces co-written with Ernest Hodder Williams, his article on Watts's portraits of literary figures is, en passant, an attack on what he was later to denounce as the 'scepticism in the sense of subjectivism', the believing in 'the line and the shadow' rather than in the subject depicted,[3] which he saw as the basis of contemporary artistic dogma: 'There is', the article begins, 'a fashion of drawing a distinction between Mr. Watts' portraits and his allegories; the school of *l'art pour l'art* especially approves

---

[2] G. K. Chesterton, 'Velasquez and Poussin', *The Bookman* (Dec. 1899), 87.
[3] See p. 173 above.

those pictures the subject of which is of the nature of portraiture, and denounces those the subject of which is allegorical, merely in order to show that it is indifferent to the subjects of pictures.' But, argues Chesterton,

All the portraits are allegories for the simple reason that all men are allegories, puzzles, earthly stories with heavenly meanings.... The profoundly original and enduring quality in Mr Watts' portraits lies in this, that he always paints the portrait of a modern man, who wears a silk hat and pays taxes, as if he were painting a purely elemental and cosmic subject....

One of the most perfect of Mr Watts' literary portraits is the portrait of Carlyle. It is interesting to notice that he does not paint the great author as Millais paints him, as a shaggy and magnificent old man, at peace with himself. It would seem as if Mr Watts saw deeper; there is a touch of something meagre and exhausted about the figure; upon every line of it is written that pathos that is worth a thousand excuses. The stroke of genius in the picture is the square and emphatic treatment of the slant forward of the beard and chin; it is worth pages of psychological discussion on Carlyle's only basic fault, the almost pitiful eagerness to scorn, the lack of patience and [of] a reverence for weakness which made the greatest of modern prophets unable, apparently, to read any further in the Bible than the Book of Malachi. Mr Watts sees all this uglier side, but it does not destroy his admiration; he paints the fearless and mournful figure of a man to whom ironic destiny had given the first requirement of a great teacher, a belief in his message, but denied the second, a belief in its universal acceptability. He gives the only quiet and perfect answer to Carlyle's lack of reverence for the weak; he paints Carlyle's weakness and paints it reverently.[4]

This is, surely, perceptive and original critical writing; its insight into Watts is at least matched by its insight into his subject, Carlyle; and his discussion of Watts's portraits of John Stuart Mill, Matthew Arnold, William Morris, Robert Browning, and Alfred, Lord Tennyson all show the same finely tuned appreciation of both artist and subject; the article is, truly, a tour de force, and demonstrates—as did much else of his journalistic output during this *annus mirabilis* of 1900—an assurance and intellectual range which go far to explain the rise to fame which was shortly to begin.

'No one ever had such friends as I had'

Chesterton's early pieces for *The Bookman* (especially those written with Ernest Hodder Williams) remind us of the part played by his friends in launching his literary career. It had been Hodder Williams (with whom

[4] G. K. Chesterton, 'The Literary Portraits of G. F. Watts R.A.', *The Bookman* (Dec. 1900), 82.

Chesterton had attended Professor Ker's lectures in English literature from
1893 to 1895) who, when his family's firm of Hodder and Stoughton had
launched *The Bookman* in 1899, had suggested that Chesterton might write
for it. Even more important was the support given—and the pressure and
encouragement exercised—by his closest friends from St Paul's. Oldershaw claimed later that '[h]e did nothing for himself till we came down
from Oxford and pushed him'.[5] This led to his debut at *The Speaker*, which
had been taken over by a group of anti-imperialist young liberals from
Oxford, and turned by them into one of the leading organs of opposition
to the Boer War. This group included Oldershaw and Bentley, who
immediately began to attempt to persuade the editor, J. L. Hammond,
and the literary editor, F. Y. Eccles, to publish articles and book reviews by
Chesterton. The second Boer War—after a protracted build-up—was
declared by Kruger on 11 October 1899, but the opposition to it was
already gaining momentum, and the pro-Boer takeover of *The Speaker* had
already taken place. On 3 October (when it was already clear that war was
imminent) Chesterton wrote to Frances that 'the *Speaker* of this week, the
first of the *New Speaker*, is coming out soon and may contain something
of mine though I cannot be quite sure. A rush of the Boers on
Natal, strategically quite possibly successful, is anticipated.'[6] Chesterton's
immediate hopes, however, were frustrated by a wholly unpredictable
impediment: Eccles refused to publish anything by him on the preposterous ground that his handwriting—an idiosyncratic form of italic script—
looked *Jewish*. Why Gilbert's friends did not simply inform Eccles that
Gilbert was not in fact Jewish at all is not clear; perhaps they thought
that this would be to dignify Eccles's prejudice: after all, the JDC had
been founded, with Chesterton, by Oldershaw and Bentley, and its
exclusive membership (controlled by them) had been one-third Jewish;
and they would certainly have been aware of Chesterton's passionate
disgust—expressed earlier in the decade in the pages of *The Debater*[7]—at
certain contemporary expressions of anti-Semitism. Eccles's objections
were not, in fact, overcome until April of the following year, when the
first of many book reviews and other articles by Chesterton appeared in
the pages of *The Speaker*.

Before we consider the content of Chesterton's rapidly burgeoning
literary output during the final year (1900) of the old century, we need

---

[5] Ffinch, *Chesterton*, 49.   [6] Ward, 105.   [7] See pp. 79–81 above.

to develop the theme of friendship; for if the launch of his literary career owed much to the practical support of his old friends, it is also true that he relied on them too, as much as ever, for his continuing emotional stability and contentment. He seems to have felt the need to include Frances in his old friendships; shortly after telling her of his hopes of publication in what he described as the *New Speaker*, he wrote her a 'colossal letter', describing a 'Grand Commemorative Meeting' of the JDC, in the form of a dinner at which everyone present made a speech. Gilbert's included the proud reflection (pardonable under the circumstances) that 'a debating club of twelve members that had given three presidents to the University Unions [including Bentley at Oxford and Langdon Davies at Cambridge] had not done badly'. 'I like', he reflected at the end of his long letter, 'to make my past vivid to you, especially this past, not only because it was, on the whole, a fine, healthy, foolish, manly, enthusiastic, idiotic past, with the very soul of youth in it. Not only because I am a victim of the prejudice, common I trust to all mankind, that no one ever had such friends as I had.'[8] Later that month, he wrote again to Frances, who had asked him about a meeting with the editor of *The Speaker*. 'Mr Hammond', replied Gilbert, 'did not turn up till after dinner . . . and before that Lucian [Oldershaw] and Bentley and I went out to dine at the "Cock"— Dr Johnson's old tavern, and ate fricasseed chicken and drank Chablis. . . . The dinner lingered, in the way that, as I fancy, men all love and women all hate. . . . We talked tremendously, we three: no one said it, but in all three hearts I know was the same thought—that we were the Triumvirate, the three who had made Clubs and Magazines and so many other things—and now were together again for a whole evening. Compared with this frivolity of profound love and knowledge Hammond sinks into insignificance.'[9]

But if his old friends were important, not only to his continuing happiness but also to the launch of his literary career, it was by his gaining of new friendships that we can perceive the extent of the growing intellectual world he was beginning to inhabit. Partly, indeed, some new friendships were the direct result of a conscious widening of his horizons, by his frequenting what he described later as the 'strange world . . . of the artistic and vaguely anarchic clubs'[10] which flourished at about that time. The Reverend Conrad Noel told Maisie Ward (by this time, forty years

[8] Ward, 107–9.   [9] *Return*, 50.
[10] *Autobiography*, 158.

later, Noel had become famous for flying the red flag over his church at Thaxted) that he and his wife 'met G.K.C. for the first time at the Stapleys' in Bloomsbury Square, at a series of meetings of the Christo-Theosophic society. He was like a very big fish out of water; he was comparatively thin, however, in those days. . . . We had been much intrigued by the weekly contribution of an unknown writer to the *Speaker* and the *Nation*—brilliant work, and my wife and I, independently, came to the conclusion when we heard this young man speak that it must be he. The style was unmistakeable.'[11] Chesterton himself remembered the meeting as having been 'at some strange club where somebody was lecturing on Nietzsche; and where the debaters (by typical transition) passed from the gratifying thought that Nietzsche attacked Christianity to the natural inference that he was a True Christian. And I admired the common sense of a curate, with dark curly hair and a striking face, who got up and pointed out that Nietzsche would be even more opposed to True Christianity than to False Christianity, supposing there were any True Christianity to oppose.'[12] The curate was Conrad Noel: and it was this encounter which finally extinguished Chesterton's youthful anti-clericalism. Noel was, wrote Chesterton later, 'an example of my preliminary prevailing impression of how stupid the anti-clericals were and how much more relatively intelligent the clerics were'.[13] Noel was due to speak in the same series a week or two later, and Chesterton wrote to him to say that he was coming to hear him; 'it was thus', Noel recalled, 'that we first became acquainted, and the acquaintance ripened into a warm friendship with us both.'[14]

Chesterton can hardly have met anyone quite like him before. Conrad le Despencer Roden Noel was born in a grace and favour residence occupied by his father, a Groom of the Privy Chamber to Queen Victoria. His family was one of the old aristocracy; his father, however, developed radical political views and resigned from his position at court. He had been intended, in the manner of younger sons, for the Church of England; but with a fastidiousness which was then far from universal he gave up this idea after contracting 'doubts about the doctrines that were then supposed to constitute Christianity'.[15] His son Conrad inherited his father's sceptical temperament, but as Robert Woodifield puts it, 'he came to give to what

---

[11] Ward, 121.   [12] *Autobiography*, 158.
[13] Ibid. 163.   [14] Ward, 121.
[15] Robert Woodifield, 'Conrad Noel', in Maurice B. Reckitt (ed.), *For Christ and the People* (London, 1968), 135.

might be termed his father's "liberal and humanist" Christianity a more "Catholic" basis and expression'.[16] The effect of Conrad Noel's society on Chesterton's religious consciousness was probably determinative. As he later put it in the *Autobiography*, 'When Noel first appeared on the horizon of my brother and myself, my brother was frankly anti-religious and I had no religion except the very haziest religiosity.' As we have seen, there is a distinct tendency in the *Autobiography* to exaggerate the extent to which, forty years before, not only during his spiritual crisis but also during its aftermath, he had fallen into agnosticism. That this was an exaggeration is clear enough: 'The Notebook', for instance, shows plainly that by 1894,[17] although Chesterton's religious feelings were far from dogmatically well defined, they amounted to something considerably more definite and powerfully experienced than can be properly described as 'the very haziest religiosity'. Meeting Conrad Noel, nevertheless, was a real turning point. Little by little, Chesterton recalled, 'I shifted nearer and nearer to the orthodox side; and eventually found myself. . . in the very heart of a clerical group of canons and curates'. This group was, in its colourful eccentricity, precisely calculated to appeal to Chesterton and his brother. It included the liturgist Percy Dearmer, who was, as Chesterton recalled, 'in the habit of walking about in a cassock and biretta which he had carefully reconstructed as being of exactly the right pattern for an Anglican or Anglo-Catholic priest; and he was humorously grieved when its strictly traditional and national character was misunderstood by the little boys in the street. Some-body would call out, "No Popery," or "To hell with the Pope," or some other sentiment of larger and more liberal religion. And Percy Dearmer would sternly stop them and say, "Are you aware that this is the precise costume in which Latimer went to the stake?" ' The eccentricity of the Anglo-Catholic party was relevant for both Chesterton brothers, according to Gilbert, 'because it really had a great deal to do with the beginning of the process by which Bohemian journalists, like my brother and myself, were drawn towards the serious consideration of the theory of a Church. I was considerably influenced by Conrad Noel; and my brother, I think, even more so.' Percy Dearmer may have been a liturgist and expert in church costume and ornament, but like Conrad Noel, he was also a fervent socialist. Most of the clergy, indeed, in whose company Chesterton now often found

---

[16] Woodifield, 'Conrad Noel', 137.
[17] See pp. 148–51 above.

himself were to some degree or other on the political left, and they included
Canon Charles Gore, later Bishop of Birmingham and founder and first
principal of Pusey House, Oxford—who was in many ways the movement's
intellectual leader—and his closest friend Canon Henry Scott Holland.
Scott Holland was the group's warmest and most vibrant personality, and
founder in 1889 of the Christian Social Union, whose stated purpose was to
'investigate areas in which moral truth and Christian principles could bring
relief to the social and economic disorder of society'. Local chapters of the
CSU were founded and meetings to further its purposes were held all over
the country. Chesterton, for a time, became involved in its activities and
sometimes spoke at its meetings, one of which, at Nottingham, he humorously immortalised in verse:

> The Christian Social Union here
> Was very much annoyed;
> It seems there is some duty
> Which we never should avoid,
> And so they sing a lot of hymns
> To help the Unemployed . . .
>
> Then Bishop Gore of Birmingham
> He stood upon one leg
> And said he would be happier
> If beggars didn't beg,
> And that if they pinched his palace
> It would take him down a peg.
>
> He said that Unemployment
> Was a horror and a blight,
> He said that charities produced
> Servility and spite,
> And stood upon the other leg
> And said it wasn't right.
>
> And then a man named Chesterton
> Got up and played with water,
> He seemed to say that principles
> Were nice and led to slaughter
> And how we always compromised
> And how we didn't orter.
> Then Canon Holland fired ahead
> Like fifty cannons firing,
> We tried to find out what he meant

> With infinite enquiring,
> But the way he made the windows jump
> We couldn't help admiring...[18]

Henry Scott Holland was a man of Chestertonian warmth. As one friend put it, '[t]he first impression Holland made on strangers was that of a man of exuberant vitality and joyousness. It was many years before I could believe that his merriment was not simply due to temperament, just as his incredible quickness of brain was a gift of nature. His fun was infectious; absolutely natural, unforced, spontaneous, so that the moment he entered a room he radiated joy into every corner without apparently knowing what he was doing.'[19]

It is unlikely that someone of Chesterton's gregariousness, intellectual predispositions, and curiosity should not have become acquainted with and to some extent influenced by the theological principles by which men of the human attractiveness and intellectual stature of Henry Scott Holland and Charles Gore—let alone Conrad Noel and Percy Dearmer—were motivated; and his own memory, that being in such company was indeed what caused him to be 'shifted nearer and nearer to the orthodox side' and 'drawn towards the serious consideration of the theory of a Church', is undoubtedly an accurate recollection, and one which, as we shall see, is borne out by other evidence, including that of his own early journalism.

'The twiformed monster . . . the Chesterbelloc'

Significantly, we have no such avowals of theological influence about another new friendship, that between Chesterton and Hilaire Belloc—whom he probably met earlier in the same year, 1900—though suggestions from later commentators, that Belloc was the principal inspiration moving him in the direction of orthodox Catholic principles, are not lacking. There are, as we shall see, good reasons why such suggestions should be resisted. But there can be no doubt that his meeting with Belloc was another turning point in his life. The bringing together of the two constituent parts of what Shaw was to call 'the Chesterbelloc' later attracted several rival claims to have effected this historic conjunction in the intellectual firmament (though

---

[18] *Autobiography*, 168–9.
[19] E. Lyttelton, *The Mind and Character of Henry Scott Holland* (London, 1926), 8.

it is worth suggesting at this point that without Shaw's famous jest, it is doubtful that they would have been naturally thought of as constituting an indivisible unit, and ironically, as we shall see,[20] Shaw was arguing the reverse). Eccles, Oldershaw (supported by Belloc himself), and Bentley all claimed to have made the introduction.[21] Chesterton himself wrote two accounts of the occasion, one claiming that they met in a restaurant, the other that the meeting took place in the street outside. Chesterton's first version was written in 1916, some twenty years before the second, so it may be more circumstantially accurate:

When I first met Belloc he remarked to the friend who introduced us that he was in low spirits. His low spirits were and are much more uproarious and enlivening than anybody else's high spirits. He talked into the night; and left behind in it a glowing track of good things. . . .

We met between a little paper shop and a little Soho restaurant; his arms and pockets were stuffed with French Nationalist and French Atheist newspapers. He wore a straw hat shading his eyes, which are like a sailor's, and emphasizing his Napoleonic chin. He was talking about King John, who, he positively assured me was not (as was often asserted) the best King that ever reigned in England. Still, there were allowances to be made for him; I mean King John, not Belloc. 'He had been Regent,' said Belloc with forbearance, 'and in all the Middle Ages there is no example of a successful Regent.' I, for one had not come provided with any successful Regents with whom to counter this generalisation; and when I came to think of it, it was quite true. I have noticed the same thing about many other sweeping remarks coming from the same source.[22]

Calling for a bottle of Moulin-à-Vent, Belloc complimented Chesterton on his writing; it is possible, since their first meeting probably pre-dated Chesterton's first appearance in the columns of *The Speaker* in April, that either Oldershaw or Bentley (both of whom Belloc knew from Oxford) had shown Belloc articles which Chesterton had submitted for publication (according to Oldershaw, Belloc had at first been prejudiced by Eccles against reading 'anything written by my Jew friend'[23]). Chesterton's later account of this first meeting, in the *Autobiography*, is more extended: it gives a similar account of Belloc's remarks about King John, but continues, interestingly, with his recollection of Belloc's views on other matters:

[20] See p. 368 below.   [21] Ward, 113.
[22] G. K. Chesterton, introduction to C. Creighton Mandell and Edward Shanks, *Hilaire Belloc: The Man and his Work* (London, 1916), pp. vii–viii.
[23] Ward, 113.

As Belloc went on talking, he every now and then volleyed out very provocative parentheses on the subject of religion. He said that an important Californian lawyer was coming to England to call on his family, and had put up a great candle to St. Christopher praying that he might be able to make the voyage. He declared that he, Belloc, was going to put up an even bigger candle in the hope that the visitor would not make the voyage. 'People say what's the good of doing that?' he observed explosively. 'I don't know what good it does. I know it's a thing that's done. Then they say it can't do any good—and there you have Dogma at once.' ... It was from that dingy little Soho cafe, as from a cave of witchcraft, that there emerged the quadruped, the twiformed monster Mr. Shaw has nicknamed the Chesterbelloc.[24]

It was to be the first of many similar Bellocian performances which reduced the younger Chesterton to dazed admiration. Belloc's ability as a speaker had been developed by his time at Oxford, where he was President of the Union, and where he had attracted the admiring attention of Oldershaw and Bentley. Not long after their first meeting, Gilbert was writing to Frances about a political debate about the Boer War, held 'in the Macgregor studio', which Belloc had addressed. 'You hate political speeches,' he wrote; 'therefore you would not have hated Belloc's. The moment he began to speak one felt lifted out of the stuffy fumes of forty-times repeated arguments into really thoughtful and noble and original reflections on history and character. When I tell you that he talked about (1) the English aristocracy (2) the effects of agricultural depression on their morality (3) his dog (4) the battle of Sadowa (5) the Puritan revolution in England (6) the luxury of the Roman Antonines (7) a particular friend of his who had by an infamous job received a political post he was utterly unfit for (8) the comic papers of Australia (9) the mortal sins in the Roman Catholic church—you may have some conception of the space that was left for the motion before the house. It lasted half-an-hour and I thought it was five minutes.'[25]

It is worth stressing that we have no account, either from Chesterton himself or from any other source, of any similar reaction by him to any other personality: if we are to trust the testimony of his friends such sentiments, indeed, were normally (unknown to Chesterton himself) directed by others towards him. According to A. N. Wilson, however, Chesterton had a strong general tendency to hero-worship: Bentley, he claims, 'always remarked in Chesterton a bump of veneration, and a desire to be rather

---

[24] *Autobiography*, 116–17.   [25] *Return*, 52.

clinging. In later years, he found these qualities vexing, and attributed them to a wholly suppressed homosexual tinge to Chesterton's make-up.'[26] In fact, 'in later years', Bentley and Chesterton met much less frequently than they had done in their youth (hardly indicating on Chesterton's part 'a desire to be clinging'); as for his alleged 'suppressed homosexuality', Wilson concedes that 'perhaps there was nothing in it': in fact—though these things can never be proved—there was almost certainly nothing whatever 'in it'. But he adds that '[i]ncontrovertibly...he was a hero-worshipper, as his account of Belloc's speech in the MacGregor studio makes abundantly clear.' But it does nothing of the sort. Belloc's dazzling abilities as a public speaker were generally recognised; at Oxford, only the legendary F. E. Smith had been able to equal him; to express admiration of one of his performances was hardly to indicate any undue 'hero-worship'. 'Listening to Belloc is intoxicating,' wrote Maisie Ward four decades later; 'I have heard many brilliant talkers, but none to whom that word can be so justly applied. He goes to your head, he takes you off your feet.... Imagination staggers before the picture of a Belloc in his full youth and vigour in a group fitted to strike from him his brightest fire at a moment big with issues for the world's future.'[27]

This picture of an inexperienced and 'unformed' Chesterton hero-worshipping the more brilliant and experienced Belloc leads A. N. Wilson to a major misjudgement. 'The meeting of the two famous men', he writes, 'was...infinitely more momentous for Chesterton than it was for Belloc. Belloc merely gained another friend with whom he could drink and laugh and talk. Chesterton gained a mentor who was to sharpen *and largely reshape*, his whole outlook on life, literature, politics and, ultimately, religion.'[28] We have seen the extent to which Chesterton's outlook on these things (hardly, by this stage 'unformed') had been developed by him alone. The development of his views on religion, as we shall see, owed virtually nothing to Belloc; and Chesterton's characteristic habit of tilting at prevailing cultural and religious assumptions was well established by the turn of the century, though it can only have been confirmed and strengthened by Belloc's company. That Belloc was to exert some influence on his views on history and politics, as we shall see, was acknowledged by Chesterton himself,

---

[26] How seriously we need take this is indicated by Wilson's source, which is given as Malcolm Muggeridge, who had no direct knowledge of either Bentley or Chesterton.

[27] Ward, 114.

[28] My italics. A. N Wilson, *Hilaire Belloc* (London, 1997), 103.

though even here we need to be cautious—he already had very decided views on history and politics, which Belloc may have enriched, but which he never fundamentally changed. Though Belloc, for instance, had already published a book on Danton and was to write two more on the French Revolution, Chesterton had written his poem about Danton's execution some eight years before, and his views on the French revolutionary and republican tradition (though completely consistent with Belloc's) were already fully formed when they met. Belloc's chief influence on Chesterton's political thinking came later, with his development of the ideas which were to lead to *The Servile State* (1912) and to his formulation of the ideology of distributism;[29] as for literature, it is clear that Chesterton knew far more (certainly about English literature) than Belloc did; in the words of Maisie Ward (with whom Belloc discussed the question of his supposed influence over Chesterton), 'Belloc has characterised himself as ignorant of English literature and says he learnt from Chesterton most of what he knows of it'.[30] She added that 'there is no doubt that Chesterton was by far the greater philosopher', and it is probably germane both to this assertion and to the wider question of their relationship to evoke, from Belloc's *Observer* obituary, his own view of Chesterton's very individual contribution as a thinker, since though it was written after his death, it is as relevant to the writings of Chesterton's first decade on the public stage as to those of his last. He had, Belloc wrote, 'an especially national character':

On the other hand, he excelled in what is not an English characteristic, but one which he could introduce to his fellow-citizens with an ease that one more alien could never have enjoyed; I mean the element of precision and of deductive reasoning. It was this, the rational process of the mind, which governed all his development in the matter of his religion.

Gilbert Chesterton's outstanding mental mark . . . was a desire to convince by proof. He was informed by the appetite for reason; it inspired all he did. To unravel, to define, to make sure, to appreciate, and to grasp—and having done this to communicate, but to communicate through an appeal to the intellect rather than the emotion, showing perpetually by example of similars why and how a thing should be approved true.[31]

Four years later, Belloc developed the arguments of his obituary, virtually paragraph by paragraph, in his little book *On the Place of Gilbert Chesterton in English Letters* (1940); his analysis of Chesterton's technique of arguing 'by

---

[29] See pp. 372–4 below.   [30] Ward, 114.
[31] Hilaire Belloc, signed obituary, *The Observer* (21 June 1936). Conlon, 533.

example of similars' becomes a discussion of Chesterton's 'Parallelism', which Belloc defines as 'the illustration of some unperceived truth by its exact consonance with the reflection of a truth already known and perceived'.[32]

In his *Observer* obituary, Belloc may well have intended a rebuttal of the *Manchester Guardian*'s obituary, which had appeared six days before and which had made a point of dismissing the widespread description of Chesterton as a 'philosopher' as 'very ill-chosen'. He had, asserted the writer, 'a profusion of fresh and original ideas, but they owed more to the spontaneous inspirations of an enormously zestful temperament than to continuous or connected thought'.[33] 'The intellectual side of him', wrote Belloc (conceivably in reply), 'has been masked for many and for some hidden by his delight in the exercise of words and especially in the comedy of words.'[34] In essence, as we shall see, this failure to perceive 'the intellectual side of him' because of the masking effect of the comedy of words had been a feature of the public response to Chesterton from the beginning; and throughout his public career it tended to obscure—even to serious critics—what Belloc calls 'the element of precision and of deductive reasoning'; this is true, perhaps, predominantly of his journalism, which in fact contained some of his most serious and original thought. It is particularly true of his use of paradox (which we will need to consider more than once, as we describe various stages of his intellectual development).

In view of the emphasis so far placed here on Chesterton's youthful admiration for Belloc's conversational ability, it may be as well to close this brief discussion of their relationship by quoting Belloc's view of Chesterton's 'power of expression . . . in conversation', which he dates 'from the first day I heard it':

His power of expression, which was, I think, his highest artistic gift . . . was inevitably stronger, being what he was, in conversation than in any other medium. Who shall determine whether a man does more in speaking or in writing, if in both he is lucid and illuminates all that he touches? . . . In Gilbert Chesterton the two were so welded that I sometimes think in reading printed sentences of his that I still hear his voice. It was a voice from which I learnt continually, from the first day I heard it until the last; acquiring from it discoveries, explanations, definitions which continue to increase my possessions.[35]

---

[32] Hilaire Belloc, *On the Place of Gilbert Chesterton in English Letters* (London, 1940), 37.

[33] *Manchester Guardian*, unsigned obituary (15 June 1936). Conlon, 523.

[34] Hilaire Belloc, signed obituary, *The Observer* (21 June 1936). Conlon, 533.

[35] Belloc, obituary; Conlon, 534.

The question of Belloc's influence on Chesterton has often been touched on (though rarely discussed at any length); that of Chesterton's on Belloc might prove just as interesting—and, possibly, just as elusive.

Paradox and the democracy of truth

The picture of Chesterton sitting in mute admiration before Belloc's unstoppable verbal flow would certainly have been seen by his friends and acquaintances as wholly untypical. He was naturally argumentative; if there was nobody else to argue with, he would argue with thin air. On one occasion, at the end of a party in the late 1890s, Mildred Wain (the fiancée of Chesterton's JDC friend Waldo D'Avigdor) found 'Gilbert walking up and down, talking rapidly. I went across to "say Goodnight" to Gilbert, but just behind him, sound asleep in the corner, was my sister Anne—she had been there most of the evening. She said Gilbert started an argument about Hottentot babies or something wild like that, and as she was not interested she merely went to sleep. I don't think Gilbert ever twigged that she was asleep, as he answered all his own questions and seemed to have enjoyed himself.'[36] Throughout his boyhood and beyond, his chief sparring partner was his brother Cecil. As Cecil's wife Ada remembered later, '[t]he brothers could—and frequently did—spend several hours in each other's company without crossing swords, but let one drop a word that challenged the other, and immediately the issue was joined, and a fresh chapter opened in their life-long discussion.' These battles took precedence over all else, even when there were guests in the house:

One evening, when we were all enjoying ourselves particularly, Cecil made a controversial remark about the problem play [a contemporary genre, designed to provoke discussion of social issues]. Immediately, Gilbert retorted that most problem plays were as unimportant and as obnoxious as the obscene domestic habits of blackbeetles. Cecil rose to the bait and for the next two hours the brothers held the floor, walking from north to south and south to north, utterly, blindly unaware of the corporal presence of the guests. It is not that in any sense they were intentionally discourteous, but the discussion of an idea actually blotted out all material considerations. They never interrupted one another, their voices were never raised, nor was there a touch of recrimination or the suspicion of rudeness. They just

---

[36] *Return*, 21.

continued the duel with such zest and brilliance that the bewildered and embarrassed onlookers were hypnotised.[37]

Chesterton was a natural debater all his life; the Junior Debating Club was almost designed around him. Later in his life, his live debates with Shaw and Wells—not to mention their mutual attacks in print—were to be justly famous as encapsulating the great culture wars of the time (the calmness and absence of recrimination of his arguments with Cecil was to be characteristic of his later battles, too). This is a key to one characteristic intellectual ability, which he possessed almost to the point of genius. It accompanied and antithesised his brilliant capacity, in Belloc's words, to show 'perpetually by example of similars why and how a thing should be approved true': it was his capacity to perceive how a statement assumed to be true was actually false, an ability which derived—again in Belloc's words—from his passion to 'unravel, to define, to make sure, to appreciate, and to grasp' the inner workings of any idea or way of thinking. It was from the combination of these two intellectual methods that he developed what was to become seen as his characteristic mode: the ability to see how a statement which on the face of it was false or irrational might actually prove to be true or rational: the Chestertonian paradox, which from the beginning of his public reputation was seen as his most brilliantly distinctive (and by his critics as his most tiresome) intellectual tendency. When a collection of his *Speaker* articles appeared at the end of 1901 under the title *The Defendant*, one reviewer attacked him on the grounds of his gross over-use of the device: 'Paradox ought to be used', wrote this critic, 'like onions to season the salad. Mr Chesterton's salad is all onions. Paradox has been defined as "truth standing on her head to attract attention." Mr Chesterton makes truth cut her throat to attract attention.'[38] His use of paradox became a ground for predominantly hostile criticism; those who praised Chesterton tended to mention it less. *The Academy*'s reviewer of *The Defendant* represented his use of paradox as a mannerism of youthful high spirits, stemming from his irrepressible (and indefensible) optimism; 'Mr Chesterton', he wrote, 'seems to think that he can make the world seem fair by proving it is so. That is a mistake. No amount of ratiocinative ingenuity of optimism, or feats of paradoxical

---

[37] Ada Chesterton, *The Chestertons* (London, 1941), 25.

[38] Ward, 136. Mr Dale Ahlquist has drawn my attention to this review, in response to a query about the source of the frequent but erroneous claim that it was Chesterton himself who wrote that paradox was 'truth standing on her head to gain attention'.

defence, can lighten the burden.' All the various subjects of the articles collected in *The Defendant* were defended by paradox, the writer argued: '[t]he paradoxical defence is the natural device of your young man excogitant. . . . It is a good device, sparingly used; but unless it is done with an almost Elian discretion and pawkiness, it is apt to suggest that the writer has adopted it as a means of laying a train of epigrammatic gunpowder with time fuses carefully adjusted.'[39]

His allegedly excessive fondness for the use of paradox in his journalism was attacked by another critic, in a letter to *The Speaker*, the following month. Chesterton replied; and since his response is (so far as I can discover) the first evidence we have that when Chesterton used paradox he did so, from the beginning, with a clear and coherent understanding of how he intended the device to reflect his philosophy of life (the term is not, it will be seen, inappropriate), his riposte is worth quoting at some length:

On the subject of paradox, I wish to speak to 'G.G.G.' [Chesterton's critic] like a father. He has got into his head that extraordinary idea that paradox is a flowery, artificial thing, invented by literary *flaneurs*. If that were all, paradox would never have become sufficiently widespread for him to be aware of its existence. Humanity would soon have exhausted the fun of the somewhat simple game of saying that black was white. The reason that paradox is continuous and ancient (the word itself dates from the time of Plato) is quite clear and sufficient. The reason is that there really is a strand of contradiction running through the universe. In proportion as men perceive it, they admit a contradiction: in proportion as men become honest they become paradoxical. Let me take, for the sake of argument, a simple example. If there be an absolutely normal thing in humanity it is the admiration of courage. It is the first virtue that the savage learns: it is the last virtue which the decadent most reluctantly abandons. . . . Here, in this matter of courage, if anywhere, there is a point of ordinary human unanimity. And yet, courage is a paradox, and can best and most easily be expressed by a paradox. I have only to say, 'Courage involves the power of being frightened,' and you have a paradox and a matter of plain common sense. For we certainly do not talk of the courage of the entomologist in boldly striking the beetle, because he does not fear it. . . . Courage involves fear, and this is only one of the million paradoxes which existed in nature ages before any literary men ever borrowed them. . . . [G.G.G.] complains that I say, 'There is nothing so natural as supernaturalism.' But what could be more plainly and prosaically true? Six typical savages live in different parts of the globe, wholly disconnected. As soon as they develop

---

[39] Unsigned article, 'The Young Man Excogitant', *The Academy* (30 Nov. 1901); Conlon, 37.

even so much intelligence as to realise that flints are sharp, or that fire warms the hands, they begin simultaneously to say that the tree is possessed by their great grandfather and that a spirit speaks in the thunder. How can this state of things be described more accurately than by saying that there is nothing so natural as supernaturalism? It is a paradox, but it is God, and not I who should have the credit of it. It may not have occurred to 'G.G.G.'—it has often occurred to me— that it was this ingrained paradox in the cosmos which led so many religions, wisely enough, to boast not that they had an explanation of the Universe, but that they had a pure, defiant paradox, like the Athanasian Creed.[40]

The response of 'G.G.G.' to this reply—that Chesterton's example of courage involving fear was no paradox but an obvious truth, like goodness involving power to do evil—drew from Chesterton the rejoinder that that was precisely his argument: 'that all these obvious truths when examined turned out to be paradoxes, both in substance and in form. It is the doctrine of old heroic myth that we are the braver for every terror. It is the doctrine of Christian holiness that we are the better for every temptation of the devil. It is the doctrine of Liberalism and free speech that we are the better for every delusion, the better for every lie.'[41]

Chesterton's denial 'that paradox is a flowery, artificial thing, invented by literary *flaneurs*', and his assertion that there is an 'ingrained paradox in the cosmos', was to be repeated in *The Ball and the Cross* (the first eight chapters of which were serialised in *The Commonwealth* in 1905–6):

Those who look at the matter most superficially regard paradox as something which belongs to jesting and light journalism. Paradox of this kind is to be found in the saying of the dandy, in the decadent comedy, 'Life is much too important to be taken seriously.' Those who look at the matter a little more deeply or delicately see that paradox is a thing which especially belongs to all religions. Paradox of this kind is to be found in such a saying as 'The meek shall inherit the earth.' But those who see and feel the fundamental fact of the matter know that paradox is a thing which belongs not to religion only, but to all vivid and violent practical crises of human living.[42]

In *Paradox in Chesterton* (1948), Hugh Kenner argues that Chesterton uses paradox in two principal ways: there is 'a metaphysical use of paradox that answers to the complexity of being, especially the Supreme Being, and a rhetorical use that answers more to the complexity of human folly. The

---

[40] 'G.K.C.', 'Bacon and Beastliness', *The Speaker* (8 Feb. 1902), 532.

[41] 'G.K.C.', 'Bacon and "G.G.G."', *The Speaker* (22 Feb. 1902), 589.

[42] G. K. Chesterton, 'A Discussion Somewhat in the Air', *The Ball and the Cross*, *The Commonwealth* (Mar. 1905).

latter is essentially verbal, and obtains its effect through the juxtaposition of unlikely words, as in G.K.'s reference to Companionate Marriage, "So-called because the people involved are not married and will very rapidly cease to be companions." [43] Although much of Chesterton's use of paradox was already of this second, rhetorical, type, it is interesting that his defence assumes a use of it which, to employ Kenner's typology, is predominantly 'metaphysical'; and it may be worth suggesting that it is misleading to see the distinction between Kenner's two types as clear-cut, since Chesterton's perception was precisely that human folly was frequently the result of a metaphysical subversion or overturning of human culture, a subversion for which at different stages of his intellectual development, he adduced various causes. It is particularly interesting, at this transitional period—during which he was in the early stages of a process of moving 'nearer and nearer to the orthodox side'—that he should evoke a text so dogmatically absolute and intellectually complex as the Athanasian Creed, as an example of the 'ingrained paradox in the cosmos' at the heart of all religion.

Chesterton's equation of 'paradox and . . . plain common sense' in his *Speaker* defence (itself a paradox) is important, and is directly connected with this metaphysical dimension of Chesterton's imagination. Such questions were grist to Chesterton's journalistic mill from the outset, and this indicates one of his most important qualities as a communicator: from the beginning of his career as a journalist, he profoundly believed he had a vocation to confront the notion that truth was the province only of an elite. His belief in democracy was nearer to being a religious conviction than it was to being a merely political stance. As he had written in one of his early articles for *The Daily News* the previous year (a review of a book on Christian mysticism), 'there was an enormous truth in the democracy of Christianity. . . . In the material world there are inequalities, gaps between the poet and the ploughman, between the prophet and the child. But in the spiritual world one all-embracing mystery knocks everything flat as with the blow of a hammer. In comparison with the infinite goodness, all differences between Shakespeare and a toadstool sink into relative insignificance.' His review begins with a characteristic paradox: 'Miss Eleanor Gregory has written a decidedly lucid and interesting account of the great mystics, in which there is little fault to be found, except that she falls into the common and natural error of regarding

---

[43] Hugh Kenner, *Paradox in Chesterton* (London, 1948), 16.

mysticism as something mysterious.' On the contrary, argues Chesterton, 'Mysticism in its noblest sense, mysticism as it existed in St John, and Plato, and Paracelsus, and Sir Thomas Browne, is not an exceptionally dark and secret thing, but an exceptionally luminous and open thing. It is in reality too clear for most of us to comprehend, and too obvious for most of us to see. Such an utterance as the utterance that "God is Love" does in reality overwhelm us like an immeasureable landscape on a clear day, like the light of an intolerable summer sun. We may call it a dark saying; but we have an inward knowledge all the time that it is we who are dark.' Mysticism, Chesterton insists, is essentially rational, even though the 'man in the street' would at first regard a mystical way of understanding material phenomena as impenetrable. But this is because, in a despiritua-lised culture, the common understanding has ceased to function naturally. It is at this point that we can begin to perceive Chesterton's equation of paradox and 'plain common sense' as being at the very heart of what has already, by this stage in his intellectual development, become a radically counter-cultural vision of his world:

It is remarkable to notice even in daily life how constant is this impression of the essential rationality of mysticism. If we went up to a man in the street who happened to be standing opposite a lamppost and addressed him playfully with the words, 'Whence did this strange object spring? How did this lean Cyclops with the eye of fire start out of unbegotten night?' it may be generally inferred, with every possible allowance for the temperament of the individual, that he would not regard our remarks as particularly cogent and practical. And yet our surprise at the lamppost would be entirely rational; his habit of taking lampposts for granted would be merely a superstition. The power that makes men accept material phenomena of this universe, its cities, civilisations, and solar systems, is merely a vulgar prejudice, like the prejudice that made them accept cock-fights or the Inquisition. It is the mystic to whom every star is like a sudden rocket, every flower an earthquake of the dust, who is the clear-minded man. Mysticism, or a sense of the mystery of things, is simply the most gigantic form of common-sense, We should not have to complain of any materialism if common-sense were only common.[44]

Paradox and common sense thus understood are inextricably connected parts of his attack on the rationalism of the modern world as being inher-ently irrational. His passion for common sense is part of his passion for rational truth; and paradox is an instrument of common sense in a world out

----

[44] G. K. Chesterton, 'The Mystery of the Mystics', *The Daily News* (30 Aug. 1901), 6.

of joint, a world in which common sense is habitually denied. Since the world has itself become a kind of permanent paradox, only paradox can unravel the truth about it. The lamp-post became for him a recurrent symbol of one particular paradox, the paradox inherent in what we can without exaggeration call Chesterton's mystical discovery, after his emergence from his period of depression and emotional instability, of the newness and imaginative liberation to be found in his own world. We have already quoted Chesterton's great post-Slade discovery (worth repeating in this new context) that

> There is one secret for life
> The secret of constant astonishment.

This is followed in 'The Notebook' by the aphorism '[t]here is one thing which gives radiance to everything, streets, houses, lamp posts, communities, politics, lives—it is the idea of something round the corner':[45] the world of everyday sense, that is to say, is the doorway to worlds as yet unknown, or even unknowable. 'Even an ordinary lamp-post', he wrote in another notebook dating from the mid-1890s, 'is indeed a thing at which poets might gaze longer than at a primrose, for it is the ensign of man's war upon Old night with fire, his stolen star.'[46] But this poet's perception is necessarily denied by the necessities of modern life; 'practical life puts a limit on mysticism, and the clerk who was stricken with a trance of worship at every lamp-post all the way up the Strand, might find his employers unsympathetic on his arrival at business.'[47] Chesterton's discovery of 'radiance' in the material expressions of an industrial culture which had come for others to embody only ugliness and indifference was to become an abiding source of paradox: where others saw only the prosaic, he discerned a new 'cosmos' which was a source of 'constant astonishment'. In another of his articles for *The Speaker*, he defended detective stories as being 'the earliest and only form of popular literature in which is expressed some sense of the poetry of modern life. Men lived among mighty mountains and eternal forests for ages before they realized that they were poetical; it may reasonably be inferred that some of our descendants may see the chimney-pots as rich a purple as the mountain-peaks, and find the lamp-posts as old and natural as the trees.'[48] In *The Napoleon of Notting Hill*, it is recounted of the

---

[45] BL MS Add. 73334.   [46] BL MS Add. 73332B.   [47] *Collected Works*, xiv. 693.
[48] 'A Defence of Detective Stories', *The Speaker* (13 July 1900).

visionary Adam Wayne that 'he saw the street-lamps as things quite as eternal as the stars; the two fires were mingled. He saw the houses as things enduring, like the mountains, and so he wrote about them as one would write about mountains.' This 'poetry of modern life,' implies Chesterton, can only be perceived if the doors of perception are cleansed, and the prosaic becomes the magical. This essential Chestertonian perception is at the heart of his paradoxical vision of the world. In clear contrast to other counter-cultural figures, like William Morris, Chesterton is not only not *hostile* to contemporary urban culture, he is a passionate proselytiser for it: 'the weak point in William Morris as a reformer', he wrote in a *Daily News* article, was that 'he sought to reform modern life, and that he hated modern life instead of loving it. Modern London is indeed a beast, big enough and black enough to be the beast in Apocalypse, blazing with a million eyes, and roaring with a million voices. But unless the poet can love this fabulous monster as he is, can feel with some generous excitement his massive and mysterious *joie-de-vivre*, the vast scale of his iron anatomy and the beating of his thunderous heart, he cannot and will not change the beast into the fairy prince.'[49] Chesterton could be moved to exasperation, even to anger, by modern man's failure to understand this poetry of modern life, as in 'King's Cross Station', one of the poems in his collection *The Wild Knight*:

> God! Shall we ever honour what we are. . . .
>
> Or must fate act the same grey farce again,
>   And wait, till one, amid Time's wrecks and scars,
> Speaks to a ruin here, 'what poet-race
>   Shot such cyclopean arches at the stars?'[50]

At the heart of Chesterton's critique of his own culture lies the paradox that despite his philosophical aversion to modernity, he has an almost sacramental attitude to the material expressions of modern life, symbolised for him repeatedly by the lamp-post, 'eternal as the stars'. There is, he senses, a poetry in such phenomena which only a world whose perceptions have been radically undermined could fail to discern. By this stage in his intellectual development, at the turn of the century and for some years afterwards, Chesterton had not come to any conclusion as to the cause of this subversion of the world's vision of reality: he was still giving it local or recent limited causes such as pessimism (Schopenhauer) or aestheticism

---

[49] G. K. Chesterton, *Twelve Types* (London, 1902), 26–7.
[50] *Collected Works*, x. 224.

(Wilde) or Impressionism (Whistler). As a Roman Catholic (indeed, by the time he wrote *Orthodoxy*) he had come to attribute it to a prior underlying historical cause—the Protestant Reformation: he now perceived the modern world as having begun not with the invention of steam or the Reform Bill of 1832, but in the sixteenth century. Nevertheless, his argument, in the 1920s, is remarkably similar to his early defence of paradox as an instrument of the restoration of 'common sense' in a cosmos which has itself been overturned. Now, however, the term 'paradox' is aligned not with common sense but with the irrational culture which has emerged from this great spiritual upheaval:

The fact that Thomism is the philosophy of common sense is itself a matter of common sense. Yet it wants a word of explanation, because we have so long taken such matters in a very uncommon sense. For good or evil, Europe since the Reformation, and most especially England since the Reformation, has been in a peculiar sense the home of paradox. I mean in the very peculiar sense that paradox was at home, and that men were at home with it. The most familiar example is the English boasting that they are practical *because* they are not logical. To an ancient Greek or a Chinaman this would seem exactly like saying that London clerks excel in adding up their ledgers, because they are not accurate in their arithmetic. But the point is not that it is a paradox; it is that paradoxy has become orthodoxy; that men repose in a paradox as placidly as in a platitude. . . . Since the modern world began in the sixteenth century, nobody's system of philosophy has really corresponded to everybody's sense of reality: to what, if left to themselves, common men would call common sense.[51]

'Gilbert Chesterton': is it a pseudonym? *Greybeards at Play* and *The Wild Knight*

Though already in some ways very close to the essentials of this world view, the Gilbert Chesterton who at the age of 26 was projected on to the public stage was in other respects still far from it. By the time his first two books were published, and the name 'Gilbert Chesterton' came to the notice of the literary world for the first time, he had, indeed, already moved on. *Greybeards at Play*, a collection of comic verses and drawings—which appeared in October 1900—and *The Wild Knight*, the title of a turgid verse drama, published the following month together with a collection of

---

[51] Ibid., ii. 513.

shorter poems, were both products of a long period of gestation which had come to an end some time before. Some poems in *The Wild Knight* are the final (and sometimes much less effective) texts of verses which appear, often in several versions, in manuscript notebooks dating from anything up to five years before. The final version of the opening verse of 'Alone', for instance—

> Blessings there are of cradle and of clan,
>   Blessings that fall of priests' and princes' hands;
>   But never blessings full of lives and lands,
> Broad as the blessing of a lonely man

is a politicised (and considerably flatter) version of a verse which first appears, in a notebook probably pre-dating his first meeting with Frances, around 1895:

> Blessings there are of cradle & of clan
>   Blessings of man & maid, of man and brute
>   But never blessing full of sun & fruit
> Broad as the blessing of a lonely man.[52]

The anti-clerical posture in the final version of this verse is echoed in 'The Wild Knight' itself. Here, as though preserved in amber, we can observe for the last time a familiar rhetorical pose, an attitude which in earlier chapters we have seen being struck in the religious poetry of *The Debater* and the passionate utterances of the post-Slade period; it was an attitude which—by the time *The Wild Knight* was published, during a period when Conrad Noel was little by little replacing Stopford Brooke as Chesterton's theological mentor—was already sinking into the dim recesses of his memories of adolescence:

> . . . I hear the crumbling creeds
> Like cliffs washed down by water, change and pass;
> I hear a noise of words, age after age,
> A new cold wind that blows across the plains,
> And all the shrines stand empty; and to me
> All these are nothing: priests and schools may doubt
> Who never have believed.[53]

---

[52] BL MS Add. 73337B, fo. 19.
[53] G. K. Chesterton, *The Wild Knight* (London, 1945), 64.

Such writing—as the book's reviewer in *Literature* noted—is very different in tone from his first published book of verse, *Greybeards at Play*. Having reviewed *Greybeards* the previous month, this critic had 'turned with delight to the author's new book', but had found to his dismay that '[t]he mature and cautious humour of the former work is in "The Wild Knight" replaced by a rash sincerity and a quite juvenile earnestness'.[54] *Greybeards* seems, nevertheless, to have attracted less attention than *The Wild Knight*, and Chesterton himself came to air-brush it from his literary career. It was not included in his *Collected Poems* (1927), and he did not mention it in the *Autobiography*. Nevertheless, it was his first work in print, and it is still worth some attention, if for no other reason than that it draws our attention once more to the benign part in his life played by his father Edward Chesterton. The book was published by Rex Brimley Johnson, and this may have been arranged, possibly even underwritten, by Mr Ed (who certainly subsidised the publication, by the firm of Grant Richards, of *The Wild Knight*). Mr Ed undoubtedly knew Brimley Johnson (who, if Frances's sister Gertrude had not been killed in a traffic accident, would have become Gilbert's brother-in-law), since at about the same time as *Greybeards at Play* he also published Mr Ed's book *The Wonderful Story of Dunder van Haeden*.

Edward Chesterton also arranged (possibly through Bentley or Older-shaw, both of whom had for many years been frequent visitors to Warwick Gardens) himself to review *Greybeards* anonymously in *The Speaker*. His review is amusingly revealing of his fatherly anxieties about Gilbert's financial viability: '[a]n original turn of mind', he wrote, 'can only with difficulty be made a remunerative thing; and indeed there are many who hold . . . that it is a permanent and insuperable bar to a decent income. Yet I do not despair of Mr Chesterton's selling his book, and what is almost as important, achieving some literary reputation by it.'[55] It was not his first effort at ensuring 'a decent income' for his impractical son. Chesterton was still working for Fisher Unwin, with whom Mr Ed had the previous year attempted to negotiate, almost as a literary agent, over his son's remuneration. Gilbert was impatient to marry; it had been a long engagement. His father could easily have afforded to give him an allowance until he had established himself. But he knew Gilbert; and he may well have decided that this would have been a disastrous encouragement to his son not to work for his own financial

---

[54] Unsigned review, *Literature* (12 Jan. 1901); Conlon, 32.
[55] 'E.C.', 'A Landmark in Lunacy', *The Speaker* (6 Oct. 1900). Conlon, 23.

independence but to rely on his support. Instead, therefore, he parleyed directly with Fisher Unwin not only over Gilbert's salary, but over a book on Paris the firm were proposing that he write. Gilbert seems to have had no diffidence in telling Frances that it was his father, and not he himself, who (apparently not for the first time) was dealing with his employers over his financial remuneration. Two months before the real beginning of Gilbert's journalistic career, with his first review in *The Bookman* in December 1899, he had written to Frances to tell her not only of his hopes of regular work on *The Speaker*, but also of his prospects in his present employment.

My father again is engaged in the critical correspondence with Fisher Unwin, at least it has begun with T.F.U. stating his proposed terms—a rise of 5/- from October, another rise possible but undefined in January, 10 percent royalty for the Paris book and expenses for a fortnight in Paris. These, as I got my father to heartily agree, are vitiated to the bone by the absence of any assurance that I shall not have to write Paris, for which I am really paid nothing, outside the hours of work for which I am paid 25/-. In short, the net result would be that instead of gaining more liberty to rise in the literary world, I should be selling the small liberty of rising that I have now for five more shillings. This my father is declining and asking for a better settlement.[56]

We do not know whether the extra 5 shillings materialised; the book on Paris did not. In any case, Chesterton was impatient to end his days as a wage slave and to plunge into the life of Fleet Street; and his two books of verse were part of his great objective, to 'rise in the literary world'.

    Greybeards at Play was his first appearance between hard covers. To publish a book of nonsense verse would not, today, be thought a sensible or practical way to launch a literary career. But *Greybeards* appeared in what was still the Victorian era (the old Queen was to live on into the following year); the names of Lewis Carroll and Edward Lear were still revered as part of an absurdist and anti-rationalist literary tradition which had deep roots in the English psyche, a tradition which was one of many strategies the Victorian mind generated in order to survive life in an industrial and Utilitarian culture which had established itself in such an atmosphere of stifling high seriousness. The most obvious influence on Chesterton in this context is likely to have been W. S. Gilbert: it will be remembered that it was as children, when, after scrapping in the school playground, Bentley had mentioned 'Dickens or the *Bab Ballads*', that they had 'plunged into a

---

[56] Ward, 105.

friendly discussion on literature' which was to continue for the rest of their lives.[57] Given Chesterton's lifelong habits, we can surmise that he probably knew many of the *Bab Ballads* by heart; and it was a literary precedent that would certainly not have discouraged him from making an entry into the world of literature as a comic poet. W. S. Gilbert was, quite apart from his relationship with the composer Sir Arthur Sullivan, enormously successful; and it was the *Bab Ballads*, rather than his early plays, that had made him not only solvent but famous. To such as the adolescent Chesterton, W. S. Gilbert's appeal is obvious enough:

> Sir Macklin was a priest severe
> In conduct and in conversation,
> It did a sinner good to hear
> Him deal in ratiocination.
>
> He could in every action show
> Some sin, and nobody could doubt him.
> He argued high, he argued low,
> He also argued round about him.
>
> He wept to think each thoughtless youth
> Contained of wickedness a skinful,
> And burnt to teach the awful truth,
> That walking out on Sunday's sinful.[58]

It is easy to understand why this essentially Victorian genre was so popular. Nonsense verse of this kind is subversive, without being revolutionary. Its challenges to rationality are conducted within strict and generally simple literary forms; indeed, the clash between invariable and hackneyed form and surrealist content is one principal source of absurdity. *Greybeards at Play* is a remarkably assured contribution to the genre. The most frequently quoted stanza is from its dedication, to Bentley:

> He was, throughout my boyhood's storm and shower,
> My best, my nearest friend;
> We wore one hat, smoked one cigar,
> One standing at each end

W. H. Auden was to write that the collection contained poems which were not merely 'enchanting', but 'some of the best pure nonsense verse in English'; he adds that 'very few of his "serious" poems are as good as

[57] See pp. 44–5 above.   [58] W. S. Gilbert, *The Bab Ballads* (London, 1979), 65–6.

these'.[59] This judgement is surely borne out from the opening verses of the
first poem, 'The Oneness of the Philosopher with Nature':

> I love to see the little stars
>   All dancing to one tune;
> I think quite highly of the Sun,
>   And kindly of the moon.
>
> The million forests of the Earth
>   Come trooping in to tea
> The great Niagara waterfall
>   Is never shy with me.
>
> I am the tiger's confidant,
>   And never mention names:
> The lion drops the formal 'Sir,'
>   And lets me call him 'James'.[60]

Mr Ed's review in *The Speaker* perceptively places the subversive dimension
of such writing in its historical context: '[t]his little book', he wrote, 'marks
a stage in the development of a kind of literature which has grown up in the
last century—that of nonsense. Slight thing as it is, it is not too much to say
that that development means a change in thought, a loosening of certain
bonds which used to be considered the proper trammels of reverence,
earnestness and dignity.'[61] This, undoubtedly, was part of his son's purpose:
but its successful attainment draws our attention to the fatal weakness of
much of the poetic diction to be found in *The Wild Knight*, which appeared
only a month later. Having with *Greybeards* helped to loosen the bonds of
'reverence, earnestness and dignity', Chesterton had fatally undermined
such utterly flat and humourless writing as predominates (despite some
striking exceptions) in his first volume of 'serious' poetry. The poetic
diction of some of the verses in *The Wild Knight* collection, after the inspired
parody of exactly this kind of writing in *Greybeards*, seems distinctly uneasy.
To go from the *Greybeards* verses just quoted to a poem from *The
Wild Knight* like 'The World's Lover' is to proceed from the absurd to the
would-be sublime in a way which can only make the young Chesterton's
attempts at high seriousness look dangerously like self-parody:

---

[59] W. H. Auden, 'The Gift of Wonder', in John Sullivan (ed.), *G. K. Chesterton: A Centenary Appraisal* (London, 1974), 78.

[60] 'The Oneness of the Philosopher with Nature', *Greybeards at Play* (London, 1974,) 16–18.

[61] 'E.C.', 'A Landmark in Lunacy'; Conlon, 25.

> My eyes are full of lonely mirth
>   Reeling with want and worn with scars,
> For pride of every stone on earth,
>   I shake my spear at all the stars.

'The World's Lover', however, is in deadly earnest and in the end this becomes clear, but it is a close-run thing: once we have understood that we are no longer in the world of comic verse but of melodrama, it is possible to avoid laughter but not, surely, to feel when reading most of this unequal collection that we are in the presence of a genuine poet. Certainly, amid the dross, there are gems. Other verses in the collection were to become justly famous; a good half-dozen of them, indeed—notably 'The Donkey', 'By the Babe Unborn', and the touching and beautiful 'A Christmas Carol'—became indispensable anthology pieces: even of these successful verses, however, the judgement of T. S. Eliot (who while seeking to praise, nevertheless places just limits on the importance we should accord even Chesterton's best verses) is unavoidable: '[h]is poetry', Eliot wrote, 'was first-class journalistic balladry, and I do not suppose that he took it more seriously than it deserved.'[62]

The contemporary reaction to *The Wild Knight* tended to be either scathing or (if favourable) sententious. In *The Speaker* (for which Chesterton was by now himself a regular reviewer), the literary editor, F. Y. Eccles, described him as 'a poet whose sonorous, tender and hope-giving voice is not to be confounded with the studious falsetto of boudoir warblers or the hoarse yell of demagogic bards'.[63] The literary critic James Douglas approvingly perceived the note of doom-laden anti-clericalism: '[t]he note of revolt predominates,' he observed, 'ringing challenges are hurled against God and Man. . . . so strong is the voice, so bold the defiance, so well-hammered the verse, that I wonder why I have never heard of "Gilbert Chesterton." Is it a pseudonym?'[64] Quieter, and more perceptive, criticism came from Rudyard Kipling in a letter to Rex Brimley Johnson, who had sent him a copy of the book's second edition, the publication of which (with the financial support of Edward Chesterton) he had taken over from Grant Richards. There was, Kipling thought, 'any amount of promise in the work', and wondered how Chesterton would develop in a few years: 'We all begin with arranging and

---

[62] T. S. Eliot, signed obituary, *The Tablet* (20 June 1936), 785; Conlon, 531.

[63] F. Y. Eccles, signed review, *The Speaker* (29 Dec. 1900); Conlon, 30.

[64] Unsigned review, 'So Nobly Fierce a Singer', *The Star* (5 Jan. 1901); Conlon, 30–1. Douglas went on to 'identify' 'Gilbert Chesterton' as the poet John Davidson.

elaborating all the Heavens and Hells and stars and tragedies we can lay our poetic hands on—later we see folk—just common people under the heavens';[65] it was a strikingly Chestertonian comment to make.

Edward Chesterton's involvement with the publication of *The Wild Knight* was probably the last occasion on which he was involved in his son's financial affairs in a protective and fatherly way; this involvement continued in a vestigial way until, in a stroke of great good fortune, a reliable literary agent (who was to look after Gilbert's affairs for the rest of his life) was found to take it over. In March 1904, Mr Ed wrote to Brimley Johnson to complain that given Gilbert's growing reputation he was doing little to give a 'push' to the book, though admitting that his son '(like many of his craft) is quite unbusinesslike to his disadvantage in practical affairs: for which reason he has (as advised by me & other friends) decided to make arrangements in future through Mr A. P. Watt, who will on our behalf communicate with you as to winding up the business of *The Wild Knight* which we have decided to do'.[66] Maisie Ward comments that 'there is something immensely pleasing in the simple but resolute figure of the older man, cutting knots that his son would vaguely have tried to loosen, as he stands against the background of Fleet Street taverns and offices'.[67]

Early journalism: *The Speaker* and *The Daily News*, 1900–1

By the end of the year 1900, Chesterton had to his credit two books, five articles in *The Bookman*, some fourteen articles in *The Speaker*,[68] and two occasional verses on political themes,[69] also in *The Speaker*. It was a

---

[65] Letter from Rudyard Kipling to Rex Brimley Johnson, Conlon, 27–8.

[66] *Return*, 62–3.

[67] Ibid. 62.

[68] 'Ruskin' (28 Apr.); 'Normandy in Black and White' (12 May) (on Percy Dearmer); 'Grant Allen' (23 June); 'Fiction' (two novels, by Anthony Hope and Gertrude Dix; 'A Manx Minstrel' (the letters and novels of T. E. Brown) (20 Oct.); 'How the Church Stands Today' (27 Oct.); 'Our Reasonable Imperialist' (Conan Doyle on the Boer War) (10 Nov.); 'Buddha versus Buddhism' (17 Nov.); 'Literature and Childhood' (24 Nov.); 'St Francis of Assisi' (1 Dec.); 'Puritan and Anglican' (15 Dec.); 'William Morris and his School' (22 Dec.); 'The Christmas Story' (29 Dec.).

[69] 'A Speech Reported' (29 Sept.) (verse attacking J. Chamberlain); 'An Election Echo' (a bitter verse on the Conservative and Liberal imperialist victory in the khaki election held between 25 Sept. and 24 Oct.) (20 Oct.).

promising beginning; but by no means yet enough to justify Cecil Chesterton's claim that '[i]n the spring of 1900 every one was asking every one
else, 'Who is "G.K.C."?' but that '[b]efore the year was over his name and
writings were better known than those of men who had made reputations
while he was still an infant.'[70] The books had had mixed reviews; and
journalistic commissions were, as yet, by no means frequent enough to
justify even the conclusion that he had established a viable journalistic
career, let alone Cecil's assertion that he was better known than such writers
as George Bernard Shaw, or even, say, Max Beerbohm. By the end of the
following year, however, Cecil's claim was on its way to fulfilment; and by
the end of 1902 we can say that Chesterton was a well-known and established writer, though not yet one of the first rank. That came with *Robert
Browning* (1903); before we are able to consider that extraordinary work,
however, we need to ask a question. How was it that John Morley, the
eminent general editor of the English Men of Letters series, came to assign
the volume on Robert Browning to such an unknown quantity as this
young journalist, who, though talented and stylish enough, had done little
except produce verses of mixed quality and an irregular stream of articles on
various topics? It was a question asked at the time: 'the world', admitted
Chesterton's friend Masterman three months before the book's appearance,
'was astonished to learn that Mr John Morley had entrusted to this unknown poet the biography of Robert Browning in that series which is
compiled by men of three-score years, knighted and with unchallenged
literary supremacy.'[71]

One part of the answer has to be that in the journalism of his earliest years
Chesterton had quickly established himself as a very considerable critic.
When he began writing for *The Daily News* (his first signed piece appeared
on 31 May 1901), he wrote invariably for the books page, and though (after
his first two signed pieces) his writings were presented as articles rather than
reviews, they were nearly all occasioned by a reference to some recently
published book, the title of which was given at the end of the article. They
were, furthermore, of some length (at least one full broadsheet column) and
except for his first two identifiable reviews (the first signed with his initials,
the second with his name, at the end),[72] they appeared with the full by-line

---

[70] Cecil, 30.
[71] C. G. Masterman, 'G. K. Chesterton: An Appreciation', *The Bookman* (Feb. 1903). Conlon, 57.
[72] 'Three Books of Verse', *The Daily News* (31 May 1901).

of G. K. Chesterton at the top of the article;[73] this was in clear distinction
from nearly all other book reviewers for *The Daily News*, whose articles
were not only short but unsigned; Chesterton was one of only three star
reviewers who were regularly given such prominence, and of these, the
only one who appeared more frequently was Arthur Quiller Couch, already
an eminent man of letters (he had produced the first *Oxford Book of English
Verse* in 1900).

Chesterton was undoubtedly accorded this prominence on the *Daily
News* books page from the beginning on the strength of the reviews he
had previously written for *The Speaker*. Though the pieces chosen from his
first year's writing to appear in book form under the title *The Defendant*
(1901) were general articles rather than book reviews, such pieces account
for considerably less than half of Chesterton's output in *The Speaker* up to
the point at which he began to write for *The Daily News* in May 1901; we
can also say that the intellectual weight of his book reviewing was substantially greater than that of such items as 'A Defence of Skeletons'. It was
amusing, perhaps, to read that 'man's horror of the skeleton is not horror of
death at all. It is man's eccentric glory that he has not, generally speaking,
any objection to being dead, but has a very serious objection to being
undignified.'[74] But such men as the editor of *The Daily News*, A. G.
Gardiner, let alone heavyweight intellectuals like John Morley, would
have been more impressed by such essays in criticism as Chesterton's review
of Edward Dowden's *Puritan and Anglican* (1900), a book which gave him
the opportunity to display his grasp of the literary, religious, and historical
issues involved. There were very few other book reviewers of any degree of
experience, let alone beginners in their first year of freelance journalism,
who could take on the legendary author of *Shakespeare, his Mind and Art*
(1875) and other weighty titles (many translated into the main European
languages), Professor of English Literature at Trinity College, Dublin, since
1874, first Taylorian lecturer at Oxford, and much else besides, with quite
such confidence as this:

While Professor Dowden fully realises the broad and noble ideals of the school
who may be called the Cavalier mystics, such as Vaughan and Sir Thomas
Browne, he does full justice to the Puritans. We hardly think, however, that

---

[73] According to John L Sullivan, Chesterton 'contributed a weekly article and occasional
reviews, many of the early ones unsigned, from Jan. 6, 1901 to Feb 1, 1913' (John L. Sullivan,
G. K. Chesterton: A Bibliography (London, 1958), 125). His weekly column did not in fact begin
until 1904, and his first identifiable *Daily News* review appeared on 14 March.

[74] 'A Defence of Skeletons', *The Speaker* (20 Apr. 1900).

he quite realises one great point of difference between the Cavalier religious movement and the Puritan religious movement. They were not only different movements, they were movements in two different senses of the word. It is highly probable that the religious ideals of Oliver Cromwell were infinitely inferior to those of Sir Thomas Browne. But the point of Puritanism was this: that however Cromwell might stand alone in genius or policy, his religious ideals practically united him with the meanest drummer in his army. On the other hand, we should laugh at the mere idea of Browne's archaeological emotions and mystical charity being shared by his butler or keeping his gardener awake at night.... The Puritan movement, if it be judged side by side with the best types of Cavalier ethics, can only appear clumsy, bitter, and offensive. If justice is to be done to it, we must remember that it was a movement in the sense that we speak of the movement that produced the Reform Bill; while the movement of Cavalier idealism was merely a movement in the sense that we speak of the movement that produced *The Yellow Book....* Of the various movements whereby new masses of men have been brought on to the stage of serious action Puritanism was one of the most remarkable. It had the unique value of theology, that it brought a philosophical problem of some sort to knock at every man's door. On the other hand, it had all the disadvantages of a revolution. Cavalier idealism had all the advantages of a fad.

Chesterton was no less confident in matters of literary judgement. Of Dowden's 'attempt to prove the spirit and theories of *Paradise Lost* to be mainly Hebraic and Scriptural' he commented that '[t]o our mind, Lecky's *European morals* and Dante's *Divine comedy* are vastly more similar than the beauty of the Old Testament and the beauty of *Paradise Lost....* The conception that gives a grand artistic unity to the Hebrew books, the conception of a great and mysterious protagonist toiling amid cloud and darkness towards an end of which only fragments are revealed to his agents, has no counterpart in Milton. The "With whom hath he taken counsel?" of the prophet is not there; the God of the Old Testament never explains himself intellectually; the God of Milton never does anything but.'[75]

'The Pessimists who ruled the culture of the age'

Chesterton's literary articles for *The Daily News* cover a wide range of topics, and they were as much about his own opinions as about the books he was reviewing—indeed, it is clear from the editorial presentation of these

---

[75] G. K. Chesterton, 'Puritan and Anglican', *The Speaker* (15 Dec. 1900), 301.

pieces that he was encouraged to take this approach, which he had already
established in *The Speaker*. His article on Dowden's *Puritan and Anglican*, for
instance, displays his belief in democracy and the common man, the anti-
Jacobite and anti-royalist prejudices which we can observe as far back as his
childhood and schoolboy writings, and his hatred for the decadents, all in
the same paragraph. It was opinionated (a word which has always conveyed
high praise on the lips of any print journalist); but it was also, nevertheless,
judicious and well-informed critical writing such as any literary editor hopes
to carry in his pages. We shall return to his early criticism in later chapters,
when we come to consider the development of his ideas, and particularly of
his religious ideas, in the early part of the decade. But we need at this stage
to consider two key themes in this early journalism, which he himself
singled out in the *Autobiography*. His later recollection was of a definite
determination to go into battle on certain specific issues, and on one issue in
particular. As he put it thirty-five years later, 'when I did begin to write,
I was full of a new and fiery resolution to write against the Decadents and
the Pessimists who ruled the culture of the age'. Though most of his early
journalism was not explicitly directed against the *fin de siècle* (which was,
after all, now over), this later recollection is borne out by the contemporary
evidence. His fire was directed principally against pessimism as such (rather
than as a by-product of the aesthetic or decadent movement in literature),
and his 'fiery resolution' pre-dates his entry into journalism. Chesterton
refers in the *Autobiography* specifically to the poem 'The Babe Unborn' (the
writing of which we can probably date around 1898 and possibly earlier)
'which imagined the uncreated creature crying out for existence and promising every virtue if he might only have the experience of life. Another
conceived the scoffer as begging God to give him eyes and lips and a tongue
that he might mock the giver of them; a more angry version of the same
fancy.'[76] This is a 'fancy' which appears strongly in 'The Notebook' from
1894 onwards; a *pensée* headed 'A pessimist' (already quoted) reads simply
'So you criticise the cosmos | And borrow a skull and a tongue to do it
with.'[77]

   This theme, a sometimes angry determination to preach the wonder of
creation and the privilege of being alive to a world apparently oblivious of
its own good fortune, continued to prepossess him into the new century,
and it underlies much of his early journalism even when he is writing on

---

[76] *Autobiography*, 92.   [77] BL MS Add. 73334, fo. 5.

apparently unrelated topics. When Chesterton came to collect a number of his *Speaker* pieces for *The Defendant*, he made it clear that the attack on pessimism was for him a major underlying theme of the book. In his introduction, he begins by imagining a desolate place, 'filled with loose rocks and boulders', which might be 'the scene of the stoning of some prehistoric prophet', 'buried under a wilderness of stones' for committing some terrible blasphemy. Such an event was now difficult to imagine:

> For in our time the blasphemies are threadbare. Pessimism is now patently, as it always was essentially, more commonplace than piety.... The pessimist is commonly spoken of as the man in revolt. He is not. Firstly, because it requires some cheerfulness to continue in revolt, and secondly, because pessimism appeals to the weaker side of everybody, and the pessimist, therefore, drives as roaring a trade as the publican. The person who is really in revolt is the optimist, who generally lives and dies in a desperate and suicidal effort to persuade all the other people how good they are.[78]

Chesterton's optimism was thus an attitude of conscious rebellion against what he took to be a prevailing secular piety. It was a key conviction, which was prone to rise to the surface at any opportunity whatever the subject might be; he defended penny dreadfuls on the ground that '[b]ooks recommending profligacy and pessimism, at which the high-souled errand-boy would shudder, lie upon all our drawing-room tables.... At the very instant that we curse the Penny Dreadful for.... encouraging the young to destroy life, we are placidly discussing whether life is worth preserving.'[79] In defending the 'discredited' virtue of humility, he took the opportunity 'to remark that this discredit has arisen at the same time as a great collapse of joy in current literature and philosophy. Men have revived the splendour of Greek self-assertion at the same time that they have revived the bitterness of Greek pessimism.'[80]

This determined optimism was criticised by his friend Masterman on the reasonable ground that if it became general it would lead to complacency and to a toleration of what was unacceptable in the modern world. 'Genial acquiescence in intolerable things', he wrote in *The Speaker*, 'is the great conservative force of the world. Mr Chesterton would urge us to believe that each man's life is illuminated by the same light that he himself discerns,

---

[78] G. K. Chesterton, *The Defendant* (London, 1901), 2–4.
[79] Chesterton, 'In Defence of Penny Dreadfuls', in *Defendant*, 15.
[80] Chesterton, 'In Defence of Humility', in *Defendant*, 99.

though it never was on sea and land. It is the pathetic fallacy, eternally untrue. "The same sun shines on the windows of the almshouse as on the windows of the castle." Never was there a profounder delusion.'[81] In the book's second edition, Chesterton added a 'Defence of Second Editions'; this was a pretext for a reply to Masterman's review—an indication, perhaps, that Masterman had struck close enough to the heart of Chesterton's deepest beliefs for it to be essential for his charge to be rebutted. His response was as close as he came to a simple statement of the world view which at this time animated all his writings about his own society:

At first sight it would seem that the pessimist encourages improvement. But in reality it is a singular truth that the era in which pessimism has been cried from the house-tops is also that in which almost all reform has stagnated and fallen into decay. The reason of this is not difficult to discover. . . . There must be some germ of good to be loved, some fragment of beauty to be admired. The mother washes and decks out the dirty or careless child, but no one can ask her to wash and deck out a goblin with a heart like hell. No one can kill the fatted calf for Mephistoph-eles. The cause which is blocking all progress today is the subtle scepticism which whispers in a million ears that things are not good enough to be worth improving. If the world is good we are revolutionaries, if the world is evil we must be conservatives. These essays, futile as they are considered as serious literature, are yet ethically sincere, since they seek to remind men that things must be loved first and improved afterwards.[82]

This was a primary Chestertonian belief which derived not only from his own deepest instincts and his own personal experience, but also from his immersion in contemporary literature and philosophy; when he reviewed books about well-known writers, he tended to have a good working knowledge of the book's subject, and if that subject was one on which he had strong views, his review became an occasion for him to express them. One of his first commissions for *The Daily News* was a review of *Schopenhauer*, by Thomas Bailey Saunders: it was a perfect opportunity for him to confront the teachings and influence of the great prophet of pessim-ism, whose fundamental tenet was that '[i]n a world like this, where there is no kind of stability, no possibility of anything lasting . . . it is impossible to imagine happiness' and that 'no man is happy; he strives his whole life long after imaginary happiness, which he seldom attains, and if he does, then it is only to be disillusioned'.[83] Jung, one of the creators of modernity to be

[81] C. G. F. Masterman, 'The Blasphemy of Opinion', *The Speaker* (26 Apr. 1902); Conlon, 43.

[82] G. K. Chesterton, *The Defendant* (London, 1902), 7–8.

[83] Arthur Schopenhauer, 'The Emptiness of Existence', in *Essays of Schopenhauer*, trans. S. H. Dircks (London, 1897), 56.

influenced by Schopenhauer, was to write that he was the first philosopher 'to speak of the suffering of the world, which visibly and glaringly surrounds us, and of confusion, passion, evil. . . . Here at last was a philosopher who had the courage to see that all was not for the best in the fundaments of the universe.'[84] Chesterton never began with 'the fundaments of the universe', but with the simplest material components of everyday life; be grateful for those, he believed, and the fundaments would take care of themselves. 'It seems strange', he wrote in his review of Bailey Saunders's book, 'that the average man should exhibit so profound a desire to believe that his bread and cheese is valueless and his beer an empty show.' Chesterton's response to Schopenhauer's fundamental assumption, that life is essentially pain and that it is a mistake to persevere in the will to live, is predictable enough: he confronts the philosopher not on his terms, but by pragmatically opposing his own experience of life as being essentially pleasure, not pain, and his consequent knowledge that to continue living requires no blind exercise of the will to live. Schopenhauer's philosophy, he argues, is a direct outcome not of any intellectual argument that needs to be seriously addressed, but of a simple moral failure, even of a defect in character; this is a contention Chesterton feels able to advance because Schopenhauer is a poet as much as a philosopher, and 'in the case of writers like Schopenhauer, Nietzsche or Carlyle, who write philosophy with the impulse of poetry, we gain a right to speak of them personally and morally which we should not have with mere philosophers':

In the case of Schopenhauer, tinging all the heavens with his own tremendous mood, it is inevitable that we should speak personally. And of all men whose souls have influenced the world, Schopenhauer seems to me the most contemptible.

He never seems to have realised that what he conceived to be an audacious photograph of existence was in truth a mere nightmare induced by lack of nerve. 'A thousand pleasures,' he quotes, 'are not worth a single torment.' They are not worth it to cowards; but that they are worth it and more to ordinary men, climbing, fighting, and a hundred other things demonstrate. In his most famous essay, 'The Misery of Life,' he moans that 'every satisfied wish begets a new one,' which seems to me the definition of happiness. . . . Schopenhauer positively complains of the fact that the heart is 'a bottomless abyss,' as if to find a bottom to it would not be the end of all human hope. In the same way, men speak of the awfulness of the idea of infinite space, as if the discovery of a place where space ended would not be too horrible for the brain to bear.

---

[84] C. G. Jung, *Memories, Dreams, Reflections* (New York, 1961), 69.

Chesterton's appeal, here as everywhere, is to 'plain common sense', to the normal experience of the ordinary man. 'When Schopenhauer declares that all good and happiness is an illusion', he protests, 'it is difficult to see what he can mean. Sport or wine or friendship are no more or less illusions than the toothache.' But Schopenhauer's failure is not merely in his remoteness from the way life is normally lived; more seriously, it derives from a fundamental imaginative defect. At this point, Chesterton evokes once more his key image of 'the babe unborn': Schopenhauer 'had not that highest order of imagination which can see the things which surround us on every side with purified and primitive eyes. Had he possessed this he would have felt as we all dimly feel that a child unborn, offered the chance and risk of so vivid and magical an experience as existence could no more resist taking it than a living child could resist opening a cupboard in which, he was told, were toys of which he could not even dream. He did not realise that the question of whether life contains a preponderance of joy or sorrow is entirely secondary to the fact that life is an experience of a unique and miraculous character, the idea of missing which would be intolerable if it were for one moment conceivable.'[85]

Patriotism and anti-imperialism I

If Chesterton's crusading instincts were aroused from the beginning by his existential hatred of 'pessimism', he came into journalism at a time when attitudes were being forged by a more immediately urgent topic: the outbreak of the second Boer War. It has, indeed, become assumed that, in the words of Michael Ffinch, 'Chesterton made his reputation largely through his writing about the Boer War.'[86] This is simply untrue; though he wrote for papers which were opposed to the war, and though his entrée to journalism was through the influence of friends who, like him, were not merely anti-war but pro-Boer, very little in his early journalism was actually about the war. Quite simply, The Speaker and The Daily News had plenty of journalists, well established on their editorial and news pages, to report the war and comment on it: they had no need of raw beginners like Chesterton. During his early years in journalism, he was mostly confined to the books pages, writing about whatever literary editors gave him to review; though

---

[85] G. K. Chesterton, 'The Great Pessimist', The Daily News (7 June 1901), 6.
[86] Ffinch, Chesterton, 83.

The Speaker did allow him to write a series of entertaining articles (most of which appeared in *The Defendant* the following year) on a variety of subjects, into which—as we have seen—serious ideas could be infiltrated. But his only successful attempts to get some kind of direct comment on current political events into print were in the form of political verses, in the run-up to, and then in the immediate aftermath of, the 'khaki' election of 16 October 1900. At the end of September, Chesterton sardonically versified about an election speech by one of his bugbears, the Liberal imperialist Joseph Chamberlain (who had formed an alliance with the Tory Prime Minister, the Marquess of Salisbury, and as Colonial Secretary had presided over the policies which had led to the declaration of the second Boer War the previous year). Chesterton may have despised Chamberlain; but he was popular in Birmingham:

> In Birmingham among my own
> Dear People I appear,
> For I was born at Camberwell,
> Not very far from here.
> And if you choose another man,
> My public life is closed:
> But you will find it difficult
> For I am unopposed.[87]

This was good humoured enough; but on 16 October, the Conservatives and Liberal imperialists were returned to power with a huge majority, having whipped up in defence of the war a great upsurge of popular patriotic sentiment. Chesterton immediately showed, for the first time in print, how very strong were his views on the war, in angry verses—published in *The Speaker* four days after the election—which exposed a bitterness rare in his writings; there was to be nothing like it until the Marconi scandal twelve years later:

> This is their triumph, ripe and rounded,
>   They have burnt the wheat and gathered the chaff;
> And we that have fought them, we that have watched them,
>   Have we at least not cause to laugh?
>
> Never so low at least we stumbled—
>   Dead we have been, but not so dead
> As these that live on the life they squandered,

---

[87] 'G.K.C.', 'A Speech Reported', *The Speaker* (29 Sept. 1900).

As these that drink of the blood they shed
We never boasted the thing we blundered,
    We never flaunted the thing that fails,
We never quailed from the living laughter,
    To howl to the dead who tell no tales. . . .
Five years ago and we might have feared them;
    Now when they lift the laurelled brow,
There shall naught go up from our hosts assembled
    But a laugh like thunder. We know them now.[88]

What angered Chesterton and his friends as much as anything else—apart
from the incompetence with which the war was being prosecuted—was the
assumption that imperialism was synonymous with patriotism. Many imperialists, indeed, had defended the war precisely because of their contempt for
small-scale patriotisms like that of the Boers; their opponents, like Chesterton, did not see how it could be argued that it was justifiable for an Englishman to love his country and be prepared to fight for its independence, but not
to accept that a Boer was entitled to love and fight for his. As he explained in
the *Autobiography*, '[t]o us it seemed obvious that Patriotism and Imperialism
were not only not the same thing, but very nearly opposite things'.[89]

And yet, it did not seem obvious to many, and probably to most, of his
contemporaries; and it is important to note that until quite recently, it had
not seemed obvious to him either. As Cecil Chesterton (who was himself an
imperialist during the war) commented later, '[t]he young Chesterton had
caught Imperialism as he had caught Socialism'. Under its influence, he
pointed out, his brother had written a poem, collected in *The Wild Knight*,
'which contains four lines such as even Mr. Kipling might have thought a
trifle extravagant':

That all our fruit be gathered,
And all our race take hands,
And the sea be a Saxon river
That runs through Saxon lands.[90]

Furthermore, he was by no means a pacifist: 'He was not in the least averse
either to violence or to bloodshed in themselves. He was passionately
patriotic, and detested all that modern theory which condemns flags and

[88] Gilbert Chesterton, 'An Election Echo', *The Speaker* (20 Oct. 1900).
[89] *Autobiography*, 129.
[90] Cecil, 39–40; 'An Alliance', *The Wild Knight*, 40.

frontiers as inherently immoral. Everything seemed to point to the prob-
ability that he would be found on the Imperialist side in that fierce controversy in regard to which hardly anyone found it possible to be impartial.'
How then was it, asked Cecil rhetorically, that he took the side of the
Boers? The key was his instinctive sympathy with the underdog. He had
learned from Stevenson that it was a fine thing

that the weak should take the sword and conquer the strong. But here we were the
strong, and we were endeavouring, without much success, to conquer the
weak. . . . Mr. Chesterton is . . . not always an entirely coherent thinker; but he
could think. And thinking was at a discount in the hot days of the war, when
men snatched up the first fragment of doctrine they could lay their hands on if it
seemed for the moment to tell in their favour. Thus Pro-Boers would denounce
patriotism as an obsolete superstition, and then go on to praise the Boers for
defending their country! Similarly the Imperialists would alternately acclaim and
decry national sentiment as it suited their turn. Now, Mr. Chesterton was one of
the comparatively few people who had on the subject a clear and definable
doctrine. He erected the sanctity of nationality into a religious dogma, and he
denied the right of any nation or Empire, on the pretence of being more civilized,
more progressive, more democratic, or more efficient, to take away from another
nation its birthright of independence.[91]

The month after the khaki election, Chesterton reviewed a book on the war
by Arthur Conan Doyle. Doyle was a supporter of the war; but unlike
Kipling, who had described the recent slaughter of General Cronje's forces
at Paardeburg as 'a satisfactory big killing', Doyle had praised their bravery
with a respectful epitaph: 'thus they passed out of their ten days of glorious
history.' Chesterton was more inclined, he wrote, 'to congratulate Mr Doyle
upon the honourable reverence that he again and again expresses for the
conquered than to argue with him about threadbare diplomatic points'.[92]

In May the following year, Chesterton published his first extended
explanation of his brand of anti-imperialist patriotism, in one of his series
of 'Defence' essays for *The Speaker*. Its opening paragraph contains some of
his most characteristic argumentation, and, towards the end, one of his most
frequently quoted aphorisms:

The decay of patriotism in England during the last year or two is a serious and
distressing matter. Only in consequence of such a decay could the current lust of
territory be confounded with the ancient love of country. . . . To one who loves his

---

[91] Cecil, 40–2.
[92] G.K.C.', 'Our Reasonable Imperialist', *The Speaker* (10 Nov. 1900), 139.

fatherland . . . our boasted indifference to the ethics of a national war is mere mysterious gibberism. It is like telling a man that a boy has committed murder, but that he need not mind because it is only his son. Here clearly the word 'love' is used unmeaningly. It is the essence of love to be sensitive, it is a part of its doom; and anyone who objects to the one must certainly get rid of the other. This sensitiveness, rising sometimes to an almost morbid sensitiveness, was the mark of all great lovers like Dante and all great patriots like Chatham. 'My country, right or wrong,' is a thing that no patriot would think of saying except in a desperate case. It is like saying, 'My mother, drunk or sober.' No doubt if a decent man's mother took to drink he would share her troubles to the last; but to talk as if he would be in a state of gay indifference as to whether his mother took to drink or not is certainly not the language of men who know the great mystery.

The terrible thing about the jingoism spawned by the Boer War, Chesterton argues, is that it has generated in the common man a debased patriotism built on a love not for his country's highest and most civilised values, but for things which, while possibly praiseworthy enough, have little to do with honour and virtue, have none of the marks of patriotism in its highest form: 'Why', asks Chesterton, 'has the adoration of our patriots been given wholly to qualities and circumstances good in themselves, but comparatively material and trivial:—trade, physical force, a skirmish at a remote frontier, a squabble in a remote continent?' The reason is that Englishmen are the only people in the world who are not taught in childhood their own literature and history. 'We have played a great and splendid part', Chesterton insists, 'in the history of universal thought and sentiment; we have been among the foremost in that eternal and bloodless battle in which the blows do not slay, but create.' And yet, he concludes, in a passage of truly majestic rhetorical force,

We have deliberately neglected this great heritage of high national sentiment. We have made our public schools the strongest walls against a whisper of the honour of England. And we have had our punishment in this strange and perverted fact that, while a unifying vision of patriotism can ennoble bands of brutal savages or dingy burghers, and be the best thing in their lives, we, who are—the world being judge—humane, honest, and serious individually, have a patriotism that is the worst thing in ours. What have we done, and where have we wandered, we that have produced sages who could have spoken with Socrates and poets who could walk with Dante, that we should talk as if we have never done anything more intelligent than found colonies and kick niggers? We are the children of light, and it is we that sit in darkness. If we are judged, it will not be for the merely intellectual transgression of failing to appreciate other nations, but for the supreme spiritual transgression of failing to appreciate ourselves.[93]

[93] 'A Defence of Patriotism', *The Speaker* (4 May 1901).

This is not yet, it will be noted, the argument against imperialism—and against socialism too—which Chesterton was to present as being at the heart of his defence of patriotism: that both imperialism and socialism 'believed in unification and centralisation on a large scale', and that '[n]either could have seen any meaning in my own fancy for having things on a smaller and smaller scale'.[94] This idea was to become, of course, a central component of Chesterton's mature vision of life; and we need, therefore, to note that by May 1901, when his 'defence of Patriotism' was published in *The Speaker*, it was not a line of argument that he had yet advanced: before he was in a position to do so, it was necessary for an intellectual development uncon-nected with politics to take place.

But that is to anticipate our narrative. For the newly married young writer who had only just begun writing for *The Daily News* and who was still struggling to become an established journalist (his famous weekly column on the paper's leader page was still some years in the future), such ideas had almost certainly yet to form themselves coherently in his mind. Much more immediate was the prospect opened up toward the end of the year by a letter which had just arrived from one of the great pillars of the liberal tradition, Gladstone's secretary and biographer, and an eminent man of letters in his own right, John Morley. Morley was General Editor of the prestigious English Men of Letters series, and his proposal (on which a representative of Macmillan's, the publishers, had already sounded Chesterton out) was that this young journalist, still struggling to establish himself in Fleet Street, should contribute a critical biography of one of Chesterton's heroes, the poet Robert Browning. Morley's letter was not wholly unexpected; but its arrival must have been, all the same, a sweet moment:

37, Elm Park Gardens, South Kensington S.W.
Dec, 1 1901

Dear Sir,
I am authorised to make a small literary proposal to you, as to which I think Mr. Colvin has said something. Would it suit you to call here at 1.30 on Tuesday next? If so, please drop me a card.

Yours faithfully,
John Morley[95]

---

[94] *Autobiography*, 109.   [95] BL MS Add. 73239, fo. 6.

Early married life

This earnest of future literary success must have been especially gratifying at this juncture in his life; for his marriage had, at last, taken place just five months previously, on 28 June. He had met Frances Blogg some time in 1896, and they had become engaged around eighteen months later in the summer of 1898; but what seems today the inordinate length of the engagement was due not to any hesitation on Chesterton's part (or on that of Frances) but to Chesterton's need to be in a position to support her. He had left the security of Fisher Unwin's not simply because he felt that he would be happier in Fleet Street but because (a more uncertain proposition) he believed that he would be able, practically speaking, to earn more in that most uncertain way of life, freelance journalism.

By the turn of the century, there had been no avoiding the fact that, for him, a career in publishing was turning out to be a dead end. 'I would stop with T.F.U. for £100 a year', he wrote to Frances in October 1899, '—but not for less. Which means, I think, that I shall not stop at all.'[96] The year 1900 did not, despite Cecil's later claim, see him famous; but it did see him making definite progress in his 'rise in the literary world'. He left Fisher Unwin's and plunged into journalism. He published *The Wild Knight* and *Greybeards at Play*. By March of the following year, he could write to Frances with a detailed account of what he thought were his practical prospects. It was at last entirely possible to begin making serious preparations for their long-delayed marriage:

The following . . . are grounds on which I believe everything will turn out right this year. It is arithmetic. 'The Speaker' has hitherto paid me £70 a year, that is £6 a month. It has now raised it to £10 a month, which makes £120 a year. Moreover they encourage me to write as much as I like in the paper, so that assuming that I do something extra (poem, note, leader) twice a month or every other number, which I can easily do, that brings us to nearly £150 a year. So much for 'The Speaker.' Now for the 'Daily News,' both certainties and probabilities. . . . I have just started a set of popular fighting articles on literature in the 'Daily News' called 'The Wars of Literature.' They will appear at least twice a week, often three times. For each of these I am paid about a guinea and a half. This makes about £3 a week which is £144 a year. Thus with only the present certainties of 'Speaker' and 'Daily News' we have £264 a year, or very likely (with extra 'Speaker' items) £288, close on

[96] Ward, 105.

£300. This again may be reinforced by all sorts of miscellaneous work which I shall get now my name is getting known, magazine articles, helping editors or publishers, reading Mss. and so on.[97]

Chesterton's optimism was not entirely realistic; in the end, writing for *The Daily News* replaced rather than augmenting his earnings from *The Speaker*. But his name was, undoubtedly, 'getting known'; there was no reason for any further delay to their marriage. The date was decided on; invitations were sent out; the presents began to arrive; Chesterton told Annie Firmin that he felt like the rich young man in the Gospel: 'sorrowful, because I have great possessions.'[98] The wedding took place in Kensington parish church. Gilbert arrived, almost correctly dressed, but he had forgotten to put on a tie; someone rushed off to buy one. They were married by Conrad Noel. As Gilbert knelt down, the label on the sole of one of his new shoes became visible; Annie Firmin caught the eye of his mother and they both dissolved into helpless laughter.

After the reception, at which, it was noted, the Chesterton brothers did not engage in one of their usual extended disputes, Lucian Oldershaw (Gilbert's best man) took their heavy luggage to the station, and put it on the train for Norfolk. The happy couple did not arrive; the train left; so did another; when they finally arrived, Gilbert explained that he had stopped on the way to drink a glass of milk in a particular shop in memory of the many times in his childhood when he had done so with his mother; and he had bought a revolver with cartridges, as he explained in the *Autobiography*, 'because it was the great adventure of my youth, with a general notion of protecting her from the pirates doubtless infesting the Norfolk Broads, to which we were bound'.[99] They followed the luggage by a slow train. On their arrival at the White Horse Inn in Ipswich, they found their luggage in their room. Gilbert saw that Frances was tired. He gave her a glass of wine; then suggested that she should lie down while he went for a walk. He had always been an enthusiastic walker; he soon found himself in open country; after a time he realised he was lost, and had to get directions back to the hotel.

All these delays have not failed to evoke a wearisomely predictable 'psychological' explanation: that both bride and groom were reluctant to come to the end of a day which could only end in one way, and that the glass of milk, the revolver and cartridges, the missed trains, and the long

---

[97] Ibid. 129.   [98] Ibid. 133.   [99] *Autobiography*, 33.

country walk were all subconscious devices to delay the moment of consummation they both feared; one writer even suggests that they indicate on Chesterton's part 'a longing to shrink back into childhood'.[100] Even this, however, is less tiresome than one notorious account—which for a time gained widespread credence because of its source—of what happened when the moment finally arrived. Some biographers follow it closely. This is Michael Ffinch's straight-faced account of the wedding night:

> When he returned eventually to the hotel...he found himself with Frances, 'utterly, unbelievably alone'. He was 'fathoms deep in love'. 'And then his whole world went crash. The woman he worshipped, whom earlier in the day he had vowed he would worship with his body, 'shrank from his touch and screamed when he embraced her'.

Finch presents this lurid account entirely uncritically. His clear implication is that it is reliable: at any rate, he assumes from it that 'it is fairly certain that when they returned to London on 3 July their marriage had not been consummated'. Dudley Barker quotes the same source, to justify (before dismissing it) a consideration, extended enough to warrant the description 'prurient', of an entirely more far-reaching claim: not only that Gilbert and Frances had their problems before all came right between them (an assumption a biographer might avoid discussing as being none of his business): but that their sexual relationship *never did come right*, that for the next thirty-five years theirs was a *mariage blanc*: a proposition impossible to ignore. Barker draws on the same source as Ffinch, but at much greater length. His quotation's final sentence is enough to convey its sense, that '[t]he final adjustment between them seems never to have been made, and Gilbert in a vital hour condemned to a pseudo-monastic life in which he lived with a woman but never enjoyed one'.[101]

　　Barker and Ffinch were both quoting *The Chestertons* (1941) by Ada Chesterton, Cecil Chesterton's widow. Ada claimed that Cecil had told her all this before his death in 1918 some seventeen years after it was supposed to have happened (she and Cecil had only married two years before). Aidan Mackey (who knew Ada Chesterton well) points out that as well as being a journalist, she 'also wrote sensational romantic fiction, of which', he suggests, 'this is a superb example'.[102] The fact, almost certainly, is either that she imagined it all and believed her own imaginings or that she

---

[100] Dudley Barker, *G. K. Chesterton* (London, 1973), 110.
[101] Ibid. 111–12.　　　[102] Aidan Mackey, unpublished memorandum.

simply made it up, consciously or unconsciously prompted by her detest-
ation of Frances and envy of her long and happy marriage (having lost Cecil
after only two years of her own marriage). This cannot be proved: perhaps
(much less likely) it was Cecil who imagined it or made it up. At the very
least, we can say that it is provably untrue, as Maisie Ward found herself
reluctantly constrained to demonstrate in an appendix to her biography,
which she declared herself to be 'Victorian enough heartily to dislike
writing'. She knew Cecil well, of course, and confessed that she found it
'impossible to imagine [him], like the bridesmaid on the honeymoon,
receiving and passing on such a story'.[103]

The thesis of *The Chestertons*, as Maisie Ward puts it, is that 'Gilbert was
an unhappy and frustrated man (a) because Frances shrank from consum-
mating their marriage, and (b) because she dragged him away from his
London life and friends to bury him in a middle class suburb'.[104] In fact,
Chesterton was always happy at Beaconsfield, the move to which was his
idea as much as that of Frances, as Maisie Ward shows. The *Autobiography*,
indeed, not only implies in one passage that his honeymoon had been a
happy one, but also demonstrates in the same passage that he and Frances
discovered Beaconsfield together and decided one day to live somewhere
like it. 'I remember', he recalled, 'that we strolled out one day, for a sort of
second honeymoon, and went upon a journey into the void.' After a railway
journey to Slough (a destination chosen at random), they walked until they
'arrived at an inn called The White Hart. We asked the name of the place
and were told that it was called Beaconsfield . . . and we said to each other,
"This is the sort of place where some day we will make our home".'[105]

As for the supposed non-consummation of their marriage, we have clear
medical evidence that this allegation was utterly fantastical. Both Frances
and Gilbert had always longed for children, but Frances simply did not
become pregnant. At last, they decided to ask for medical advice. The
problem was gynaecological; an operation (which was unfortunately—
even tragically—unsuccessful) was advised: clearly, no such medical intervention would have taken place without having being preceded by some
years of normal sexual relations. Her doctor recalled the case clearly some
forty years later, unsurprisingly perhaps, since, as he recalled in a letter to
Maisie Ward,

---

[103] Ward, 559–60. [104] Ibid. 559. [105] *Autobiography*, 220.

I well remember an incident which occurred during her convalescence from that operation. I received a telephone call from the matron of the Nursing Home in which Mrs. Chesterton was staying, suggesting that I should come round and remonstrate with Mr. Chesterton. On my arrival I found him sitting on the stairs, where he had been for two hours, greatly incommoding passers up and down and deaf to all requests to move on. It appeared that he had written a sonnet to his wife on her recovery from the operation and was bringing it to give her. He was not however satisfied with the last line, but was determined to perfect it before entering her room to take tea with her.[106]

The simple fact is that Chesterton was *not* an unhappy and frustrated man; as he put it in the *Autobiography*, his life had always been 'indefensibly fortunate and happy;[107] and Frances, with whom all his life he remained deeply in love, was central to that happiness. There is no evidence whatever of any sexual difficulty at any time, even on their honeymoon: there is only impertinent (and almost ludicrously insubstantial) conjecture, like that of Ffinch, who having taken Ada Chesterton's lurid account of the couple's wedding night seriously quotes a letter from Chesterton to his parents as supporting evidence: 'I have a wife, a piece of string, a pencil and a knife: what more can any man want on a honeymoon.'[108] Of this, Ffinch solemnly observes that '[p]erhaps only his mother *might* have seen in this remark that things had not gone very smoothly' (my emphasis).[109] There is in fact no substantial reason to suppose anything but that the honeymoon was as happy as Chesterton later remembered it as being.

On their return to London, they lived at first in a house in Edwardes Square, very close to Warwick Gardens, and then, after only a few months (the house had been borrowed from a friend to live in while they looked for something more permanent), in an apartment in Battersea in a great Victorian block, Overstrand Mansions, where they were to spend the rest of the decade. It was here that Maisie Ward first came to know them; she paints a fascinating picture of life across the river from the more prosperous part of London where Chesterton had grown up. Battersea Park was flanked by mansion flats, including the one where the Chestertons lived. Behind these mansions were street upon street of the tiny houses of the poor. A little further from the river was Clapham, where meat was much cheaper and where vegetables could be bought from barrows. 'A shilling in those days went as far south of the river as

---

[106] Ward, 210.   [107] *Autobiography*, 331.
[108] Ward, 134.   [109] Ffinch, *Chesterton*, 96.

half a crown to the north of it', Maisie Ward comments.[110] Most of Chesterton's neighbours in Overstrand Mansions were as impecunious as they were. A couple called Saxon Mills became close friends. 'When we were short, they used to feed us', remembered Mrs Saxon Mills years later; 'when they were short, we used to feed them'.[111] Another close friend was Rann Kennedy, who used to meet Chesterton, writing articles on his cuffs, on the stairs (Overstrand Mansions had no lift). One day, Chesterton said, 'Isn't it jolly out in the park there'; Kennedy replied, 'Yes, it is lovely, have you just been there?' The following day, when they met on the stairs, Kennedy remarked, 'did you notice when we saluted yesterday we both greeted each other in a choriambus and a hypermetric?' The two men delightedly embraced, and another friendship was sealed.[112]

Here, Frances set about developing what was to become her particular vocation in life: the channelling and practical management of Chesterton's vast but chaotic literary energies, and the invention and maintenance of his public persona. She famously dealt with his sartorial untidiness by covering it over with a great cloak and placing a wide-brimmed floppy hat over the whole phenomenon; if Gilbert could not be neat, he would be picturesque.[113] This sartorial stratagem caused some to see him as a poseur: Robert Blatchford, with whom he was to conduct a famous extended controversy in defence of the Christian religion, said that he 'always felt Chesterton was an actor. He played a part and dressed for a part.'[114] Within a few years, Cecil noted that 'he has certainly become a public personality'. He was, nevertheless, entirely unselfconscious: his general comportment simply reflected, in Cecil's words, 'that incurable romanticism which is so marked a feature of all that he has written':

The scenes which he haunts are not generally regarded as very perilous. Both Battersea and Fleet Street are, I believe, adequately policed. But Mr. Chesterton insists on traversing them armed with a sword-stick, and generally carrying a revolver in his pocket. This is not an affectation; he does not parade it to the world as a self-advertizer would. He hugs it to himself as did the lantern-bearing boys in Stevenson's delightful essay. He does it because he is really romantic, the essence of romance being a sense of the unexplored possibilities of life. I believe that in his heart of hearts G.K.C. hopes that one day some impossible thing will happen

---

[110] *Return*, 68. [111] Ibid. [112] Ibid. 68–9.
[113] Ward, 138–9. [114] *Return*, 80.

to him, and compel him to use his lethal weapons. At any rate, the sense of having them to use if he wanted to gladdens his secret heart.[115]

If one part of Frances's function was the daily assembly of this 'public personality', her most vital calling, at this period of her life, was to act as a kind of private secretary; for much of Chesterton's career the necessary correspondence with A. P. Watt, his literary agents, was to be conducted by her (at first, this relationship was managed by Mr Ed, who set it up in 1904; but from 1907, it was assumed by Frances).[116] It was only with the arrival of Dorothy Collins in 1926 that Frances's responsibility for administering his daily affairs was taken over.[117] In Battersea, it was Frances who made sure he would be in the right place at the right time: the famous and probably apocryphal story of his telegram 'Am in Market Harborough stop where should I be' conveys an important truth: for it was only Frances who could be relied on to *know* where he should be. She made most of the practical decisions in their lives (including where they would go on holiday), often without consulting him. This led to comment: some said she behaved like a 'schoolmarm' towards him; others that she suffered greatly from his impracticality and intellectual self-absorption. Maisie Ward records censorious gossip of 'Frances waiting up at night for him, tying his shoe-laces, cleaning off the food spilt on his clothes, waiting on him hand on foot with patient devotion. Of the endless hours when he sat at table talking instead of eating; of the broken engagements and the forgotten promises for which she had to supply an excuse or to apologise.' Blatchford recalled with contempt an occasion when he went out in the rain to get a cab for his wife, while Frances went out to get a cab for her husband;[118] almost certainly, he was deep in conversation and unaware even that it was raining, let alone that it was time to go anywhere.

An 'atmosphere of males and journalistic males at that', remembers Maisie Ward, 'pervaded the Battersea years'. This meant endless talk, and late nights: such, indeed, was the beginning of the Chestertons' friendship with Saxon Mills and his wife. Cecil Chesterton already knew them, and took his brother downstairs to introduce him. The inevitable argument ensued; Saxon Mills's wife went to bed. At two she woke; the argument was still going on; it continued until five. In the morning, the room was in

---

[115] Cecil, 248–9.
[116] BL MSS Add. 73200–Add. 73213 (1907–38).
[117] Ward, 459.   [118] *Return*, 80–1.

chaos, 'with cigar butts, empty glasses and siphons scattered everywhere and the smell of stale smoke hanging over it like a pall'.[119] Frances was not generally part of Chesterton's extended disputations, many of which took place in Fleet Street. But it would be wrong to assume, nevertheless, that theirs was a relationship between a genius and a dim and self-effacing woman whose role in life was simply to look after him and remain silent except when she was organising the practicalities of his life. It is clear from the letters Chesterton wrote to her during their long engagement (there is, for obvious reasons, virtually no correspondence during the marriage itself) that he respected Frances intellectually, that theirs was a relationship of the mind as much as of the heart, indeed, that mind and heart were inseparable; there is no 'dissociation of sensibility' here, these are love letters in which two intellects are clearly engaged, and two literary intellects at that. 'There is nothing in God's earth', Chesterton writes to her in July 1899, 'that really expresses the bottom of the nature of a man in love except Burns' songs. To the man not in love they must seem inexplicably simple. When he says, "My love is like the melody that's sweetly played in tune," it seems almost a crude way of referring to music. But a man in love with a woman feels a nerve move suddenly that Dante groped for and Shakespeare hardly touched. What made me think of Burns, however, was that one of his simple and sudden things, hitting the right nail so that it rings, occurs in the song of "O a' the airts the wind can blaw," where he merely says that there is nothing beautiful anywhere but it makes him think of the woman. That is not really a mere aesthetic fancy, a chain of sentimental association—it is an actual instinctive elemental movement of the mind, performed automatically and instantly.'[120]

The two write to each other constantly about books and writers. Frances decides to read Herodotus and asks if Gilbert knows a good translation. 'So glad you want to read that fascinating old liar, the Father of History', he replies:

I don't know why he was called the Father of History, except that he didn't pay much attention to it: may be said to have cut it off with a shilling.

To take a literal translation first, there is, of course the inevitable Bohn. There is a complete translation of Herodotus in Bohn's classical Library. . . . it is probably about the dullest translation you are likely to find. However, it is complete and quite accurate. I read a lot of Bohns once. And, as the prophet Ezekiel said, the

[119] Ibid. 68.   [120] Ward, 100.

Bohns were very dry. About the best book you could get I think would be
Church's 'Stories of the East from Herodotus', and 'Stories of the Persian War
from Herodotus'.... Though they only profess to be tales, they are practically
translations, but much more refreshing and literary than the above. I myself can
remember reading them with great delight.[121]

Staying near Ilkley with the Steinthals, through whom Chesterton was later
to meet Father John O'Connor, Frances writes that 'Mrs Steinthal is abusing
Omar Khayyam and says she doesn't believe you really like it . . . though you
may admire it intellectually.' Chesterton replies (an interesting response in
view of his later swingeing attack in *Heretics*):

that I hold myself absolutely free to admire Omar Khayyam intellectually and enjoy
him too, if I thought his philosophy (as it sometimes is) as hateful as the slime of
hell. It is a poor, panic-stricken virtue which fears to touch a thing even for the
good it can give, and although I certainly think the highest kind of poetry that
which is in unison with spiritual veracity, I should no more think of saying that a
man could not be a good poet because he was spiritually infamous than of saying
that he could not be a good tight-rope dancer because he was an atheist or a
habitual liar.[122]

In a long letter on the novelist George Meredith he argues that '[y]ou would
not mind through whatever psychological inferno you went, if your Virgil
and conductor were Browning or Stevenson. Have you ever read Meredith's poetry, where, as in all poetry, the man's general theory comes out?
The whole of his fiction is a study of the various sides of the requirement

> That from flesh unto spirit men grow
> Even here upon sod under sun.'[123]

Chesterton's letters to Frances could be quoted here at much greater length,
not only from Maisie Ward's two biographical volumes but also, perhaps
more illuminatingly, directly from the Chesterton papers: Ward is necessarily selective and tends to concentrate more on the lyrical and sentimental
than the intellectual aspects of this correspondence between engaged lovers.
What we need to register here, perhaps, is not only that it is clear from these
letters that this was as much a relationship of the mind as of the emotions
and the affections, but also that (both before and after their marriage)
Frances's religious influence on Chesterton is otherwise inexplicable,

---

[121] BL MS Add. 73193.   [122] Ibid.   [123] Ibid.

given the rigorously intellectual character of his religious preoccupations. Above all, perhaps, as Maisie Ward puts it, the letters reveal that during their long engagement, '[t]he two got to know each other with a close intimacy: they were comrades as well as lovers and carried both these relationships into married life'.[124]

[124] Ward, 96.

6

The Man of Letters as Defender of the Faith, 1903–4: *Robert Browning*; Blatchford I; *The Napoleon of Notting Hill*

John Morley's 'small literary proposal' that Chesterton should write a critical biography of Robert Browning marks a decisive landmark in his life. Before it arrived, he was a rising young journalist, whose prospects were entirely happily bounded by Fleet Street. After the publication of *Robert Browning* in May 1903, Chesterton was to enter, in the words of the anonymous reviewer of *Vanity Fair*, 'on a new phase of his career as a writer'; he now belonged, the reviewer pronounced, 'to the men of letters as apart from the journalists'.[1] He already had, it needs to be stressed, a growing reputation, and established writers were already seeing him as one of themselves. On the day the letter from Macmillan's confirming the proposal arrived, he was due to lunch with Max Beerbohm; on hearing the younger writer's news, Beerbohm said, 'in a pensive way: "A man ought to write on Browning while he is young."' 'I did not know what Max meant at the time,' commented Chesterton later, 'but I see now that he was right; as he generally is.' His own assessment of the book, thirty years afterwards (he had almost certainly not reread it in the interim), has probably had an undue effect on later critical assessments of it, and like most of his own self-criticisms should be treated with considerable caution:

I will not say that I wrote a book on Browning; but I wrote a book on love, liberty, poetry, my own views on God and religion (highly undeveloped), and various

---

[1] Unsigned review, 'Mr Chesterton's Browning', *Vanity Fair* (28 May 1903); Conlon, 60.

theories of my own about optimism and pessimism and the hope of the world; a book in which the name of Browning was introduced from time to time, I might almost say with considerable art, or at any rate with some decent appearance of regularity. There were very few biographical facts in the book, and those were nearly all wrong. But there is something buried somewhere in the book; though I think it is rather my boyhood than Browning's biography.[2]

This is simply not to be taken seriously: as his latest biographer, Ian Finlayson, puts it, Chesterton's book, though 'now and again' it gets 'strict biographical fact' wrong, is still valuable 'for consistently inspired and constantly inspiriting psychological judgments about the poet and his work, which he gets right'. His overall assessment is that 'Chesterton's *Robert Browning* has never been bettered.'[3] Like all Chesterton's critical works, the book had its share of misquotations (a result of his lifelong habit of quoting from memory), many of which were spotted by Macmillan's; the Irish writer Stephen Gwynn, one of those who had recommended Chesterton for the project, was sent for by the firm's senior partner, who was 'in a white fury, with Chesterton's proofs corrected in pencil; or rather not corrected; there were still thirteen errors uncorrected on one page; mostly in quotations from Browning'.[4] Gwynn wrote to Chesterton to tell him that the firm thought that the book 'was going to disgrace them'; but the critical response was overwhelmingly favourable. The *Manchester Guardian* found it 'wonderfully fresh . . . recalling in its vividness, its gaiety and assurance, its alert play of mind the exuberant youth of Browning himself. *Mutatis mutandis*, it is such a book as Browning at thirty might have written upon some *Doppelganger* in the previous century. Mr Chesterton has some undoubted affinities of temperament with his subject which carry him in some important points straight to the mark.'[5] The *Westminster Gazette* called it 'a strong, live piece of work, a study of Browning which will rank high among the many studies that have been written;[6] *The World* commended John Morley for his 'editorial courage and perspicacity' in commissioning Chesterton to write it.

The book is a lively and perceptive biography; it is also a work of popular criticism of the highest originality, one which seeks always to teach and to

---

[2] *Autobiography*, 96–7.
[3] Iain Finlayson, *Robert Browning: A Private Life* (London, 2004), 9.
[4] Ward, 145.
[5] Unsigned review, *Manchester Guardian* (12 Aug. 1903); Conlon, 77.
[6] Unsigned review, 'Browning and Mr Chesterton', *Westminster Gazette* (15 Sept. 1903); Conlon, 79.

explain rather than to dazzle. He was writing, of course, not simply as a critic, but as a practitioner (even if he was not in the same league as his subject); and he did not hesitate to resort to parody to make his point:

This, then, roughly is the main fact to remember about Browning's poetical method, or about any one's poetical method—that the question is not whether that method is the best in the world, but the question whether there are not certain things which can only be conveyed by that method. It is perfectly true, for instance, that a really lofty and lucid line of Tennyson, such as—

'Thou art the highest, and most human too'

and

'We needs must love the highest when we see it'

would really be made the worse for being translated into Browning. It would probably become

'High's human; man loves best, best visible,'

and would lose its peculiar clarity and dignity and courtly plainness. But it is quite equally true that any really characteristic fragment of Browning, if it were only the tempestuous scolding of the organist in 'Master Hugues of Saxe-Gotha'—

'Hallo, you sacristan, show us a light there!
Down it dips, gone like a rocket.
What, you want, do you, to come unawares,
Sweeping the church up for first morning-prayers,
And find a poor devil has ended his cares
At the foot of your rotten-runged rat-riddled stairs?
Do I carry the moon in my pocket?'

—it is quite equally true that this outrageous gallop of rhymes ending with a frantic astronomical image would lose in energy and spirit if it were written in a conventional and classical style.

For, though this statelier version might be excellent poetry of its kind, argues Chesterton—having produced a stanza of cod Tennyson—is it not obvious that 'it would lose all the swing, the rush, the energy of the preposterous and grotesque original'?[7]

There was, of course, more than one view of Browning's exercise of 'the preposterous and grotesque'. Chesterton's own book must have been nearing

---

[7] G. K. Chesterton, *Robert Browning* (London, 1903), 146–8.

completion when, in September 1902, he reviewed *Browning*, by his old
theological mentor, Stopford Brooke. The contrast between the two men's
attitudes to the grotesque in Browning's poetry is significant. 'Mr Stopford
Brooke tends not precisely to ignore it,' Chesterton noted in *The Daily News*,
'but to explain it away in various directions, and to break it up under various
heads. Sometimes, for instance, he appears to treat the grotesque in Browning
as a mere ebullition of humour. But the grotesque is not necessarily humorous; it may be serious, it may be tragic.... Sometimes again, Mr Stopford
Brooke sees the grotesque as a piece of powerful and necessary realism. But
the grotesque is not necessarily realistic. It seeks the fantastic as an ideal, not
merely as a phenomenon. Its heaven and its fairyland are as queer as the
biology of the earth. If the owl and the frog had not existed already, Browning would have invented them.'[8] Reviewing Chesterton's *Robert Browning*,
the poet Alfred Noyes saw both Browning's and Chesterton's affinity with
the ugly and the grotesque as issuing from a particular quality of spiritual
insight in their respective imaginations: 'it is the element of strangeness in
familiar things,' he perceptively observed, 'rather than that of beauty, that is
most potent to bring Mr. Chesterton into the heart of the world's mystery.... A star needs no apology, forgiveness or commentary. But what, in
God's name, is a toadstool? Surely it is a bountiful token of the infinite pity
and mercy of the Everlasting that there should be such miracles of material
ugliness on the earth.'[9] James Douglas, too (though in a rather different way),
saw the two men's love of the grotesque as being at the heart of a spiritual
vision common to them both, a 'perception of that grotesque element in
existence which is the true basis of optimism.... For Browning is the laureate
of cosmic incongruity, the singer of the central laughter of the central soul.
Call that laughter what you will, it is in its essence spiritual, and the absolute
antithesis of the laughter of the cynic, which indeed is not true laughter at all,
but a kind of miserable counterfeit.'

Noyes's phrase 'the element of strangeness in familiar things' indicates not
merely an important element in Chesterton's love of the grotesque, but an
animating principle of his imagination. It was a principle that was to be
increasingly central to his vision of life. According to Arthur Clayborough
in a chapter on Chesterton in his book *The Grotesque in English Literature*
(1965), '[t]he chief point of interest in Chesterton's remarks on the grotesque

[8] G. K. Chesterton, 'Mr Stopford Brooke's "Browning"', *The Daily News* (25 Sept. 1902).

[9] Alfred Noyes, 'In White Cotton Nightcap Country', *The Speaker* (13 June 1903); Conlon, 68.

is the idea that the grotesque may be employed as a means of presenting the world in a new light without falsifying it'.[10] Mark Knight rightly points to Chesterton's short story 'The Coloured Lands' as an early example of this theme;[11] and as we have already suggested—and as we shall see—it reaches its natural fulfilment in the first chapter of *Orthodoxy*. But there is no stage in Chesterton's development at which this process of imaginative rediscovery is not central.

Robert Browning was Chesterton's first real book, his first, that is, written as such (his books so far had been collections of articles or verse), and he researched it laboriously, spending much time in the majestic circular reading room of the British Museum. Around this great travail, legends arose. According to one story, finding himself hungry and penniless, he drew a pathetic figure blasted by famine, which he then showed other readers with a silent appeal for funds; when he had gathered enough he went to a nearby hostelry in search of nourishment.[12] His concentration on the book probably accounts for the fact that between 18 February and 21 July 1902, there is no article by him in *The Daily News*, even though in the weeks leading up to this prolonged silence his pieces had become increasingly frequent, appearing by mid-February as little as four days apart. Certainly, by June, he appears to have made sufficiently good progress to have arrived at an overall idea of how the book should be written, and he wrote to John Morley to report progress and to seek his approval. Morley gave him carte blanche to write the book as he saw fit:

June 10, 1902
Dear Mr Chesterton,
I incline to think it best you should follow your own suit. I don't insist, but when you have finished the book, of course I'm at your service for advice. It is good news that you have made such way.
Yours sincerely,
John Morley

The book is still worth reading for three distinct reasons. First, for its critical judgments on individual poems, as fresh today as when they were first arrived at; secondly for its biographical insights—not least because, as Finlayson puts it, 'he was closer in time and thought to the Victorian age, more attuned to the

[10] Arthur Clayborough, *The Grotesque in English Literature* (London, 1965), 60.
[11] Mark Knight, *Chesterton and Evil* (New York, 2004), 70–1.
[12] Michael Ffinch, *G. K. Chesterton: A Biography* (London, 1986), 110.

Browning period and the psychology of the protagonists than we are now, closer to the historical literary ground than we can be'.[13] The third reason the book is still of interest is for what it tell us of Chesterton's own spiritual development. This is *not* to accept his own assessment that the book is simply about 'my own views on God and religion . . . and various theories of my own about optimism and pessimism and the hope of the world'. This is, it needs to be stressed, a book whose principal focus is the life and poetry of Robert Browning, and whose principal value lies in its acute and durable judgements on the poet and his oeuvre: it is worth remembering that the year after the book's publication (and almost certainly because of it), Sir Oliver Lodge—the first Vice-Chancellor of Birmingham University—invited Chesterton to become a candidate for the University's new chair of English literature. But no work of literary criticism is written in a vacuum (I. A. Richards notwithstanding), and the book's success was due, not least, to what the *Manchester Guardian* called Chesterton's 'undoubted affinities of temperament with his subject'. 'In following Mr Chesterton's vigorous analysis of Browning's mental and spiritual composition', commented *The World*, '—his invincible optimism, his vehement energy, his overmastering passion for the grotesque—one is none the less convinced of its passionate accuracy because the analyst himself manifestly shares, and as manifestly delights in, the attributes which he discovers in his hero.'[14] As James Douglas noted in *The Bookman*, 'There have been some misfits in the new series of English Men of Letters, but Mr Chesterton's brilliant essay on Browning is not one of them. It was a delicate feat of imaginative wit on the part of Mr John Morley to choose him for this task, not only because he brings out the best in Browning but because Browning brings out the best in him.' Douglas's judgement, as we shall see, is as relevant to Chesterton's later works of criticism (notably, for our purpose, to *G. F. Watts* and *Charles Dickens*) as to *Robert Browning*:

Criticism is a revelation of the critic as well as of the creator. The better the critic the more subjective the criticism, for criticism is an art of spiritual reverberations as well as an art of spiritual judgements. Life and literature, which is life in language, are things too nervously alive to be arranged, as a numismatist arranges coins, without passion and without prejudice. The spiritual blow struck by a poet is struck afresh on the soul of every reader, and criticism is the echo of these spiritual blows. Browning strikes Mr Chesterton on that part of his soul which is most resonant, and

[13] Finlayson, *Browning*, 9.
[14] Unsigned review, *The World* (2 June 1903); Conlon, 65.

the reverberating clang is deep and full and clear. The explanation of this is an explanation of Browning, on the one hand, and of Mr Chesterton on the other.[15]

We have seen already one overmastering personal reason why Chesterton should feel such a close empathy with Browning: along with Whitman and Stevenson, he was one of that small group of writers who for him had embodied optimism and hope in the darkest days of his period of mental instability and frequent despair at the Slade School of Art. It is not insignificant that in *Robert Browning*, when he seeks for a contrast to Browning's philosophy of life, he naturally lights upon what, at the Slade, had been for him the artistic and literary embodiments of his depression:

Browning's conception of the Universe can hardly be better expressed than in the old and pregnant fable about the five blind men who went to visit an elephant. One of them seized its trunk, and asserted that an elephant was a kind of serpent; another embraced its leg, and was ready to die for the belief that an elephant was a kind of tree.... This ... is the whole theology and philosophy of Browning. But he differs from the psychological decadents and impressionists in this important point, that he thinks that although the blind men found out very little about the elephant, the elephant was an elephant, and was there all the time.... there is a vital distinction between the mystical view of Browning, that the blind men are misled because there is so much for them to learn, and the purely impressionist and agnostic view of the modern poet, that the blind men were misled because there was nothing for them to learn. To the impressionist artist of our time we are not blind men groping after an elephant and naming it a tree or a serpent. We are maniacs, isolated in separate cells, and dreaming of trees and serpents without reason and without result.[16]

This is not the only reference in *Robert Browning* to Chesterton's cultural *bêtes noires* as embodying mental dis-ease; I have already cited, in an earlier chapter, how Chesterton described the responsibility of Elizabeth Barrett's father for her ill health by declaring that 'The truth was that Edward Barrett was living emotionally and aesthetically, like some detestable decadent poet, upon his daughter's decline.'[17] Browning was the antidote, for Chesterton as for Elizabeth Barrett; he recounts in the *Autobiography* that, as he had been hanging on to religion 'with one thin thread of thanks', '[t]his way of looking at things, with a sort of mystical minimum of gratitude, was ... assisted by those few of the fashionable writers who were not pessimists; especially by Walt Whitman, by Browning and by

---

[15] James Douglas, 'Personality in Literature', *The Bookman* (July 1903); Conlon, 73.
[16] Chesterton, *Browning*, 175–6.   [17] Ibid. 60.

Stevenson'; he was thinking particularly of Browning's line (from 'Pippa Passes') 'God must be glad one loves his world so much.'[18] Browning's optimism was hardly, of course, Chesterton's discovery; it was the general consensus that, just as Carlyle personified the stoical pessimism of the Victorian age, so Browning epitomised its energy and confidence; in the words of Henry Jones, Professor of Philosophy at Glasgow University, writing in 1891, 'Carlyle's cry of despair is turned by Browning into a song of victory. . . . [Browning] has the consciousness of battling against a retreating foe; and the conviction of coming triumph gives a joyous vigour to every stroke.'[19] For Chesterton, the battle against despair had been a matter of deeply felt personal experience; and his depression had given way to the sense that there was 'radiance' in 'everything, streets, houses, lamp posts, communities, politics, lives . . . '.[20] Here is the key to the 'undoubted affinities of temperament' he had with Browning: it was his own love of the immediate human and material experiences of life that caused him to respond so personally to Browning's gratitude for the sensual accidents of human existence:

this quality of Browning's optimism, the quality of detail, is also a very typical quality. Browning's optimism is of that ultimate and unshakeable order that is founded upon the absolute sight, and sound, and smell, and handling of things. . . . if he . . . had simply answered the question 'Is life worth living?' with the real, vital answer that awaited it in his own soul, he would have said as likely as not, 'Crimson toadstools in Hampshire.' Some plain, glowing picture of this sort left on his mind would be his real verdict on what the universe had meant to him. . . . His mysticism was not of that idle and wordy type which believes that a flower is symbolical of life; it was rather of that deep and eternal type which believes that life, a mere abstraction, is symbolical of a flower. With him the great concrete experiences which God made always come first; his own deductions and speculations about them always second.[21]

This is the precise obverse of Chesterton's judgement on Schopenhauer, as he had explained it in his *Daily News* essay on the philosopher of pessimism; Schopenhauer 'had not that highest order of imagination which can see the things which surround us on every side with purified and primitive eyes'.[22] In his attitude both to Browning's optimism and to Schopenhauer's pessimism, he is appealing to a dimension of human experience—which Browning

[18] *Autobiography*, 92.

[19] Henry Jones, *Browning as a Philosophical and Religious Teacher* (London, 1891), 84.

[20] BL MS Add. 73334, fo. 40.

[21] Chesterton, *Browning*, 182.

[22] See pp. 208–10 above.

personified and from which Schopenhauer had excluded himself—which he would have described as mystical, one by which the small, common, material things of everyday life undergo an instinctive process of imaginative trans-figuration. This was all—still, nearly a decade later—part of his post-Slade rediscovery of the imaginative intensity of his childhood vision of the world, of the 'submerged sunrise of wonder' which he had suddenly realised was '[t]he object of the artistic and spiritual life'.[23] As we have seen, it was a vision in the formation of which George MacDonald's *The Princess and the Goblin* had played a central part. Shortly after he had emerged from 'the abysses', indeed, George MacDonald had almost inevitably returned to his mind: in one of the post-Slade notebooks, he had suggested the way in which his own recovered love of 'the absolute sight, and sound, and smell, and handling of things' was for him the natural antithesis of the nightmare world from which he had now emerged. As in other notebooks of the period (from 1894), the person of Christ naturally came to the forefront of his mind. 'Like his Master Jesus,' Chesterton noted, 'George MacDonald has an intense attraction for what may be called the simplicities of nature: for the grandeur of plain primal materials, he takes pleasure not, like a decadent, merely in sensuous harmonies and schemes of colour, but like a poet, in the substance corn, in the substance grass: in the substance fire, in the substance water.'[24]

Alfred Noyes, unlike most of the reviewers of *Robert Browning*, saw Chesterton's book—as indeed he saw Browning's poetry—as an essentially religious exercise. 'In some ways,' he wrote, 'the best possible criticism of Mr Chesterton's book is that wonderful poem by Robert Browning himself—*Johannes Agricola in Meditation*. Mr Chesterton's cry throughout is, "I intend to get to God" and that, in brief is what he wishes the rest of the world to do. . . . He makes it his mission to interpret to us the infinite love and mercy of that secret but very present God.'[25] Noyes saw more in the book than others saw, and almost certainly more than Chesterton intended; but he was on to something, nevertheless. Those 'undoubted affinities of temperament' perceived by the critic of the *Manchester Guardian* operated at a deeper spiritual level than he perhaps understood. There was, of course, nothing specifically Christian in this shared spirituality. Browning's religious sense corresponded to the pre-dogmatic and pre-ecclesial phase in Chesterton's own development, the phase reflected, say, in his manuscript

[23] *Autobiography*, 91–2.   [24] BL MS Add. 73333B.
[25] Noyes, 'In White Cotton Nightcap Country'; Conlon, 67.

Fragments for a Life of Christ (*c*.1895)[26] in which he had seen the love of mankind as a gateway to God:

To Browning, probably the beginning and end of all optimism was to be found in the faces in the street. To him they were all the masks of a deity, the heads of a hundred-headed Indian god of nature. Each one of them looked towards some quarter of the heavens, not looked upon by any other eyes. Each one of them wore some expression, some blend of eternal joy and eternal sorrow, not to be found in any other countenance. The sense of the absolute sanctity of human difference was the deepest of all his senses. He was hungrily interested in all human things, but it would have been quite impossible to have said of him that he loved humanity. He did not love humanity but men. . . . Browning believed that to every man that ever lived upon this earth had been given a definite and peculiar confidence of God. Each one of us was engaged on secret service; each one of us had a peculiar message; each one of us was the founder of a religion. Of that religion our thoughts, our faces, our bodies, our hats, our boots, our tastes, our virtues, and even our vices, were more or less fragmentary and inadequate expressions.[27]

The 'drift towards orthodoxy'

By 1903, however, it is clear that Chesterton's own ideas about religion had moved on, and that they had become both more corporate and more doctrinal than *Robert Browning* reflects. By the end of the year this was to become strikingly apparent in Chesterton's headlong engagement in a vigorous public controversy over the integrity of the Christian religion, an episode which had probably become an increasingly inevitable outcome of his intellectual history during the previous three years.

As we have seen, from around the middle of the year 1900 his friendship with Conrad Noel had, little by little, drawn him into 'the very heart of a clerical group of canons and curates', under whose influence he had 'shifted nearer and nearer to the orthodox side';[28] together with much else, his new acquaintances brought him to 'the serious consideration of the theory of a Church'.[29] Among other strange new ideas, it drew him into the world of Anglican 'comprehensiveness', with its implied pressures to choose between high (or 'Anglo-Catholic'), low (or 'Evangelical'), and broad (or 'liberal') 'churchmanship'. Chesterton's first instincts were always to look for the

---

[26] See pp. 145–8 above.   [27] Chesterton, *Browning*, 186–7.
[28] *Autobiography*, 172.   [29] Ibid. 166.

strengths in any particular position; it was what made him such a formidable debater when he decided against it. At first, the evidence appears to be that though he found himself more and more in Anglo-Catholic company, his primary impulse was to avoid sectarian allegiances. This seems to be reflected in a review for *The Speaker* published in December 1900, of a book entitled *The Crisis in the English Church*, in which he gives it as his 'definite and even earnest opinion'

that this discussion will never have either profit or solution until each party abandons identifying Protestantism with Mr Kensit or Catholicism with the idiots above mentioned ['who flog nuns almost to death'], and, frankly, admits the really interesting historic fact that Catholicism and Protestantism are two moral and intellectual forces standing for tendencies that are as old as life and equally worth living. Catholicism stands for the instinct for clothing the unutterable in noble systems, enduring images and worthy language, Protestantism for the recurrent necessity of rending the loveliest veils and refreshing human nature in the terrible simplicity of monotheism.[30]

At some point—it is difficult to know exactly when—this neutrality between the Catholic and the Protestant views was abandoned, though to a general audience Chesterton always maintained an uncommitted posture whenever he could. But when he was addressing a meeting of the Anglo-Catholic Christian Social Union, or writing for the CSU's organ *The Commonwealth* (edited by the movement's founder, Henry Scott Holland), he could express himself more freely. Certainly, by the middle of 1904 (and as we shall see, probably well before) he had identified himself with the 'churchmanship' of Scott Holland, of Conrad Noel, of Percy Dearmer, and of Charles Gore (all of them by now personal friends as well as fellow contributors to *The Commonwealth*); it was also, of course, the 'churchmanship' of his wife, who became part of the same Anglo-Catholic set. At first, it may seem difficult to understand why someone of Chesterton's bohemian temperament and habits should have been attracted by the company of clergymen, and it is important to understand the exuberance, as well as the seriousness, of such circles. In March, Frances Chesterton recorded Gilbert's attendance at a CSU debate in her diary:

Gilbert was to speak on 'Education' at a CSU meeting at Sion College, but a debate on the Chinese Labour in South Africa was introduced instead and went excitingly. . . . When the meeting was over we adjourned to a tea-shop and had immense

---

[30] G.K.C., 'How the Church Stands Today', *The Speaker* (27 Oct. 1900).

fun. Gilbert, Percy Dearmer and Conrad Noel walked together down Fleet Street, and never was there a funnier sight. Gilbert's costume consisted of a frock coat, huge felt hat and walking stick brandished in the face of the passers-by, to their exceeding great danger. Conrad was dressed in an old lounge suit of sober grey with clerical hat jauntily stuck on the back of his head (which led someone to remark, 'Are you here in the capacity of a private gentleman, poor curate, or low-class actor?'). Mr Dearmer was clad in wonderful clerical garments of which he alone possesses the pattern. . . . They swaggered down the road, talking energetically. At tea we talked of many things, the future of *The Commonwealth* chiefly.[31]

It seems clear that by this time, he shared not only the frequent company of Anglo-Catholics like Dearmer and Noel, but their theological presupposi-tions too. Thus, in engaging with the intellectual legacy of 'Darwin's bulldog', Thomas Huxley (who despite his own 'agnosticism'—he coined the word—had nevertheless promoted the teaching of the Bible in schools for its literary and moral value), Chesterton now felt himself able to do so from an avowedly 'Catholic' perspective. 'What Huxley and the men of his time said to themselves', he told a meeting of the CSU in the chapter house of St Paul's in May 1904,

was really this: 'Let us make decent and reasonable provision for a dying superstition.' At the back of their minds—at the back of the minds of most men of that generation I ever knew—was the assumption that Catholic theology was doomed. Well, they were wrong. Everything that was Catholic is returning on our civilisation, the belief in unity, the belief in ritual, the feeling that tradition is living and documents dead. Even where the modern world does not abandon the rationalism of Huxley, it abandons his Protestantism.[32]

This profession of belief in a specifically 'Catholic theology' had already, as we shall see, been reflected in articles in *The Commonwealth* and *The Daily News* the previous year, and was to emerge again in *The Ball and the Cross* (the first eight chapters of which were to be serialised, significantly in *The Commonwealth*, during 1905–6). But in the very early years of the decade, he had not reached a stage of development at which anything as complex as a 'theology', thus definable, had emerged in his mind, and his writings at this time reflect a growth of belief in very much more basic Christian doctrines. The key dogma was that of the divinity of Christ, towards which, as we have seen, he had seemed briefly to be moving around 1896 in 'The

---

[31] Ward, 147.
[32] G. K. Chesterton, 'The Two Compromises', *The Commonwealth* (June 1904).

Notebook',[33] but in which there is little evidence of his convinced and consistent belief much before the turn of the century. By the end of the year 1900, however, he seems to have embraced not only the particular doctrine of Christ's divinity but also—a real sign that he had now definitively shaken off the tutelage of Stopford Brooke, for whom these were key doctrinal whipping boys—a belief in the operation of the supernatural and the miraculous in human history. Brooke had repeatedly rejected the doctrine that 'Jesus Christ is God', since it 'predicates the miraculous'. 'It is not according to reason', he argued, 'that the absolute God and a man who lived and died as we live and die, should form one person.'[34] Chesterton now made it plain that he accepted the miraculous, and that he believed in the divinity of Christ. In a review of a life of Jesus for children, he praised the author for 'avoiding dogma without the error of dogmatising against dogma' (this could itself be seen as an attack on Brooke's brand of anti-dogmatic theological liberalism), and for her equal success 'in eluding the bigotry which is in mortal fear of bigotry, the pompous orthodoxy of the agnostic. Wherever a frankly theological or supernatural story obviously assisted the portraiture of the Divine figure, she has employed it fearlessly and with incomparable common sense. The terror in which many excellent educationalists stand of the supernatural in religious narrative certainly finds no welcome in Mrs Rye *or in us*' (my italics). These same educationalists, Chesterton continued, excluded 'the imaginative and merciful wonders told in the book which has made our literature, the stories which no one can ignore who wishes to understand three sentences of our plainest prose-writers'; the author, he went on, 'has realised . . . that water being turned into wine is not, upon the whole, so incredible as a cloud being turned into water'.[35]

The Christian religion, however, is not, as such, a subject which predominates in the journalism of Chesterton's first three years in Fleet Street (1900–2). For the most part, Chesterton reviewed the books he was given by the literary editors of *The Speaker* and then, from 1901, of *The Daily News*. Some of these had a religious content; if they did, he took the opportunity to make his opinions clear, if he could, however tortuously, make a case for these opinions being relevant to his subject. Reviewing a book on Buddhism in November 1900, for instance, he took the opportunity to defend Christianity

[33] See pp. 155–6 above.
[34] Stopford A. Brooke, *Jesus and Modern Thought* (London, 1894), 1.
[35] G. K. Chesterton, 'The Christmas Story', *The Speaker* (29 Dec. 1900).

against misrepresentation by Schopenhauer, on the slightly tortuous ground that 'Christianity is as often accused of nihilism by its enemies as Buddhism is accused by its friends':

Schopenhauer, with that brilliant futility which made him so striking considered merely as a literary man, maintains that Christianity is akin to his own pessimism because it rejects the vanities of the world. The remark is a good instance of that class of ingenious observations against which we can say nothing except that they are obviously not true. Any one can see that a man floating in visions of certain felicity is not in the same state of mind as a man who believes all felicity impossible: and the two are not made essentially any more similar by the accident that they both take the same attitude toward something else.[36]

Defender of the faith I: the Blatchford controversy (1903)

After over three years during which Chesterton perceived himself more and more as being on the side of the Christian faith against the modern world, he suddenly saw his opportunity to defend it against an opponent who was worthy of his mettle and who could be relied on to answer back. Two months before the publication of *Robert Browning*, Chesterton came across an enthusiastic review in the *Clarion* newspaper, written by the paper's founder and editor, Robert Blatchford, of a recent reprint of an attack on Christianity by the well-known zoologist Ernst Haeckel (who used the theory of evolution to justify racism, aggressive nationalism, and social Darwinism and whose arguments were later used in Germany to justify National Socialism). In the course of his article, Blatchford challenged Christians to respond to his own attack; and Chesterton duly responded with an article in *The Daily News* which inaugurated a pitched battle in print which was to continue, intermittently, until the end of the following year, involving the two men in numerous good-humoured but slashing attacks on each other in *The Daily News*, *The Commonwealth*, and *The Clarion*, and which prompted—as by-products of the carnage—the publication of three books, two attacking Christianity and one defending it.

By the time the controversy had run its course, Chesterton had clearly established his role, in his own mind at least, as a committed apologist for the Christian religion. Like the publication of *Robert Browning*, which established

---

[36] G.K.C., 'Buddha versus Buddhism', *The Speaker* (17 Nov. 1900).

him as a man of letters rather than a mere journalist, the Blatchford campaign
was, as he put it in the *Autobiography*, 'naturally a landmark in my life'.[37] It was
the point at which he first, openly and with deliberation, declared himself as a
believing Christian: and his first article, entitled 'The Return of the Angels',
contained not merely the opening salvoes in what was to be a prolonged
engagement, but what amounted to a kind of personal manifesto, a public
declaration of his former loss of faith in, and his present commitment to, the
Christian religion (though Christianity is not specifically alluded to in this first
article, the context makes it clear that this is what is meant). This article,
I suggest, is one of the most important documents in his intellectual and
spiritual history. Previous writers on Chesterton have either ignored it or (in
a few cases) simply referred to it in passing. 'The Return of the Angels',
nevertheless, represents the point in Chesterton's life at which he realised
that the time had come when he had to take sides. There had grown up, he
said, a habit of avoiding the subject of religion; and he declared that '[i]t is time
that this nonsense stopped'. Blatchford, he went on, had made an effort to stop
it, and had called on Christianity to defend itself. The great silence had been
broken; and Chesterton made a clear personal commitment to picking up the
gauntlet of 'these rationalistic challenges':

For during the silence many things have happened. During the silence, at one time,
it really did happen that numberless young men passed over from religion to
irreligion. I happened to be among them, and I believe that the time has come to
talk about it. I write these remarks with one great hope, that of arousing controversy.

Chesterton explained not only his own recovery of faith, but also the
possibility of a general recovery of religious belief in a scientific age, by
appealing to current scientific methodology. The greatest of all the discoveries of modern science, he argued, was not of a fact, but of a method,
which was 'the mother of innumerable facts. That method is, of course,
what is known in scientific theory as the method of the hypothesis.' This, he
goes on, is how we believe in evolution: '[o]f the thousands of brilliant and
elegant persons like ourselves who believe roughly in the Darwinian doctrine, how many are there who know which fossil or skeleton . . . is really
believed to be the conclusive example and absolute datum of natural
selection?' 'We know', he goes on, 'hardly any of the Darwinian facts that
lead to conversion: what we know is much more important: the Darwinian

facts that come after conversion. What we know, to use a higher language, are the fruits of the spirit. We know that with this idea once inside our heads a million things become transparent as if a lamp were lit behind them.' Proof becomes irrelevant: 'if we walked up to the nearest rationalist we know and asked him to prove evolution, he would be dazed, like a man asked to defend justice.' The ground has now been laid for Chesterton's personal confession of religious faith; having established an analogy from the natural and physical world, he applies it to the supernatural and spiritual world which he and, he claims, many others have now rediscovered:

it is most emphatically by this method, this method of the successful hypothesis, of the theory that justifies itself, that so large a number of the young in this generation have returned to a certain doctrine of the spiritual. What this doctrine is it may be right to state as baldly and as briefly as possible: it is that the world, clearly examined, does point with an extreme suggestiveness, to the existence of a spiritual world, of a world of agencies, not apparently produced by matter, capable to some extent of controlling and inspiring, capable to some extent of being known. It ought, I say, to be plainly stated that numbers of us have returned to this belief: and that we have returned to it, not because of this argument or that argument, but because the theory, when it is adopted, works out everywhere.

Chesterton is emphatic on this point: rationalists imagine that 'we found such a tremendous doctrine on a few desperate quibbles'. On the contrary, says Chesterton: [if] a man believes in God because the Missing link is still missing, because flaws have been found in the Darwinian school...he is...a fool'. The return to the spiritual view of life depends on no particular argument. 'It rests, like the movement towards evolution, on the fact that the thing works out. We put on the theory, like a magic hat, and history becomes translucent like a house of glass.'[38]

There was, of course, a personal symbolism for Chesterton in taking on Robert Blatchford as the incarnation of the unbelief he was now so publicly renouncing, for Blatchford had been a personal hero, whose book *Merrie England* had converted him to socialism a decade before and about whom he had written at the time to Oldershaw with such jubilation: 'A Blatchford! A Blatchford! St Henry George for "Merrie England" and down with everything.'[39] He had, even more to the point, nailed his religious colours to the mast by publishing, in 1895, his poem 'Easter Sunday', which can be

---

[38] G. K. Chesterton, 'The Return of the Angels', *The Daily News* (14 Mar. 1903).
[39] See pp. 99–100 above.

described as being ambiguously in favour of Christ but unambiguously hostile to Christianity: this was precisely Blatchford's position, and it is by no means insignificant that it was in Blatchford's paper, *The Clarion*, that Chesterton had chosen to publish it. The poem is worth quoting in full at this point, since it dramatically exhibits the full extent of Chesterton's volte-face:

> The Christ is risen the preachers say
>   'Cry, for today is Easter Day'.
>
> Yea; if the dead might rise; then he
>   Might rise for one thing verily.
>
> He has not heard the mouths that moved
>   The faint and fallen that he loved
>
> The wheels that rack, the lips that rave
>   Stern is God's guard about the grave.
>
> Peace—for the priests in gold array—
>   Peace—for today is Easter day.
>
> The bannered pomp: the pontiffs wise
>   (Great God—methinks he might arise)
>
> Might break for once from death's eclipse
>   To smite these liars on the lips.[40]

This is more than merely anti-clerical (it is significant, perhaps, that it is not included in *The Wild Knight*), and it is interesting that neither Chesterton, nor Blatchford, who after all had published it, made any allusion to it in the controversy which now ensued; perhaps they had both simply forgotten it. Blatchford, indeed, showed little sign that he thought Chesterton was any particular threat. His own obsessive onslaughts against Christianity had been going on for some time now; they usually occupied a whole broadsheet page of his newspaper, sometimes on the front page; in them, Blatchford usually peppered a wide range of targets. His reply to Chesterton's *Daily News* piece came well down the fourth column of a five-column article, and briefly dismissed his arguments before passing on to other matters: 'His article is witty and brilliant,' he wrote, 'but it amounts to little more than a statement that Mr Chesterton believes in some form of spiritual life because nearly all men believe in something of the kind.'[41] But Chesterton was not going to be thus lightly dismissed. He let three months go by and then returned to the charge with a series of six articles in *The Commonwealth*, which were to be

---

[40] *Collected Works*, x. 35.
[41] R. Blatchford, 'Religion and Science', *The Clarion* (27 Mar. 1903).

supplemented by a barrage of articles and letters in *The Daily News* and *The Clarion* itself, which continued unabated for the next six months. Chesterton made sure in the opening paragraph of his first piece in the July issue of *The Commonwealth* that this time Blatchford was going to give him a proper fight: 'The recent attacks which Mr Blatchford has made on Christianity', he provocatively began, 'have done great good to freedom of thought, great good to Christianity, great good to everything, except perhaps Mr. Blatchford himself, whose talents are for another kind of work.' This was unlikely to be ignored. Chesterton made sure of his man by humorously discounting the great crusade of Blatchford's life, for the establishment of a socialist state, as existing only in Mr Blatchford's dreams. Christianity, where it had failed, had failed after centuries of application to concrete historical situations, because it had been repeatedly betrayed by sinful men; but socialism could not fail because it had never been tried: it did not exist in the real world. In making this argument it is worth noting that Chesterton does not—as he had done in his first *Daily News* article—defend Christianity in some unspecific way, as being simply a belief in a spiritual rather than a merely material world; he is now defending a clearly defined belief in a God who is 'the word made flesh', one who was incarnate and crucified. If socialism did ever become more than simply a world of dreams, Chesterton insisted, it too would display the folly and wickedness of men:

the Socialistic State has a grandeur far above any ... reason or potency; it has a most impregnable purity and strength. It does not exist. It dwells in those perfect and innocent meadows which are the playground of the babe unborn. It dwells in a place where there are no tangles or temptations, no mistaken orders and no unscrupulous instruments. . . . There the wicked cease from troubling and the weary are at rest. . . . It is the noble country of words: there are all the words of Mr Blatchford, with all the splendid words of Plato, the words of Sir Thomas More, the words of Godwin and of Morris. But our word was made flesh and dwelt among us. Our ideal has trusted itself to human nature and been battered and defiled; Christianity in the suffocating bewilderment of life, has been the oppressor; just as its God, in His daring and divine experiment received the insult of nakedness and the greater insult of the purple. Mr Blatchford is an experienced man and he is not likely to be under the delusion that if Socialism became a historic fact it would be free from the shame that lies heavy on all the historic systems of the earth.

'[T]hrowing the practice of Christianity in our teeth', therefore is not an argument that has any weight, Chesterton argues; 'Christianity has committed crimes so monstrous that the sun might sicken at them in heaven.... She has committed them and will commit them, just as every living mortal has committed them and will commit them.' Blatchford's secularism is merely theoretical: '[h]istoric Christianity is a positive system, which hangs together: Secularism is only a chaos of miscellaneous objections. Thomas Aquinas builds a Cathedral: Mr Blatchford merely throws a brick.'

Chesterton now moves on to the particular controversy which was to dominate much of the argument between them, that between determinism and free will; this was, for Blatchford, the heart of the matter. For him, as for Chesterton, this was a specifically theological argument: it is important to establish this, since the suggestion has been made that in choosing to fight Blatchford on this particular battlefield, Chesterton was simply engaging in a philosophical dispute rather than defending the Christian religion as such. This impression has been fostered (like many other erroneous judgements) by Chesterton's own recollections thirty years later: 'what I was defending', he wrote in the *Autobiography*, 'seemed to me a matter of ordinary human morals... It was the question of Responsibility, sometimes called the question of Free Will, which Mr Blatchford attacked.... It was not that I began by believing in supernormal things. It was that the unbelievers began by disbelieving in even normal things.' Dudley Barker accepts this uncritically, and argues that the view Chesterton was defending fell considerably short of full belief in Christianity as such. 'Blatchford, certainly,' he concedes, 'was attacking Christianity'; but, he argues, 'the view that Chesterton disputed with him was his determinism; and for this Chesterton required, as he himself showed, only a limited definition of a Christian'.[42] This is not a view which can be sustained in the face of the evidence; in particular, it ignores entirely the articles and letters Chesterton wrote between March and December 1903 and July and August 1904: as we shall see, it is impossible to understand this substantial body of writing as being anything but a full declaration of belief in 'orthodox' Christianity. On 22 July 1904, for instance, he writes of the world's discovery of 'the sane path' between Nature worship and 'the hopeless stoics' of ancient Rome: 'It was the Christian God. He made Nature but he was Man.'[43] As for Chesterton's attack on Blatchford's determinism, it has to be understood that Blatchford was arguing against free will in specifically anti-Christian terms: determinism was for him principally an argument

---

[42] Dudley Barker, *G. K. Chesterton: A Biography* (London, 1973), 168.

[43] G. K. Chesterton, 'We are All Agnostics until—', *The Clarion* (22 July 1904); *Collected Works*, i. 385.

against the idea that God created morally autonomous beings who were therefore capable of either sin or virtue: Man, argued Blatchford, cannot sin against God, since God made him as he is. As he was to put it in his famous anti-Christian polemic *God and my Neighbour* (1903), 'Man never did, and never could, sin against God. For man is what God made him; could only act as God enabled him or constructed him to act, and therefore was not responsible for his act, and could not sin against God.'[44] Ultimately, the conflict between determinism and free will was argued out by Chesterton and Blatchford as a dispute over the doctrine of original sin, that is, over the very basis of Christianity itself. The controversy was thus essentially and not peripherally a theological one.

It is very noticeable that in his first strike against Blatchford's contention that man could not sin, in the first *Commonwealth* article of this anti-Blatchford series, Chesterton did so in similar terms to those of his attack on Thomas Huxley's supposed 'Protestantism'; that is, from a self-consciously 'Catholic' perspective:

Mr Blatchford wrote on a poster four foot high the words 'Why Man Cannot Sin Against God,' and devoted an article to deriding the possibility of such a sin. I am a very vague Agnostic compared to Mr Blatchford, and cannot rise to this Papal certainty, but the one thing that struck me about his remarks was that it was quite evident that he had never heard of the Catholic doctrine of free will. He said that a man cannot sin against God because man being a creature, all his acts are merely the acts of God. I am not now discussing which is right, the free will of Catholicism or the Calvinism of Mr Blatchford; I only say that the Catholic doctrine brings the discussion a step further, and that Mr Blatchford has never thought of that step. To one like myself who is mainly engaged in turning off twopenny opinions of his own, there is a certain pleasure in spending a few moments in reciting, not for the benefit of the readers of this newspaper but solely for the benefit of Mr Blatchford, an ancient piece of thinking which may be right or wrong but which is brilliant, lucid, and noble.[45]

Blatchford's response was a typically swingeing, knockabout performance, spreading itself over four broadsheet columns, which reproduced a large part of Chesterton's article, and ended with a renewed defence of his arguments that man was incapable of sin, and that God did not intervene in human life:

---

[44] R. Blatchford, *God and my Neighbour* (London, 1904), 123–4.
[45] G. K. Chesterton, 'The Dogmas of Free Thought: I', *The Commonwealth* (July 1903).

If, as Mr Chesterton owns, God *makes* man, and gives to him 'some of his power,' then man can no more sin against God than a cannon I have made can sin against me.

God *made* the man. You admit it. God *gave* him certain powers. You admit it. Has man any power of body or of mind which he himself (man) has made? No. . . .

If God gives a man a weak will, is the man blamable? No.

Who does give men their wills? God.

Who then is responsible for those wills? God.

How, then can a man sin against God? He cannot.[46]

Blatchford's piece was published on a Friday; Chesterton replied the following day in his now fortnightly Saturday piece for *The Daily News*. Blatchford, he argued, had confused several different meanings of the word 'will'; in particular, he had confused the ordinary use of the word with the philosophical use of it. Blatchford talked about a 'weak will'. But the philosophical argument had never had anything to do with strong wills or weak wills, it had always been concerned with whether anyone had a will of any sort. Blatchford had asked whether God would be justified in asking of human wills more than they could perform. But, said Chesterton, who ever said that he had? To take a symbolic case, who ever said that Adam's temptation was beyond Adam's strength? It was a perfectly philosophical position to say that in the nature of things Adam might have had no will at all. But it was 'simply childish' to say, as Blatchford said, that he had, indeed, a will, but that it was so weak and limited that he was not responsible for his use of it. Of course he was not responsible for the will or the character of the will. But he *was* responsible for his use of it up to its own limits, or it was not a will at all. The very definition of will included a certain limited responsibility.[47]

Blatchford's response was predictable enough; he simply ignored Chesterton's definition of will as involving personal responsibility; will, he said, was 'the power to choose'; was not the power given by God? If the 'power' were to choose ill, was not the ill choice the result of the action of the 'power' God gave? Chesterton, claimed Blatchford, had evaded the real question:

Let us consider the symbolical case he chooses: the case of Adam. Adam had to choose between eating and rejecting the apple offered to him by Eve. How would his mind (his God-given mind) work? He would desire the apple. He would know that God forbade him to eat the apple. He took the apple, and he disobeyed God.

[46] R. Blatchford, 'A Wolf in Lamb's Clothing', *The Clarion* (10 July 1903).

[47] G. K. Chesterton, 'On Calling a Spade a Spade', *The Daily News* (11 July 1903).

That was because his desire for the apple overcame his reluctance to disobey God. His desire overcame his obedience.

Now, then, did God make Adam? He did. Did God make the faculties of his brain? He did. Did God make his curiosity strong and his obedience weak? He did. Then, if this man Adam was so made that his desire would overcome his obedience, was it not a foregone conclusion that he would eat that apple? It was. In that case, what becomes of the freedom of his will?

'To crystallise my arguments into a sentence,' Blatchford concluded his piece, 'I contend that: *Since God is responsible for man's existence, He is responsible for all his acts*' (original italics).[48] Chesterton, however, was not ready to accept that the argument was over. Three weeks later, *The Clarion* printed his response, in the form of a lengthy letter. In it, Chesterton replied to Blatchford's absolute assertion that nobody but God could be praised or blamed for any human act, by quoting another article by Blatchford, which had so far formed no part of the argument between them, and in which Blatchford had admitted that blame could attach to one man for his conduct to another. The passage quoted by Chesterton was from an article published on 20 March, over four months before: 'But he (man) can be unjust and cruel and base and mean towards his fellow man, and he often is. He can sin against his fellow man and he often does.' Chesterton now deployed this brief quotation against Blatchford's argument that man is incapable of sin against God:

I do not quite understand now what this passage means. Action against God, you say, cannot be called 'sin,' because man is not responsible for any of his acts. But why, then should action against man be called 'sin,' for that is one of the acts for which is he not responsible? If sin involves responsibility, why do you, on your view, apply the term to any human acts? If it does not, why do you object to apply it to Adam? The real conclusion from your last article is clear enough—that there is no such thing as human sin.

And even though Blatchford claims not to believe in sin, says Chesterton, in the conduct of his newspaper he acts as though he does: 'The Christian fantasy crops up even in the most unlikely places. Even in the *Clarion*, for instance, I have seen writers distributing a grave and tender blame to their political opponents and to those who adulterate milk and butter and rack-rent slums. But you, on your principles hold all these men guiltless. The fact is, argues Chesterton, that 'You are not now attacking Christianity at all:

---

[48] R. Blatchford, 'Wolf!! Wolf!! Wolf!!', *The Clarion* (18 July 1903).

you are attacking Civilisation. . . . What is the point of insisting that a man cannot say that Adam fell, when by the same argument a man cannot even say, "Please pass the mustard"? For "please" means "if you please," and that is free will.' There follows a passage of impassioned rhetoric, in Chesterton's most powerful and effective vein; its effectiveness comes from its combination of oratorical dash with a perfectly judged understanding of the particular weakness of his opponent, who was a campaigner for socialism greatly given to the denunciation of tyrants and oppressors:

Do you know now what I meant when I said that there had never been a civilisation founded on your principles? Can you imagine one—a civilisation in which no one could be praised or blamed? Above all, can you imagine it humane and democratic, after your own heart? Can you believe that men would be better off when they could not even denounce or disgrace an oppressor? Do you think tyrants would be more tender when their victims could not even curse them? Have you found the rulers of the earth so sweet and tactful that they can be trusted in a world without a whisper of blame? I can imagine such a world only wildly—men moving about with faces shining with a horrible innocence, and murdering men as children pick flowers.[49]

Blatchford replied the following week: characteristically, he simply repeated his argument about God being responsible for the acts of the creature he had created, and insisted (in the teeth of the published evidence to the contrary) that Chesterton 'had failed to make his objection good'. To the passage I have just quoted, he replied that 'I have heard of men "moving about with faces shining with a horrible innocence, and murdering men (and women and little babies) as children pick flowers," and these horrible men were generally religious, and did their murders to the glory of God'—a clever debating point but hardly an argument in defence of determinism. The debate had by now established the lines on which it was to be conducted: repetitive restatements of the arguments for determinism and free will, together with miscellaneous sideswipes, some pertinent, others wildly off target. Chesterton's *Commonwealth* articles for August, September, and October for the most part reported for his Anglo-Catholic readers the arguments of the dispute being conducted in the Nonconformist *Daily News* and atheist *Clarion*, but took the opportunity also to introduce other themes. In the September issue of *The Commonwealth*, Chesterton introduced the subject of the relationship of Christianity with modern science,

---

[49] G. K. Chesterton, 'Mr Blatchford and Free Will', *The Clarion* (7 Aug. 1903).

arguing as much with his own coreligionists as with Blatchford and Haeckel—'(dear old Haeckel, his name revives me)', he interjects at one point—by denying what not only Blatchford but also 'many like him, including archbishops, bishops, priests, archdeacons and deans have thought, that science and theology can be in some sort of opposition'. What Chesterton is concerned with here (a theme to which he returned several times in this phase of his argument with Blatchford) is the nature of faith itself:

As Mr Blatchford is fond of dogmas, I will lay down a dogma which seems to me self-evident, and for which I will fight when and where he pleases. The whole notion of a fight between science and theology is not merely impossible but unthinkable. No conceivable discovery could contradict any conceivable religious dogma. . . . For instance it is a religious doctrine that man is the image of God. Not only could not science dispute that man was the image of God, but it could not dispute that a giraffe was the image of God. Science cannot attack religion even when religion is wrong.[50]

In October, he returned to the same argument, this time addressing *The Commonwealth*'s audience in specifically Catholic language. Religious statements, he argued, 'cannot be tested by any material knowledge; for the simple reason that it does not make any assertions at all about any material things; and that is the nature of all religions. . . . For instance, strictly and absolutely, all that a man of science could say against Transubstantiation is that the wafer appears to be bread, and as the Catholic does not deny it for a moment, there is no possibility of the conversation going any further.'[51] The word 'Catholic' to this kind of Anglican readership, it should be noted, did not mean 'Roman Catholic'; later in the same article, Chesterton refers to Bishop Charles Gore's preaching 'a new and vigorous Catholicism': this was, we need to understand, how such men as Henry Scott Holland and Conrad Noel—and by now, we can almost certainly say Gilbert Chesterton—defined themselves: not as 'Anglo-Catholics', but as 'Catholics', *tout court*. Roman Catholic writers understandably ignorant of the internal culture of Anglicanism have often been confused by this: when Cecil, for instance, wrote in 1908 of his brother's having become 'the avowed champion of a strict Catholic orthodoxy' he is simply assumed by them to have made a mistake: 'later critics of Chesterton', writes David Dooley, 'will

[50] G. K. Chesterton, 'The Dogmas of Free Thought: III', *The Commonwealth* (Sept. 1903).
[51] G. K. Chesterton, 'The Dogmas of Free Thought: IV', *The Commonwealth* (Oct. 1903).

protest that Cecil made many mistakes in chronology and in the interpretation of his brother's intellectual and spiritual development. After all, G.K. was to become a Catholic convert only in 1922.'[52] There was no mistake.

In his November article for *The Commonwealth*, Chesterton focused on four of Blatchford's arguments, each of which he numbered and dismissed 'in about two sentences':

1. Blatchford's obsessive references to 'Christians killing and roasting heretics' are countered with the cruelties of 'the French Revolutionists, who founded democracy', and the question 'Does Mr Blatchford excuse Christianity, or does he reject democracy?'

2. Blatchford's insistence that the infinite world of solar systems revealed by science is far nobler than the limited world of Genesis is dismissed by Chesterton as 'Spiritual Imperialism; the delusion that the larger thing is the greater'.

3. Blatchford's triumphant references to 'the sins of Biblical heroes, apparently under the notion that heroes, Biblical or other, were supposed to be sinless' are dealt with by Chesterton's dismissive quip that 'It is Mr Blatchford's dogma, that God cannot do what any seamstress may do—love a man in spite of his faults.'

4. Blatchford declares that 'many modern men like himself are moral without the use of Christianity. Again, two sentences will do it. Were Blatchford and Mr John Morley brought up as members of a Christian civilisation? There are hundreds of good men brought up in the Moslem civilisation; only they massacre Armenians because that is the Moslem civilisation.'[53]

Blatchford wearily replied in *The Clarion* only to the first two of these arguments ('as I am not as smart as he is I will leave the other brace');[54] Chesterton rebutted his arguments in a letter to *The Clarion*[55] and in *The Commonwealth*—in the final article, the sixth, of his series.[56] The Punch and Judy slogging match of the previous six months was running out of energy by now, and the chief interest of what was now the end game—not of the

[52] David Dooley, foreword, *Collected Works*, i. 9.

[53] G. K. Chesterton, 'The Dogmas of Free Thought: V', *The Commonwealth* (Nov. 1903).

[54] R. Blatchford, 'Clerical Logic', *The Clarion* (13 Nov. 1903).

[55] G. K. Chesterton, letter, 'Mr Blatchford, Persecution and Other Things', *The Clarion* (20 Nov. 1903).

[56] G. K. Chesterton, 'The Dogmas of Free Thought: VI', *The Commonwealth* (Dec. 1903).

controversy between the two men, which was to resume toward the end of the following year, but of its first phase—lies in two *Daily News* pieces by Chesterton, in which he attempts to go beyond the immediate theological pugilism of his disagreement with Blatchford to more substantial reflections on the nature of faith itself. The first article was a review of Blatchford's long-expected (and in *The Clarion* much-puffed) new book *God and my Neighbour*; this naturally involved the by now familiar dog-fights over determinism and the theory of evolution. But he moves on to ask a new question. 'All this is secondary,' he says; 'What is primary? The primary thing is a thing of plain human experience. It is the thing out of which religion necessarily arose; but Mr Blatchford...cannot see the necessity. Religion arose because there are incurable contradictions, impossible paradoxes in existence itself.' Toward the end of this first piece, he develops this theme: Blatchford, he says, 'has caught no glimpse of those awful questions out of which religion rose, those terrible contradictions in mere existence.... Let him doubt more and he will believe more; for belief was always born out of doubt. Once before, the world went through an equinox of doubt, of cultured, serious, philosophical, cosmopolitan doubt; the result was Christianity.'[57]

According to Fr. Stanley Jaki, 'Chesterton meant to deal in another article with other details in Blatchford's book that cried out for a recognition of the practical paradox of the nature of faith.... That second [article] was never written';[58] in fact, it was written. Two weeks later, Chesterton returned to Blatchford's failure to perceive that 'there are vital riddles in life itself'. 'The true religion', Chesterton continued, 'is not that which has no difficulties. It is that which has difficulties where common sense has difficulties. We have to swallow mysteries with it. But we have to swallow the same mysteries without it.' Chesterton now repeated the assertion about the nature of religious belief that he had made in his first anti-Blatchford piece the previous March: that faith is a hypothesis which, once tested, can become a means of perception, making sense of what was previously obscure; in particular, it is a key to the understanding of human history— as he had put it seven months before, '[w]e put on the theory, like a magic hat, and history becomes translucent like a house of glass'.[59] As he neared the

[57] G. K. Chesterton, 'Mr Blatchford and my Neighbour', *The Daily News* (14 Nov. 1903).
[58] Stanley L Jaki, 'Chesterton's Landmark Year: The Blatchford–Chesterton Debate of 1903–4', *Chesterton Review*, 10/4 (Nov. 1984), 416.
[59] G. K. Chesterton, 'The Return of the Angels', *The Daily News* (14 Mar. 1903).

end of the controversy's first phase, in his article of 28 November, he was using the same argument to defend the whole of Christian history against Blatchford's vague and untested modern humanitarianism; and he does this by asserting that he is in a position to understand these things in a way that Blatchford—the prisoner of a rationalist civilization—cannot; since, once faith has been understood as a means of perceiving what cannot be seen without it, the controversy becomes, quite simply, an argument about what is visible between a blind man and a man who can see:

The whole matter really at issue is one that my respected opponent does not ever really succeed even in getting near. It is simply this: Are there or are there not certain powers and experiences possible to the human mind which really occur when that mind is suitably disposed, but for which that mind, in our particular civilisation, is not suitably disposed? Is the religious history of mankind a chronicle of accidental lies, delusions and coincidences? Or is it a chronicle of real things, which we happen not to be able to do, and real visions, which we happen not to be able to see? If it is the latter, the list of all its popes, councils, persecutions, martyrdoms, cathedrals, sacraments, and massacres is no longer what it is in Mr. Blatchford's eye—a rococo and rather incredible fuss about nothing. It becomes a perfectly business-like and natural record of actions, good, bad, and indifferent, taken in connection with a quite intelligible aim; it becomes a thing like Egyptian research, or the Stock exchange.

Chesterton now pursues this last apparently bizarre comparison with a striking example of what Belloc was to describe as his capacity for 'parallelism'.[60] Imagine the inhabitants of a country without commerce or paper money. 'The Stock Exchange would then appear to them not in the least as a sordid market, but as an assembly of wild saints. Their Blatchfords would point out how in the dark ages of the 19th century men speculated so much about the Unknown and the Unknowable that they actually bought and sold invisible things—things that they could not see and handle. Such was the hypnotic trance of their religion, that they seem to have believed that they had bags of gold or bales of wool in their hands, whereas to the rational eye their hands were entirely empty and stuck in their trousers' pocket.'

The question, says Chesterton, is simple to state: is there, or is there not, a 'normal human power' called the power of faith, and are there human experiences which follow this, 'experiences which range from receiving assurances to working miracles'? To say that there is no evidence for any such thing is simply futile: there is the evidence of all those who themselves

---

[60] Hilaire Belloc, *On the Place of Gilbert Chesterton in English Letters* (London, 1940), 37.

have undergone such experiences. 'What these people really mean', says Chesterton, ' . . . is this, that they themselves take the responsibility of setting aside this kind of evidence, as a judge in a court of law would set aside corrupt or drunken evidence.' And they set it aside for a reason which has every appearance of rationality: that those who have such visions or experiences are not only credulous, but boast of their credulity: 'they pride themselves on the fact that they have a preliminary and delirious certainty that they will receive what they finally receive. In short, the rationalist puts aside this world-old chorus of witness-bearing upon the not unreasonable ground that it is avowedly not impartial.' This ground, however, though apparently reasonable, is flawed. Impartiality cannot be a criterion:

If a Salvationist hears a call, if a nun has a vision . . . the rationalist school says that this is ignorant evidence. So far from being ignorant evidence, it is expert evidence. Upon the particular matter which we have to discuss, which is—do certain results follow on belief—they are specialists like Sir Robert Ball [the astronomer] and Sir Frederick Treves [the surgeon]. Only, unfortunately, they are obviously partial. This is a difficulty which of necessity besets experts. Mr Chiozza-Money [the financial statistician and fellow contributor to the *Daily News*, who was to be elected as a Liberal MP in the landslide of 1906] knows more about the fiscal problem than the Llama of Thibet. But the Llama is unquestionably more impartial. Any man you may meet in the street is more impartial; more impartial than the man who understands the subject. . . . Experts fight as theologians fight; but none of them is impartial.

Rationalists are entitled to assert, Chesterton concedes, that they will never submit their intellect as men of faith submit theirs. But by doing so, they have disqualified themselves from the argument: '[for] by refusing to experience faith they have refused to test it. They are in the position of people who have retired from a demonstration at a hospital because it was too disgusting.' Chesterton concludes this remarkable piece with the flourish of a debater who has won the argument, triumphantly taking his seat at the end of the evening: 'I respect their sentiment: but I will not accept their report.'[61]

The following week, Blatchford moved away from the argument as it had developed, and attempted, as he put it, to 'get to business' by demanding that Chesterton should 'give us plain and serious answers to the following questions:

---

[61] G. K. Chesterton, 'Faith and the Fantastic', *The Daily News* (28 Nov. 1903).

1. Are you a Christian?
2. What do you mean by the word Christianity?
3. What do you believe?
4. Why do you believe it?'[62]

Two weeks later, Chesterton gave his answer. To the first question, he replied: 'certainly'; answering the second, he defined Christianity as '[t]he belief that a certain human being whom we call Christ stood to a certain superhuman being whom we call God in a certain unique transcendental relation which we call sonship'. To the question 'what do you believe?', he replied 'a good number of things. That Mr Blatchford is an honest man, for instance, and (though less firmly), that there is a place called Japan. If he means, what do I believe in religious matters, I believe the above statement (answer no 2) and a large number of other mystical dogmas ranging from the mystical dogma that man is the image of God to the mystical dogma that all men are equal, and that babies should not be strangled.' To the final question, 'why do you believe it?', he gave an answer which was to confuse a number of commentators—including Cecil Chesterton—who have, I believe, radically misunderstood it: 'I believe it because I perceive life to be logical and workable with these beliefs, and illogical and unworkable without them.' According to Cecil, 'That defence was wholly pragmatic. He makes no adequate attempt to show that the Christian creed is an intellectually coherent and reasonable explanation of the Universe. He almost admits that it is not so. But he contends that it is a philosophy by which men can live.' Cecil shows no knowledge of anything else Chesterton had written and was to write in the course of his voluminous contribution to this controversy. Neither does Barker, who echoes and extends Cecil's judgement, and appears to be quoting from Cecil's book rather than from the article itself. 'The careful distinction', he writes, 'between "human being" and "superhuman being" in the second answer, and the pragmatism of the fourth, are clear indications of Chesterton's reservations at that time.'[63] This is, it is clear, a major misjudgement. Against his first assertion, that Chesterton is here making a 'careful distinction' between the humanity of Christ and the superhumanity of God—in other words that at this stage in his life he still believed that Jesus was not himself divine—I have already discussed evidence which tends strongly to the opposite conclusion.[64] But what Chesterton went on to write during the same month also shows clearly

---

[62] R. Blatchford, 'A Few Arrears', *The Clarion* (4 Dec. 1903).
[63] Barker, *G. K. Chesterton*, 169.   [64] See pp. 156 and 238.

that by this time Chesterton had no 'reservations' about basic Christian doctrine. This is even true of *The Daily News* article we are now considering. In it, he goes on to reject Blatchford's question and answer method of argument as being hopelessly simplistic, since '[t]he more honest a man is, the more he will feel the mystery of truth and the inadequacy of language'. He then makes it clear that, so far as he is concerned, 'Christianity is so generally and solidly true that I do not care at what end one takes hold of it or by what path one approaches it or how one turns it upside down or inside out.'[65] A month before, in a letter to *The Clarion*, he had defined a Christian as someone who 'gets it inside his head that the doctrine of the Trinity is true'.[66] Two weeks later, on Boxing Day, he related the doctrine of Christmas to the season's festivities, making quite clear his belief that what is involved in them is the celebration of a miraculous event, and also, and more importantly, of an incarnational relationship between the material and the spiritual, which has to be understood in the context of the fully elaborated basic doctrine of the Christian Church. The seriousness with which Chesterton wrote it may be indicated by the fact that in 1905 he incorporated it verbatim into the text of *Heretics*:[67]

Christmas is, as a matter of fact, the standing example of the proposition which I have been lately maintaining; I mean the proposition that without the superhuman we are not human. Rationally there appears no reason why we should not scream over lighted puddings in honour of anything, the birth of Michael Angelo or the opening of Euston Station. But, as a fact, people only become thus splendidly, thus greedily and gloriously material about something spiritualistic. It seems odd that a pudding should depend on a doctrine. It seems strange that a dogma of mystics should be the only thing which will make grown-up people play Blind Man's buff. But so it is. Take away the Nicene Creed . . . and you do some strange wrong to the sellers of sausages.[68]

As for the alleged pragmatism of Chesterton's answer to Blatchford's second question—why Chesterton believed the Christian religion—that 'I believe it because I perceive life to be logical and workable with these beliefs, and illogical and unworkable without them', it needs to be insisted that this can only be represented as a merely 'pragmatic answer' if—like Barker—we

---

[65] G. K. Chesterton, 'On Irrelevancy', *The Daily News* (19 Dec. 1903).
[66] Chesterton, 'Mr Blatchford, Persecution and Other Things'.
[67] *Collected Works*, i, p. xx.
[68] G. K. Chesterton, 'The Feast of Christmas Day', *The Daily News* (26 Dec. 1903).

ignore its context within the overall controversy (of which he appears to be entirely ignorant). As we have seen, Chesterton had begun his involvement with Blatchford by defining faith as a means of perception, metaphorically evoking the scientific notion of the hypothesis, and drawing a parallel with the theory of evolution: 'We know that with this idea once inside our heads a million things become transparent as if a lamp were lit behind them.' Numbers of young men, he asserted, had returned to belief in 'a spiritual world...capable of being known...because the theory, when it is adopted, works out everywhere'. This is precisely the same proposition as 'I believe it because I perceive life to be logical and workable with these beliefs'. By the end of the controversy, as we have seen, he was using the same argument to defend the whole of Christian history—and by implication, doctrine: he gives the examples specifically of 'the Creation or the Incarnation' as essentials.[69] Thus, by the end of 1903, far from believing in some crudely pragmatic and non-doctrinal quasi-Christianity, he had on the contrary arrived at a set of quite comprehensive beliefs about both the content and the nature of Christian faith, beliefs which were consistent with the ecclesiological and dogmatic assumptions of the clerical circles in which he was moving.

Patriotism and anti-imperialism II

The end of 1903 is thus a suitable point in his career at which to assess how far he had moved in what his brother Cecil was to describe, nearly five years later, as his 'drift to orthodoxy'. The first thing to note, perhaps, is how misleading is Cecil's word 'drift'—with its implication that his brother was unthinkingly carried along by a current of events or influences not of his own making. It is clear from Chesterton's challenges to Blatchford that he was involved in a process of defining his own position by challenging a predominant current of thought, one which Blatchford represented but did not create: there was no 'drift'; on the contrary, Chesterton was swimming vigorously against the tide. This posture of challenge was evident from the beginning; in his early reviews of books in some way touching on Christian themes, he tended to clarify his own evolving thinking by challenging those who denied some article of orthodox belief: as we have seen, for instance, by the end of the year 1900

---

[69] Chesterton, 'Faith and the Fantastic'.

he was defending the author of a children's life of Christ for defying, 'fearlessly and with incomparable commonsense', those educationalists who excluded any 'frankly theological or supernatural story'; and when he referred, in the same article, to Christ as 'the Divine figure', he was not using the phrase in any spirit of unthinking pietism, but as a clear and defiant statement of what had relatively recently become his own belief.[70] By the end of 1903, he had come to believe in a specifically Catholic 'theory of a Church' (the phrase he used in the *Autobiography* when describing the influence over him of Conrad Noel, Henry Scott Holland, and the other Anglo-Catholics among whom, from around mid-1900 on, he found himself moving), and *The Daily News* piece of 28 November 1903 makes this clear: the history of the Church, he says in it, is 'a chronicle of real things' and 'real visions'—realities from which, says Chesterton, a secularist culture has cut itself off, impotent to engage with them. To the eye of faith, 'the list of all [Christianity's] popes, councils, persecutions, martyrdoms, cathedrals, sacraments, and massacres ... becomes a perfectly business-like and natural record of actions, good, bad, and indifferent, taken in connection with a quite intelligible aim'.[71] The very fact that his onslaught against Blatchford in *The Daily News* and *The Clarion* took place in the overall setting of the six pieces he wrote, under Scott Holland's editorship, for *The Commonwealth*—a clearly partisan publication, part of whose implicit agenda was to further a particular theology within Anglicanism—itself demonstrates that though certain themes (notably the argument between determinism and the doctrine of original sin) predominate, so far as Chesterton is concerned, his defence is now being conducted within the overall context of what he more than once describes as a Catholic theology. 'Free will'—the core belief at the heart of his defence of Christianity—is described unambiguously in one of the *Commonwealth* articles as a specifically 'Catholic doctrine'; and his use of sacramental language in another *Commonwealth* article (in which he discusses Transubstantiation) confirms this overall orientation. David Dooley concludes that 'he wrote as a convinced and orthodox Christian' and that '[i]f Chesterton was not "the avowed champion of a strict Catholic orthodoxy" in 1903 and 1904 ... he was certainly an avowed champion of Christianity'.[72] I think we can probably go further than this, to say that within a particular Anglican context, Chesterton by now saw himself, though not as a defender of a 'strict' orthodoxy of any

---

[70] Chesterton, 'The Christmas Story'.   [71] Chesterton, 'Faith and the Fantastic'.
[72] Dooley, foreword, *Collected Works*, i. 20.

kind, certainly as being a writer whose views on questions of faith were formed by a theology which—to an audience of those who thought as he did—he had no hesitation in describing as 'Catholic'.

These developments in Chesterton's theological understanding can be seen to have had a clear and definable effect on other key Chestertonian ideas—ideas which he had acquired in a specifically secular context, but which now evolved further in a way which invites speculation as to the general influence of theology over his social and political ideas. One of these key ideas has to do with his feelings about patriotism, a subject to which he now returned, in a long chapter ('The Patriotic Idea') in a book entitled *England: A Nation*, published by a body called the Patriots' Club (invented by Chesterton and a group of like-minded friends for the purpose[73]) and which appeared the following year, 1904—a year which was to see also the publication of his first novel *The Napoleon of Notting Hill*, to which, as we shall see, the ideas of patriotism it develops are directly relevant.

We have already considered Chesterton's ideas about patriotism, as they were formed in order to articulate his hostility to imperialism in general and to the second Boer War in particular. His first and clearest argument was that it was incoherent for an Englishman to claim that his own patriotism was based on his love for his own country but that others—in this context, particularly, the Boers—were not entitled to an equal love of theirs, and an equal right to enjoy an independent national existence. In fact, he claimed, the imperialists tended to despise patriotism of this kind, and to define English patriotism not as a love of country, but as a right to subjugate others. For Chesterton, therefore, patriotism defined itself in the first place as anti-imperialism. As we have seen, he developed this argument passionately in a piece for *The Speaker*, reprinted the following year in *The Defendant* as 'A Defence of Patriotism', in which he describes his own idea of patriotism as being based on his country's real contributions to civilization, and his opponents' as being based on a crude and bullying coercion of other cultures.

Nowhere, yet, however, had Chesterton put the argument which he was later to present as the key to his defence of small nations and his opposition

---

[73] According to Cecil Chesterton, '[t]he Patriots' Club was Mr. Chesterton's own idea; its aim was to provide a rallying point for those who disapproved alike of the Cosmopolitan and the Imperialist ideals. It never did anything as far as I know except to produce the aforesaid volume, which contained contributions from persons as diverse and typical as Mr. Masterman, Mr. Ensor, Mr. Hugh Law, M.P., Mr. Nevinson, Mr. Hammond, Mr. Reginald Bray, and the Rev. Conrad Noel on various aspects of the Nationalist doctrine.' Cecil, 43.

to 'cosmopolitanism', and which, so far as I can discover, he first developed in his lengthy essay in *England: A Nation*, edited by Lucian Oldershaw and published some two years after the end of the war. Before examining Chesterton's chapter more closely, however, we need to return to another of his contributions to the debate on patriotism, in an article written after 'A Defence of Patriotism' but two years before *England: A Nation*. It was, perhaps significantly, written for *The Commonwealth*, and published at the beginning of 1902. It is entitled 'The Mystery of Patriotism', and we can see it as his first public exploration of the spiritual or religious dimensions of this theme. It develops an idea he had first touched on the previous year, in *The Daily News* article in which he had equated paradox, mysticism, and common sense.[74] The idea of patriotism, he argued, like all ideas that have entered into practical politics, is an essentially mystical idea:

The practical man and the mystic are much akin, because mysticism and common sense are so nearly akin as to be almost identical. Mysticism and common sense both represent those certainties which always come off worse in argument and best in life. Logic may show by some trick of words that life is evil, that death is good, that leaves are grey in spring-time, and that a donkey has five legs. But... the mystic still believes that existence is holy, and the man of common sense still believes that a donkey's legs are numerically confined to four. Patriotism is an idea of this character. It rests upon the conception that an attachment felt by the inhabitants of a certain area for that area is not a thing which it is necessary to describe as expedient or wise, or even good: it is simply a thing that will happen. The idea of nationality is like almost all the ideas that have practically affected humanity, an idea of sanctity.

Such ideas cannot always be understood, says Chesterton. We may come across an utterly repellent man in a train, '[w]e see him practically every day, and from the crown of his head to the sole of his foot, there is not one atom of evidence that the world would not go on with a slightly increased cheerfulness if we broke his head with a pickaxe'. What restrains us is 'the mystical idea, chiefly the product of Christianity, the idea of the sanctity of an individual life'. The same idea arose, Chesterton continues, with the rise of liberalism in connection with the individual life of a nation. There has, however, arisen a particular problem. 'The reverence due to the national identity of other States has been found to be inconvenient... in the struggle for existence in the modern world.' But this should not have been allowed to become an argument against it. Something worth believing in should be

[74] G. K. Chesterton, 'The Mystery of the Mystics', *The Daily News* (30 Aug. 1901).

held to, even if it leads to disaster: 'To the false patriot England will be at the best a sanity: to the true patriot, she will be a sanctity. The false patriot will boast about the constant increase of England and sing songs about the accidents of her prosperity. The true patriot will boast of her last battle and sing the song of her heroic fall.'[75]

By the time Chesterton wrote once more about patriotism, in *England: A Nation*, he had developed a public theological language whose principal outlines may be briefly described. He had written publicly in defence of the miraculous and of the 'mystical'. He held a Christian doctrine of Creation. He believed in the divinity of Christ and the doctrine of the Incarnation. He had written repeatedly about free will and the doctrine of original sin. He had a clearly Catholic doctrine of the Church; he even saw Protestantism as being in a kind of alliance with the unbelief of Huxley and Blatchford. There are hints that by now he also believed in the Catholic sacramental system, though even for the Anglo-Catholic readership of *The Commonwealth* he fought shy of diving too whole-heartedly into theological areas that might be considered by the outsider as arcane. This was, of course, a principle he adhered to throughout his life; but the existence of this principle does not, of course, mean that we can assume that the theological ideas Chesterton generally avoided discussing in his published writings had no effect on the development of ideas which *were* intended for the public forum. In particular, though he only rarely referred to Catholic sacramental theology, there is good reason to suppose that sacramental principles are implicit in his attitude to the material world, and particularly in the way he saw material realities as being the gateway to the spiritual realities he believed them to convey.

One of the most tantalising problems of studying Chesterton's intellectual development lies in the difficulty of establishing the external influences which nurtured it. It is, for instance, clear that there must have been considerable influence exercised over him by such figures as Henry Scott Holland, Charles Gore, and in the early years of the century above all, perhaps, Conrad Noel: but we can search their writings in vain for literary evidence that such and such a passage influenced Chesterton in writing this or that. Almost certainly, this influence was mostly exercised through the medium of private conversation, through probably endless discussions and arguments, often extending into the small hours of the morning. This is one of the main ways Chesterton absorbed

---

[75] G. K. Chesterton, 'The Mystery of Patriotism', *The Commonwealth* (Jan. 1902).

ideas. It is, of course, true also that he was a great reader; but personal contact, *cor ad cor*, was his lifeblood; that is why he remained obstinately a journalist, and rejected, without a second thought, the notion of becoming a Professor of English Literature. Occasionally, however, we come across a literary text which does pose questions about intellectual influence; and one of these is Conrad Noel's contribution to *England: A Nation*. For, what Noel argues is not merely a defence of patriotism which bears striking similarities with Chesterton's *as it had developed since 1902*, posing questions about Noel's part in the process of development; the point, here, is that Noel defends patriotism by relating it specifically to Catholic sacramental theology in a way which raises questions as to whether such a theological perspective should, by now, be seen as an essential defining feature in Chesterton's own intellectual and spiritual hinterland.

Reading Conrad Noel, we can imagine him, in company with Chesterton and others, or perhaps *tête-à-tête* with him; which of them, for instance, first broached with the other the subject of Tolstoy's hostility to patriotism? Both of them attack Tolstoy early in their essays; and they do so in a way which—though they both make very much the same point—suggests not so much that one of them may have read the other's essay before submitting their own to Oldershaw, but that the subject had, probably more than once, arisen in discussions in which they had both taken part. Tolstoy's interpretation of the Christian faith, argues Conrad Noel, 'Notwithstanding its evident sincerity, its systematized morality, its insistence upon a kind of universal love,'

leaves upon one's mind an ineradicable impression of inhumanity, of a system superimposed in avowed opposition to the instincts of the race—witness its warfare with sex and with nationality. . . . It is when we come to his interpretation of [the supreme law of love as the living force of life] that we begin to rub our eyes. By failing to acknowledge the development of Christian universalism from the nationalism of Israel and the naturalism of common loves and desires, his final conception of world-love is twisted into a caricature. . . . Tolstoy's Christ is Salvator Mundi. So is ours; but ours was born at Nazareth, and was, also, Saviour of Israel.[76]

'Tolstoy', says Chesterton, ' . . . has succeeded in founding a school which . . . has all the characteristics of a great religion. . . . This important and growing sect . . . directly impugn the idea of patriotism as interfering

---

[76] Conrad Noel, 'Patriotism and Christian Faith', in L. Oldershaw (ed.), *England: A Nation* (London, 1904), 237–41.

with the larger sentiment of the love of humanity. To them the particular is always the enemy of the general.'[77] The opposite, argues Chesterton, is actually the case: we can only understand the general if we begin with the particular: '[t]he truth is ... that real universality is to be reached rather by convincing ourselves that we are in the best possible relation with our immediate surroundings.... The fundamental spiritual advantage of patri- otism and such sentiments is this: that by means of it all things are loved adequately because all things are loved individually.'[78] Chesterton had not advanced this particular defence of patriotism before; and he was essentially arguing what Conrad Noel also argued. 'Countless historical instances', asserts Noel, 'might be cited in support of this pre-eminently Christian doctrine of the expansiveness of local affections, of this pre- eminently Christian method of stressing both the particular and the univer- sal, or rather, the *universal in the particular*' (original italics). Noel goes on to concentrate on one particular instance of this principle, one which is clearly so important to his own understanding of the 'universal in the particular' that his argument is worth quoting at some length, if for no other reason than that it is a powerfully argued elucidation of a way of thinking which was the common currency of the ecclesiastical circles in which Chesterton was now moving, a milieu which by his own account had had, over the previous three or four years, such an important influence over the devel- opment of his thought. The most striking witness is born to the idea of the 'universal in the particular', argues Noel,

by sacramental beliefs common to almost all Christian schools, and treated as fundamental by the Catholic world—instance the rites of Baptism, Confirmation, Orders and, above all, the Blessed Sacrament of God's Body.

How close a parallel can be traced between its history and the history of nationalism! Is it not, for instance, those very cosmopolitan sects, Tolstoyans and the like, who, shocked at the corruptions of nationalism and of the Mass, and confusing their abuses with their essential character, have rejected both, their vision of God becoming vague and blurred? And are not the corruptions of the one and of the other almost identical in nature? The Divine Presence in the Mass, adored as a Presence distinct, exclusive, cut off from and incompatible with God's universal presence in the world, becomes an insupportable heresy. So, too, with the love of country. A worship of the nation that is narrow, and excludes admiration for the traditions and heroisms of other countries, that is in effect a denial of the universal

---

[77] G. K. Chesterton, 'The Patriotic Idea', in Oldershaw (ed.), *England: A Nation*, 1–2.
[78] Ibid. 4–5.

workings of God's Spirit, is the turning of a great and legitimate sacrament into a blasphemous fable and dangerous deceit.

That God is contained within wafer or country is as necessary a proposition as it is orthodox. That He is circumscribed or limited by either the one or the other is rank heresy.... *The fact is that human nature is so constituted that it can get no real hold on the universal excepting through its particular and instinctive expressions* [my italics]. How full a recognition of this is found in the Gospel of Jesus Christ when one remembers that to the Founder of our religion the natural corollary of His words—'Woman, believe Me the hour cometh, and now is, when ye shall neither in this mountain nor yet at Jerusalem worship the Father, for God is a Spirit'—was the taking of bread, the definite and common substance of everyday life, and blessing it, and giving it to His disciples, saying, '*This is My Body.*' To those disciples and to their children's children it became clearer and clearer that in Him they had found all that was meant by the word 'God'; that He and their Father were one; that His body was the body of the universal God; and, further, that just as it was only in contact with the definite human being that they had found God, so, in future it would be only through this or that definite friendship, place, saint, shrine, sacrament that they would keep in touch with the Sacred Heart of the universe, the Soul of the souls of men.[79]

There can, I suggest, be little doubt that the sacramental underpinning of Conrad Noel's defence of patriotism has a direct relevance, not only to the development of Chesterton's own defence of patriotism, but also to his whole world view. This is not to say that we can necessarily assert that there was a direct and demonstrable influence of one mind over the other (though I would be astonished if there had not been). But that in a particular 'clerical group of canons and curates' he had discovered an intellectual atmosphere which was to him deeply congenial; that he wrote on theological questions under Scott Holland's editorship (and therefore, to some extent, under his tutelage); that other members of the same group did so too; that he appeared on the same platforms; that he regarded them as allies: all these things are not vague suggestions but clear and demonstrable facts. And his argument in defence of patriotism in *England: A Nation* is both new to him and identical with Conrad Noel's, except for the fact that he makes no specific reference to the sacramental underpinning of Noel's exposition. The fact that he does not do so, however, in no way weakens Noel's relevance to Chesterton's argument. Chesterton's argument is now that we cannot love the universal until we love the particular first; this is identical to Noel's explanation of the wider relevance of the sacramental principle: that 'human nature is so

---

[79] Noel, 'Patriotism', 249–52.

constituted that it can get no real hold on the universal excepting through its particular and instinctive expressions'. Chesterton's argument, already quoted, that 'real universality is to be reached rather by convincing ourselves that we are in the best possible relation with our immediate surroundings'[80] represents a vision which might have been described without exaggeration as 'sacramental' even without any knowledge of the eucharistic beliefs of the circle under whose influence he had, by his own account, 'shifted nearer and nearer to the orthodox side'. We have, of course, already seen many examples of this instinct to 'begin the praise of the world at the nearest thing', in his oft-repeated love for the immediate tangible expressions of material existence. Conrad Noel's essay, however, allows us a glimpse of what had by now become a significant element in the theological context by which that instinct was now informed.

His belief in patriotism, which in his *Speaker* essay 'A Defence of Patriotism' had been based on a simple love for what was best in one's own national culture, had now become a belief in the limited and knowable as having its own kind of sanctity. To some extent, as we have seen, this notion has roots in Chesterton's childhood: 'all my life', he was to write, 'I have loved frames and limits; and I will maintain that the largest wilderness looks larger seen through a window.' Interestingly, he goes on to express his belief that 'in feeling these things from the first, I was feeling the fragmentary suggestion of a philosophy I have since found to be the truth'.[81] The development of his ideas on patriotism allows us to understand, perhaps, one element in the formation of that philosophy. His belief in the special character of nations, especially small nations, was still defined by his antagonism to empires. But there is now another element, one that we have to describe as 'spiritual' or 'religious': 'it is true', he argues in 'The Patriotic Idea', that 'empire often looks strong and nationality often looks weak, but that is because the things that are eternal always look weak. That simple discovery has been the seed of all religions.'[82]

The Napoleon of Notting Hill

The context of this *aperçu* is a general attack on the absorption of small nations by large ones, a theme Chesterton was to explore in his first novel, *The Napoleon of Notting Hill*, which was published later that year.

---

[80] Chesterton, 'The Patriotic Idea', 5–6.   [81] Ibid. 21.   [82] Ibid.

Parts of 'The Patriotic Idea', indeed, read almost like a commentary on the novel:

Many good men believe that a great conglomeration of peoples, like the British Empire, may be a unification of varied merits. They believe that by it may be extracted the best from the Sepoy, the Australian, the Irishman, the Dutchman, the negro and the Cockney. All these, they say, may thus grow in one orchard, and civilization can gather the best fruit from each.

   Now, this kind of empire has many beauties; it is varied, fascinating, and instructive. But it has one defect: it does not exist. It is emphatically not true that when we conquer peoples we get the good out of them. So far from that, the reverse is rather true: that when we conquer peoples we lose them forever.[83]

This anticipates the passage in *The Napoleon of Notting Hill* in which Juan del Fuego, the ex-President of Nicaragua (whose country has been absorbed by some kind of large imperial confederation), is told by an imperialist that 'We moderns believe in a great cosmopolitan civilization, one which shall include all the talents of all the absorbed peoples'; del Fuego's answer is that

When you say you want all peoples to unite, you really mean that you want all peoples to unite to learn the tricks of your people. If the Bedouin Arab does not know how to read, some English missionary or schoolmaster must be sent to teach him to read, but no one ever says, 'This schoolmaster does not know how to ride on a camel; let us pay a Bedouin to teach him.' You say your civilization will include all talents. Will it? Do you really mean to say that at the moment when the Esquimaux has learnt to vote for a County Council, you will have learnt to spear a walrus?. . . . If you are going to include all the talents, go and do it. If not, permit me to say, what I have always said, that something went from the world when Nicaragua was civilized.[84]

This nationalist philosophy is now taken by Chesterton to a *reductio ad absurdum*. King Auberon (who has been chosen king by a system of random selection) has decided, in a spirit of satirical pseudo-medievalism, to give to the different parts of London their own independent governments. The spirit of playfulness in which he does so reminds us strongly of one side of Chesterton himself:

The King was happy all that morning with his cardboard and his paint-box. He was engaged in designing the uniforms and coats-of-arms for the various municipalities of London. . . .

---

[83] Ibid. 26–7.   [84] G. K. Chesterton, *The Napoleon of Notting Hill* (London, 2001), 21.

'I cannot think,' he said, 'why people should think the names of places in the country more poetical than those in London.

Shallow romanticists go away in trains and stop in places called Hugmy-in-the-Hole, or Bumps-on-the-Puddle. And all the time they could, if they liked, go and live at a place with the dim, divine name of St. John's Wood. I have never been to St. John's Wood. I dare not. I should be afraid of the innumerable night of fir trees.'[85]

This is a self-mocking version of Chesterton's own quite genuinely held urban romanticism; when, therefore, Auberon unintentionally convinces the serious and fanatical Adam Wayne, who has become Provost of Notting Hill by the same absurd random process as that by which he has become king, that his 'Great Proclamation of the Charter of the Free Cities' is an entirely serious document, and that he has the right to defend the independence of his 'city', if necessary to the death, Wayne can be seen to represent Chesterton no less than Auberon does. The issue which first defines Wayne's Notting Hill patriotism is a destructive road scheme, and Wayne conceives his opposition to it in chivalric terms: 'This leadership and liberty of Notting Hill is a gift from your Majesty,' he tells Auberon, 'And if it is taken from me, by God! it shall be taken in battle, and the noise of that battle shall be heard in the flats of Chelsea and in the studios of St. John's Wood.' This is the same Chesterton who could imagine some distant future enquirer asking, amid the ruins of King's Cross Station, 'what poet-race | Shot such cyclopean arches at the stars?', who could upbraid William Morris for hating modern urban life instead of perceiving its poetry, and who in his dedication of *The Napoleon of Notting Hill* to Belloc could contrast Belloc's love of the countryside with his own passionate love of London and also with his own childhood dreams:

> Far from your sunny uplands set
> I saw the dream; the streets I trod
> The lit straight streets shot out and met
> The starry streets that point to God.
> This legend of an epic hour
> A child I dreamed, and dream it still,
> Under the great grey water-tower
> That strikes the stars on Campden Hill.[86]

The mystic symbolism of the lamp-post for Chesterton has already been touched on; and we need to recall here, once more, the quasi-sacramental

[85] G. K. Chesterton, *The Napoleon of Notting Hill* (London, 2001), 47–8.   [86] Ibid., p. ii.

character of his ideology of patriotism, the particular love of country which begins 'the praise of the world at the nearest thing': in *The Napoleon of Notting Hill*, the nearest thing is the street, epitomised here by one street in particular, Pump Street, within which the essentials of the nation are contained within a row of five shops:

> They were a grocer's, a chemist's, a barber's, an old curiosity shop, and a toy-shop that sold also newspapers. . . . If Notting Hill was the heart of the universe, and Pump Street was the heart of Notting Hill, this was the heart of Pump Street. The fact that they were all small and side by side realized *that feeling for a formidable comfort and compactness which, as we have said, was the heart of his patriotism and of all patriotism.* (my italics)[87]

The battle between Notting Hill and the other municipalities takes place, with Notting Hill gaining a great victory and establishing an empire; this one ends in disaster, as Chesterton insisted all empires must, with a rebellion against Wayne's rule which leads to his bloody downfall. The novel ends with Wayne, the fanatic, telling Auberon, the satirist, that they 'are two lobes of the same brain, and that brain has been cloven in two'. Auberon demurs: 'Yet nothing can alter the antagonism . . . the fact that I laughed at these things and you adored them.' Wayne replies with an exposition of what we can now see is Chesterton's own personal philosophy of life, one in which, in an unending paradox, conviction must always be yoked with humour and humour must be always yoked with conviction, for otherwise humour becomes decadent and conviction becomes fanatical. The paradox proposed here is of an essentially Chestertonian type: that is, it is synonymous with that mystical entity, 'common-sense':

> I know of something that will alter that antagonism, something that is outside us, something that you and I have all our lives perhaps taken too little account of. The equal and eternal human being will alter that antagonism, for the human being sees no real antagonism between laughter and respect, the human being, the common man, whom mere geniuses like you and me, can only worship like a god. When dark and dreary days come, you and I are necessary, the pure fanatic, the pure satirist. We have between us remedied a great wrong. We have lifted the modern cities into that poetry which every one who knows mankind knows to be immeasurably more common than the commonplace. But in healthy people there is no war between us. We are but the two lobes of the brain of a ploughman. Laughter and love are everywhere. The cathedrals, built in the ages that loved God, are full of

---

[87] Ibid. 80.

blasphemous grotesques. The mother laughs continually at the child, the lover laughs continually at the lover, the wife at the husband, the friend at the friend.[88]

There has, in fact, already been a discussion between the two men, over the clash between their respective visions of life: Auberon asks Wayne if 'the sacred Notting Hill' is not somewhat absurd; Wayne replies that Notting Hill is 'a rise or high ground of the common earth, on which men have built houses to live, in which they are born, fall in love, pray, marry, and die. Why should I think it absurd?' The King responds vaguely that 'It is generally felt to be a little funny.' Wayne now makes a declaration which we can, I suggest, understand as representing the essentials of Chesterton's vision of life as it has developed by this stage in his religious and intellectual development, even though, it should be acknowledged in passing, there is documentary evidence that he had been working on this book for many years: according to Cecil Chesterton—who in his anonymous review cited the notebooks—parts of it go back to his schooldays;[89] the extant manuscript evidence certainly shows him working on the book between 1897 and 1902.[90] Nevertheless, not only does the final text establish Chesterton's brand of quasi-sacramental local patriotism as lying within a fundamentally Christian world view; it includes, too, a poetic reassertion of the Catholic ecclesiology he had declared the previous November in his *Daily News* article on the nature of faith. It is a passage which has been generally unremarked; but it must surely be noted, at least in passing, in any survey of the growth of Chesterton's religious ideas. Here, it is Wayne who is arguing, though with savage irony, for a humorous understanding of a subject normally approached with total solemnity:

'I suppose,' said Adam, turning on him with a fierce suddenness, 'I suppose you fancy crucifixion was a serious affair?'
'Well, I . . .' began Auberon, 'I admit I have generally thought it had its graver side.'
'Then you are wrong,' said Wayne, with incredible violence. 'Crucifixion is comic. It is exquisitely diverting. It was an absurd and obscene kind of impaling reserved for people who were made to be laughed at . . . for slaves and provincials . . . for dentists and small tradesmen, as you would say. I have seen the grotesque gallows-shape, which the little Roman gutter-boys scribbled on walls as a vulgar joke, blazing on the pinnacles of the temples of the world. And shall I turn back?'

---

[88] G. K. Chesterton, *The Napoleon of Notting Hill* (London, 2001), 182–3.
[89] Cecil Chesterton, unsigned review, *Vanity Fair* (7 Apr. 1904); Conlon, 92.
[90] BL MS Add. 73342C.

The King made no answer.

Adam went on, his voice ringing in the roof.

'This laughter with which men tyrannize is not the great power you think it. Peter was crucified, and crucified head downwards. What could be funnier than the idea of a respectable old Apostle upside down? What could be more in the style of your modern humour? But what was the good of it? Upside down or right side up, Peter was Peter to mankind. Upside down he still hangs over Europe, and millions move and breathe only in the life of his Church.'[91]

[91] *The Napoleon of Notting Hill*, 66–7.

7

The Critic as Polemicist, 1904–6: *G. F. Watts*; Blatchford II; *Heretics*; *The Ball and the Cross*; *Charles Dickens*

Chesterton's growing fame, recorded his brother Cecil, had 'carried him into new circles, and made him acquainted with men of what may roughly be called the governing class, with bishops and cabinet ministers, members of parliament, and men eminent in letters and art'.[1] This new celebrity seems to have come upon him as something of a curiosity, and not one that was always entirely agreeable. Frances began keeping a diary at the beginning of 1904; she inaugurated it with the observation that 'Gilbert and I meet all sorts of queer, well-known, attractive, unattractive people and I expect this book will be mostly about them'. Of an 'At Home' on 17 February, she wrote that 'it was rather jolly but too many clever people there to be really nice. The clever people were Mr Joseph Conrad, Mr Henry James, Mr Laurence Binyon, Mr Maurice Hewlitt, and a great many more.'[2] Other occasions were more to her taste. The Literary Fund Dinner in May was '[a]bout the greatest treat I ever had in my life'; she happily recorded that '[i]t is wonderful the way in which they all accept Gilbert, and one well-known man told me he was the biggest man present'. J. M. Barrie was 'so splendid and so complimentary'. Four days later, they went to see Max Beerbohm's caricature at the Carfax Gallery: 'G.K.C.—Humanist— Kissing the World'. In June, Frances recorded a political At Home at Mrs Sidney Webb's, where they met Winston Churchill and Lloyd George.[3]

---

[1] Cecil, 252.   [2] Ward, 147.   [3] Ibid. 148.

Entries for June and July the following year (*Heretics* appeared in June) show that Chesterton's new fame was no passing phenomenon:

June 5th. Granville Barker came to see Gilbert, touching the possibility of a play.
June 29th. A garden party at the Bishop's House, Kennington. The Bishop told me that A. J. Balfour was very impressed with *Heretics*. Guild of St. Matthew Service and rowdy supper. Gilbert made an excellent speech.
July 5th. Gilbert dined at the Asquiths; met Rosebery. I think he hated it.
July 16th. Gilbert went to see Mrs. Grenfell at Taplow. He met Balfour, Austen Chamberlain and George Wyndham. Had an amusing time, no doubt. Says Balfour is most interesting to talk to but appears bored. George Wyndham is delightful.

In such circles, wrote Cecil in 1908, 'he has, I always fancy, something of the air of a man who has strayed into an environment interesting and even congenial, but at bottom alien to him', for, '[h]is type of life is still the journalistic type. The atmosphere really native to him is still the atmosphere of Fleet Street. And he is never more at his ease, never more amusing, never more wholly himself, than when he is talking to his old brothers of the craft.'[4]

Congenial to him or not, the beginnings of Chesterton's real fame as a writer of the first rank coincided with a period of extraordinary creativity. Between May 1903 and August 1906 he published three major works of criticism, a collection of short stories, a novel, and a polemical tour de force: *Robert Browning* (1903), *The Napoleon of Notting Hill* (1904), *G. F. Watts* (1904), *The Club of Queer Trades* (1905), *Heretics* (1905), and *Charles Dickens* (1906). During the same period, his journalistic output (which, of course, included his voluminous contributions to the Blatchford controversy) grew exponentially; at the beginning of it, his *Daily News* articles were frequent enough but irregular, and mostly confined to the books page; in 1903 he began a regular column, every other Saturday, on the leader page. The following year, this became his famous weekly column; it was soon realised that on the day it appeared, there was a detectable rise in circulation. In October 1905, in addition to his *Daily News* column, he began a weekly column in the *London Illustrated News*. His productivity, by now, was unremitting and apparently effortless. Writing books and journalism at the same time is a feat not many can carry off; as we have seen, Chesterton himself gave up writing for *The Daily News* for several months during the writing of *Robert Browning*. For the most part, however, he seems to have

[4] Cecil, 252–3.

experienced little difficulty in engaging in the two different kinds of writing concurrently.

Shortly after *The Napoleon of Notting Hill*, which appeared in March 1904, Chesterton produced what, though it is one of his least appreciated books, is in many ways one of his most characteristic: *G. F. Watts*, which appeared in the autumn. The book functions on two almost (but not quite) distinct levels. There is the level of pure art criticism, which reveals, as we might expect, a considerable knowledge of other Victorian painters—Burne-Jones, Millais, Rossetti, and (rather different) Whistler—and an ability to make the appropriate comparisons and contrasts between them. There is also the level on which a book about Watts, in Chesterton's hands, was bound to become an appropriate occasion for wider reflections on the culture wars of the Victorian age and of the post-Victorian world to which the book is directly addressed. Watts was the almost perfect subject for an Edwardian anti-modernist whose disaffection from his own age was increasingly strongly based on that age's withdrawal from its own religious and philosophical roots: 'I make no apology', he begins the book's final paragraph, 'if I have asked the reader, in the course of these remarks, to think about things in general. It is not I, but George Frederick Watts, who asks the reader to think about things in general.'[5] He had prefaced this with a remarkable statement of what by now had become his own personal vision of the world. He began it by talking of Watts's own expansiveness of vision, as part of an explanation for his own apparent 'straying from the subject' during the course of the book: Watts, he says, has attempted, 'whether he has succeeded or no, to paint such pictures of such things that no one shall be able to get outside them; that everyone should be lost in them for ever, like wanderers in a mighty park'. Without any intervening modulation, Chesterton now suddenly changes key:

Whether we hide in a monastery or thunder on a platform, we are still standing in the Court of Death. . . . This is the great pathos and the great dignity of philosophy and theology. Men talk of philosophy and theology as if they were something specialistic and arid and academic. But philosophy and theology are not only the only democratic things, they are democratic to the point of being vulgar, to the point, I was going to say of being rowdy. They alone admit all matters; they alone lie open to all attacks. . . . There is no detail, from buttons to kangaroos, that does not enter into the gay confusion of philosophy. There is no fact of life, from the

⁵ G. K. Chesterton, *G. F. Watts* (London, 1904), 168.

death of a donkey to the General Post Office, which has not its place to dance and sing in the glorious Carnival of theology.[6]

Behind this broad assertion, there is a very specifically Christian subtext, which Chesterton had spelled out in the immediate aftermath of the first phase of the Blatchford controversy, in December 1903. At a time when he must have been either contemplating *G. F. Watts* or actually writing it, he wrote this in *The Daily News*:

You cannot evade the issue of God; whether you talk about pigs or the binomial theory, you are still talking about Him. . . . Things can be irrelevant to the proposition that Christianity is false, but nothing can be irrelevant to the proposition that Christianity is true. Zulus, gardening, butcher's shops, lunatic asylums, housemaids and the French Revolution—all these things not only may have something to do with the Christian God, but must have something to do with Him if He really lives and reigns.[7]

There is a real sense in which we can say that after this 'landmark' year of 1903, in which for the first time Chesterton publicly, persistently, and sometimes aggressively confessed his faith, nothing he ever wrote about again was 'irrelevant to the proposition that Christianity is true'. This does not mean, of course, that all his writings from this point on were either overtly or covertly about the Christian religion (though often they were); but it does mean that from now on his own perceptions of the real world and everything in it were transformed by his Christian presuppositions; as he had put it in one of his early anti-Blatchford pieces, after conversion, 'with this idea once inside our heads a million things become transparent as if a lamp were lit behind them'. Many, and probably most, of his pre-Christian assumptions and instincts remained unchanged (they were mostly, after all, either consistent with Christianity or were part of what had brought him to embrace it). His view of Watts, and certainly of the school of *l'art pour l'art* of which he was the living antithesis, remained unaltered:

The salient and essential characteristic of Watts and men of his school was that they regarded life as a whole. They had in their heads, as it were, a synthetic philosophy which put everything into a certain relation with God and the wheel of things. Thus, psychologically speaking they were incapable not merely of holding such an opinion, but actually of thinking such a thought as art for art's sake; it was to them like talking about voting for voting's sake, or amputating for amputating's

---

[6] Ibid. 167–8.
[7] G. K. Chesterton, 'A Universal Relevance', *The Daily News* (12 Dec. 1903).

sake.... The idea of following art through everything for itself alone, through extravagance, through cruelty, through morbidity, is just exactly as superstitious as the idea of following theology for itself alone through extravagance and cruelty and morbidity. To deny that Baudelaire is loathsome, or Nietzsche inhuman, because we stand in awe of beauty, is just the same as denying that the court of Pope Julius was loathsome, or the rack inhuman, because we stand in awe of religion.[8]

But though in some respects this could have been written by the pre-Christian Chesterton of, say, 1899, we need to register a change of perspective. There had been a cultural shift between the age in which it was possible for a painter like Watts to be an iconic figure, and the age which Chesterton was now addressing: and it was a shift which Chesterton now understood in a new way. The modern portrait painter, notes Chesterton, merely attempts to identify what makes his subjects' facial features unique, 'to paint the mouth whose grimace is inimitable, the eyes that can only be on one head'. There has been a shift to a focus on the merely superficial aspects of a subject's physical appearance, and it has taken place, he insists, because there has been a loss of vision, not merely by individual painters, but by their whole culture: 'It is the misfortune of the non-religious ages that they tend to cultivate a sense of individuality, not only at the expense of religion, but at the expense of humanity itself. For the modern portrait painter not only does not see the image of God in his sitters, he does not even see the image of man.'[9] Elsewhere, he points out that for Watts, the personal appearance of his sitters was never the most important consideration. His famous portrait of Cardinal Manning is singled out, as the most notable of many examples of Watts not concerning himself with making the most of his sitters' looks, but rather of their characters, perceived *sub specie aeternitatis*:

To the ordinary onlooker there was behind the wreck of flesh and the splendid skeleton, the remains of a very handsome English gentleman; relics of one who might have hunted foxes and married an American heiress. Watts has no eyes for anything except that sublime vow which he would himself repudiate, that awful Church which he would himself disown. He exaggerates the devotionalism of Manning. He is more ascetic than the ascetics; more Catholic than Catholicism.[10]

Watts, like Browning, is an optimist, says Chesterton; and he is an optimist for very similar reasons (reasons which naturally invite comparison with

[8] Chesterton, *G. F. Watts*, 21–2.   [9] Ibid. 157.   [10] Ibid. 163–4.

Chesterton's own optimism): 'an illimitable worship and wonder directed towards the fact of existence'. This is an optimism of a very particular kind, Chesterton asserts:

There is a great deal of difference between the optimism which says that things are perfect and the optimism which merely says . . . that they are very good. . . . One optimism says that this is the best of all possible worlds. The other says that it is certainly not the best of all possible worlds, but it is the best of all possible worlds that a world should be possible. Watts . . . is dominated throughout by this prehistoric wonder. A man to him, especially a great man, is a thing to be painted as Fra Angelico painted angels, on his knees. He has indeed, like many brilliant men in the age that produced Carlyle and Ruskin, an overwhelming tendency to hero-worship. . . . To the Carlylean the hero, the great man, was a man more human than humanity itself.

This idea of an optimism based not on the world's perfection but on the 'prehistoric wonder'—attributed by Chesterton here to Watts but undoubtedly also personal to him—that a world, any world, 'should be possible—had been expressed by Chesterton over a decade before in what I have called the Slade Notebook, at a time when he was still going through his own personal battle against 'pessimism':

The optimism which talks about this as 'the best of all possible worlds' misses the point altogether. The precise fact which makes the world so wonderful and valuable is the fact that you cannot compare it with anything. It is everything; it is our father and our mother. It is not the best of all possible worlds: but it is the best of all possible things that a world should exist.[11]

The 'Catholic' theological mindset we have already noted being intermittently reflected in Chesterton's language in 1903–4 is by no means frequently evident in *G. F. Watts*, for obvious reasons. The same can be said, of course, about all his writings which were directed toward the general public rather than the ecclesial subculture represented by *The Commonwealth* and the Christian Social Union. But there are a surprising number of examples in which it makes itself apparent elsewhere; and it may be worth noting one here: 'In worshipping [the great man], he continues, 'you were worshipping humanity in a sacrament: and Watts seems to express in almost every line of his brush this ardent and reverent view of the great man.'[12] This shows Chesterton's newly

---

[11] 'From the Note-books of G.K.C.', *The Tablet* (4 Apr. 1953).
[12] Chesterton, *G. F. Watts*, 148–9.

Catholicised conceptual understanding of a principle he had already perceived as being exemplified by Watts in his *Bookman* review of December 1900: 'all [Watts's] portraits', he had written, 'are allegories for the simple reason that all men are allegories, puzzles, earthly stories with heavenly meanings.... The profoundly original and enduring quality in Mr Watts' portraits lies in this, that he always paints the portrait of a modern man, who wears a silk hat and pays taxes, as if he were painting a purely elemental and cosmic subject.'[13] In 1900, Chesterton had seen Watts's attitude to his subjects as being simply allegorical; by 1904 he has enlarged Watts's vision by perceiving it as being sacramental. It is an imaginative shift we have already observed taking place in other ways.

   G. F. Watts embodies also, it should be noted, Chesterton's defence not merely of art for morality's sake (that was nothing new) but also of the dogmatic principle—that great *sine qua non* of Catholic theology and bug-bear of the liberal mind—as a necessary element in its vindication. Watts and the other great Victorians, he says, 'were ingrainedly ethical; the mere idea of thinking anything more important than ethics would have struck them as profane.... [Watts] simply draws the line somewhere, as all men ... draw it somewhere; he is dogmatic, as all sane men are dogmatic.'[14]

Defender of the faith II: the Blatchford controversy (1904)

In July 1904, probably between the writing and the publication of *G. F. Watts*, Chesterton returned to the business of specifically focused Christian apologetics. Though he had, so he probably supposed, finished expounding the case for Christianity against Robert Blatchford, *The Clarion* had not finished with him. In December 1903, Blatchford had thrown open the pages of his newspaper to what he charmingly described as 'his friends, the enemy'. He put the whole operation in the hands of a Christian Socialist colleague, George Haw, suggesting that he 'deal with all articles and letters on the Christian side sent to the *Clarion* office, restricting the writers to a discussion of the two points, What they believed and Why they believed [it]'. Haw decided instead to invite a number of writers of various denominations; and every week for six months, three full columns of *The Clarion* were devoted to the defence of

---

[13] G. K. Chesterton, 'The Literary Portraits of G. F. Watts R.A.', *The Bookman* (Dec. 1900), 82.
[14] Chesterton, *G. F. Watts*, 69–70.

Christianity: Chesterton was invited to wind the series up with three articles. Later in the year, all the articles appeared in a book entitled *The Religious Doubts of Democracy*.

Only Chesterton's articles are of interest today. He begins by making a point which, though it does nothing to further his argument, says a good deal about what was to be perceived as a great Chestertonian paradox: that on the one hand his defence of the Christian religion could seem so lighthearted that it could be, and frequently was, dismissed as mere buffoonery; on the other, his idea of faith was, nevertheless, so massively influential over such intellectual heavyweights as C. S. Lewis and J. R. R. Tolkien. It was a problem Chesterton was already aware of: but it was not one he had any intention of solving by becoming uncharacteristically solemn: for him, indeed, solemnity was almost the enemy of faith. The passage is worth quoting, since it shows how complete and without reservations his conversion was by now; it was no longer for him a question of working his way through intellectual problems in personal isolation: it was now a matter of the euphoria of becoming, for the first time, part of a living historical community of faith:

I have begun to realise that there are a good many people to whom my way of speaking about these things appears like an indication that I am flippant or imperfectly insincere. Since, as a matter of fact, I am more certain of myself in this affair than I am of the existence of the moon, this naturally causes me some considerable regret; but I think I see the naturalness of the mistake, and how it arose in people so far removed from the Christian atmosphere. Christianity is itself so jolly a thing that it fills the possessor of it with a certain silly exuberance, which sad and high-minded rationalists might reasonably mistake for mere buffoonery and blasphemy; just as their prototypes, the sad-minded Stoics of old Rome did mistake the Christian joyousness for buffoonery and blasphemy. This difference holds good everywhere, in the cold Pagan architecture and the grinning gargoyles of Christendom, in the preposterous motley of the Middle Ages and the dingy dress of this Rationalistic century.[15]

This recalls, perhaps, Scott Holland's 'exuberant vitality and joyousness' (in the *Autobiography*, Chesterton described him as 'a man with a natural surge of laughter within him, so that his broad strong mouth seemed always to be shut down on it in a grimace of restraint'[16]) and the 'immense fun' Frances recorded Gilbert having, 'talking energetically' with Percy Dearmer

---

[15] G. K. Chesterton, 'Christianity and Rationalism', *The Clarion* (22 July 1904); *Collected Works*, i. 374.

[16] *Autobiography*, 170.

and Conrad Noel;[17] this is what Chesterton meant by 'the Christian atmosphere'; it reminds one, perhaps, of the similar experience, a generation later,
recorded by C. S. Lewis in *Surprised by Joy*.

When Chesterton agreed to write 'one or two' more articles for *The
Clarion*, he may well have supposed that he would simply have to summarise
what he had already written the previous year. His first article, however,
deals first with an argument to which, though Blatchford had advanced it at
the time,[18] Chesterton had failed to respond. Blatchford and his school, said
Chesterton, pointed out that there were many myths parallel to the Christian story; 'that there were Pagan Christs, and Red Indian Incarnations, and
Patagonian Crucifixions, for all I know or care'. This was, of course, an
argument against Christianity that was already fashionable, largely through
the influence of Frazer's *The Golden Bough* (1890). Frazer's thesis was that
ancient religions were fertility cults that centred around the worship of, and
periodic sacrifice of, a sacred king who was the incarnation of a dying and
reviving god. Frazer claimed that this legend was central to all the world's
mythologies, and included Christianity as an example on the same footing as
all his pagan fertility cults; this caused great scandal among Christians and
jubilation among aggressive secularists like Blatchford.

Chesterton's invariable answer appears here for the first time: that if the
Christian God really made the human race, then the human race would
naturally be drawn to 'rumours and perversions' of the Christian God. It is a
characteristic example of what Belloc called his 'appetite for reason', and of
'the rational process of the mind, which governed all his development in the
matter of his religion':[19]

The story of a Christ is very common in legend and literature. So is the story of two
lovers parted by Fate. So is the story of two friends killing each other for a woman.
But will it seriously be maintained that, because these two stories are common as
legends, therefore no two friends were ever separated by love or no two lovers by
circumstances? It is tolerably plain, surely, that these two stories are common
because the situation is an intensely probable and human one, because our nature
is so built as to make them almost inevitable. . . .

Thus . . . when learned sceptics come to me and say, 'are you aware that the Kaffirs
have a story of Incarnation?' I should reply 'speaking as an unlearned person,

[17] Ward, 147.
[18] R. Blatchford, 'Christianity before Christ', *The Clarion* (28 Aug. 1903).
[19] Hilaire Belloc, signed obituary, *The Observer* (21 June 1936). Conlon, 533.

I don't know. But speaking as a Christian, I should be very much astonished if they hadn't.'[20]

Next, Chesterton addressed the argument that Christianity had been 'a gloomy and ascetic thing', the source of a 'procession of austere or ferocious saints who have given up home and happiness'. This fact becomes, in Chesterton's hands, an argument for the substantial existence of that for which these gloomy ascetics had sacrificed everything. It is a characteristic example of his unfailing capacity for standing his opponents' arguments on their heads: the secularist, he argues, 'tries to prove that there is no such thing as supernatural experience by pointing at the people who have given up everything for it. He tries to prove that there is no such thing by proving that there are people who live on nothing else.' These men may, of course have been eccentrics who loved unhappiness for its own sake: 'But it seems more in accordance with commonsense to suppose that they had really found the secret of some actual power or experience which was, like wine, a terrible consolation and a lonely joy.'[21]

The next Blatchfordian argument is one he had already addressed at some length in *The Commonwealth*:[22] that 'Christianity produces tumult and cruelty'; but for his first *Clarion* piece, he produced a different argument to rebut it. The previous year, he had argued simply that all human institutions, being human, were equally guilty. Now, he contended, perhaps somewhat less persuasively, that 'men commit crimes not only for bad things, far more often for good things', like 'the food of their children, the chastity of their women, or the independence of their country'. The same thing is true of some new and 'sudden vision': 'the chance of winning it, the chance of losing it, drives them mad. It has the same effect in the moral world that the finding of gold has in the economic world. It upsets values, and creates a kind of cruel rush.' He gives the secular example of the effect of the longing for Liberty, Equality, and Fraternity, and concludes: 'Thus . . . when the learned sceptic says: "Christianity produced wars and persecutions," we shall reply: "Naturally." '[23] It is a more sophisticated defence; but a more risky one, perhaps.

This first *Clarion* piece ends with a rebuttal of a less central objection: the local origins of both the Jewish and Christian religions. This, Chesterton

---

[20] G. K. Chesterton, 'Christianity and Rationalism', *The Clarion* (22 July 1904); *Collected Works*, i. 375.

[21] Chesterton, 'Christianity and Rationalism'; *Collected Works*, i. 376.

[22] See p. 257 above.

[23] Chesterton, 'Christianity and Rationalism'; *Collected Works*, i. 378.

effortlessly inverts, with something very like Conrad Noel's 'sacramental' argument for patriotism: 'if there really are some higher beings than our-selves, and if they . . . really revealed themselves to rude poets or dreamers in very simple times, that these rude people should regard the revelation as local, and connect it with the particular hill or river where it happened, seems to me exactly what any reasonable human being would expect. It has a far more credible look than if they had talked cosmic philosophy from the beginning. If they had, I should have suspected "priestcraft" and forgeries and third-century Gnosticism.' So, concludes Chesterton, '[w]hen the learned sceptic says: "The visions of the Old Testament were local, and rustic, and grotesque," we shall answer: "Of course. They were genuine."'

Chesterton pulls this necessarily rather bitty article together with a rhetorical thrust which was to be a habitual part of his debater's arsenal over the years ahead: that all the arguments Blatchford had made for *not* believing in Christianity were precisely the arguments that convinced him that Christianity was true: 'He has undoubtedly set up these four great guns of which I have spoken. . . . I can only say that . . . he has set up those four pieces of artillery . . . with the mouths pointing at himself.'[24]

Chesterton's second article was an attempt to explain the positive char-acter of his faith, on the basis of his perception that his difficulty with Blatchford 'very largely lies in the fact that he, like masses of clever people nowadays, does not understand what theology is'.[25] First, he argues for the dogmatic principle as a practical necessity, and one which everyone in practice actually lives by, whether they realise it or not. We all need to believe something; so we are all agnostics until we discover that agnosticism does not work. 'Then we adopt some philosophy . . . ' Blatchford's philoso-phy is no more agnostic than a Christian's: '[t]he Agnostic would say that he did not know whether man was responsible for his sins. Mr Blatchford says that he knows that man is not.' And here, asserts Chesterton, 'we have the seed of the whole huge tree of dogma':

Why does Mr Blatchford go beyond Agnosticism and assert that there is certainly no free will? *Because he cannot run his scheme of morals without asserting that there is no free will.* He wishes no man to be blamed for sin. Therefore he has to make his disciples quite certain that God did not make them free and therefore blamable. No wild Christian doubt must flit through the mouth of the Determinist. No demon

[24] Chesterton, 'Christianity and Rationalism'; *Collected Works*, i. 379.
[25] G. K. Chesterton, 'We are All Agnostics until—', *The Clarion* (22 July 1904); *Collected Works*, i. 381.

must whisper to him in some hour of anger that perhaps the company promoter was responsible for swindling him into the workhouse. (original italics)[26]

The argument for free will that Chesterton now propounds is a familiar one, and there is no need to repeat it here. From it, however, he can move on naturally to write about the doctrine of the fall of Man, and the Christian insistence that all men are called to higher things than their instincts often dictate. And here, once more, we return to that insistent Chestertonian theme, the mysticism of common sense, for, he says, 'the Fall like every other large part of Christianity is embodied in the common language talked on the top of an omnibus': 'If you wanted to dissuade a man from drinking his tenth whisky you would slap him on the back and say, "Be a man." No one who wished to dissuade a crocodile from eating his tenth explorer would slap it on the back and say, "Be a crocodile." For we have no notion of a perfect crocodile.' But we *have* been given, implies Chesterton, a notion of a perfect man, and a civilisation that has lost sight of him will soon begin to believe in a terrible perversion of the idea of human perfection. He now goes on to give a prophetic warning of what was to come in the twentieth century—a warning surely remarkable for its date—together with an equally prophetic (and, doctrinally, unambiguously and fully Christian) response to his own warning:

if a man came up to us (as many will soon come up to us) to say, 'I am a new kind of man. I am the super-man. I have abandoned mercy and justice'; we should answer, 'Doubtless you are new, but you are not nearer to the perfect man, for he has already been in the mind of God. We have fallen with Adam and we shall rise with Christ; but we would rather fall with Satan than rise with you.'[27]

Chesterton's final article for *The Clarion*, 'Mr Blatchford's Religion', falls naturally into two parts; indeed, when his articles were reprinted in *The Religious Doubts of Democracy*, Haw split it into two separate chapters, which he entitled 'Miracles and Modern Civilisation' and 'The Eternal Heroism of the Slums'. In the first part of the article, he developed arguments he had already put forward in his *Daily News* piece of 28 November the previous year, in which he stated that one of the human experiences which may follow 'the power of faith', together with 'receiving assurances', was 'working miracles'.[28] In *The Clarion*, he dealt with the philosophical objections to

---

[26] Chesterton, 'We are All Agnostics until—'; *Collected Works*, i. 382–3.
[27] Chesterton, 'We are All Agnostics until—'; *Collected Works*, i. 385.
[28] G. K. Chesterton, 'Faith and the Fantastic', *The Daily News* (28 Nov. 1903).

such miracles. To assert simply that the universe is governed by laws, he argues, is no objection, since we cannot know what all the laws are: if Blatchford 'does not know about the laws how can he possibly know about the exceptions'? The fact that a thing happens seldom is no proof that it is against natural law. The philosophical case against miracles, contends Chesterton, is easily dealt with:

There is no philosophical case against miracles. There are such things as the laws of Nature rationally speaking. What everybody knows is this only. That there is repetition in nature. What everybody knows is that pumpkins produce pumpkins. What nobody knows is why they should not produce elephants or giraffes.[29]

Blatchford argues that 'Science is against it'. That means that 'so long as pumpkins are pumpkins, their conduct is pumpkiny and bears no resemblance to the conduct of a coach'. The idea of scientific 'law' is itself not scientific but metaphorical:

What Christianity argues is merely this. That this repetition in nature has its origin not in a thing resembling a law but a thing resembling a will. Of course its phase of a Heavenly Father is drawn from an earthly father. Quite equally, Mr Blatchford's phase of a universal law is a metaphor from an Act of Parliament. But Christianity holds that the world and its repetition came by will or Love as children are begotten by a father, and therefore that other and different things might come by it.[30]

The historic case against miracles, argues Chesterton, consists of calling miracles impossible, then saying that no one but a fool believes impossibilities. When we take all the records of the human race and say 'here is your evidence', the reply is 'But these people were superstitious, they believed in impossible things.' 'The real question', Chesterton insists, 'is whether our little Oxford Street civilisation is certain to be right and the rest of the world certain to be wrong. Mr Blatchford thinks that the materialism of nineteenth century Westerns is one of their noble discoveries. I think it is as dull as their coats, as dirty as their streets, as ugly as their trousers, and as stupid as their industrial system.' Having established, as clearly as he knows how, his grounds for believing in the possibility of miracles, Chesterton now makes it clear that they should not be advanced as a reason for Christian belief, simply accepted as one of its inevitable accompaniments. What Chesterton

[29] G. K. Chesterton, 'Mr Blatchford's Religion', *The Clarion* (5 Aug. 1904); *Collected Works*, i. 386.
[30] Chesterton, 'Mr Blatchford's Religion'; *Collected Works*, i. 387.

thought *was* essential to Christian belief he now makes clear: and yet again, it is worth stressing that there were, by this period in his life, no reservations about his faith and that it was based on a clear and unambiguous belief in the Godhead of Christ:

What matters about a religion is not whether it can work marvels like any ragged Indian conjurer, but whether it has a true philosophy of the Universe. The Romans were quite willing to admit that Christ was a god. What they denied was that He was the God—the highest truth of the cosmos. *And this is the only point worth discussing about Christianity.* (my emphasis)[31]

To conclude the article—and, indeed, his entire series of articles against Blatchford, which had begun eighteen months before, in March 1903—he returns to the central argument in their dispute: the contention between Blatchford's determinism and what Chesterton had called 'the Catholic doctrine of Free Will'. There is no need here to repeat reasoning which had already become repetitive twelve months before. But it is worth noting the strength of Chesterton's personal feeling on the matter. It was not simply the argument that determinism denied the existence of a God who had created Man in his own image, and who had given him moral freedom, that Chesterton hated: it was the implied contempt for humanity, and particularly for the poor, in Blatchford's insistence that sin was the inevitable product of squalid environments and that if human environments were perfected, then sin would disappear. Coming from Blatchford—the famous Nunquam, champion of the poor—this seemed particularly offensive; and Chesterton's angry response was all the more striking from a controversialist who was already famous for the sweetness of his temper:

As for the great part of the talk of Mr. Blatchford about sin arising from vile and filthy environments, I do not wish to introduce into this discussion anything of personal emotion, but I am bound to say that I have great difficulty in enduring that talk with patience. Who in the world is it who thus speaks as if wickedness and folly raged only among the unfortunate? Is it Mr Blatchford who falls back upon the old contemptible impertinence which represents virtue to be something upper-class, like a visiting card, or a silk hat? Is it Nunquam, who denies the eternal heroism of the slums? The thing is almost incredible, but so it is. Nunquam has put as a coping stone upon his Temple, this association of vice with poverty, the vilest and the oldest and the dirtiest of all the stones that insolence has ever flung at the poor.[32]

---

[31] Chesterton, 'Mr Blatchford's Religion'; *Collected Works*, i. 393.
[32] Chesterton, 'Mr Blatchford's Religion'; *Collected Works*, i. 393–4.

Chesterton's controversy with Blatchford, as he later put it, served 'to divide all this part of my life into two distinct periods'.[33] By the time it had run its course, he had realised not only the extent to which disbelief in the Christian religion had become endemic in English culture; but, much closer to home, he had come to understand how much he had now isolated himself from the presuppositions of nearly everyone in the literary and journalistic world of which he was now a recognised part. He first realised this, he recorded in the *Autobiography*, at a dinner party:

I remember that there was, sitting next to me at this dinner, one of those very refined and rather academic gentlemen from Cambridge who seemed to form so considerable a section of the rugged stalwarts of Labour. There was a cloud on his brow, as if he were beginning to be puzzled about something; and he said suddenly, with abrupt civility, Excuse my asking, Mr. Chesterton, of course I shall quite understand if you prefer not to answer, and I shan't think any the worse of it, you know, even if it's true. But I suppose I'm right in thinking you don't really believe in those things you're defending against Blatchford? I informed him with adamantine gravity that I did most definitely believe in those things I was defending against Blatchford. His cold and refined face did not move a visible muscle; and yet I knew in some fashion it had completely altered. Oh, you do, he said, I beg your pardon. Thank you. That's all I wanted to know. And he went on eating his (probably vegetarian) meal. But I was sure that for the rest of the evening, despite his calm, he felt as if he were sitting next to a fabulous griffin.[34]

Heretics: why 'man can be defined as an animal that makes dogmas'

One of the 'things' Chesterton had been 'defending against Blatchford' had been the dogmatic principle, not merely in religion, but as a common necessity of life. We are all agnostics, he had argued, until agnosticism fails us; '[t]hen we adopt some philosophy'. The dogmatic principle was not, however, in itself a defence of any particular truth: the assailant of Christianity was as dogmatic as the Christian apologist. Blatchford's attack on free will and responsibility was as dogmatic as Chesterton's argument for the doctrine of original sin, necessarily so, for '[n]o wild Christian doubt must flit through the mouth of the Determinist'.[35] Dogmas might be orthodox: but they might equally be heretical.

[33] *Autobiography*, 180.   [34] Ibid. 181.
[35] Chesterton, 'We are All Agnostics until—'; *Collected Works*, i. 382–3.

Despite the continuing existence of dogmatism on all sides, however, the general belief was, Chesterton perceived, that it survived only among religious believers of the most illiberal or superstitious kind. It was here that he had come to realise that he was most out of step with the modern world: his intellectual transgression was not so much that he believed that *Christianity* was true; but that he believed that anything could be absolutely true—and, therefore, that anything incompatible with it was necessarily false. This was the underlying theme of *Heretics*, which appeared in June the following year (1905): there had been a time, Chesterton argued in the book's opening chapter, when it had been taken for granted that the truth was worth fighting for; a man 'was proud of being orthodox, was proud of being right':

> If he stood alone in a howling wilderness he was more than a man; he was a church. He was the centre of the universe; it was round him that the stars swung. All the tortures torn out of forgotten hells could not make him admit that he was heretical. But a few modern phrases have made him boast of it. He says, with a conscious laugh, 'I suppose I am very heretical,' and looks round for applause. The word 'heresy' not only means no longer being wrong; it practically means being clear-headed and courageous. The word 'orthodoxy' not only no longer means being right; it practically means being wrong.[36]

The rise of doctrinal relativism, Chesterton had sensed (though it was not a word he ever used), was what really distinguished modern culture from what it had replaced; in this sense, Blatchford, with his dogmatic determinism, was as much an outsider as he was. This had been one of the underlying themes of *G. F. Watts*. Watts, Chesterton had written, had 'the one great certainty which marks off all the great Victorians from those who have come after them: he may not be certain that he is successful, or certain that he is great, or certain that he is good, or certain that he is capable: but he is certain that he is right.' It is this, Chesterton says, that has disappeared from modern culture: 'it is...the very element of confidence which has in our day become least common and least possible. We know we are brilliant and distinguished, but we do not know that we are right.'[37]

The first priority of *Heretics*, therefore, was to re-establish the notion that believing 'that we are right' was not only possible, but the only sane and practical objective in human life; not only that, but that whatever they had said, those who had most effectively assailed the notion of orthodoxy

[36] *Collected Works*, i. 39.   [37] Chesterton, *G. F. Watts*, 13.

actually operated according to their own notions of it. Thus, in his opening chapter, 'The Importance of Being Orthodox'—(a heading which was itself, of course, a sideways thrust at one particular form of heresy, that of 'the green carnation')—he gave notice of his intention to deal with his opponents 'not personally or in a merely literary manner, but in relation to the real body of doctrine which they teach':

I am not concerned with Mr. Rudyard Kipling as a vivid artist or a vigorous personality; I am concerned with him as a Heretic—that is to say, a man whose view of things has the hardihood to differ from mine. I am not concerned with Mr. Bernard Shaw as one of the most brilliant and one of the most honest men alive; I am concerned with him as a Heretic—that is to say, a man whose philosophy is quite solid, quite coherent, and quite wrong. I revert to the doctrinal methods of the thirteenth century, inspired by the general hope of getting something done.[38]

The bringing into disrepute of the notion of orthodoxy, Chesterton argued in this opening chapter, had had an unintended and paradoxical consequence. When Victorian liberals 'removed the gags from all the heresies', their intention had been that there would be a growth in intellectual freedom. Their view 'was that cosmic truth was so important that every one ought to bear independent testimony. The modern idea is that cosmic truth is so unimportant that it cannot matter what any one says. [The Victorians] freed inquiry as men loose a noble hound; [the modern age] frees inquiry as men fling back into the sea a fish unfit for eating. Never has there been so little discussion about the nature of men as now, when, for the first time, any one can discuss it. The old restriction meant that only the orthodox were allowed to discuss religion. Modern liberty means that nobody is allowed to discuss it.'[39]

This was, of course, precisely the point he had made in the opening stages of the Blatchford campaign: a great silence had fallen on the subject of religion, which he now committed himself to breaking. 'I write these remarks with one great hope', he had announced: 'that of arousing controversy.'[40] There is thus an important sense in which we have to see *Heretics* as a continuation and expansion of the Blatchford campaign he had begun two years before. Then, he had defended his faith, for eighteen months, in single combat against a contumacious atheist: now, he decided to raise the polemical

[38] *Collected Works*, i. 46.   [39] Ibid. 40–1.
[40] G. K. Chesterton, 'The Return of the Angels', *The Daily News* (14 Mar. 1903).

stakes by taking on the most prominent secularisers of the age. His technique, however, was to be very different: rather than disputing over particular doctrines with an opponent he expected to answer back, this was to be a brief but intensive guerrilla strike directed against multiple targets. Some of them did indeed answer back later; *Heretics* has to be seen, for example, as one of the opening shots in his lifelong debate (and possibly the inauguration of his lifelong friendship) with George Bernard Shaw. The real distinction between Blatchford and Chesterton's targets in *Heretics* was that few of them regarded Christianity as an adversary that needed any particular sustained or detailed attention; they had moved into the empty territory its supposed collapse had liberated, each in his own way, and not necessarily with any aggressively secularist intention (though of course there were exceptions, like the renegade priest Joseph McCabe). Chesterton's task now was therefore more various and more intellectually challenging. In his final *Daily News* article at the end of the Blatchford controversy (already quoted), he had laid down his new rules of engagement. The defence of Christianity could not effectively be a continuous guerrilla war fought on the devastated battlefield over which religion-baters like Blatchford roamed, seeking targets for his weekly cannonades against believers in miracles or the doctrine of original sin. If Christianity was true, there was nothing that was irrelevant to it, for '[y]ou cannot evade the issue of God; whether you talk about pigs or the binomial theory, you are still talking about Him.... nothing can be irrelevant to the proposition that Christianity is true.'[41] And if Christianity was true, then those who had abandoned it would believe what was false: the abandonment of orthodoxy had had consequences, not always well understood, for individuals and for the culture they had created. *Heretics* is a necessarily discursive and haphazard survey of that culture. It was, implicitly and partly unconsciously, a survey he had been making in his journalism for some years now. He may not have written about pigs or the binomial theorem; but he had written about Shaw and Kipling and other subjects clearly relevant to 'the proposition that Christianity is true'. David Dooley suggests that '[o]ne way of distinguishing *Orthodoxy* from *Heretics* is by saying that there is more of the *Clarion* controversy in the later book.'[42] There is a very good reason why this should be so: it is that much of *Heretics* had already appeared as articles (mostly in *The Daily News*) before the *Clarion* controversy began, and was therefore

[41] Chesterton, 'A Universal Relevance'.
[42] David Dooley, foreword, *Collected Works*, i. 27.

both chronologically more distant and intellectually less focused: the direct line of Chesterton's intellectual development as a Christian apologist (rather than as a general commentator on secular culture) leads from the journalism of his early years to the campaign against Blatchford and then onwards to the great apologetic base camp of *Orthodoxy*, from which future ascents to the theological summits of *The Everlasting Man* and *St Thomas Aquinas* were to set out. The *Clarion* controversy was the first time he had been called upon to defend the Christian religion, and he summoned up all his considerable powers of reasoning to do so. The articles on which Chesterton drew for the chapters on individual writers in *Heretics* were necessarily more various and less disciplined; and some of them pre-dated the 'landmark year' in which for the first time Chesterton set himself to defend his faith in a consistent way—though others are contemporaneous with the Blatchford controversy (1903–4), and yet others appeared after it.[43] All the 'thematic' chapters are post-Blatchford; that is, perhaps, why—for instance—the final chapter, 'Concluding Remarks on the Importance of Orthodoxy', seems to have more in common with the direct and relatively more disciplined reasoning of some of his anti-Blatchford pieces than with the more discursive essay-writing style of his chapters on Kipling or Wells. *Heretics* is not, in the same way that *Orthodoxy* was to be and that his contributions to the *Clarion* controversy of 1903–4 had been, an example of consistently focused Christian apologetics. But we need to say, nevertheless, that neither is the book simply a ragbag of old articles, held together by new material. David Dooley argues that '[t]here are many types of Christian apologetics . . . and *Heretics* is an example of one of them. By showing what heresy implies, Chesterton illustrates what orthodoxy implies.'[44] This is true up to a point: but it has to be said, too, that in *Heretics*, discussions of 'what heresy implies' several times become occasions for spelling out Chesterton's view that orthodoxy was identical with the teachings of the Christian tradition, and for indicating this view, furthermore, explicitly and unambiguously rather than in some subtle or implicit fashion.

This is particularly striking in the book's chapter on the Irish writer and art historian George Moore, a link for Chesterton with the Slade period and his confrontation with the 'diabolist'—in which, it will be recalled, he had declared that 'I am becoming orthodox . . . because I have come, rightly or wrongly . . . to the old belief that heresy is worse than sin.' The writings

---

[43] David Evans, 'The Making of G. K. Chesterton's *Heretics*', *Yearbook of English Studies*, 5 (1975), 207–13.

[44] Dooley, foreword, *Collected Works*, i. 22.

of George Moore had been an identifiable inspiration behind what he had then come to see as heresy. As we have discussed,[45] Moore had been a major influence over the English understanding of Impressionism (most relevantly to Chesterton's own understanding of it, he had been a strong formative influence over the Slade's principal, Fred Brown). Moore had praised particularly the way in which Impressionists like Whistler had, in Moore's words, 'helped to purge art of the vice of subject and [of] belief that the mission of the artist is to copy nature',[46] or as Chesterton was to characterise the philosophy of Impressionism, 'if all that could be seen of a cow was a white line and a purple shadow, we should only render the line and the shadow; in a sense we should only believe in the line and the shadow, rather than in the cow': this, Chesterton described as 'scepticism in the form of subjectivism'.[47] Moore, therefore, had been a key figure in the intellectual and artistic subculture against which Chesterton had reacted by raising, for the first time, the banner of 'orthodoxy'. Chesterton had at that stage still been five or six years away from any consistent belief in most of Christianity's basic doctrines; nevertheless, 'orthodoxy' was always for him religious in character, and its earliest meaning for him was inseparable from belief in God and gratitude for his creation—this is the unambiguous message of the notebooks he kept from 1894 onwards.[48] In his salvation from the *fin de siècle*, he had 'hung on to religion by one thin thread of thanks'.[49] He was recalling, perhaps, this period in his life when, just after the end of the Blatchford controversy, he reflected in a *Daily News* piece on the consequences for any human culture of cutting itself off from God:

We maintain that man is not only a part of God, but God is a part of man: a thing essential, like sex. We say that (in the light of actual history) if you cut off the supernatural what remains is the unnatural. We say that it is in believing ages that you get men living in the open and dancing and telling tales by the fire. We say that it is in ages of unbelief that you get emperors dressing up as women and gladiators or minor poets wearing green carnations and praising unnameable things. We say that, taking ages as a whole, the wildest fantasies of superstition are nothing to the fantasies of rationalism.[50]

If Chesterton's revolt against the *fin de siècle* in 1894 was still far from being consistently Christian, by 1903 (and probably sooner), the connection had been made: 'orthodoxy' now meant the Catholic tradition as it was

---

[45] See p. 105 above.   [46] George Moore, *Modern Painting* (London, 1893), 23–4.
[47] *Autobiography*, 88–9.   [48] See p. 234 above.   [49] *Autobiography*, 91.
[50] G. K. Chesterton, 'What Happens to Rational Persons', *The Daily News* (12 Dec. 1903).

understood from within a particular Anglican perspective. Thus, in *Heretics*, Chesterton interestingly relates Moore's hostility to the idea of objective truth, his 'scepticism in the form of subjectivism', as much to his rejection of the Catholicism in which he had been brought up as to his adoption of the aestheticism of the *fin de siècle*:

> His account of his reason for leaving the Roman Catholic Church is possibly the most admirable tribute to that communion which has been written of late years. For the fact of the matter is, that the weakness which has rendered barren the many brilliancies of Mr. Moore is actually that weakness which the Roman Catholic Church is at its best in combating. Mr. Moore hates Catholicism because it breaks up the house of looking-glasses in which he lives. Mr. Moore does not dislike so much being asked to believe in the spiritual existence of miracles or sacraments, but he does fundamentally dislike being asked to believe in the actual existence of other people. Like his master Pater and all the aesthetes, his real quarrel with life is that it is not a dream that can be moulded by the dreamer. It is not the dogma of the reality of the other world that troubles him, but the dogma of the reality of this world.

Chesterton now illustrated the weaknesses in Moore's judgements on particular writers—as Moore had expounded them in his book *Confessions of a Young Man* (1888)—by relating them specifically to his rejection of Catholic ethical teaching. This was doing a good deal more than simply showing obliquely 'what orthodoxy implies'; Chesterton was self-consciously asserting what orthodoxy explicitly teaches:

> The truth is that the tradition of Christianity (which is still the only coherent ethic of Europe) rests on two or three paradoxes or mysteries which can easily be impugned in argument and as easily justified in life. One of them, for instance, is the paradox of hope or faith—that the more hopeless is the situation the more hopeful must be the man. Stevenson understood this, and consequently Mr. Moore cannot understand Stevenson. Another is the paradox of charity or chivalry that the weaker a thing is the more it should be respected, that the more indefensible a thing is the more it should appeal to us for a certain kind of defence. Thackeray understood this, and therefore Mr. Moore does not understand Thackeray. Now, one of these very practical and working mysteries in the Christian tradition, and one which the Roman Catholic Church, as I say, has done her best work in singling out, is the conception of the sinfulness of pride. Pride is a weakness in the character; it dries up laughter, it dries up wonder, it dries up chivalry and energy. The Christian tradition understands this; therefore Mr. Moore does not understand the Christian tradition.[51]

    51 *Collected Works*, i. 106–7.

In the opening chapter of *Heretics*, Chesterton had insisted—against the modern 'habit of saying that [a man's] philosophy does not matter'—that 'it is far more practical to begin at the beginning and discuss theories'. One important component of the overall context in which this was to be done, it is clear, was the defence of the practical viability of the Christian tradition. In November 1903, in *The Daily News*, he had described the long list of Christianity's 'popes, councils, persecutions, martyrdoms, cathedrals, sacraments, and massacres' as being 'a perfectly business-like and natural record of actions, good, bad, and indifferent, taken in connection with a quite intelligible aim'.[52] That had been in the context of an openly apologetic defence of historic Christianity; but it is an error to suppose that in *Heretics* this emphasis was to become implicit rather than explicit. As he now expressed it in his first chapter, 'The Importance of Being Orthodox', 'I see that the men who killed each other about the orthodoxy of the *Homoousion* [i.e. the doctrine that Jesus was 'of one substance with the Father'] were far more sensible than the people who are quarrelling about the [1902] Education Act. For the Christian dogmatists were trying to establish a reign of holiness, and trying to get defined, first of all, what was really holy. But our modern educationists are trying to bring about a religious liberty without attempting to settle what is religion or what is liberty.'[53] In *Heretics*, he continued to assail modernist ideas in pointedly, even triumphalistically, Christian language. The previous year, in *The Clarion*, he had contemptuously dismissed Nietzsche's superman by saying that it was a perversion of the idea of the perfect human being which had already been 'in the mind of God'.[54] In *Heretics*, he challenges Shaw's Nietzschean proselytising by evoking the Christian virtue of humility and the Christian doctrine of creation, for, he argues, 'blessed [are] the meek, for [they] shall inherit the earth' and '[u]ntil we realize that things might not be we cannot realize that things are':

Mr. Shaw cannot understand that the thing which is valuable and lovable in our eyes is man—the old beer-drinking, creed-making, fighting, failing, sensual, respectable man. And the things that have been founded on this creature immortally remain; the things that have been founded on the fancy of the Superman have died with the dying civilizations which alone have given them birth. When Christ at a symbolic moment was establishing His great society, He chose for its corner-stone neither the brilliant Paul nor the mystic John, but a shuffler, a snob, a coward—in a word, a man. And upon this rock He has built His Church, and the gates of Hell

[52] Chesterton, 'Faith and the Fantastic'.   [53] *Collected Works*, i. 45.
[54] G. K. Chesterton, 'We are All Agnostics until—'; *Collected Works*, i. 385.

have not prevailed against it. All the empires and the kingdoms have failed, because of this inherent and continual weakness, that they were founded by strong men and upon strong men [only]. But this one thing, the historic Christian Church, was founded on a weak man, and for that reason it is indestructible.[55]

The more we register not only the underlying assumptions of *Heretics*, but the book's clear indications—intermittent but unambiguous—of their Christian origins, the more necessary it becomes to qualify the general view among commentators on Chesterton that, as Garry Wills argues it, Chesterton's aim in the book was, in a purely secular way, to help re-establish certitude and philosophical realism and that his Christian apologetic was to be written later.[56] Certainly, this was one of the book's primary aims; this was not apologetics in the same sense that the Blatchford campaign had been. Nevertheless, 'philosophical realism', for Chesterton, by now *meant* Christianity: nothing was irrelevant to 'the proposition that Christianity is true'. That would still have been the case even if, in assembling *Heretics*, he had deliberately suppressed all mention of Christian teachings, or all illustrations for his arguments based on Christian ideas or imagery. But he did not; Christian arguments and ideas are not obsessively introduced in *Heretics*, and there are chapters where they are not overtly introduced at all; but where they arise— and when they do, they are as often as not of a specifically Catholic complexion—they are used naturally and unapologetically. In chapter 18, 'The Fallacy of the Young Nation', he argues that religious rituals in which the universal is symbolised by the concrete and material correspond to a basic human instinct: 'The most ferocious opponent of the Christian ceremonials must admit that if Catholicism had not instituted the bread and wine, somebody else would most probably have done so. Any one with a poetical instinct will admit that to the ordinary human instinct bread . . . and wine . . . [symbolise] something which cannot very easily be symbolised otherwise.' In chapter 2, 'On the Negative Spirit', we read that 'A young man may keep himself from vice by continually thinking of disease. He may keep himself from it also by continually thinking of the Virgin Mary. There may be question about which method is the more reasonable, or even about which is the more efficient. But surely there can be no question about which is the more wholesome.' He goes on to evoke the 'body and substance' of Christ in the consecrated eucharistic elements against a

---

[55] *Collected Works*, i. 69–70.
[56] Garry Wills, *Chesterton: Man and Mask* (New York, 1961); discussed by Dooley, foreword, *Collected Works*, i. 22.

contention that to show a picture of a drunkard's liver would be more efficacious in preventing alcoholism than prayer or any other kind of religious intervention. This contention, says Chesterton, 'perfectly embodie[s] the incurable morbidity of modern ethics':

In that temple the lights are low, the crowds kneel, the solemn anthems are uplifted. But that upon the altar to which all men kneel is no longer the perfect flesh, the body and substance of the perfect man; it is still flesh, but it is diseased. It is the drunkard's liver of the New Testament that is marred for us, which we take in remembrance of him.[57]

The Christian religion is nowhere systematically expounded in *Heretics*: that was not the book's purpose. But Christianity was undoubtedly and openly the foundation on which the whole structure was erected. It was hardly conceivable that it should have been otherwise, for Christian belief was by now the foundation on which not merely Chesterton's thinking but his whole life was built. The name of Christ appears only intermittently in Chesterton's writings at this stage in his religious development (as we have seen, it is wildly untrue to say that it does not appear at all). But that does not indicate his indifference to it. There was, in a man of his generation, a certain natural reticence to be observed; the holy name was not lightly to be bandied about. But his passionate commitment could emerge at any time. At one of his by now frequent speaking engagements, at about the time *Heretics* was published, a Canon Barnett recalled that a member of the audience 'spoke discourteously of Christ':

Mr Chesterton bore him for the allotted time, and then slipping off his indifference like a loose coat, sprang to his feet and, with glorious eloquence and rapidity, told of his own faith, stripped the incidents of time and circumstance from the Character which has transfigured history, and declaimed that reverence and humility were the paths all men should keep open, for they alone led to the evolution of the true. I never now read anything by Mr. Chesterton without seeing him on that platform defending, in a physical elephantine rage, his spiritual angelic surety.[58]

As Chesterton puts it in the opening chapter of *Heretics*, 'the most practical and important thing about a man is still his view of the universe'; this is certainly true of Chesterton himself and it would be strange if his faith did not emerge in the course of a book whose purpose is to justify this assertion. And in fact, this proves to be the case, despite Cecil Chesterton's judgement (surely as flawed

---

[57] *Collected Works*, i. 48. [58] *Return*, 75.

on *Heretics*—and in much the same way—as his judgement on the ·*Clarion* controversy had been): 'Mr. Chesterton', opined Cecil, 'criticizes his opponents with much vigour and acumen. But he does not [in *Heretics*] very clearly define, much less defend, his own position. Doubtless that position can be roughly deduced from his criticisms of others, but from one who lays such stress upon the importance of clearly defined doctrines we have a right to expect something more than this negative method of definition.'[59] This is much the same judgement as Dooley's, that 'by showing what heresy implies, Chesterton illustrates what orthodoxy implies'. Margaret Clarke, in an article to which it will be necessary to return, is even more sweeping: until he became a Catholic in 1922, she claims, 'Chesterton's propaganda for "Christianity", "Christendom", and "Orthodoxy", does not admit of Christ in Person. . . . The sacramental side of Christianity is conspicuous by its absence in Chesterton.'[60] Such judgements simply cannot survive even the most cursory knowledge of the Blatchford campaign (particularly of Chesterton's contributions to *The Commonwealth*) or of the text of *Heretics*; and it is perhaps at this stage in our survey of Chesterton's religious development that we need initially to address the matter (it will arise again when we come to consider *Orthodoxy*). If the test is admitting of 'Christ in Person' or in registering the existence of 'the sacramental side of Christianity', a much stronger case could be made for the proposition that, by the time he produced *Heretics*, both 'Christ in Person' and Christ in the sacraments of the Catholic Church (of which he undoubtedly believed, by this date, that Anglicanism was an organic part), were for Chesterton not only the fires warming and animating his whole vision of human life, but realities to be openly proclaimed where it was appropriate to do so. In his polemic against Omar Khayyám and the fatalistic tradition he represented (chapter 7), they blaze forth triumphantly, in one of Chesterton's splendid oratorical bursts. The rhetoric of this passage is built up by a dramatic repetition of the word 'Drink', which comes to its climax with a direct quotation from the words of institution of the eucharist as they appear in the Book of Common Prayer, 'Take this, all of you and drink from it, for this is my Blood of the New Testament, which is shed for you and for many for the remission of sins':

Jesus Christ . . . made wine, not a medicine, but a sacrament. But Omar makes it, not a sacrament, but a medicine. He feasts because life is not joyful; he revels because he is

[59] Cecil, 152.
[60] Margaret Clarke, 'Chesterton the Classicist', *Dublin Review*, 209 (1955), 51–67.

not glad. 'Drink,' he says, 'for you know not whence you come nor why. Drink, for you know not when you go nor where. Drink, because the stars are cruel and the world as idle as a humming-top. Drink, because there is nothing worth trusting, nothing worth fighting for. Drink, because all things are lapsed in a base equality and an evil peace.' So he stands offering us the cup in his hand. And at the high altar of Christianity stands another figure, in whose hand also is the cup of the vine. 'Drink' he says 'for the whole world is as red as this wine, with the crimson of the love and wrath of God. Drink, for the trumpets are blowing for battle and this is the stirrup-cup. Drink, for this my blood of the new testament that is shed for you. Drink, for I know of whence you come and why. Drink, for I know of when you go and where.'

The sacramental principle—according to which, as Conrad Noel had explained it, 'human nature is so constituted that it can get no real hold on the universal excepting through its particular and instinctive expressions'[61]— was always to be a primary animating tenet both of Chesterton's argumentation and of his imaginative life. Nearly always, however, overtly biblical or devotional language of the kind we have quoted above is avoided in his writings. His *Heretics* chapter on Kipling is an obvious example. Chesterton reprises his arguments against imperialism and in favour of patriotism, as we have already considered them. He begins with what we might call his pre-sacramental argument, as he had advanced it in 'In Defence of Patriotism', that patriotism should be based on love of one's country, not on pleasure in her capacity for coercing others: Kipling 'admires England, but he does not love her; for we admire things with reasons, but love them without reasons. He admires England because she is strong, not because she is English.' This, says Chesterton, puts his devotion in an altogether different category from that of the Boers 'whom he hounded down in South Africa'. Chesterton now moves on to what we have described as his quasi-sacramental argument, as he had expounded it in *England: A Nation*: that 'real universality is to be reached . . . by convincing ourselves that we are in the best possible relation with our immediate surroundings'.[62] Kipling loves the universal, but has no knowledge of the particular. He knows no country well enough truly to love her; and since he has no intimate knowledge of one country, his knowledge of the world itself has no concrete reality: 'He is a perfect master of that light melancholy with which a man looks back on having been the citizen of many communities, of that light

[61] Conrad Noel, 'Patriotism and Christian Faith', in Lucian Oldershaw (ed.), *England: A Nation* (London, 1904), 249–52.
[62] G. K. Chesterton, 'The Patriotic Idea', in Oldershaw (ed.), *England: A Nation*, 5–6.

melancholy with which a man looks back on having been the lover of many women. He is the philanderer of the nations':

Astronomically speaking, I understand that England is situated on the world; similarly, I suppose that the Church [which teaches that we should keep ourselves 'unspotted from the world'] was a part of the world, and even the lovers [who talk of the 'world well lost'], inhabitants of that orb. But they all felt a certain truth—the truth that the moment you love anything the world becomes your foe. Thus Mr. Kipling does certainly know the world; he is a man of the world, with all the narrowness that belongs to those imprisoned in that planet. He knows England as an intelligent English gentleman knows Venice. He has been to England a great many times; he has stopped there for long visits. But he does not belong to it, or to any place; and the proof of it is this, that he thinks of England as a place. The moment we are rooted in a place, the place vanishes. We live like a tree with the whole strength of the universe.

This image of putting down roots in a particular soil and gaining thereby 'the whole strength of the universe' is one that springs from an imagination which has always been instinctively, and now has become consciously, essentially sacramental. As we have seen in a number of ways, this manifests itself constantly in Chesterton's writings, both in his rational elucidations of his world view, and in his use of imagery and metaphor, and it is necessary to insist that Margaret Clarke's view, that '[t]he sacramental side of Christianity is conspicuous by its absence in Chesterton' at this period,[63] is simply untenable. Nevertheless, the primary objective of *Heretics* is not directly to put the argument for Christianity in any of its aspects, but to achieve, rather, a necessary preliminary objective: the re-establishment of an understanding that any particular world view has a theoretical basis which needs imperatively to be understood: for 'nothing can be more dangerous than to found our social philosophy on any theory which is debatable but has not been debated'.[64] There is also, Chesterton argues, another objection to this evasion of theory: that it is an obstacle to real rather than illusory human progress. Man cannot live without convictions, any more than he can live without intellectual boundaries. As he explains in the book's final chapter, in a passage which can be seen as central, not only to the argument of *Heretics* but to an understanding of the stage in Chesterton's intellectual development it represents,

The vice of the modern notion of mental progress is that it is always something concerned with the breaking of bonds, the effacing of boundaries, the casting away

[63] Clarke, 'Chesterton the Classicist'.   [64] *Collected Works*, i. 196.

of dogmas. But if there be such a thing as mental growth, it must mean the growth into more and more definite convictions, into more and more dogmas. The human brain is a machine for coming to conclusions; if it cannot come to conclusions it is rusty. . . . Man can hardly be defined, after the fashion of Carlyle, as an animal who makes tools; ants and beavers and many other animals make tools, in the sense that they make an apparatus. Man can be defined as an animal that makes dogmas.[65]

The Ball and the Cross

Heretics was published in June 1905. In March of the same year (probably after he had sent the text of the book to the publishers, John Lane) he had begun publishing a novel, *The Ball and the Cross*, in serial parts. What were to become the first eight chapters of the novel appeared in monthly instalments, significantly in Scott Holland's magazine *The Commonwealth*, until April of the following year; two final instalments appeared in June and November 1906 and the serialisation then fizzled out when, as it appears, Chesterton lost interest in it. It was to be salvaged later, and it was published, duly completed, between hard covers in 1910. The unfinished version is worth some passing attention at this point, however, since it not only neatly enacts Chesterton's emerging character, in the middle of the decade, as a controversialist, but also casts light on his personal religious convictions at this time. The novel concerns a violent confrontation between Evan MacIan, a fanatical Scottish Catholic, and Turnbull, an equally fanatical Scot, who is editor of an anti-Christian newspaper called *The Atheist*. The identification of MacIan as Chesterton and Turnbull as Blatchford (*The Atheist* is obviously *The Clarion*) is surely irresistible; and the underlying theme of the novel is that of *Heretics*: the hostility or indifference of the modern world to questions involving real belief. The novel's protagonists are both men seized by the dogmatic principle, like Chesterton and those of his contemporaries whom he polemically confronted: as he put it in *Heretics*, 'I hold that I am dogmatic and right, while Mr. Shaw is dogmatic and wrong.' When MacIan smashes *The Atheist*'s office window because of what he perceives as a blasphemy against the Blessed Virgin Mary, the police who arrest them both for causing an affray find Turnbull just as incomprehensible as his attacker: 'the editor's fine rational republican appeals to his respect for law, and his ardour to be tried by his fellow citizens, seemed to the police

---

[65] Ibid.

quite as much gibberish as Evan's mysticism could have done. The police were not used to hearing principles, even the principles of their own existence.' When the magistrate asks MacIan why he has smashed Turnbull's window, his answer is unintelligible to him:

'He is my enemy,' said Evan, simply; 'he is the enemy of God.' Mr. Vane shifted sharply in his seat, dropping the eye-glass out of his eye in a momentary and not unmanly embarrassment. 'You mustn't talk like that here,' he said, roughly, and in a kind of hurry, 'that has nothing to do with us.' Evan opened his great, blue eyes; 'God,' he began. 'Be quiet,' said the magistrate, angrily, 'it is most undesirable that things of that sort should be spoken about—a—in public, and in an ordinary Court of Justice. Religion is—a—too personal a matter to be mentioned in such a place.... to talk in a public place about one's most sacred and private sentiments—well, I call it bad taste. (Slight applause.) I call it irreverent. I call it irreverent, and I'm not specially orthodox either.' 'I see you are not,' said Evan, 'but I am.'[66]

As Chesterton had put it in the opening chapter of *Heretics*, '[t]he old restriction meant that only the orthodox were allowed to discuss religion. Modern liberty means that nobody is allowed to discuss it. Good taste, the last and vilest of human superstitions, has succeeded in silencing us where all the rest have failed.'[67] MacIan and Turnbull are both determined, not only not to be silenced, but to fight, in the name of their principles, to the death. The world is determined to prevent them, on the ground that what divides them is not worth fighting about. Whether *The Ball and the Cross* says more about these themes (or says them better) than Chesterton had already said in his polemical writings of the previous three years may be doubted. As he himself put it in the *Autobiography* thirty years later, 'I could not be a novelist; because I really like to see ideas or notions wrestling naked'—an apt description of the Blatchford campaign and of *Heretics*—'and not dressed up in a masquerade as men and women. But I could be a journalist because I could not help being a controversialist.'[68] *The Ball and the Cross* was one of the novels he had in mind when he came to this conclusion: it 'had quite a good plot', wrote Chesterton, 'about two men perpetually prevented by the police from fighting a duel about the collision of blasphemy and worship, or what all respectable people would call, "a mere difference about religion"'. Its theme—'that the modern world is organised in relation to the most

---

[66] G. K. Chesterton, 'The Religion of the Stipendiary Magistrate', *The Commonwealth* (June, July 1905).
[67] *Collected Works*, i. 41.   [68] *Autobiography*, 298.

obvious and urgent of all questions, not so much to answer it wrongly, as to prevent it being answered at all'—had 'a great deal in it'; but he was doubtful 'about whether [he] got a great deal out of it'. His novels, Chesterton continued, 'were not as good as a real novelist would have made them'; not only that, they were not as good as he might have made them himself if he had really been trying to be a novelist.[69]

The novel form, nevertheless, permitted Chesterton the exploration of certain non-polemical and imaginative themes, themes which can be seen to reveal important aspects of his spiritual world at this period of his life; and in anything but a novel, it is doubtful that they would have been explored, in any literary sense, at all. *The Ball and the Cross* is a novel about the mutual incomprehension of a deeply religious 'Cradle Catholic' and an unbelieving world: it was therefore inevitable that it would in some ways reflect Chesterton's own situation as a self-consciously 'Catholic' convert who was himself coming to terms with his own conflict with an increasingly relativist secular culture. Chesterton's attempts to evoke Evan MacIan's childhood spiritual formation necessarily reflect his own adult conversion. Chesterton's picture of MacIan's childhood world looks like nothing so much as an unconscious grafting of a retrospective cradle Catholicism on to his own happy childhood memories 'of white light on everything, cutting things out very clearly'. Chesterton was to stress the clarity and the reality of his recollections: the point was, he insisted, 'that the white light had a sort of wonder in it, as if the world were as new as myself; but not that the world was anything but a real world. . . . There was something of an eternal morning about the mood.'[70] If to this we add the memory of the enchanted landscapes he had seen (and continued to see throughout his adult life) through the proscenium arch of his father's toy theatre, and if we then remember the fairy-tale world of George MacDonald's *The Princess and the Goblin*, presided over by an unageing and beautiful magical grandmother (whom Chesterton was later to identify with the Blessed Virgin Mary[71]); if we then add to this imaginative melting pot Chesterton's personal Marian devotion, which we can see powerfully expressed as early as 1892, in 'Ave Maria' (his final poem for *The Debater*), we begin to have some idea of why Chesterton invests Evan MacIan's childhood with such a powerful emotional charge. *Heretics* and the Blatchford controversy give us a much clearer

---

[69] Ibid. 297–8.   [70] Ibid. 45.
[71] Introduction to Greville M. MacDonald, *George MacDonald and his Wife* (London, 1924), 9–11.

understanding of the 'ideas wrestling naked' which engaged Chesterton's intellect; but *The Ball and the Cross* presents us with a different and more expressive articulation of Chesterton's new faith:

Evan lived like a man walking on a borderland, the borderland between this world and another. Like so many men and nations who grow up with nature and the common things, he understood the supernatural before he understood the natural. He had looked at dim angels standing knee-deep in the grass before he had looked at the grass. He knew that Our Lady's robes were blue before he knew the wild roses round her feet were red. The deeper his memory plunged into the dark house of childhood the nearer and nearer he came to the things that cannot be named. All through his life he thought of the daylight world as a sort of divine debris, the broken remainder of his first vision. The skies and mountains were the splendid off-scourings of another place. The stars were lost jewels of the Queen. Our Lady had gone and left the stars by accident.[72]

It is important to understand that the way in which Chesterton here describes MacIan's devotion to the Blessed Virgin Mary is in no way intended as the comment, *de haut en bas*, of an urban sophisticate on the faith of an ignorant and superstitious man. On the contrary: it is clear that in his simplicity, MacIan is to be admired, since it has given him immunity to the false sophistication of a merely secular culture. It is clear, too, that MacIan's devotion to the Blessed Virgin mirrors Chesterton's own. This was nothing new: as we have seen, in a sense, Chesterton believed in Mary as an object of worship before he believed in Jesus. In 'Ave Maria' (1892), he sees her as epitomising values of strength and purity endangered in an age in which traditional moral (probably specifically sexual) restraint is being lost:

> O Woman, O Maiden and Mother, now also we need Thee to greet
> Now in ages of change and of question I come with a prayer to thy feet
> In the earthquake and cleaving of strata, the lives of low passions we see,
> And the horrors we bound in dark places rejoice, having hope to be
>   free;
> Wild voices from hills half-forgotten laugh scorn at all bonds that
>   restrain:
> O queen of all tender and holy, come down and confound them
>   again![73]

A few years later, at a time when he was still writing scornfully about priests and pontiffs, he was writing in the most traditionally Roman Catholic style

[72] Chesterton, 'The Religion of the Stipendiary Magistrate'.   [73] *The Debater*, ii. 95.

about the Blessed Virgin. 'A Christmas Carol' can probably be dated around 1896–8:

> At Bethlehem, that city blest
> Did Our Lady take her rest
> Mary, fair and undefiled
> There conceived and bore a Child
>   Mater sanctissima
>   Ora pro nobis
>
> And Saint Joseph, when he saw
> Christ asleep upon the straw,
> In great love he worshipped there
> Mary and the Child she bore
>   Ave plena gratia
>   Ave Rosa Mundi.[74]

Throughout his career, Chesterton wrote poems bearing witness to his rather touching Marian devotion, often but not always about Christmas, including 'The Nativity' (1897),[75] another poem entitled 'A Christmas Carol' collected in *The Wild Knight* (1900),[76] 'The Neglected Child' (*c.*1907),[77] 'The House of Christmas' (*c.*1908),[78] 'A Christmas Rhyme' (1910),[79] and '*Regina Angelorum*' (1925).[80] In the circles in which Chesterton moved as an Anglican, his Marian devotion was not unusual; but once beyond the invisible walls of the Anglo-Catholic ghetto, he was to find his singularity in this respect, as in others, increasingly irksome, and when in the end he was received into the Roman Catholic Church, he was grateful to find his Catholic eccentricities normalised as he joined the mainstream. As he explained in the *Autobiography*, 'I do not want to be in a religion in which I am *allowed* to have a crucifix. I feel the same about the much more controversial question of the honour paid to the Blessed Virgin. If people do not like that cult, they are quite right not to be Catholics. But in people who are Catholics, or call themselves Catholics, I want the idea not only liked but loved and loved ardently, and above all proudly proclaimed. . . . I want to be allowed to be enthusiastic about the existence of the enthusiasm; not to have my chief enthusiasm coldly tolerated as an eccentricity of myself.'[81] This was written thirty years after *The Ball and the Cross*; but it undoubtedly applies not only to the period immediately preceding Chesterton's conversion to Rome but also to this earlier period in

---

[74] *Collected Works*, x. 125.   [75] Ibid. 146.   [76] *The Wild Knight* (London, 1900), 27.
[77] *Collected Works*, x. 150.   [78] Ibid. 139.   [79] Ibid. 128.
[80] Ibid. 156.   [81] *Autobiography*, 251.

Chesterton's life, when he had himself become one of those who—as he later put it—'call themselves Catholics'. Evan MacIan's ardent Marian piety is a reflection of the devotion Chesterton himself felt for the Blessed Virgin for at least the last four decades of his life.

Liberal politics and liberal principles: the general election of 1906

By 1906, Chesterton had undergone a revolution in his religious views; but in his politics he was still a steadfast Liberal, not merely in his political principles, but in his support for the Liberal party. This divergence between his former theological liberalism and his continuing political liberalism is worth remarking at this point, since there can be little question that his youthful attitudes to politics and religion had a common source: we have quoted his brother Cecil's recollection that '[t]he politics and religion of his parents were emphatically Liberal' and we need to remember Cecil's judgement that it was from this family tradition that his early sympathy not only for Stopford Brooke's hostility to traditional Trinitarian Christianity but also for the Gladstonian political tradition were derived:

The politics of the family bore some resemblance to its religious atmosphere. They were not Jacobin, but they were decidedly Liberal. The childhood of G.K.C. coincided more or less with the St. Martin's Summer of Liberalism, from 1880 to 1885. Political controversy was so much in the air of the household that even as an infant he must have heard echoes of that last stand of Gladstonian Liberalism; he was certainly beginning to be politically conscious when the 'flowing tide' in which Gladstone had trusted suddenly turned and overwhelmed him.[82]

By the middle of the first decade of the new century, his theological liberalism had utterly collapsed; but his political liberalism remained intact. There was nothing intrinsically incongruous in this; Gladstone himself, of course, was a devout Anglican high churchman. All Chesterton's friends, furthermore, and one in particular, were Liberal party supporters; two of them, indeed, were elected in the general election of January 1906. Hilaire Belloc was returned as Liberal Member of Parliament for Salford South. A sudden shower of delirious letters and postcards arrived in London, announcing his imminent triumphant return to the capital:

[82] Cecil, 9.

I have, as you will have seen, pulled it off by 852. It is huge fun. I am now out against all Vermin. . . . The Devil is let loose: let all men beware. H.B.

Tomorrow Monday Meet the Manchester train arriving Euston 6.10 and oblige your little friend HB—St. Hilary's Day.

Don't fail to meet that train. Stamps are cheap! HB

I beg you. I implore you.—Meet that 6.10 train—HB

Stamps are a drug in the market. 852

Meet that train! Stamps are given away now in Salford.[83]

Masterman, too, formed part of the new Liberal government's landslide majority; Chesterton had, indeed, canvassed for him in this triumphant election campaign of 1906 as he had in the 1903 Dulwich by-election. Chesterton had remained loyal to his party 'in the desert', as he put it, and was to remain so throughout much of the decade, though within 18 months of the 1906 election he had written *Orthodoxy*, with its famous declaration that 'As much as I ever did, more than I ever did, I believe in Liberalism. But there was a rosy time of innocence when I believed in Liberals.'[84] He maintained a residual tribal loyalty to the Liberal party, nevertheless, until the Marconi scandal led to his final repudiation of all party politics. As a young journalist at the outset of his career, his passionate belief in political liberalism—which emerges strongly in a letter he wrote to J. L. Hammond, editor of the pro-Boer paper *The Speaker*—is unmistakable: but so, perhaps, is the inevitability of his eventual disillusion. Already, his impatience with purely party political loyalties was clear enough:

The Speaker is a party paper and does not profess to be otherwise. But here I am sure we are mistaking our mission. What *The Speaker* is (I hope and believe) destined to do, is to renovate Liberalism, and though Liberalism (like every other party) is often conducted by claptrap, it has never been renovated by claptrap, but by great command of temper and the persistent exposition of persuasive and unanswerable truths. It is while we are in the desert that we have the vision: we being a minority, must be all philosophers: we must think for both parties in the State. It is no good our devoting ourselves to the flowers of mob oratory with no mob to address them to. We must, like the Free Traders, for instance, have discoveries, definite truths and endless patience in explaining them. We must be more than a political party or we shall cease to be one. Time and again in history victory has come to a little party with big ideas: but can anyone conceive anything with the mark of death more on its brow than a little party with little ideas?[85]

---

[83] Ward, 248.   [84] *Collected Works*, i. 249.   [85] BL MS Add. 73346B.

Masterman remembered Chesterton engagingly but impractically practising this 'persistent exposition of persuasive and unanswerable truths' while canvassing during general elections. Masterman would go down one side of a street and up the other, and would find Chesterton at the first house, still arguing 'the philosophy of government' with the first voter he had canvassed. Chesterton later admitted that he had '[begun] electioneering under the extraordinary delusion that the object of canvassing is conversion'. As he explained in the *Autobiography*, '[t]he only real reason for people being pestered in their own houses by party agents is quite unconnected with the principles of the party . . . it is simply that the agents may discover from the words, manner, gesticulations, oaths, curses, kicks or blows of the householder, whether he is likely to vote for the party candidate, or not to vote at all.'[86] Nevertheless, even by his second general election as a canvasser in the Liberal interest, though Chesterton had by now learned the real purpose of going from door to door, he seems not entirely to have lost the ambition of converting uncertain voters; as he put it in his *Illustrated London News* column during the run-up to the 1906 election, though '[t]he canvasser comes rather to reconnoitre the ground than to conquer it' and 'aims rather at knowing the proportion of his friends and enemies for future operations than at immediately and individually endeavouring to alter that proportion'; even so, 'he is hunting for the half-converted man—the man who is worth arguing with. When he sees him, he bursts into tears of joy and pulls out forty-three pamphlets.'[87] We need to remember the mystical weight carried for Chesterton by the word 'democracy'. The electoral process, for him, had a profound religious significance, and canvassing was a kind of ritual enactment of it: as he was to put it in *Orthodoxy*, two years later, 'To say that voting is particularly Christian may seem somewhat curious. To say that canvassing is Christian may seem quite crazy. But canvassing is very Christian in its primary idea. It is encouraging the humble; it is saying to the modest man, "Friend, go up higher." '[88]

The *Illustrated London News* was politically neutral; so, therefore, was Chesterton's pre-election column. His weekly column for *The Daily News* was a different matter. *The Daily News* was a Liberal paper, and he himself had, after all, been in the thick of the battle; as he recorded in his column on 27 January, 'my patriotism obliges me to plunge into and labour in the

---

[86] *Autobiography*, 126.

[87] G. K. Chesterton, 'Canvassing in Elections', *Illustrated London News* (13 Jan. 1906); *Collected Works*, xxvii. 109.

[88] *Collected Works*, i. 325.

political struggle (chiefly by sitting on crowded platforms and grinning) and necessitates that all the random notes I have snatched for this paper during the last fortnight should be, so far as they could be coherent at all, concerned with the national event'.[89] Voting in the 1906 election took place on different dates in different parts of the country, between 12 January and 6 February. Chesterton wrote three articles on the election campaign in January; or rather, he wrote three articles in which the election campaign figured but which, like all his articles, are really about the ideas he felt politics ought to be about rather than the ideas they were actually about. It was not only 'in the desert' that, as he had written to Hammond in 1901, he felt that 'we should all be philosophers': it was also in the midst of 'the political struggle'. As he wrote on 13 January, '[i]t is said that when we are in the thick of a battle it is no time to talk of our general aims and ideas. . . . But this election battle is in its nature a battle to persuade; it may be a rather ramping, raging persuasion, but it is persuasion. And in persuasion we have nothing to do except to try and show that we are right. Our aims and ideals are the only weapons we have to fight with.' The article that follows reads more like an attack on all party politics than anything one might expect from someone still engaged in 'sitting on crowded platforms and grinning' and going from door to door canvassing for votes:

are we really fighting for any persuasive idea? The fight is something less than most of us think it if it is really only a few criticisms of the ineptitudes of a single government. We know all that is to be said about the inefficiencies of Mr Balfour and the inaccuracies of Mr Chamberlain. But suppose that we had sufficient imagination to conceive of an efficient Balfour? Suppose that we were such poets as to have pictured an accurate Chamberlain? Should we not be passionately opposed to both of them? I hope we should; but why should we? Because the politics loosely called Imperialistic for the last fifteen years have really meant something.

By 'Imperialism', Chesterton might be supposed to be thinking particularly about the second Boer War—to which, as we have seen, he had been so bitterly opposed at the time—and its aftermath. Balfour had successfully brought the war to an end in 1902, but not before public opinion had turned against it; there was widespread revulsion at the burning of Boer homesteads and the conditions in the so-called 'concentration camps'; the inhumane use of Chinese labour in the new colony after the war also aroused considerable outrage. All this undoubtedly contributed to the

---

[89] G. K. Chesterton, 'One Last Remark I Wish to Make', *The Daily News* (27 Jan. 1906).

spectacular collapse in electoral support for the Conservative party in 1906. But none of this is what Chesterton, even in the heat of the electoral battle, appears to mean by 'the politics loosely called Imperialistic'. His interest in the topic, even in the midst of an election in which he is heavily involved, is on an altogether more theoretical basis: '[t]he thing that called itself Imperialism', he wrote, 'asked us to be satisfied with the fact that the area of action was great.... But the nature of the thing is that the bigger becomes the Empire the fewer become the Emperors. And our policy is the opposite. The creation of that local intensity in which the space is little, but the People is great.' Whether this was in fact 'our policy' (that is, the policy of the Liberal party) rather than Chesterton's personal political vision may be doubted. Chesterton's theme here has little to do with the real issues of this election, though his piece refers to some of them in passing: the ugly drama of the Boer War and the financial interests involved in bringing it about and 'the pale and hideous procession of Oriental slaves' which had caused such public revulsion. But there is no mention of issues like free trade or the rise the Labour party, both (especially, for obvious reasons, the latter) highlighted in an article by one of the new Labour members, Philip Snowden, in an article on the same page. The underlying theme of Chesterton's piece was one which he had first explored politically two years before, in his defence of patriotism in *England: A Nation*. His theme is still that 'real universality is to be reached . . . by convincing ourselves that we are in the best possible relation with our immediate surroundings'.[90] As the article proceeds, Chesterton describes an increasingly fantastic political scenario; by the end of it, he is evoking something remarkably like the dream-world of *The Napoleon of Notting Hill*:

The idea of the last fifteen years has been Imperialism, that is, the desire to advance outwards. It is our new conception to advance inwards. We must be continually narrowing our circles until we come at last to the secret and centre, the unknown and actual life of a man. The Imperial conception was that when a man had got Battersea, he wanted Chelsea, and then he looked with insatiate eyes upon the purple cliffs of Pimlico. It would be hardly an exaggeration to say that our ideal conception would be even the reverse. We might say that a man who had ruled England was almost worthy to rule in Battersea.

And we might say that when a man had ruled Battersea, he should have another step of advancement; he should be promoted to rule half Battersea, and he would find it a new world. Then he would come to a corner of Battersea which would open

⁹⁰ Chesterton, 'The Patriotic Idea'.

before him like elfland, full of dragons to be slain; and finally, perhaps, he might find himself in the room in which I am sitting, inspired with the insane ideal of making it tidy.[91]

It was hardly the work of a man seized by the party political spirit, for all his canvassing and sitting on party platforms. It was only the following week, when the election was virtually over, that he brought himself to produce anything like party political polemic, with an ironical appreciation of the collapse, in the moment of defeat, of his opponents' pseudo-progressive political rhetoric; and even then, he went out of his way to avoid anything approaching an unpleasant tone. 'The pretence of the last twenty years has all but collapsed', he wrote at the end of January; 'the man who called himself a Tory democrat now defends Toryism on the ground that it is not democracy'. The election result, he perceived, had brought reality back to politics:

In a sense . . . the thing can be put impartially, even pleasantly. For the development means really this: in our relief and exultation we are apt to say that this election is the re-emergence and resurrection of the Liberal Party. But it is something much more than that. It is also the re-emergence and resurrection of the Conservative Party. It has done with its unnatural antics and entirely alien programmes. The Conservative Party comes back as the Conservative Party; it comes back honourable, courageous, consistent, logical. The Conservative Party comes back to conserve.[92]

For the most part, Chesterton never had the animus against his political opponents that a real party man needs, though there were a very few exceptions: he maintained, for instance, a lifelong contempt for Joseph Chamberlain. He positively liked Balfour, whom as we have seen, he had met the previous year and whose conversation he had found 'most interesting'; in the *Autobiography* he described him as 'obviously preferring any philosophers with any philosophies to his loyal followers of the Tory Party'.[93] There seems to have been a natural intellectual sympathy between them: the Bishop of Southwark had told Chesterton shortly after the publication of *Heretics* that Balfour approved of it (partly, perhaps, because in it he had himself been described as 'too gentlemanly to be called merely clever, and just too clever to be called merely a gentleman). Two days after the long drawn-out voting was finally over, Chesterton was rending Joseph

[91] G. K. Chesterton, 'The Root of the Quarrel', *The Daily News* (13 Jan. 1906).
[92] Chesterton, 'One Last Remark I Wish to Make'.
[93] *Autobiography*, 270.

Chamberlain (who had been re-elected) with passionate allegations of political cowardice and lack of integrity, but defending Balfour (who had lost his seat). 'Whatever the merits of the Tory philosophy,' he wrote, 'Mr Balfour has at least done his best for it like a man. And of all the base results of the cowardly philosophy taught for the last fifteen years there has been none baser than the conduct of those men who have turned their tails upon him because he turned his face to the enemy.'[94] As the passions of the election receded into the past, however, the consistent impression conveyed by Chesterton's journalism over the months that followed is of his relief at being able to address once more the issues that really concerned him: the ultimate questions of human existence and, specifically, the defence of the Christian tradition against the vagaries of the passing age. On 3 March he was defending the Middle Ages against the charge of the illiteracy of the faithful; on 10 March he was writing about one modern form of the sin of pride ('We know where the men are who of all men believe most in themselves. They are all in lunatic asylums'[95]); on 14 April, he was writing about the spiritual impoverishment of secular materialism, which 'in its full vision of a featureless fate does not merely teach us that we shall not exist hereafter; it teaches essentially that we do not exist now'.[96] On 28 April, he returned to politics with an article on the bill which had been brought forward by the new government to reform the 1902 Education Act; but the article was in the end inevitably more about religion than politics. The 1902 Act, passionately opposed by Nonconformist opinion, had integrated denominational schools into the state system. This had overwhelmingly benefited the Anglican Church more than any other; Nonconformists complained that it was unfair that they should subsidise Anglican schools through their taxes. The new Liberal government twice attempted to revise the Act, but was frustrated in the Lords. *The Daily News* published a leading article supporting the government's arguments for the proposed legislation; in his own leader-page piece on the same day, however, Chesterton (though in favour of the bill) attacked the government's arguments on theological grounds, grounds which he revealingly identifies as deriving from his own Anglo-Catholic perspective:

Those who most instinctively and generally support the new Education Bill are constantly saying things with which no Catholic or Anglo-Catholic can agree. That is quite natural. But they never say so unmistakeably things with which no Catholic

[94] G. K. Chesterton, 'On Certain Politicians', *The Daily News* (10 Feb. 1906).
[95] G. K. Chesterton, 'On Believing in Oneself', *The Daily News* (19 Mar. 1906).
[96] G. K. Chesterton, 'The God of the Tribe', *The Daily News* (14 Apr. 1906).

can agree as when they think they are saying things with which everybody must agree. . . . As a matter of conscience we cannot have, at any price, those parts of [Augustine Birrell's] speech which he evidently thought were indisputable and obvious. . . . Mr Birrell began his whole speech . . . by the comfortable statement that the question of creed in education had become the main problem of education, but that it was not the most important part of education. The teaching of cleanliness, the teaching of handicrafts were, he said, the real question. This he apparently meant as an amicable introduction, and with this I for one should violently disagree. I think it obvious that creed is by far the most important part of education. I cannot understand the proposition that teaching a child how to wash his hands, or even how to use his hands on chemicals or pottery, can be so important as teaching him what he is or what sort of world he is living in. How can it be more important to teach a child how to avoid disease than how to value life? . . . The reason why the religious problem should be taken out of State education is not because the religious problem is not the most important; it is because the religious problem is too important to be entangled in anything else. It is not because creed and dogma are too small a matter for the State; but because they are too large a matter for the State; because they have survived a hundred States; because heaven and earth shall pass away, but creed and dogma shall not pass away.[97]

It was as succinct—and as passionate—a summary of what Chesterton believed in by this stage in his intellectual development as it would be possible to give. It is, above all, a clear expression of his absolute belief in the primacy of religion over politics. And like Evan MacIan in *The Ball and the Cross*, Chesterton had clearly arrived at a determination that he, at least, would not be silenced as so many other believers had been: as he put it in a *Daily News* piece in June, 'Faith has not faded like a fable; faith is concealed like a sin. Religion is not now the mask; religion is the guilty secret.'[98] It was the new hypocrisy: and he was going to have no part of it.

Charles Dickens and the triumph of 'vulgar optimism'

The twin-path polemical struggle, both to establish that religion was intellectually respectable and to define man 'as an animal that makes dogmas', had been the explicit purpose of *Heretics* as it was also the message of his

[97] G. K. Chesterton, 'Something to Avoid', *The Daily News* (28 Apr. 1906).
[98] G. K. Chesterton, 'The New Hypocrite', *The Daily News* (9 June 1906).

much less convincing fiction *The Ball and the Cross*—of which it is difficult
not to conclude that its serialisation petered out because Chesterton was
already discovering the shortcomings of the novel as a means of engaging
in controversy. As he was to put it in the *Autobiography*, 'among many . . .
abject reasons for not being able to be a novelist, is the fact that I always
have been and presumably always shall be a journalist', a *métier* which was
possible only 'because I could not help being a controversialist'. And he
insisted that 'it was not the superficial or silly or jolly part of me that made
me a journalist. On the contrary, it is such part as I have in what is serious
or even solemn.'[99] By now, however, it was not in his journalism that
Chesterton's real seriousness as a writer was most clearly recognised by his
contemporaries: it was in his literary criticism. By the time the serialisation
of *The Ball and the Cross* had faded away in November 1906, one of
Chesterton's greatest works was being widely acclaimed. *Charles Dickens*
was published by Methuen at the end of August. It had, in fact, been
completed the previous year, but its publication had been delayed after
Dickens's daughter, Kate Perugini, had asked for an alteration to one
paragraph.[100] The work had probably had a long period of gestation; one
of Chesterton's notebooks contains a short essay on *Bleak House*, possibly
in preparation for the relevant chapter in *Charles Dickens*; we can date this
about three years before the book, since two pages later there are four draft
stanzas of the poem 'The Wise Men', published in the *Daily Mail* on
Christmas Day, 1903.[101] *Robert Browning*, too, had not been one of those
works which Chesterton wrote quickly and apparently without effort.
John Morley commissioned it in December 1901; it was not published
until May 1903. Like *Robert Browning*, *Charles Dickens* was an immediate
critical success. *Public Opinion* opined that, though Chesterton's *Robert
Browning* had been one of 'the most stimulating books of its kind written
within recent years', his 'study of Dickens marks the definite entry of its
author into the serious walks of literature'.[102] 'As a critic', judged the *Pall
Mall Gazette*, 'Mr Chesterton has never sparkled better or to more purpose'.[103] James Douglas, in *The Throne*, compared him with Dr Johnson
(this was a comparison that was to become ever more inevitable with the

---

[99] *Autobiography*, 298.
[100] Letter from Frances Chesterton to Algernon Methuen, BL MS Add. 73231, fos. 4^{r-v}.
[101] *Bleak House* essay, BL MS Add. 73353C, fo. 1; *Daily Mail* poem, fos. 3, 4, 5.
[102] Unsigned review, *Public Opinion* (7 Sept. 1906); Conlon, 124–5.
[103] Unsigned review, *Pall Mall Gazette* (30 Aug. 1906); Conlon, 112.

passing of the years).[104] The book was not simply a critical success: it led to a popular revival of interest in Dickens's writings, and to the publication of the Everyman edition of his works from 1907 to 1911, with individual introductions to every novel by Chesterton himself (collected in 1911 in *Appreciations and Criticisms of the Works of Charles Dickens*).

The natural sympathy between Chesterton and his subject was widely noted by the critics; indeed, the anonymous reviewer of *The World* adduced it as evidence of lack of proper critical impartiality. 'By those who are acquainted with the socio-political creed which Mr Chesterton loses no opportunity of expounding, his profound veneration for Dickens the democrat, Dickens the practical optimist, Dickens the persistent asserter of the dignity and blessedness of low estate, will have been taken for granted, long before the appearance of this book. His sympathy with the novelist's attitude, standpoint, and mental idiosyncrasy is, in fact, so intense that it dominates his work to the detriment of its critical balance.'[105]

Most reviewers, however, failed to notice some of the ways in which in *Charles Dickens* Chesterton continued to probe—as he had in *Robert Browning* and in a rather different way in *G. F. Watts*—many of the same underlying social and religious prepossessions as he had explored in the books that had preceded it. This is not to say that *Charles Dickens*, any more than *Robert Browning* had been, was simply a vehicle for Chesterton's own ideas. But Chesterton's emerging philosophy of life made him receptive to certain themes in Dickens's novels that others had not perceived. The central theme of both *Heretics* and *The Ball and the Cross* had been the indifference of the modern world to questions of real belief, and the declared purpose of both books had been the defence of the dogmatic principle. This was not the underlying theme of *Charles Dickens*: but it was an idea that had been at the forefront of Chesterton's mind for the previous three years; and it inevitably had its part to play in directing Chesterton's intellectual focus now. Thus, though it was unavoidable that Chesterton should recognise that Dickens had 'a dislike of defined dogmas', he was concerned to detach him from any taint of cultural or moral relativism: Dickens's dislike of defined dogma simply meant that in keeping with 'all the prejudices of his time', he had a 'preference for *unexamined*

[104] James Douglas, *The Throne* (8 Sept. 1906); Conlon, 127.
[105] Unsigned review, *The World* (1 Sept. 1906); Conlon, 117.

dogmas'.[106] Dickens was himself, on this reading, instinctively dogmatic, though in no inflexible or doctrinaire sense: his was the dogmatism inseparable from that mystic and democratic power, Common Sense: 'perhaps the best evidence of [Dickens's] steadiness and sanity', argues Chesterton, 'is the fact that, dogmatic as he was, he never tied himself to any passing dogma: he never got into any *cul de sac* or civic or economic fanaticism: he went down the broad road of the Revolution.' This last assertion places Dickens in the same tradition as Chesterton himself, as a firmly anti-ideological liberal (Chesterton's hostility to the twentieth century's growing tendency to ideology was later to be an essential element in his developing anti-modernism[107]). Dogma and ideology, indeed, are clearly distinguished at this point: what follows can be seen as an account of Dickens's instinctive dogmatism by means of an extended exposition of his (and Chesterton's) hostility to the way in which ideologies could narrow and even destroy human sympathy:

He never admitted that economically, we must make hells of workhouses, any more than Rousseau would have admitted it. He never said the State had no right to teach children or save their bones, any more than Danton would have said it. He was a fierce Radical; but he was never a Manchester Radical. He used the test of Utility, but he was never a Utilitarian. While economists were writing soft words he wrote Hard Times, which Macaulay called sullen Socialism, because it was not complacent Whiggism. But Dickens was never a Socialist any more than he was an Individualist; and, whatever else he was, he certainly was not sullen. He was not even a politician of any kind. He was simply a man of very clear, airy judgment on things that did not inflame his private temper, and he perceived that any theory that tried to run the living State entirely on one force and motive was probably nonsense. Whenever the Liberal philosophy had embedded in it something hard and heavy and lifeless, by an instinct he dropped it out. He was too romantic, perhaps, but he would have to do only with real things. He may have cared too much about Liberty. But he cared nothing about *Laissez Faire*.[108]

As we have seen, one particular dogmatic belief which had been at the forefront of Chesterton's mind over the previous two years had been the Christian doctrine of original sin. This undoubtedly had its effect on his reading of Dickens. The doctrine's positive consequence, that a man, even imprisoned by poverty or vice, still has the power to transcend his own nature

[106] *Collected Works*, xv. 163.
[107] See John D. Coates, *Chesterton and the Edwardian Cultural Crisis* (Hull, 1984), 24 ff.
[108] *Collected Works*, xv. 113–14.

and circumstances, is expounded in *Charles Dickens* as the 'mystical contradiction' which, Chesterton insisted, 'goes deep into Dickens's social reform': that
'[i]f we are to save the oppressed.... We must think the oppressed man
intensely miserable, and at the same time intensely attractive and important.'
The contradiction must, Chesterton insists, be maintained: 'The optimists will
say that reform is needless. The pessimists will say that reform is hopeless. We
must apply both simultaneously to the same oppressed man; we must say that
he is a worm and a god; and we must thus lay ourselves open to the accusation
(or the compliment) of transcendentalism. This is, indeed, the strongest
argument for the religious conception of life.... If we are idealists about the
other world we can be realists about this world.'[109] The necessary background
to this passage is Chesterton's eighteen-month battle with Blatchford over the
doctrine of original sin, and particularly his final assault against Blatchford's
determinist argument that the 'earthly degradation' of the poor, and particularly the prevalence among the poor of crime and vice, was simply a result of
their environment. This, Chesterton had argued, was to deny 'the eternal
heroism of the slums': 'this association of vice with poverty' was 'the vilest and
the oldest and the dirtiest of all the stones that insolence has ever flung at the
poor'. Chesterton's contention that, even when humanity is in its most
degraded state, there is also a glory in it, is a vital part of his argument for the
doctrine of original sin: 'Man that is born of a woman has but short days and is
full of trouble', Chesterton continues: 'but he is a nobler and a happier being
than this would make him out.... Man has something in him always which is
not conquered by conditions.... There is a liberty that has made men happy in
dungeons, as it may make them happy in slums. It is the liberty of the mind,
that is to say, it is the one liberty on which Mr Blatchford has made war.'[110]
This perception, Chesterton saw, was fundamental to Dickens's view of
human society:

The pessimistic reformer points out the good elements that oppression has
destroyed; the optimistic reformer, with an even fiercer joy, points out the good
elements that it has not destroyed.... The first describes how bad men are under
bad conditions. The second describes how good men are under bad conditions. Of
the first class of writers, for instance, is Gorky. Of the second class of writers is
Dickens.[111]

[109] Ibid. 193–4.
[110] G. K. Chesterton, 'Mr Blatchford's Religion', *The Clarion* (5 Aug. 1904); *Collected Works*,
i. 393–4.
[111] *Collected Works*, xv. 194–5.

The sympathy between Chesterton and Dickens, it is important to establish at this point, is thus of a broader and more comprehensive kind than can be conveyed by simply pointing to their common predilections or political instincts. Just as, even in his earliest criticism, Chesterton had manifested his inclination to write about both an author and his subject, so now he manifested the same impulse in his approach to Dickens, a writer whose subject is nothing less than humanity itself. The subject of *Charles Dickens* is human life as both Dickens and Chesterton perceived it: and humanity—and Dickens himself—are seen through the eyes of Chesterton, inevitably, by this stage of his imaginative journey, *sub specie aeternitatis*. It is worth returning once more here (not for the last time) to that pivotal declaration from the end of 1903: 'You cannot evade the issue of God.... Things can be irrelevant to the proposition that Christianity is false, but nothing can be irrelevant to the proposition that Christianity is true.'[112] Whatever else he wrote about, that was now the determining perspective, even when it was firmly excluded from the openly examined presuppositions of Chesterton's writing. It is worth noting that it was not excluded from *Charles Dickens*: 'The issue of God', indeed, is raised in the book's very first paragraph together with a by now characteristic assertion of the mystical force of the concrete and the commonplace:

Much of our modern difficulty, in religion and other things, arises merely from this: that we confuse the word 'indefinable' with the word 'vague.' If some one speaks of a spiritual fact as 'indefinable' we promptly picture something misty, a cloud with indeterminate edges. But this is an error even in commonplace logic. The thing that cannot be defined is the first thing; the primary fact. It is our arms and legs, our pots and pans, that are indefinable. The indefinable is the indisputable. The man next door is indefinable, because he is too actual to be defined. And there are some to whom spiritual things have the same fierce and practical proximity; some to whom God is too actual to be defined.[113]

This is one of the few occasions on which the word 'God' occurs in the text bearing a theological rather than a merely rhetorical sense; but it is, nevertheless, one of the keys to *Charles Dickens*, if for no other reason than that it has become one of the keys to the book's author. One imaginative result—or, at least, accompaniment—of this development (a matter, as we have said, of perceiving humanity *sub specie aeternitatis*) was Chesterton's impulse to make critical comparisons transcending time and culture. Thus,

---

[112] Chesterton, 'A Universal Relevance', *The Daily News* (12 Dec. 1903).
[113] *Collected Works*, xv. 39.

in making the judgement that uniquely among his contemporaries 'Dickens will dominate the whole England of the nineteenth century', he does so by a daring literary parallel: just as 'wise and scholarly men', he argues, 'do from time to time return to the lyrists of [the] French Renascence, to the delicate poignancy of Du Bellay: so they will go back to Thackeray. But I mean that Dickens will bestride and dominate our time as the vast figure of Rabelais dominates Du Bellay, dominates the Renascence and the world.' This comparison should remind us, perhaps, of the way in which Professor W. P. Ker,[114] whose influence Chesterton was to recall in the *Autobiography*,[115] 'could'—according to another of his former students—'illuminate one author by reference to another, and often one of a different period and country'; it should remind us, indeed, of the way in which Ker had himself, in a lecture we have already quoted at length, compared Rabelais with Cervantes and Shakespeare, pointing out that they had 'the enormous and unfair advantage over other writers that . . . they had the whole abandoned region of medieval thought and imagination to take over and appropriate'.[116] That was, indeed, precisely what Chesterton himself, with great imaginative daring, now did in *Charles Dickens*: not only did he colonise that 'abandoned region of medieval thought and imagination'; he repopulated it by introducing into it Dickens and his whole created world. It was upon Dickens, claimed Chesterton, and 'not upon the pallid mediaevalists who thought they were reviving it', that 'the real tradition of "Merry England"' had descended:

The Pre-Raphaelites, the Gothicists, the admirers of the Middle Ages, had in their subtlety and sadness the spirit of the present day. Dickens had in his buffoonery and bravery the spirit of the Middle Ages. He was much more mediaeval in his attacks on mediaevalism than they were in their defences of it. It was he who had the things of Chaucer, the love of large jokes and long stories and brown ale and all the white roads of England. Like Chaucer he loved story within story, every man telling a tale. Like Chaucer he saw something openly comic in men's motley trades. Sam Weller would have been a great gain to the Canterbury Pilgrimage and told an admirable story. . . .

In fighting for Christmas he was fighting for the old European festival, Pagan and Christian, for that trinity of eating, drinking and praying which to moderns appears irreverent, for the holy day which is really a holiday. . . . He cared as little for mediaevalism as the mediaevals did. He cared as much as they did for lustiness

---

[114] See pp. 92–4 above.   [115] *Autobiography*, 97.
[116] B. Ifor Evans, *W. P. Ker as a Critic of Literature* (Glasgow, 1955). 12–13.

and virile laughter and sad tales of good lovers and pleasant tales of good livers. He would have been very much bored by Ruskin and Walter Pater if they had explained to him the strange sunset tints of Lippi and Botticelli. He had no pleasure in looking on the dying Middle Ages. But he looked on the living Middle Ages, on a piece of the old uproarious superstition still unbroken; and he hailed it like a new religion. The Dickens character ate pudding to an extent at which the modern mediaevalists turned pale. They would do every kind of honour to an old observance, except observing it. They would pay to a Church feast every sort of compliment except feasting.[117]

This is reminiscent of his *Daily News* article in defence of Christmas over two years before;[118] then, it will be recalled, he had been arguing not that a festive Christmas was essentially Christian but that a Christian Christmas was essentially festive: '[i]t seems strange', he had argued, 'that a dogma of mystics should be the only thing which will make grown-up people play Blind Man's buff. But so it is. Take away the Nicene Creed . . . and you do some strange wrong to the sellers of sausages.'[119]

Ian Ker, in the only indispensable critical analysis of *Charles Dickens*, identifies one of Chesterton's entry points to the Middle Ages as the grotesque, particularly in the form of the gargoyle.[120] Gargoyles were, in fact, a frequently used Chestertonian emblem for Christian exhilaration and generosity, usually proposed in contrast with secularist or pagan meanness of spirit. We have already seen how, in his controversy with Blatchford, Chesterton had contrasted the exuberance of Christendom with 'the sad-minded Stoics of old Rome', holding that '[t]his difference holds good everywhere, in the cold Pagan architecture and the grinning gargoyles of Christendom, in the preposterous motley of the Middle Ages and the dingy dress of this Rationalistic century'.[121] In *Heretics*, he claims that the Salvation Army, 'though their voice has broken out in a mean environment and an ugly shape, are really the old voice of glad and angry faith, hot as the riots of Dionysus, wild as the gargoyles of Catholicism'.[122] In *The Napoleon of Notting Hill*, he puts into the mouth of Adam Wayne the insight that '[l]aughter and love are everywhere. The cathedrals, built in the ages that

---

[117] *Collected Works*, xv. 131–2.   [118] See p. 255 above.

[119] G. K. Chesterton, 'The Feast of Christmas Day', *The Daily News* (26 Dec. 1903).

[120] Ian Ker, *The Catholic Revival in English Literature, 1845–1961* (Notre Dame, Ind., 2003), 87.

[121] G. K. Chesterton, 'Christianity and Rationalism', *The Clarion* (22 July 1904); *Collected Works*, i. 374.

[122] *Collected Works*, i. 85.

loved God, are full of blasphemous grotesques.'[123] We have quoted Arthur Clayborough's judgement that '[t]he chief point of interest in Chesterton's remarks on the grotesque is the idea that the grotesque may be employed as a means of presenting the world in a new light without falsifying it':[124] so it is that Chesterton can claim that Dickens uses the grotesque as a means of establishing not only the vividness but the truthfulness of his characters: '[w]hen a Dickens character becomes excited,' he asserts, 'he becomes more and more himself. . . . As he rises he grows more and more into a gargoyle or grotesque.'[125] In *Dombey and Son*, 'Major Bagstock is a grotesque, and yet he contains touch after touch of Dickens's quiet and sane observation of things as they are.' It is 'a deadly error', Chesterton continues, ' . . . to suppose that lies are told with excess and luxuriance, and truths told with modesty and restraint. . . . Many official declarations are just as dignified as Mr. Dombey, because they are just as fictitious. On the other hand, the man who has found a truth dances about like a boy who has found a shilling; he breaks into extravagances, as the Christian Churches broke into gargoyles.'[126] Chesterton's idea of the Middle Ages is not of a remote and inaccessible historical period, but of a kind of parallel dimension, into which imaginative forays can be made at any time, an accessible universe in which truthfulness and humanity perpetually and exuberantly flourish.

Chesterton's linking of Dickens with the 'lustiness and virile laughter' of the Middle Ages reminds us once more of his defence (in the Blatchford campaign) against the accusation that when writing about religion he was 'flippant or imperfectly sincere': it was that 'people so far removed from the Christian atmosphere' would naturally fail to see that 'Christianity is itself so jolly a thing that it fills the possessor of it with a certain silly exuberance, which sad and high-minded rationalists might reasonably mistake for mere buffoonery and blasphemy'.[127] Dickens was, of course, as Chesterton recognised, hostile to the Middle Ages in the same way as most Victorians, lacking as he did both self-knowledge and understanding of the past: '[h]e supposed the Middle Ages to have consisted of tournaments and torture-chambers, he supposed himself to be a brisk man of the manufacturing age, almost a Utilitarian. But for all that he defended the mediaeval feast which was

---

[123] *The Napoleon of Notting Hill*, p. xx.

[124] Arthur Clayborough, *The Grotesque in English Literature* (London, 1965), 60.

[125] *Collected Works*, xv. 180–1.

[126] Ibid. 144–5.

[127] Chesterton, 'Christianity and Rationalism'; *Collected Works*, i. 374.

going out against the Utilitarianism which was coming in. He could only see all that was bad in mediaevalism. But he fought for all that was good in it.'[128] It was Chesterton's ability to make the imaginative leap of placing Dickens in the world of Chaucer that allowed him to see—in a way that Dickens himself could never have seen—that Dickens's anti-Catholicism was a superficial and second-hand bias, one existing at the level of the cheap slogan and the unexamined prejudice. And Chesterton perceived this, partly because he perceived also, as he put it in a later chapter, that 'Dickens's "confidence in the value of existence and the intrinsic victory of virtue" . . . is not optimism but religion':[129] not, perhaps a religion that existed for Dickens at any ecclesial or openly dogmatic level, but (as with Chesterton's understanding of Browning's religious instinct) at the level it had existed for Chesterton himself between 1894 and the turn of the century (Dickens, indeed, had considerable sympathy, as Chesterton had then, with Unitarianism, partly under the influence of his friends John Forster and W. J. Fox; Fox summed up his own creed as 'Belief in the supremacy of God the Father and in the humanity and divine mission of Jesus of Nazareth';[130] that probably conveyed Dickens's own conscious religious beliefs well enough).

Chesterton sensed that Dickens as an *homme moyen sensuel* understood much less than as a genius he discerned; and he saw the gulf between the two levels of perception as a kind of tragedy. Dickens's weaknesses, he seems to have concluded, particularly his tendency to sentimentality, were due to a failure consistently to see life in the context of eternity. This perspective suggested to Chesterton not only how great Dickens was, but how much greater he might have been. It is at this point that we can see most clearly, perhaps, Chesterton's own greatness as a critic, particularly evident in his analysis of Dickens's characters: his treatment of Mr Micawber exhibits—in a way which celebrates Dickens's genius even as it points to his imperfections—not only Dickens's lack of perception at the level of conscious art but at the same time his infinitely more important penetration of the *comédie humaine* at the almost sublime level of which he was himself, almost tragically, consciously unaware:

The whole meaning of the character of Mr. Micawber is that a man can be always almost rich by constantly expecting riches. The lesson is a really important one in

---

[128] *Collected Works*, xv. 131–2.   [129] Ibid. 190.

[130] Thomas Wright, *Life of Charles Dickens* (London, 1935), 155. See also Edgar Johnson, *Charles Dickens: His Triumph and Tragedy* (New York, 1952), i. 464.

our sweeping modern sociology. We talk of the man whose life is a failure; but Micawber's life never is a failure, because it is always a crisis. We think constantly of the man who if he looked back would see that his existence was unsuccessful; but Micawber never does look back; he always looks forward, because the bailiff is coming to-morrow. You cannot say he is defeated, for his absurd battle never ends; he cannot despair of life, for he is so much occupied in living. All this is of immense importance in the understanding of the poor; it is worth all the slum novelists that ever insulted democracy. But how did it happen that the man who created this Micawber could pension him off at the end of the story and make him a successful colonial mayor? Micawber never did succeed, never ought to succeed; *his kingdom is not of this world.* (my emphasis)[131]

This is to be placed with Chesterton's defence—significantly directed against 'one of the plays of the decadent period'—of Dickens's 'vulgar optimism' on the ground that '[i]n a world in which physical distress is almost the common lot', it is extraordinary to complain 'that happiness is too common.... [w]hen we consider what the conditions of the vulgar really are, it is difficult to imagine a stranger or more splendid tribute to humanity than such a phrase as vulgar optimism.'[132] The reference here to 'the decadent period' is important, and not merely as one of the almost obsessive references—many of which we have noted—throughout Chesterton's first decade as a published writer, to the hopelessness he associated with 'the green carnation', a hopelessness he had not only perceived in the literary and artistic culture of the *fin de siècle*, but which had also at times almost engulfed him personally. But now, all that was in the past; there were in Chesterton's life now deep and abiding sources of hope; and for the rest of his life he celebrated their manifestations wherever they were to be found in life or art or history. Dickens embodied for him the optimism of early Victorian England, an optimism which he celebrated pointedly for its contrast with what he perceived as the languor and hopelessness of 'the age of Dorian'. The early Victorian period 'was full of evil things, but it was full of hope.... the *fin de siècle*, was even full (in some sense) of good things. But it was occupied in asking what was the good of good things. Joy itself became joyless; and the fighting of Cobbett was happier than the feasting of Walter Pater.'[133] Yet again, we need to register the almost visceral revulsion Chesterton still felt for the *fin de siècle*: in certain of his characters, he notes, 'Dickens does, in the exact sense, make the flesh creep; he does not, like the

---

[131] *Collected Works*, xv. 192.   [132] Ibid. 190.   [133] Ibid. 41–2.

decadents, make the soul crawl.'[134] Just as Browning, Whitman, and Stevenson had done, Dickens takes his place for Chesterton in a cultural pantheon whose members had not only held the decadents at bay (in the case of Dickens and Stevenson, before the event) but had also shown the way back to the sanity which more and more Chesterton fears that his own age has lost:

The hour of absinthe is over. We shall not be much further troubled with the little artists who found Dickens too sane for their sorrows and too clean for their delights. But we have a long way to travel before we get back to what Dickens meant: and the passage is along a rambling English road, a twisting road such as Mr. Pickwick travelled. But this at least is part of what he meant; that comradeship and serious joy are not interludes in our travel; but that rather our travels are interludes in comradeship and joy, which through God shall endure for ever. The inn does not point to the road; the road points to the inn. And all roads point at last to an ultimate inn, where we shall meet Dickens and all his characters: and when we drink again it shall be from the great flagons in the tavern at the end of the world.

Chesterton's focus on Dickens's early novels has been seen by some later critics as one of the book's failings, Chesterton exemplifying for them a school of criticism which was allegedly too much impressed by 'the image of a Pickwickian Dickens' and which 'looked into the later novels for saving remnants of Dickensian "character" and of what Chesterton called "the great gusto"'—the alternative being the school of criticism 'for whom Edmund Wilson may stand as the type' who 'looked into the earlier novels for foreshadowings of the "darker" Dickens and of the elaborate symbolic techniques of the later, greater, novels'.[135] Edmund Wilson himself wrote that Chesterton's analysis was 'always melting away into that peculiar pseudo-poetic booziness which verbalises with large conceptions and ignores the most obtrusive actualities; Chesterton celebrated the jolly Dickens.'[136] Wilson's view that Dickens was essentially a darker figure than Chesterton was prepared to contemplate is based in part on the psychological importance he attached to the crucial formative trauma of Dickens's childhood, his father's financial collapse and his own consequent employment in a blacking factory in the East End (in a sense, the Dickensian

[134] *Collected Works*, xv. 208–9.

[135] Lauriat Lane, Jr., 'Dickens and Criticism', in *The Dickens Critics* (Ithaca, NY, 1961), 4.

[136] Edmund Wilson, 'Dickens: The Two Scrooges', in *The Wound and the Bow* (London, 1941), 2.

equivalent of Chesterton's time at the Slade).[137] But Chesterton, too, at even greater length than Wilson, described this trauma, and drew conclusions (which, anti-Freudian that he was, were very different) about its importance for Dickens as a creative writer. 'Dickens worked [at the blacking factory] drearily,' Chesterton wrote, 'like one stunned with disappointment.... To a child excessively intellectualised... the coarseness of the whole thing—the work, the rooms, the boys, the language—was a sort of bestial nightmare.... He never spoke of the whole experience except once or twice, and he never spoke of it otherwise than as a man might speak of hell.' Chesterton commented that 'It need not be suggested... that this agony in the child was exaggerated by the man.' Chesterton goes on to discuss the 'desolate finality of Dickens's childhood mood' at some length, and concludes that 'I think we can imagine a pretty genuine case of internal depression. And when we add to the case of internal depression the case of the external oppression, the case of the material circumstances by which he was surrounded, we have reached a sort of midnight.... About any early disaster there is a dreadful finality; a lost child can suffer like a lost soul.'[138] Whatever we may think of Edmund Wilson's supposedly seminal essay on Dickens, his loftily dismissive judgement of Chesterton's *Charles Dickens*, we may reasonably judge, is worthless. It may, of course be that what Wilson—like other later critics—cannot forgive Chesterton is the moral he draws from the end result of Dickens's desperate childhood: that '[i]f his school of thought was a vulgar optimism, this is where he went to school. If he learnt to whitewash the universe, it was in a blacking factory that he learnt it.' Chesterton's conclusion reminds one of his memorable phrase 'the eternal heroism of the slums' in his final attack on Blatchford:

As a fact, there is no shred of evidence to show that those who have had sad experiences tend to have a sad philosophy. There are numberless points upon which Dickens is spiritually at one with the poor, that is, with the great mass of mankind. But there is no point in which he is more perfectly at one with them than in showing that there is no kind of connection between a man being unhappy and a man being pessimistic.[139]

The resolution of the probably false opposition between critics who see an optimistic 'Pickwickian' Dickens, and those who perceive him as a 'dark' and essentially pessimistic writer, lies beyond the scope of the present work; but it may be observed in passing that given both Chesterton's personal

[137] Ibid. 4–7.   [138] *Collected Works*, xv. 56–7.   [139] Ibid. 60–1.

philosophy and his love of his subject, a Schopenhauerian Dickens was never likely to emerge from the pages of any book written by him. It may also be noted that the critical reputation of Chesterton's *Charles Dickens* stands high among Dickens critics a century after it first appeared; like T. S. Eliot (who had written on Chesterton's death that it was the 'best essay on that author that has ever been written'[140]). Peter Ackroyd recently concluded that Chesterton was 'perhaps Dickens's best critic';[141] there, perhaps, the matter may be left.

[140] T. S. Eliot, signed obituary, *The Tablet* (20 June 1936), 785; Conlon, 531.
[141] Peter Ackroyd, *Dickens* (London, 2002), 154.

8

Battles in the Last Crusade, 1907–8: *The Man who was Thursday* and *Orthodoxy*

With *Orthodoxy*, Chesterton saw himself as having reached, as he had with his campaign against Blatchford, 'a landmark in my life'[1]—a milestone at which he needed once more to take stock of his life and beliefs: the book was, he declared, 'a sort of slovenly autobiography'.[2] The same mood of self-assessment and remembrance is reflected in other writings of the same period. In the dedicatory verses of *The Man who was Thursday* (the writing of which overlapped that of *Orthodoxy*) he meditatively addressed his friend Bentley, almost in the tones of an old man looking back over a long life—though he was only 33 when he wrote these lines:

> Between us, by the peace of God, such truth can now be told;
> Yea, there is strength in striking root and good in growing old.
> We have found common things at last and marriage and a creed,
> And I may safely write it now, and you may safely read.

In the preface to *Orthodoxy*, he invites comparison with John Henry Newman in one respect at least (though as we shall see, there are other parallels): he had, he claims, 'been driven back upon somewhat the same difficulty as that which beset Newman in writing his *Apologia*; he has been forced to be egotistical only in order to be sincere'. It was his purpose, Chesterton declared, 'to attempt an explanation, not of whether the Christian Faith can be believed, but of how he personally has come to believe it'.[3] There is, of course, a

---

[1] *Autobiography*, 181.   [2] *Collected Works*, i. 215.
[3] G. K. Chesterton, *Orthodoxy* (London, 1908), p. i. (The Ignatius Press *Collected Works* unaccountably omits Chesterton's preface.)

transparent agenda here: we are invited to identify with Chesterton in his own discovery of Christianity, and the book is an explanation of how we too, even in the midst of an aggressively secularist culture, and with the habits of mind which such a culture has inevitably formed, can come to believe it. But the autobiographical mode is no mere literary or apologetic device but the expression of a deep-rooted instinct; and in this appeal to his own experience and perceptions, *Orthodoxy* is typical of all his writings, and particularly of his journalism, which depends heavily on Chesterton's self-projection as a protagonist, a *dramatis persona* (partly artificially constructed, mostly entirely genuine) who, swordstick in hand, goes into battle in the various ideological, political, and theological skirmishes which he enacts for his audience.

The idiom of autobiography, of explicit and sequentially described remembrance, was particularly, it seems, an irresistible one at certain key points in his life. The famous opening sentences of his *Autobiography* ('I am firmly of opinion that I was born on the 29th of May, 1874, on Campden Hill, Kensington; and baptised according to the formularies of the Church of England in the little church of St. George opposite the large Waterworks Tower that dominated that ridge. I do not allege any significance in the relation of the two buildings; and I indignantly deny that the church was chosen because it needed the whole water-power of West London to turn me into a Christian'[4]) was reworked from a long autobiographical letter he had written to Frances, probably around the time of their engagement, four decades earlier. The letter's last two sentences read: 'Here ends my previous existence. Take it: it led me to you'; it begins

Gilbert Keith Chesterton was born of comfortable but honest parents on the top of Campden Hill, Kensington. He was christened at St. George's Church which stands just under that more imposing building, the Waterworks Tower. This place was chosen, apparently, in order that the whole available water supply might be used in the intrepid attempt to make him a member of Christ, a child of God and an inheritor of the Kingdom of Heaven.[5]

His marriage, too, prompted memories of childhood, and a kind of ritual farewell to his 'previous existence'. After the ceremony, he stopped to drink a glass of milk in one shop and to buy a revolver with cartridges in another. His explanation was that the pistol represented 'the great adventure of my youth, with a general notion of protecting her from the pirates doubtless infesting the Norfolk Broads, to which we were bound'. The pistol was a

---

[4] *Autobiography*, 5.   [5] Ward, 90–4.

stage property in a kind of ceremonial reminiscence of boyhood yarns (above all, perhaps, those by Stevenson); the glass of milk was a more distant but no less powerful memory of early childhood. He stopped at that particular dairy because he had always drunk a glass of milk there when walking with his mother; and it seemed to him 'a fitting ceremonial to unite the two great relations of a man's life'. 'Outside the shop', he remembered, 'there was the figure of a White Cow as a sort of pendant to the figure of the White Horse; the one standing at the beginning of my new journey and the other at the end. But the point is here that the very fact of these allegories having been acted over again, at the stage of marriage and maturity, does in a sense transform them.'[6]

This recurrent instinct for the remembrance and consequent transformation of things past can be seen powerfully to reassert itself during the years 1907 and 1908 in a number of Chesterton's writings. This period was marked by the final merging, into a new and powerfully flowing mainstream, of two intellectual currents, one personal and introspective, the other springing from his journalist's response to external events and controversies. He found himself taking stock of his own life; at the same time, his understanding of what it was to defend the Christian tradition in the modern world moved into a new phase against the background of current theological disputes. The fruits of these ruminations were two very remarkable and, at first sight, wholly incongruent books, which appeared the following year: *The Man who was Thursday* (published in February 1908) and *Orthodoxy* (published six months later in September).

I have already considered, in some detail, two documents from 1907 which might be described as accounts of emotion recollected, less in tranquillity than with a vivid remembrance of past anxieties: the *Daily News* article 'The Diabolist' (published in November)[7] and the dedicatory verses to *The Man who was Thursday* (the Bentley dedication),[8] which since the novel was published in February 1908 were probably written some time before 'The Diabolist': perhaps they even triggered it off. Both texts recall his confused and often depressed time at the Slade School of Art and also his sudden emergence, at the end of his year there, from the time when for him 'huge devils hid the stars, yet fell at a pistol flash';[9] and though I have quoted from them extensively

[6] *Autobiography*, 33.
[7] G. K. Chesterton, 'The Diabolist', *The Daily News* (9 Nov. 1907). See pp. 118–21 above.
[8] See pp. 113–14 above.
[9] G. K. Chesterton, *The Man who was Thursday* (London: Penguin, 1986), 5–7.

in the context of the period to which they directly refer, it is worth returning
to these two interesting texts in the personal and historical context in which
they were written. At both of these turning points—the summer of 1894,
when we can assume the confrontation with 'the diabolist' took place, and
1907, when Chesterton recalled and vividly described this experience—he was
going through a phase both of energetic engagement with what had come
before and of forward movement towards what lay ahead. Both 'The Diabolist' and the Bentley dedication vividly evoke the *fin de siècle*: but they are
illuminating also about the period of their composition, two years after the
publication of *Heretics* (June 1905) and some months before (perhaps even
partly concurrent with) the writing of *Orthodoxy*. Both in 1894 and in 1907,
Chesterton's understanding of 'heresy' and 'orthodoxy' is central. Though
both texts look back to what Chesterton recalled in 1907 as a time of confusion
and danger followed by one of new clarity and tranquil release, they clearly
relate also to present conflicts, less introspectively personal in character,
conflicts exemplified for Chesterton particularly (as we shall see) by
R. J. Campbell's *The New Theology* (1907)—which he attacked in a speech
given in July, a report of which appeared in Scott Holland's *Commonwealth* the
following month—and by the response to Campbell of one of Chesterton's
theological mentors, Charles Gore, in *The New Theology and the Old Religion*
(published at the end of the same year). For Chesterton, the terms 'orthodoxy'
and 'heresy' had, by this date, obviously enough, taken on a weight and
intellectual content hardly conceivable in the summer of 1894. It is, all the
same, interesting that over a decade later he was to remember the intellectual
and cultural warfare for which even then, an undergraduate in his final year, he
was beginning to prepare himself, as having been drawn up along battle-lines
identically defined. 'The diabolist', he remembered, had '... asked me abruptly why I was becoming orthodox.... "I am becoming orthodox," I said,
"because I have come, rightly or wrongly, after stretching my brain till it
bursts, to the old belief that heresy is worse even than sin." '[10]

The Man who was Thursday

The question is what Chesterton can have meant in 1894 by 'heresy', and
what relation that bore to his understanding of the same word in 1907. Part
of the answer seems clear, and has to do, as we have seen, with the powerful

[10] 'The Diabolist', *The Daily News* (9 Nov. 1907).

effect on him of the intellectual atmosphere prevailing at the Slade School of Art at the time he was a student there, an atmosphere which was, for him, part of an accumulation of unhappy memories which could come back, as he expressed it in a disquisition on memory in the *Autobiography*, 'sharply and suddenly, piercing the protection of oblivion'.[11] We have more than once had occasion to refer to the passage in the *Autobiography* in which Chesterton identified Impressionism as one of the philosophies which had contributed to the mood of 'unreality and sterile isolation that settled at this time upon [him]'.[12] He added that he thought the same mood had also settled 'upon many others'. The 'unreality' of Impressionism, its alleged capacity to distort or diminish a sane perception of things, returned to Chesterton's mind more than once during 1907. 'A blind and deaf man would only know that a ship was moving by the fact that he was seasick,' he wrote in a *Daily News* article published in January. 'This is the thing called "impressionism" ... Impressionism means shutting up all of one's nine million organs and avenues of appreciation except one. Impressionism means that, whereas Nature has made our senses and impressions support each other, we desire to suppress one part of perception and employ the other.' His remarks were prompted, significantly, by an exhibition of medieval illuminations in the George Rylands Museum in Manchester: in contrast to ' "impressionism," that typically modern thing', he insisted, '[i]f these old artists draw a ship, everything is sacrificed to express the "shipish-ness" of the ship. If they draw a tower, its whole object is to be towering.'[13] I have suggested that his understanding of Impressionism was influenced by the way in which it was understood and propagated by his teachers at the Slade, probably (certainly in the case of the principal, Fred Brown) under the influence of George Moore,[14] who it will be remembered praised Whistler (for Chesterton the most representative Impressionist) because he had, in Moore's words, 'helped to purge art of the vice of subject and [of] the belief that the mission of the artist is to copy nature';[15] of the belief, that is to say, precisely that if they draw a ship their mission ought to be 'to express the "shipishness" of the ship'. This entirely explains Chesterton's conviction (sometimes puzzling today) that 'Impressionism naturally lends itself to the metaphysical suggestion that things only exist as we perceive

---

[11] *Autobiography*, 31.   [12] Ibid. 89.

[13] G. K. Chesterton, 'The Grave-digger', *The Daily News* (26 Jan. 1907).

[14] John D. Coates, *Chesterton and the Edwardian Cultural Crisis* (Hull, 1984), 196 ff.

[15] George Moore, *Modern Painting* (London, 1893), 23–4.

them, *or that things do not exist at all*' (my italics).[16] The subtitle of *The Man who was Thursday* is 'A Nightmare'; according to its dedicatory verses, it is 'a tale of . . . old fears': one of these 'old fears', certainly, was that 'things do not exist'—a remembered dread which contributes much to the novel's nightmarish atmosphere, and one which, significantly, Chesterton makes a point of identifying, in the course of the narrative, in the precisely defined intellectual context of his personal understanding of Impressionism. The passage in question vividly evokes the 'mood of unreality'—intensely visually perceived—of this art student of the early 1890s:

Was anyone anything? This wood of witchery, in which men's faces turned black and white by turns, in which their figures first swelled into sunlight and then faded into formless night, this mere chaos of chiaroscuro (after the clear daylight outside), seemed to Syme a perfect symbol of the world in which he had been moving. . . .

   Was not everything, after all, like this bewildering woodland, this dance of dark and light? Everything only a glimpse, the glimpse always unforeseen, and always forgotten. For Gabriel Syme had found in the heart of that sun-splashed wood what many modern painters had found there. He had found the thing which the modern people call Impressionism, which is another name for that final scepticism which can find no floor to the universe.[17]

In one important sense, we can see *The Man who was Thursday* as enacting the struggle of its principal protagonist, Gabriel Syme, to escape from this nightmare of the early 1890s, a nightmare which in its new context in Edwardian secularist culture has come to incorporate new threats to Chesterton's vision of sanity. Syme represents Chesterton: but Chesterton the mature Christian apologist, as much as Chesterton the youthful near-agnostic verging on astonished theism. In one sense, that is to say, we need to see *Heretics* and *Orthodoxy* as being among the essential keys to *The Man who was Thursday*. Cecil Chesterton, indeed, in his book on his brother (published in 1908, just before the publication of *Orthodoxy*), claimed that 'none of his excursions into theological controversy throw so clear a light on his fundamental religious beliefs as the "Nightmare" of *The Man who was Thursday*'.[18] The key-word 'anarchy' in *Thursday*, it is clear, is close to being synonymous with 'heresy'. Early in the novel, Syme complains that 'the modern world has retained all those parts of police work which are really oppressive and ignominious' but that it has given up 'the punishment

[16] *Autobiography*, 88–9.   [17] *Thursday*, 126–7.   [18] Cecil, 178–9.

of . . . powerful heresiarchs'. Syme continues: 'The moderns say we must not punish heretics. My only doubt is whether we have a right to punish anybody else.' As a result of this avowal, he is recruited by Scotland Yard to fight what is called 'anarchy', a term which clearly has a much wider philosophical remit than the low-key political terrorism of the period, and includes not only Impressionism (as we have seen) but also another facet of what was for Chesterton part of the same essentially un-English intellectual culture, Wildean aestheticism ('the green carnation' as he calls it in the book's dedicatory verses). In a newspaper interview given over a decade later on the occasion of *Thursday*'s being produced as a play,[19] Chesterton inaccurately but revealingly described Gregory, 'the real anarchist', as 'a decadent artist' (in *Thursday* he is actually a poet); and he interestingly dated the writing of the novel, not at the end of the previous decade, but in the early 1890s, that is, the period in which the story appears to be set. The decadent artist, he continued, 'was very much with us *at the time I wrote the book*. It was a poisonous period, when all the ordinary ways of living were regarded as silly, and young men who spent most of their time in drinking strange liquors and imagining stranger sins—impeached God for not having made a universe to suit them' (my italics). Chesterton's apparent slip in claiming that he had written *Thursday* in the early 1890s was not entirely a misremembering of the past. There survive writings from that period which can be seen as first attempts at themes which come to their fruition in the novel. In one fragment, for instance, probably dating from 1894, a poet called Gabriel Hope is represented as writing a story entitled 'a prophetic policeman', in which among other philosophical gems the policeman in question pronounces that 'It has long been my belief that the greatest theoretic mistakes have arisen from supposing that the six days of Creation were over', that 'when Eden is built' will come 'the . . . most overpowering thought ever thought by man. . . . The rest of God', and that policemen are 'the chivalry of law, the knight errantry of London, the heralds of the perfect peace': all fairly obvious prefigurings of the knight-errant policeman Gabriel Syme, of the six days represented by the anarchist council, and of the 'overpowering thought' which is Sunday's identification of himself as 'The Peace of God'. We have already referred to a story (published in 1896) called 'A Picture of Tuesday', which contains a description of 'a huge

---

[19] Interview in the *Illustrated Sunday Herald*, reprinted in *G. K. Chesterton Quarterly*, 5 (Winter 1997), 5–6.

human figure' which like Sunday on more than one occasion is seen 'with its back to the spectator',[20] and to an entry in what Maisie Ward called The Notebook—from about the same period—referring to Sunday (the day) as 'the most tremendous thought ever thought by Man . . . the rest of God'.[21]

These seminal ideas continued to germinate. In a letter to Frances, probably dating from around 1898, he refers to 'The Novel—which though I have put it aside for the present—yet it has become too much a part of me not to be constantly having chapters written—or rather growing out of the others'.[22] This may be a reference to an early version of *Thursday* (though it may conceivably be a reference to early versions of *The Napoleon of Notting Hill*, on which there is surviving manuscript evidence of work between 1897 and 1902[23]). Whatever the accuracy of such speculations, it is clear that the period of gestation of *The Man who was Thursday* began in what we might call Chesterton's post-diabolist but pre-Christian phase, the period of joyful discovery in which he was writing (in The Notebook) such astonished utterances as 'Have you taken in the conception | Of the tremendous Everything which is anywhere?'[24] It was a period of transition: he had emerged from the 'poisonous period' through which he had been living; and he was finding his way towards an understanding of what that 'tremendous Everything' might be. For the Chesterton of 1907, the values of Christendom had become the clear and natural resolution of the intellectual discordances and confusions of the *fin de siècle*: after his enrolment into Scotland Yard's special counter-anarchist corps, Syme is given a small blue card on which is written 'The Last Crusade'. Not the least of those values Syme is defending is what, during the Blatchford controversy, Chesterton had called 'the eternal heroism of the slums' and in *Thursday* he describes as 'the irrational valour of the poor, who in all those unclean streets were all clinging to the decencies and the charities of Christendom'. These

---

[20] 'A Picture of Tuesday', *Collected Works*, xiv. 62.

[21] BL MS Add. 73334, fo. 8ᵛ.

[22] Ward, 70.

[23] BL MS Add. 73342C. Both of Chesterton's first two novels clearly had extended periods of gestation. For *Thursday*, we can pick up the trail once more in 1905, with a story called 'The Appalling Five', about an 'inner council' of five members, the president of which shows only his back (one member of the council describes it as 'a significant back', another, 'A back which accuses the civilisation of Europe' (BL MS Add. 73354B)). We also have a list of contents and notes for the novel from about the same period, which shows that its plot was virtually complete about three years before its publication (BL MS Add. 73354C).

[24] BL MS Add. 73334, fo. 20.

decencies are epitomised for Syme by the sound of the barrel-organ, the indomitable music of the poor; he is possessed by 'an ultimate certainty that the [anarchists were] wrong and that the barrel-organ was right. There clanged in his mind that unanswerable and terrible truism in the song of Roland—"Pagens ont tort et Chretiens ont droit".'

The novel's surreal plot describes Gabriel Syme's warfare beneath this heraldic device. Having been recruited as part of 'The Last Crusade' he is led by Lucian Gregory, the anarchist poet (whose aim is 'to abolish God') to a local anarchist meeting place. Displacing Gregory, Syme contrives to be elected to the Anarchist Central Council. The Council consists of seven men, each known by the name of a day. Syme becomes 'Thursday' (interestingly, as part of his induction into this role, he symbolically assumes various items of distinctly Chestertonian gear, including a revolver, a swordstick, and a cloak). There is a prolonged chase, which begins as part of an operation to prevent the assassination of the Tsar and ends as an effort to escape an increasingly nightmarish and apparently universal conspiracy, controlled by the forces of 'anarchy' under the control of the literally larger-than-life President of the Council, Sunday (who is significantly described at one point in Nietzschean terms as a 'Super-man'). As the story unfolds, Syme discovers that five of the other six members are also undercover detectives; each was recruited in the same way in a darkened room by a man with his back to them. Only Sunday remains as the epitome of the evil they are all fighting: but Sunday proves invincible. At the end of an extended dreamlike denouement of great beauty, Sunday reveals that he is not the enemy but 'the peace of God', perhaps even God himself. Chesterton confirmed this identification in the newspaper interview already quoted, in which he briefly but illuminatingly summarised the novel's meaning:

You ask me who Sunday is. Well, you may call him Nature if you like. But you will notice that I hold that when the mask of Nature is lifted you find God behind. All that wild exuberance of Nature, all its strange pranks, all its seeming indifference to the wants and feelings of men, all that is only a mask. It is a mask which your Lucien Gregorys paint, but can never raise. Mind you, I think it is well that we should not know all about those around us, that we should fight in the dark, while having the faith that most men are on the right side, for to possess courage the soul of men must be lonely until at last it knows all.[25]

---

[25] Interview in the *Illustrated Sunday Herald*, reprinted in *G. K. Chesterton Quarterly*, 5 (Winter 1997), 5–6.

The identification of Sunday as God—and in a very particular way, as God incarnate—is confirmed in the text of the novel: Syme asks the question 'have you ever suffered?' Sunday grows in size until he blots out the light; and in the frightening darkness that follows, 'in the blackness before it entirely destroyed his brain he seemed to hear a distant voice saying a commonplace text that he had heard somewhere, "Can ye drink of the cup that I drink of?"'—this 'commonplace text' is, of course, Mark 20: 22, and it inevitably evokes another, Matthew 26: [26–56]: Christ's appeal in the Garden of Gethsemane to 'let this cup pass from me'. All this recalls an important passage in *Orthodoxy*, in which Chesterton approaches 'a matter more dark and awful than it is easy to discuss': 'what happened in Gethsemane' says Chesterton, is that Christ 'passed in some superhuman manner through our human horror of pessimism. When the world shook and the sun was wiped out of heaven, it was not at the crucifixion, but at the cry from the cross: the cry which confessed that God was forsaken of God.' The Christian—and by now the Chestertonian—instinct is that it is only by first identifying with this ultimate dereliction that an authentic 'optimism' may be attained: and there is, in Chesterton's discernment of the divine experience of 'our human horror of pessimism', a deeply personal application to his own passing through and emergence from this particular 'human horror': the use here of the word 'pessimism' is significant. What distinguishes Chesterton's vision is the gaiety and the vitality with which that emergence is celebrated. He summed up his own experience in the *Autobiography*, nearly three decades after *Orthodoxy*, in a passage already quoted in the context of the period to which it refers: 'no man knows how much he is an optimist, even when he calls himself a pessimist, because he has not really measured the depths of his debt to whatever created him and enabled him to call himself anything. At the back of our brains, so to speak, there was a forgotten blaze or burst of astonishment at our own existence.'[26] When Syme finally emerges from his own ordeal, he finds himself in Saffron Park, a setting easily identifiable as Bedford Park, the home of Chesterton's Anglo-Catholic fiancée Frances, and for him the symbolically charged *locus* of the beginning of his post-Slade pilgrim's progress towards Christian belief. Syme's state of mind is clearly identifiable as that peculiar to religious conversion:

while he could always remember afterwards that he had swooned before the face of Sunday, he could not remember having ever come to at all. He could only

---

[26] *Autobiography*, 92.

remember that gradually and naturally he knew that he was and had been walking along a country lane with an easy and conversational companion. That companion had been a part of his recent drama; it was the red-haired poet Gregory. They were walking like old friends, and were in the middle of a conversation about some triviality. But Syme could only feel an unnatural buoyancy in his body and a crystal simplicity in his mind that seemed to be superior to everything that he said or did. He felt he was in possession of some impossible good news, which made every other thing a triviality, but an adorable triviality.[27]

It is a crucially important passage, not merely in the context of the novel, but for any understanding of Chesterton himself. Chesterton has become entirely possessed by the convert's knowledge that he is living suspended between two worlds. For him now, everything can be, inevitably must be, understood in two entirely different ways, which must somehow be reconciled. Everything has two meanings: that which can be known or experienced by human reason and the material senses; and that which may be perceived only when the world is seen, however dimly, *sub specie aeternitatis*. He is 'in possession of' the 'impossible good news' which transforms 'every other thing': and almost all his writings may now be seen as an attempt—often unspoken, sometimes declared—to create a bridge, across which some part at least of this good news may be carried. Above all, he is motivated by the imperative to convey the essential ambiguity of all human experience: this, undoubtedly, is one of the keys to *The Man who was Thursday*:

'Listen to me,' cried Syme with extraordinary emphasis.
'Shall I tell you the secret of the whole world? It is that we have only known the back of the world. We see everything from behind, and it looks brutal. That is not a tree, but the back of a tree. That is not a cloud, but the back of a cloud. Cannot you see that everything is stooping and hiding a face? If we could only get round in front—'[28]

Chesterton, the convert, has got 'round in front'; he is perceiving the same world, the same cloud, the same tree; but now his perception has been transformed by a wholly new and previously unimaginable perspective. This notion of being able to see both the visible and the invisible faces of human reality is present throughout his apologetic writings: in 'The Return of the Angels', his very first anti-Blatchford article—in a sense his apologetic manifesto—the idea is understood in terms of the imagery of transparency: once we have assumed the truth of 'the spiritual view of life', once we have

---

[27] *Thursday*, 183–4.   [28] Ibid. 170.

'put on the theory, like a magic hat', 'history becomes translucent like a house of glass'. Earlier in the article, he proposes the parallel of the scientific hypothesis: 'We know that with this idea once inside our heads a million things become transparent as if a lamp were lit behind them.'[29]

The war over the creeds: Gore, Scott Holland, and Campbell

In the first chapter of *Orthodoxy*, Chesterton defines his terms: 'When the word "orthodoxy" is used here', he declares, 'it means the Apostles' Creed, as understood by everybody calling himself Christian until a very short time ago and the general historic conduct of those who held such a creed.'[30] This leads the reader to suppose that the articles of the creed will at some point be asserted or at least defended. But no such process of assertion or defence ever materialises: this is not a systematic defence of Christian doctrine, though certain key doctrines inevitably feature as being at the heart of Chesterton's evolving personal beliefs. The Apostles' Creed is flourished here as a kind of banner, one which has flown through the ages over an historical community of faith, a community with which Chesterton here aligns himself. It is also, implicitly, an indication of where he stood in a particular Anglican controversy, the terms of which had been defined some time before by Charles Gore, since 1905 Bishop of Birmingham, whom Chesterton had known since the beginning of the decade as one of the 'clerical group of canons and curates' (Gore was then a canon of Westminster) 'in the very heart' of which he had found himself moving 'nearer and nearer to the orthodox side'.[31]

Others had had an equal, and at first possibly greater influence than Gore. A more immediate inspiration, perhaps, certainly in the early years of the century had been Conrad Noel (then still a curate), on the face of it, perhaps, not an influence one might have expected to tend towards strict orthodoxy: Conrad Noel described himself as a 'Liberal Catholic' and later—under the influence of the (Roman) Catholic modernist movement of the early years of the new century—as a 'Catholic modernist'. He was refused ordination on doctrinal grounds by two bishops; it was only when

---

[29] G. K. Chesterton, 'The Return of the Angels', *The Daily News* (14 Mar. 1903).
[30] *Collected Works*, i. 215.   [31] *Autobiography*, 172.

the then Canon Gore intervened that he was finally ordained as an Anglican priest. The long delay in his ordination was probably due less to his 'Liberal Catholic' theology than to his preaching that socialism was its essential expression. As we have seen (and as he was to demonstrate many times in the years that followed, more than once at around the time he was writing *Thursday* and *Orthodoxy*[32]), Chesterton had already moved away from his own youthful socialism at the time he met Conrad Noel; and Noel was certainly theologically more liberal than Chesterton was to become. Nevertheless, in 1900, to someone in Chesterton's half-formed theological condition, Noel was still distinctly nearer to mainstream orthodoxy than he was; Noel would, for instance, have had little trouble with the Apostles' Creed: he would almost certainly have affirmed the belief of his hero, the Catholic modernist Father George Tyrrell, that even though it is not the Church's principal business to translate faith into rational language, there is nevertheless a need for the Church to be held together on some kind of dogmatic foundation. In Tyrrell's words, 'It is not . . . directly as an expression of my own private judgment and spiritual orientation that I say the Credo, but as an expression of the Church's collective Faith, which I desire to share and appropriate, and which I acknowledge as a rule or norm.'[33]

Gore's defence of the Credo was an altogether steelier business. Faced by the growing liberalism of the Anglican clergy, Gore had been insisting since 1887 (when he published *The Clergy and the Creeds*) that the clergy ought to be required to subscribe to the historic creeds: what was involved, he said, was 'the whole question of what is really true, and claims to be permanent in Christianity': in particular, he insisted that those clergy who shared the view of the liberal biblical critics, that the miraculous facts enshrined in the creeds were incredible, were lacking in the sincerity that ought to attach to their office.[34] Gore's position today seems paradoxical, since in the teeth of the opposition of traditionalist Anglicans like Henry Liddon (for whom *Lux Mundi*, a collection of essays edited by Gore, had been a body blow from which he never recovered) he had insisted that the validity of the so-called 'higher criticism'—the foundation of the theological liberalism of the late nineteenth century and the modernism of the early twentieth—had to be

---

[32] See pp. 372ff below.

[33] George Tyrrell, *Lex Credendi: A Sequel to Lex Orandi* (London, 1906), 4. See Allan Savage, 'George Tyrrell: Modernist Theologian (1861–1909): What he Said he Said', *Quodlibet Journal*, 4/1 (Winter 2002), <http://www.Quodlibet.net>.

[34] Charles Gore, *The Clergy and the Creeds* (London, 1887), 28.

accepted. Gore's insistence that biblical criticism was consistent with credal orthodoxy was easier for him to maintain, perhaps, than it would have been had he not applied it mainly to the Old Testament. At any rate, it was as an embattled defender of credal orthodoxy that Chesterton knew him: and despite the fact that Gore is often classified as a 'Liberal Catholic' within the Anglican tradition, the defence of the historic creeds became a cause for which he is now, perhaps, remembered as much as for *Lux Mundi*. His name, wrote James Carpenter, 'is perhaps too exclusively mentioned in connection with the credal controversy in which he played so prominent a part'.[35] Gore returned to the theme in two sermons, published in 1905 as *The Permanent Creed and the Christian Idea of Sin*, in which he summed up his attitude to the creeds in a way which explains much of his influence in the development of Chesterton's religious ideas during this decade: his language here is very similar to that in which, in *Orthodoxy*, Chesterton was to express his understanding of the Apostles' Creed 'as understood by everybody calling himself Christian until a very short time ago and the general historic conduct of those who held such a creed':

There is, after all, a faith which has been held *semper, ubique, ab omnibus* in such sense that what fragments of the Christian body have not held it hardly count in the total effect. What records we have of human life redeemed and consecrated have been redeemed and consecrated in the profession of this faith, and what lies outside this profession can be left out of reckoning without the general effect being altered, or the result for human life appreciably affected. And this impression of unity through all differences, and permeating all divisions, is impressive in a very high degree. It generates in the mind a sense of indissoluble coherence—a feeling that this Creed and Christianity are one and the same thing, or as root and fruit. There may be great differences between the Christian beliefs of the twentieth, and the tenth, and the fourth, and the second century, but the differences will not touch the great central body of faith.

This is wholly congruent, for instance—though less picturesquely expressed—with Chesterton's attack in *Orthodoxy* on the 'imbecile habit' that 'has arisen in modern controversy of saying that such and such a creed can be held in one age but cannot be held in another' and his scornful rejection of the notion that '[s]ome dogma . . . was credible in the twelfth century, but is not credible in the twentieth'.[36] Two ideas in particular may usefully be singled out at this point as central to Gore's importance for Chesterton: his

---

[35] James Carpenter, *Gore: A Study in Liberal Catholic Thought* (London, 1960), 105.
[36] *Collected Works*, i. 278.

defence of the miraculous assertions in the creed, particularly the Virgin Birth and the Resurrection, disbelief in which, he argued, simply proved the disbeliever to be sceptical about whether God did or even could intervene in the world: 'the question whether these recorded events actually happened,' argued Gore in *The Permanent Creed*, 'miraculous and supernatural as they are, will almost always be answered in accordance with what a man's mind is as to the probabilities of Divine action',[37] an argument refined in *Orthodoxy* in Chesterton's aphorism '[a] miracle only means the liberty of God'.[38] The second area of theological congruence that can be singled out is indicated by Gore's growing attack on the immanentism of such liberal Protestants as the Revd R. J. Campbell, whose book *The New Theology* (1907) was something of a *succès fou*. Campbell's book was nothing less than a radical recasting of Christian theology: the Incarnation, in particular, was seen by Campbell as no more than the supreme example of God's immanence; in his thinking, the distinction between God and man was dissolved in a comprehensive pantheism.[39] Gore's response, *The New Theology and the Old Religion* (published the same year), was altogether more intellectually substantial. As James Carpenter comments, 'Campbell was not a profound theologian at all, but Gore perceived that he was the most popular exponent of the immanental trend in the theology of that day and that his teaching had to be reckoned with speedily and effectively.'[40] Gore had until a few years before seen the nineteenth-century trend towards immanence as a necessary corrective to the deistical thought of the previous century; but as the trend grew more and more dominant in the new century, he recognised its dangers and came increasingly to stress the transcendent character of God and of Christ in the Gospels.[41] Campbell's views were crudely Hegelian: God, he believed, finds his expression in the world and in man: quite simply, he asserted, humanity is integral to the very being of God.[42] In Campbell's assertion that there was no dividing line between the being of God and the being of man,[43] Gore perceived a claim that God and man were of one substance.[44] In response, he stressed the separateness of God and human beings; it was, he insisted,

[37] Charles Gore, *The Permanent Creed and the Christian Idea of Sin* (London, 1905), 10.
[38] *Collected Works*, i. 332.
[39] J. K. Mozley, *Some Tendencies in British Theology* (London, 1951), 34.
[40] Carpenter, *Gore*, 78.
[41] Ibid. 154.
[42] R. J. Campbell, *The New Theology* (London, 1907), 18, 20, 21.
[43] Ibid. 34.
[44] Charles Gore, *The Old Theology and the New Religion* (London, 1907), 43.

'quite impossible' that there should be 'any identification of themselves with God':[45] there was 'no breath of pantheistic identification of Godhead with manhood . . . in the New Testament'.[46] Gore's insistence here is reflected— or at least paralleled—in one of the major themes of *Orthodoxy*, Christianity's 'dogmatic insistence that God was personal, and had made a world separate from Himself'.[47] In the ancient world, asserts Chesterton, '[t]hat transcendence and distinctness of the deity which some Christians now want to remove from Christianity, was really the only reason why any one wanted to be a Christian.'[48]

Campbell's one-sided immanental theology, Gore believed, was even further removed from the Bible and the creeds than Unitarianism. It was similar enough, however, and something very like the New Theology was nothing new for Chesterton; as Cecil pointed out in his book on his brother, published the year after *The New Theology*, it had been in the Bedford chapel, under Stopford Brooke, that 'more than fifteen years ago, the young Chesterton learned from the lips of a genuine poet and orator the whole of that system of religious thought which has been discovered by certain Nonconformist ministers within the last eighteen months, and is now emphatically called "The New Theology" '.[49] In particular, Campbell's ideas about the nature of Christ must have seemed to Chesterton very reminiscent of Stopford Brooke's. 'Nothing in Mr. Campbell's exposition of the New Theology', comments Kenneth Mozley, 'gave greater offence than his apparent refusal to allow that Jesus was divine in any other way than was possible for every man, however much it was true that the harmony of the divine and the human was perfect in Jesus beyond what had come to pass in any other man.'[50] Chesterton was quick to respond to Campbell's book, in a speech to the Saltley Christian Fellowship in July. 'He took exception', reported *The Commonwealth* in August, 'to the idea that divinity was contained within, and not without. Certainly that was not the point upon which Christianity had achieved its greatest triumphs. Take, for illustration, a large Buddha idol and the picture of some mediaeval saint— two actual figures—and there might be noted several differences. Buddha

[45] Charles Gore, *The Old Theology and the New Religion* (London, 1907), 47.
[46] Ibid. 48.
[47] *Collected Works*, i. 282.
[48] Ibid. 281.
[49] Cecil, 8–9.
[50] Mozley, *Some Tendencies in British Theology*, 35.

had his eyes closed and was looking for God, as it were, in the regions of his soul, while the Christian stared outward to something beyond himself.'[51] It was an idea that Chesterton developed in *Orthodoxy*:

Buddhism is on the side of modern pantheism and immanence. And it is just here that Christianity is on the side of humanity and liberty and love.... This is the meaning of that almost insane happiness in the eyes of the mediaeval saint in the picture. This is the meaning of the sealed eyes of the superb Buddhist image. The Christian saint is happy because he has verily been cut off from the world; he is separate from things and is staring at them in astonishment. But why should the Buddhist saint be astonished at things?—since there is really only one thing, and that being impersonal can hardly be astonished at itself.[52]

Though, unlike Gore, Chesterton was no longer a socialist, he still believed, as Gore did, that orthodoxy in theology had social consequences. In his Saltley speech he insisted that 'whatever influence there might be in the new movement... would be against and not in favour of Social Reform'. In *Orthodoxy*, he explained why Campbell's immanentism would be so inimical to social change:

If we want reform, we must adhere to orthodoxy: especially in this matter (so much disputed in the counsels of Mr. R. J. Campbell), the matter of insisting on the immanent or the transcendent deity. By insisting specially on the immanence of God we get introspection, self-isolation, quietism, social indifference—Tibet. By insisting specially on the transcendence of God we get wonder, curiosity, moral and political adventure, righteous indignation—Christendom.[53]

Of the 'clerical group of canons and curates' who had had such a powerful influence on Chesterton's spiritual and theological development in the years leading up to the writing of *Orthodoxy*, Gore was probably the most intellectually weighty (and certainly the most prolific). But we should not forget Henry Scott Holland, with whom Chesterton probably had as much or more personal contact, and who had a much warmer and more magnetic personality than the austere and somewhat forbidding Gore. These two men were among the most influential Anglican thinkers of their day. Of the contributors to *Lux Mundi*, '[g]reatest of all', asserts Michael Ramsey, 'were the two prophets, Henry Scott Holland and Charles Gore'. While Scott Holland's writings 'were but sermons and occasional pieces... they contain flashes of a theological

[51] Unsigned report, 'The New Theology and the Social Movement', *The Commonwealth* (Aug. 1907), 238.

[52] *Collected Works*, i. 337–8.   [53] Ibid. 339–40.

creativity which amounts to genius'.[54] Scott Holland's writings, certainly, are full of a passion and a colour which must have appealed to Chesterton, and whether he read Scott Holland's views on *The New Theology*, or heard them in conversation (or both), they probably formed part of the general mix of ideas from which his own reactions to Campbell's book were developed. Scott Holland responded to Campbell's book with an article in *The Commonwealth* entitled 'Theologies: New and Old'. Unlike Chesterton, Scott Holland reasserts the traditional Catholic view according to which immanence was denied when it was 'absolute' but affirmed when it was 'relative', seen, in the words of the *Catholic Encyclopaedia*, as 'a subjective preparation which shall dispose the individual for the act of faith by exciting in him the desire to enter into relations with the transcendent God'. As Scott Holland puts it in his article,

When you have come to the end of all that you can know about the Divine Immanence in man, you will still be in need of the word that will tell you why the Divine Immanence is so precious and so effectual. The Divine Immanence points away beyond itself. Its religious value lies in its perpetual witness to the Divine Transcendence. Out of the play of the one into the other springs the eternal significance of the Incarnation.[55]

In *Orthodoxy*, immanence is seen simply as a threat; and in this, it has to be said, Gore and Chesterton were probably more representative of traditionalist Catholic opinion—Roman or Anglican—at the time, than Scott Holland. The year 1907 was also, of course, that in which Pius X condemned the immanentism of Catholic modernism in his encyclical *Pascendi Dominici Gregis*. The similarities between liberal Protestants and Catholic modernists were many (though it should be noted that there were different strains among Catholic modernists); 'Baron von Hugel', writes Michael Ramsey, 'was with the modernists in his conviction that historical criticism must be pursued with uncompromising integrity: but he was suspicious of the immanentist doctrine which he sensed in Loisy, and his own religion was rooted in the conviction of divine transcendence'[56]). *Pascendi* nowhere preaches a sense of the immanence of God as being part of a balanced spirituality, as does Scott Holland (reflecting St Augustine and St Thomas Aquinas). 'Immanence' was a bogey that had to be extirpated: the most radical modernists were not interested in a theology which would leave intact an ultimate belief in divine transcendence or in a revelation that was not vulnerable to historical criticism. 'On any

---

[54] Michael Ramsey, *From Gore to Temple* (London, 1960), 12.

[55] Henry Scott Holland, 'Theologies Old and New', *The Commonwealth* (Mar. 1907), 82.

[56] Ramsey, *From Gore to Temple*, 64.

showing', argues Michael Ramsey, 'the conflict with papal authority was inevitable.'[57] *Pascendi* is sometimes seen today as part of an oppressively authoritarian exercise of papal power, and it was attacked, indeed, in *The Commonwealth* at the time for reviving 'in its most arrogant and relentless form the conception of religion as mere submission . . . to a chosen and rigid system';[58] Gore's insistence, nevertheless, as Bishop first of Worcester, then of Birmingham and later of Oxford, that his own clergy subscribe without any personal reservations to the Catholic creeds, was by Anglican standards no less 'relentless'. And both Gore and Chesterton reacted to the challenge of liberal Protestantism in remarkably similar terms to those in which Pius X condemned Catholic modernism. The doctrine of divine immanence, argues *Pascendi*, leads directly to pantheism:

For does it, We ask, leave God distinct from man or not? If yes, in what does it differ from Catholic doctrine, and why reject external revelation? If no, we are at once in Pantheism. Now the doctrine of immanence in the Modernist acceptation holds and professes that every phenomenon of conscience proceeds from man as man. The rigorous conclusion from this is the identity of man with God, which means Pantheism.[59]

The author of the encyclical might almost at this point be responding to *The New Theology*; and his critique of immanentism is precisely that of both Gore and Chesterton: that it leads to 'the identity of man and God and thence to pantheism'; as Chesterton puts it in *Orthodoxy*, 'according to orthodox Christianity [the] separation between God and man is sacred. . . . That a man may love God it is necessary that there should be not only a God to be loved, but a man to love him.'[60]

Becoming Everyman

The parallel between Chesterton's hostility to 'The New Theology' (and the current secularisms it echoed) and the Catholic anti-modernism of which *Pascendi* was the spearhead was noted by one distinguished Roman Catholic observer. In an extended review of *Orthodoxy* in the *Dublin Review*, Wilfrid Ward, Newman's first biographer, noted that though Chesterton's stance was not 'necessarily identical with Catholicism', 'its affinities to Catholicism are

---

[57] Ibid.
[58] A. L. Lilley, 'The Encyclical "Pascendi" ', *The Commonwealth* (Dec. 1907), 364.
[59] *Pascendi Dominici Gregis*, § 39.   [60] *Collected Works*, i. 337.

very close'. A review of *Orthodoxy* at such length was justified in a Catholic journal, Ward insisted, because Chesterton's work was 'an attempt in [the] English literature of the hour at doing what a sympathetic spectator from another planet would regard to be one great work of the Church at present—namely, bringing to bear all available guns against a perverse philosophy of life, which is being preached in the name of progress':

> In her official action the Church emphasises . . . the defects and dangers of modern thought. She notes that weak man may easily be absorbed by the new and lose his grasp on the old. Our faculties are in danger of losing what they have already grasped and possessed—truth which is substantial and divine—while they pursue shadows. . . . Such an attitude is undoubtedly reinforced by some of Mr Chesterton's best pages. And it is likely to be as unpopular in many quarters as the Church is ever unpopular with the world.[61]

Chesterton, Ward has already indicated, 'disclaims novelty for his views'.[62] What gives his arguments their special force is that they have emerged in a mind formed by the modernity it now confronts: it is precisely the autobiographical element in *Orthodoxy* that gives Chesterton's defence of the tradition its special 'vividness and reality': 'Novel . . . his views are not. Original in him they most certainly are . . . He tells us, indeed, that he has never read the chief Christian apologetic writings at all. He has discovered his arguments for himself, and herein lies half the interest and value of his book. . . . The depth of the Christian philosophy met the difficulties of an active and penetrating mind that had again and again found the shibboleths of typical modern speculative thinkers incoherent, mutually destructive, or even self-destructive. (Chesterton's claim to have generated his arguments in a literary vacuum, however, is perhaps disingenuous: asked to draw up a 'scheme of reading' for 1908, he suggested Butler's *Analogy*, Coleridge's *Confessions of an Enquiring Spirit*, Newman's *Apologia*, St Augustine's *Confessions*, and the *Summa Theologica* of St Thomas Aquinas.)[63]

Much of the significance of *Orthodoxy* for Ward lay in Chesterton's analytical capacity to perceive the errors of modern thought. As much as Chesterton's intellectual rigour in *Orthodoxy*, he registered, too, 'the drama of personal conviction and history' that lay behind it. It is a drama we have already seen partly acted out in *The Man who was Thursday*, a novel which, I have suggested, needs to be placed in the general context of the autobiographical mode which

---

[61] Wilfrid Ward, 'Mr Chesterton among the Prophets', *Dublin Review*, 144 (Jan. and Apr. 1909), 32.
[62] Ibid. 3.   [63] Ibid. 3–4; Ward, 170.

was such a powerful shaping force in Chesterton's imagination during 1907 (when the final version of *Thursday*—with its long memory-filled dedication—was written) and the early months of 1908 (when *Orthodoxy* was completed). I have argued that we need to see *Heretics* and *Orthodoxy* as being among the essential intellectual keys to *The Man who was Thursday*; it is just as much the case that *Thursday* is an emotional key to the underlying personal drama of *Orthodoxy*; in a sense, it is the first act in that drama, evoking as it does the period in Chesterton's life when he was emerging from the confusion and 'pessimism' of his first year at University College into the 'sunrise of wonder' of his second and final year, a sequence which was the necessary prelude to the decade-long search for meaning of which *Orthodoxy* is the remarkable eventual outcome. This sequence is vividly evoked in the final chapters of *The Man who was Thursday*, in which the 'Nightmare' of *Thursday* fades into a tranquil waking state of 'crystal simplicity' in the mind of the novel's protagonist, Gabriel Syme.

The same kind of correspondence between Chesterton's personal experience and the imaginative and intellectual dynamic of his writing can be observed in an even more comprehensive way throughout *Orthodoxy*—in a way, indeed which is so openly avowed that it becomes the book's defining literary convention: 'I have attempted,' he tells the reader at the beginning of the first chapter, 'in a vague and personal way, in a set of mental pictures rather than in a series of deductions, to state the philosophy in which I have come to believe. I will not call it my philosophy; for I did not make it. God and humanity made it; and it made me.' The process by which 'it made me' is the stuff from which the book is formed: it is 'not an ecclesiastical treatise but a sort of slovenly autobiography'. The autobiographical process is, indeed, already under way: *Orthodoxy*, as I have suggested, begins at the biographical point at which *Thursday* ends, for, just as the novel draws on a period in Chesterton's life which can be dated roughly from 1892 to 1894, so the first chapter in this 'slovenly autobiography' can be seen to look back to a period which begins just *after* Chesterton's emergence from his final ordeal.

It was a period full of youthful exhilaration at the recovery of his childhood's sense of perpetual wonder. 'At the back of our brains', he puts it in a later chapter of the *Autobiography* (in a passage to which it has been necessary to return more than once), '. . . there was a forgotten blaze or burst of astonishment at our own existence.' Chesterton is very clear here about the defining importance of this recovery of 'astonishment' to his own identity as a writer: for him, it is the *fons et origo* of an imaginative and intellectual dynamic which underpins all his writing. '*The object of the artistic and spiritual life*', he continues, 'was to dig for this submerged sunrise of wonder' (my italics).[64]

This perception was to be his creative driving force for the rest of his life. A key document linking the beginnings of this process of 'digging' with what can be seen in many ways as its fulfilment in *Orthodoxy* is the short story, unpublished during Chesterton's lifetime, entitled 'Homesick at Home' (*c.*1896), which we have already discussed, in passing, in the context of its period, but to which we now need to return as (moving through the text of *Orthodoxy*) we begin what will be a sequence of similar returns to successive earlier periods in Chesterton's life.

The first chapter is in this sense out of sequence, beginning not with the story of the gradual unfolding of Chesterton's religious and spiritual consciousness (this begins, chronologically, with his childhood in chapter 4, 'The Ethics of Elfland') but with the personal origins of the central dramatic idea which will drive the book forward: that is, the rediscovery of forgotten realities within the known and familiar. After a brief journalistic chat on the supposed occasion for the writing of the book, Chesterton gives us what is its real opening, the famous sentence which inaugurates the series of 'mental pictures' which form the drama of his spiritual life thus far: 'I have often had a fancy for writing a romance about an English yachtsman who slightly miscalculated his course and discovered England under the impression that it was a new island in the South Seas.' The idea that all exploration—geographical or spiritual—is a homeward journey occurs repeatedly at this point in Chesterton's life, but also later, for instance at the end of *The New Jerusalem* (1920), which describes his return to England after a journey to the Holy Land. In *Manalive* (1912), Innocent Smith circumnavigates the globe, travelling through the steppes of Russia, the forests of China, and the mountain villages of California, in order to find his way home; he breaks into his own house to see what it is really like; he elopes repeatedly with his own wife. In the first chapter of *Orthodoxy*, Chesterton develops this basic idea doctrinally: the fresh 'discovery' of what he already knew is likened to his imagined invention of a new 'heresy' followed by the chastened realisation that it was after all the old orthodoxy: not only is he is 'the man who landed (armed to the teeth and talking by signs) to plant the British flag on that barbaric temple which turned out to be the Pavilion at Brighton';[65] later in the same chapter, still in 'autobiographical' mode, he

[64] *Autobiography*, 92.   [65] *Collected Works*, i. 211.

develops this idea. 'I am the man', he asserts, 'who with the utmost daring discovered what had been discovered before...this book explains how I fancied I was the first to set foot in Brighton and then found I was the last.... *I freely confess all the idiotic ambitions of the end of the nineteenth century. I did, like all other solemn little boys, try to be in advance of the age. Like them I tried to be some ten minutes in advance of the truth. And I found that I was eighteen hundred years behind it*' (my italics).[66] In fact, this account of Chesterton's intellectual journey goes well beyond the point at which the facts of his life can support it. As we have seen, even at school he never had any sympathy with 'the idiotic ambitions of the end of the nineteenth century', nor (his brief flirtation with socialism apart) did he attempt to be 'in advance of the age'; he was, indeed, profoundly repelled by many of those who did. But the underlying idea—of the rediscovery as though it were new and unexpected of an old reality or tradition, lost or weakened through the contempt bred of excessive familiarity—was true to Chesterton's experience, and *Orthodoxy* was not the only expression during 1907 of this idea's re-emergence in his mind. He also explored it, for instance, in his *Daily News* column, as he prepared in June that year for a real-life journey, not around the world, but around Europe. 'More than a month ago,' he told his readers in July,

When I was leaving London for a holiday, a friend walked into my flat in Battersea and found me surrounded with half-packed luggage.

'You seem to be off on your travels,' he said. 'Where are you going?'

With a strap between my teeth I replied, 'to Battersea.'

'The wit of your remark,' he said, 'wholly escapes me.'

'I am going to Battersea,' I repeated, 'to Battersea, via Paris, Belfort, Heidelberg, and Frankfort. My remarks contained no wit. It contained simply the truth. I am going to wander over the whole world until once more I find Battersea. Somewhere in the seas of sunset or sunrise, somewhere in the ultimate archipelago of the earth, there is one little island which I wish to find: an island with low green hills and great white cliffs. Travellers tell me that it is called England...and there is a rumour that somewhere in the heart of it there is a beautiful place called Battersea.'

Chesterton's explanation of this *jeu d'esprit* illuminates not only these apparently whimsical remarks about his projected European travels, but also the opening chapter of *Orthodoxy*, which he may have been planning or even writing at about this time. 'I cannot see any Battersea here', he continues; 'I cannot see any London or any England. I cannot see that door. I cannot see

---

[66] Ibid. 214.

that chair: because a cloud of sleep and custom has come across my eyes. The only way to get back to them is to go somewhere else.'[67]

'Homesick at Home', written twelve or thirteen years earlier, begins with a similar fancy:

One, seeming to be a traveller, came to me and said, 'What is the shortest journey from one place to the same place?' ...
'Surely,' I said, 'to stand still.'
'That is no journey at all,' he replied. 'The shortest journey from one place to the same place is round the world.'

The story's rather tiresome protagonist, White Wynd, after many years living in a White Farmhouse by a river, has grown weary of what he has always known: 'he seemed to be able to see other homes, but not his own. This was merely a house. Prose had got hold of him: the sealing of the eyes and the closing of the ears.'[68] He decides to travel in order to find his true home, 'far away at the end of the world'. Having left his real home, after long and weary travels, he rediscovers the joys of the created order: 'He felt like Adam newly created. He had suddenly inherited all things, even the sun and the stars. Have you ever been out for a walk?'[69]

The tone here is very similar to many of the entries in what Maisie Ward calls 'The Notebook', which we have considered at some length in Chapter 4. 'Homesick at Home' is, indeed, contemporary with The Notebook, which chronicles not only Chesterton's joyful rediscovery of the Creation but also his return to belief in—and the search for engagement with—a Creator:

Have you ever known what it is to walk
Along a road in such a frame of mind
That you thought you might meet God at any turn of the path?[70]

The Notebook is more explicit in its spiritual quest than 'Homesick at Home'; but it is clear enough that the story is written against the background of the same notion of a joyful return to an abandoned religious tradition; it is clear, too, that the tradition in question is in some broad sense Christianity. Even though we know, as we have seen in Chapter 4, that at this period Chesterton's religious understanding was very far from the orthodoxy he was defending some twelve years later, 'Homesick at

[67] G. K. Chesterton, 'The Riddle of the Ivy', *The Daily News* (6 July 1907).
[68] *Collected Works*, xiv. 64.
[69] Ibid. 66.
[70] BL MS Add. 73334, fo. 13.

Home' is set within a specifically indicated religious culture: 'He had come to the end of the world. Every spot on earth is either the beginning or the end, according to the heart of man. . . . It was his home now. But it could not be his home until he had gone out from it and returned to it. Now he was the Prodigal Son.'[71] This key Chestertonian theme of the need to retrieve a sense of the wonder of creation from the deadness of custom and inertia is not, of course, his own invention, and it needs to be placed in the general context of romantic and Victorian literary tradition. It reminds us particularly, perhaps, of Coleridge writing about Wordsworth's aim, in the *Lyrical Ballads*, 'to excite a feeling analogous to the supernatural, by awakening the mind's attention to the lethargy of custom, and directing it to the loveliness and the wonders of the world before us; an inexhaustible treasure, but for which, in consequence of the film of familiarity and selfish solicitude, we have eyes, yet see not, ears that hear not, and hearts that neither feel nor understand.'[72]

Chesterton's emphasis on the importance of his childhood, and on the freshness of his childhood vision 'of a sort of white light on everything', a 'white light [which] had a sort of wonder in it, as if the world were as new as myself', can hardly fail to remind us of the opening lines of Wordsworth's 'Intimations of Immortality from Recollections of Early Childhood', in which he evokes 'a time when meadow, grove, and stream, | The earth, and every common sight, | To me did seem | Apparelled in celestial light'. Like Wordsworth, Chesterton sees the recovery of early memories as a mainspring of his creative life, so much so that that he asserts in the *Autobiography* that the '[t]he object of the artistic and spiritual life [is] to dig for this submerged sunrise of wonder'.[73] In particular, there is an obvious parallel between the intentions of *Orthodoxy* and those of Wordsworth's *Prelude*, which is a kind of spiritual autobiography whose purpose is to prepare for a substantial philosophical work, in his case never completed. In *Orthodoxy*, the two stages are achieved together: spiritual autobiography becomes the literary convention within which Chesterton achieves a fully articulated personal philosophy which turns out to be indistinguishable from—or at least wholly consistent with—a recognisable version of Catholic Orthodoxy.

---

[71] *Collected Works*, xiv. 67–8.

[72] S. T. Coleridge, *Biographia Literaria*, ed. with his aesthetical essays by J. Shawcross (Oxford, 1817), ii. 6.

[73] *Autobiography*, 91–2.

The opening chapter of *Orthodoxy* explains two things: the general imaginative and philosophical aim of the book, and the implications of this approach for religious belief in general and Christian apologetics in particular. 'The main problem for philosophers, and...in a manner the main problem of this book' is how to answer a very clearly articulated question: 'How can we contrive to be at once astonished at the world and yet at home in it? How can this queer cosmic town, with its many-legged citizens...how can this world give us at once the fascination of a strange town and the comfort and honour of being our own town?'[74] In *Orthodoxy*, Chesterton is clear about the apologetic implications of this question. Chesterton's projected audience is 'any average reader' (we have repeatedly observed his Whitmanesque reverence for 'the average man'). His question represents a universal human need: and it is comprehensively answered, he claims, by the Christian tradition, by what he describes later in the book as 'the romance of orthodoxy':

I wish to set forth my faith as particularly answering this double spiritual need, the need for that mixture of the familiar and the unfamiliar which Christendom has rightly named romance.... The thing I do not propose to prove, the thing I propose to take as common ground between myself and any average reader, is this desirability of an active and imaginative life, picturesque and full of a poetical curiosity, a life such as western man at any rate always seems to have desired.... nearly all people I have ever met in this western society in which I live would agree to the general proposition that we need this life of practical romance; the combination of something that is strange with something that is secure. We need so to view the world as to combine an idea of wonder and an idea of welcome. We need to be happy in this wonderland without once being merely comfortable. It is *this* achievement of my creed that I shall chiefly pursue in these pages.[75]

The next two chapters are described by Chesterton as a 'rough review of recent thought';[76] this part of the book is for the most part a return to the negative mode of *Heretics*. 'In front of me, as I close this page,' Chesterton tells us at the end of chapter 3, 'is a pile of modern books that I have been turning over for the purpose—a pile of ingenuity, a pile of futility. By the accident of my present detachment, I can see the inevitable smash of the philosophies of Schopenhauer and Tolstoy, Nietzsche and Shaw, as clearly as an inevitable railway smash could be seen from a balloon.'[77] Chesterton

---

[74] *Collected Works*, i. 212.   [75] Ibid. 212–13.
[76] Ibid. 246.   [77] Ibid.

(surely correctly) describes these two chapters as the 'dullest business of this book';[78] certainly, the negative analysis of these chapters tends to delay the book's forward movement, and I shall delay considering their content until we can do so in a rather different context.

Chesterton's 'rough review', though, is preceded by a short passage on the imagination to which it is worthwhile to give some attention in passing. Contrary to common belief, Chesterton argues, the imagination is a means of attaining sanity; this is especially true of what he describes as 'mystical imagination'. The idea that imagination is dangerous to man's mental balance is a simple reversal of the truth: poets, he says, are spoken of as 'psychologically unreliable'; but facts and history contradict this view; '[m]ost of the very great poets have been not only sane, but extremely business-like; and if Shakespeare ever really held horses, it was because he was much the safest man to hold them'; it is mathematicians and chess-players who go mad; the only poet who went mad was Cowper, who was 'definitely driven mad by logic, by the ugly and alien logic of predestination. Poetry was not the disease, but the medicine; poetry partly kept him in health.' This contention leads Chesterton to one of *Orthodoxy*'s key assertions ('key' because it unlocks much else): 'The general fact is simple. Poetry is sane because it floats easily in an infinite sea; reason seeks to cross the infinite sea, and so make it finite.' This recalls Keats's famous definition of 'negative capability' (one of the necessary attributes of the poet): 'that is, when a man is capable of being in uncertainties, mysteries, doubts, without any irritable reaching after fact and reason.'[79] The idea of the poetic imagination as a means of knowing a truth which is superior to 'fact and reason' has to be placed within the general anti-rationalist context of romantic theory, and with the romantic certainty (as Keats expresses it) of 'nothing but the holiness of the heart's affections, and the *truth* of imagination'. We need, finally, to recall romantic ideas, especially, perhaps, those of Wordsworth (to which we have already referred) and Blake, about the special insights of childhood as being a time, in Blake's words, of 'the opening morn' when we can see the '[i]mage of truth new-born'.[80]

Chapter 4 of *Orthodoxy*, 'The Ethics of Elfland', returns to this 'opening morn' in Chesterton's own life, and its underlying assumption is that 'truth

---

[78] Ibid.

[79] John Keats, Letter to George and Thomas Keats (22 Dec. 1817), *Keats' Letters*, compiled and annotated by Tohru Matsuura (Tokyo, 1969), 14.

[80] William Blake, 'Voice of the Ancient Bard', in *Songs of Innocence*, ed. Michael Mason (Oxford, 1994), 66.

new-born' is a great deal more than a kind of pre-rational apprehension of the world, whose attraction is mainly that of a fresh unsullied innocence. On the contrary: 'truth', here, has to do with a particular way of looking at the world which, Chesterton insists, is valid throughout life. 'My first and last *philosophy*,' says Chesterton, 'that which I believe in with unbroken certainty, I learnt in the nursery' (my italics):

The things I believed most then, the things I believe most now, are the things called fairy tales. They seem to me to be the entirely reasonable things. They are not fantasies: compared with them other things are fantastic. Compared with them religion and rationalism are both abnormal, though religion is abnormally right and rationalism abnormally wrong. Fairyland is nothing but the sunny country of common sense.[81]

Though Chesterton seems here to be implying that the expression 'common sense' means 'normal' or 'unremarkable', we are aware by now that such assertions should make us wary; we are approaching the marshy territory, here, of Chestertonian paradox, where it would be wise to suspect that common sense may turn out to mean profoundly uncommon sense. And so it proves. This inversion of 'common sense', indeed, was already by now well established in Chesterton's personal lexicon. As early as 1902 he had argued that '[t]he practical man and the mystic are much akin, because mysticism and common sense are so nearly akin as to be almost identical' and that '[m]ysticism and common sense both represent those certainties which always come off worst in argument and best in life';[82] that this notion was not a passing journalistic whimsy is shown by the reappearance of precisely the same ideas five years later in March 1907 (in Chesterton's *Daily News* column) when he argued in almost identical terms that '[c]ommon sense has all the qualities of pure mystical religion' and that 'Like religion, common sense is unexplainable.'[83] Chesterton's assertion in *Orthodoxy* that 'Fairyland is nothing but the sunny country of common sense' was akin to an idea he had already tried out in *The Daily News* in June 1907, interestingly in the context of a current controversy about religious instruction in schools. Nonconformist opinion tended to be that such instruction should be 'non-denominational' and limited to unadorned biblical instruction. Chesterton's response to a letter to this effect from

[81] *Collected Works*, i. 252.
[82] G. K. Chesterton, 'The Mystery of Patriotism', *The Commonwealth* (Jan. 1902).
[83] G. K. Chesterton, 'Common Sense in Politics', *The Daily News* (16 Mar. 1907).

one of his readers was that of a declared Anglican Catholic gently teasing a Protestant adversary. He suggested 'that we would have simple Bible teaching in the schools if he would have simple coloured statues of the Virgin and the Saints in school as well', as a prelude to suggesting as an alternative that 'the children should learn nothing but fairy tales, which really are like Science, unsectarian, and which really are like Religion, fundamental, human, and eternal. But when I tried to persuade a biologist and a theologian that "Jack and the Beanstalk" might be a very reasonable substitute for both their studies, they did not agree with me.'[84]

That which is 'fundamental, human and eternal' for Chesterton naturally and indispensably includes that which is astonishing. Childhood is a state of perpetual astonishment: that is why the vision of childhood is one he is constantly and instinctively engaged in excavating from beneath the intervening layers of adult consciousness. 'We all like astonishing tales because they touch the nerve of the ancient instinct of astonishment', he says in *Orthodoxy*; '[t]his is proved by the fact that when we are very young children we do not need fairy tales: we only need tales. Mere life is interesting enough. A child of seven is excited by being told that Tommy opened a door and saw a dragon. But a child of three is excited by being told that Tommy opened a door.'[85]

Chesterton, nevertheless, as a child of 3, had lived in an imaginative world of which dragons were a natural part, as were giants, fairies, and other fabulous beings; and we have no need to rely on his adult memories (whether those of his early thirties in *Orthodoxy* or his sixties in the *Autobiography*) or on any other speculation or reminiscence to establish this. At the age of 18, it will be remembered, he had argued that 'a creative instinct exists in [every child, who] has . . . a series of imaginary characters, whose proceedings he details at enormous lengths'.[86] Whether this is true of every child may be doubted; but it was undoubtedly true of little Gilbert Chesterton, whose creative instincts had been duly noted and nurtured by the adults around him: mainly by his parents but also by his Aunt Rose, to whom, at the age of 3 years, he dictated a short story, in two chapters. Aunt Rose kept this evidence of precocious talent in a safe place, and it is rightly preserved, with due solemnity, in the British Library's Chesterton collection. The story is entitled *The History of Kids*, and its first chapter, entitled 'The Birth of Kids', is worth quoting in full:

---

[84] G. K. Chesterton, 'A Plea for Popular Philosophy', *The Daily News* (22 June 1907).
[85] *Collected Works*, i. 257.   [86] *The Debater*, iii. 89.

Kids' father heard a trumpet's blast which seemed to say there was some boars and dragons and giants in a forest near there, and the King, (Kids' father) went out to fight them, and the first thing he met was a large dragon, the next thing he met was a large giant, and when he came home, 'Kids' was born. Then there was a fairy and she kept waving her wand, and a little sprite appeared, and the sprite kept growing prettier and prettier until at last he was a boy, and his name was Valimal. Then a Prince appeared and then the fairy waved her wand again and the Prince appeared like a Roman soldier. Then she waved her wand again and a horse appeared. Then the Roman soldier saw some Ancient Britons coming along in the distance, and the fairy said to the soldier: 'that horse is yours.' So the Roman soldier jumped on the horse—he had just gone about 100 miles when he saw a giant before him, so he drew his dagger and struck the giant on the head, and the giant caught hold of his long sword—so the King (Kids' father) said: 'Run, run and get one more.' But the Roman soldier wouldn't, but he drew his short dagger and fought for the long one, and when he'd fought he got it, and killed the giant. When the King saw the wounded giant he said the Soldier had won. And so he had.
This is the end of the birth of Kids.[87]

Even as a small child, Gilbert Chesterton seems to have seen play and fantasy as a serious business: the second chapter of his tale is entitled 'The Boyhood of Kids', and it begins with Kids 'dressed up for fun in armour, with a short dagger by his side, and *his father* thought it would be only for fun, *but Kids marched off* . . .'. He has gone to join the army, and is soon 'a little speck 100 miles off'; 'He fought', declares the 3-year-old Gilbert, 'and conquered' (my italics).

'Of all forms of literature', he wrote in one of his early book reviews (1902), 'it seems to me, fairy tales give the *truest* picture of life [my italics]. . . . We learn first and foremost that all doors fly open to courage and hope. We learn that the world is bound together in mysterious bonds of trust and compact and prevision, and that even green dragons keep their promises.'[88] We learn, in short, the strength of moral tradition: the 'chivalrous lesson' of *Jack the Giant Killer*, as Chesterton wrote in *Orthodoxy*, five years later, is that giants should be killed as a 'manly mutiny against pride as such'. The lesson of *Cinderella* is that of the *Magnificat*: that the humble shall be lifted up, *exaltavit humiles*. The lesson of *Beauty and the Beast* is that 'a thing must be loved *before* it is loveable'. But Chesterton is not concerned,

---

[87] BL MS Add. 73307; G. K. Chesterton, 'The History of Kids', *Chesterton Review* (Oct. 1996). Since this is taken down from the young Gilbert's dictation, the punctuation of the MS we have is Aunt Rose's, and I have therefore thought it permissible to adjust it so as to make the text more coherent.

[88] Review of *The Violet Fairy Book* by Andrew Lang, *The Speaker* (12 Oct. 1901).

he goes on, with the 'separate statutes of elfland', but with 'the whole spirit of its law':

It might be stated this way. There are certain sequences or developments (cases of one thing following another), which are, in the true sense of the word, reasonable. They are, in the true sense of the word, necessary. Such are mathematical and merely logical sequences.... But as I put my head over the hedge of the elves and began to take notice of the natural world, I observed an extraordinary thing. I observed that learned men in spectacles were talking of the actual things that happened—dawn and death and so on—as if *they* were rational and inevitable.... [But]... [t]here is an enormous difference by the test of fairyland; which is the test of the imagination. You cannot *imagine* two and one not making three. But you can easily imagine trees not growing fruit; you can imagine them growing golden candlesticks or tigers hanging on by the tail.[89]

The general basis of Chesterton's essentially romantic project to foster the credibility of the imagination and undermine the power of rationalist assumptions is beginning to be apparent. The idea of scientific 'law' had already attracted his hostile scrutiny in the course of his extended engagement with Blatchford, as part of a defence of Christian belief in miracles. The idea of scientific law, he had argued, is itself not scientific but metaphorical: '[w]hat Christianity argues is merely this. That this repetition in nature has its origin not in a thing resembling a law but a thing resembling a will.'[90] In *Orthodoxy*, however, he is at pains to make no such argument at this point: at the end of the chapter, he insists that all this time he 'had not thought of Christian theology'. He is careful at this stage simply to question the use of the term 'law' to describe a pattern of observed repetition of certain sequences of events. We cannot say why an egg may turn into a chicken any more than we can say why a bear could turn into a fairy prince. Certain transformations do happen: we should regard them in 'the philosophic manner of fairy tales' and not in 'the unphilosophic manner of science and the "Laws of Nature"'.

When we are asked why eggs turn to birds or fruits fall in autumn, we must answer exactly as the fairy godmother would answer if Cinderella asked her why mice turned to horses or her clothes fell from her at twelve o'clock. We must answer that it is *magic*.... It is no argument for unalterable law (as Huxley fancied) that we

---

[89] *Collected Works*, i. 253–4.
[90] G. K. Chesterton, 'Mr Blatchford's Religion', *The Clarion* (5 Aug. 1904); *Collected Works*, i. 386.

count on the ordinary course of things. . . . All the terms used in the science books, 'law,' 'necessity,' 'order,' 'tendency,' and so on, are really unintellectual, because they assume an inner synthesis, which we do not possess. The only words that ever satisfied me as describing Nature are the terms used in the fairy books, 'charm,' 'spell,' 'enchantment.' They express the arbitrariness of the fact and its mystery. A tree grows fruit because it is a *magic* tree. Water runs downhill because it is bewitched. The sun shines because it is bewitched.[91]

Wonder before the Created order, that is to say, is or should be the normal state of things: and wonder necessarily leads to a sense that life is a precious gift, for which it is natural to thank the giver. His strongest emotion, Chesterton remembers, 'was that life was as precious as it was puzzling...We thank people for birthday presents of cigars and slippers. Can I thank no one for the birthday present of birth?' As he puts it, later in the chapter, 'I had always believed that the world involved magic: now I thought that perhaps it involved a magician. And this pointed a profound emotion always present and sub-conscious; that this world of ours has some purpose; and if there is a purpose, there is a person. I had always felt life first as a story: and if there is a story there is a story-teller.'

Chesterton now enunciates what he calls 'the second great principle of the fairy philosophy', which he calls 'the Doctrine of Conditional Joy':

The note of the fairy utterance always is, 'You may live in a palace of gold and sapphire, *if* you do not say the word "cow";' or 'You may live happily with the King's daughter, *if* you do not show her an onion.' The vision always hangs upon a veto. . . . the true citizen of fairyland is obeying something that he does not understand at all. In the fairy tale an incomprehensible happiness rests upon an incomprehensible condition. A box is opened, and all evils fly out. A word is forgotten, and cities perish. A lamp is lit, and love flies away. A flower is plucked, and human lives are forfeited. An apple is eaten, and the hope of God is gone.[92]

Chesterton goes on to confirm, unintentionally, what I have already suggested: that his confession (in chapter 1) that he had espoused 'all the idiotic ambitions of the end of the nineteenth century' is simply not borne out by the facts of his life, for he now insists that he 'never could join the young men of [his] time in feeling what they called the general sentiment of *revolt*'. He had never, he says, subscribed to 'the common murmur of that rising generation against monogamy, because no restriction on sex

91 *Collected Works*, i. 255–6.   92 Ibid. 258–9.

seemed so odd and unexpected as sex itself. . . . Keeping to one woman is a
small price for so much as seeing one woman.' The *fin de siècle*, he says, had
wallowed in its enjoyment of beauty without accepting any moral limitations (here, as so often, it is the 'green carnation' which is Chesterton's
touchstone for the disfunction of modernity): 'the aesthetes', he continues,
'touched the last insane limits of language in their eulogy on lovely things.
The thistledown made them weep; a burnished beetle brought them to
their knees. Yet their emotion never impressed me for an instant, for this
reason, that it never occurred to them to pay for their pleasure in any sort
of symbolic sacrifice. . . . Surely one might pay for extraordinary joy in
ordinary morals. Oscar Wilde said that sunsets were not valued because we
could not pay for sunsets. But Oscar Wilde was wrong; we can pay for
sunsets. We can pay for them by not being Oscar Wilde.'[93] The idea of
paying 'for extraordinary joy in ordinary morals', of the wonder of human
life being impossible to grasp without accepting some sacrifice in personal
freedom, even the fairy-tale notion that 'incomprehensible happiness rests
upon an incomprehensible condition' were all undoubtedly part of what
he asserts was his refusal, some fifteen years before, to 'join the young men
of [his] time in feeling what they called the general sentiment of *revolt*', a
claim for which we have the clearest evidence in his Slade notebook
(*c*.1893), in which he goes so far as to assert the intrinsic benefit of
limitations *per se*:

Men made limitations at random, first of all, as they made joys at random. And
they were right. They felt (by an instinct as deep and dim as the sea) that limitation
is a necessity to joy. Limitation as limitation is good. Any limitation makes
something, as any outline takes some shape. This is the true and thrilling meaning
of the tale of Adam and Eve. God put something forbidden in their garden because
without limit things are without form and void. The dark stem of the strange tree
threw up all the green and gold. But they clamoured for 'infinity'. . . . They
destroyed the outline of Eden. They ate the one thing that kept everything
else sacred. Immediately they had everything and therefore nothing.[94]

This pivotal chapter is summed up in an important passage, whose
meaning we can see as central to the underlying message of *Orthodoxy*:
that the doctrines of the Christian religion are not imposed on reality from
without, but are, on the contrary, the key which unlocks life's real meaning.

---

[93] Ibid. 261.
[94] G. K. Chesterton, 'From the Notebooks of G.K.C.', *The Tablet* (4 Apr. 1953).

By discovering himself, Chesterton claims, he has discovered mankind's immemorial instincts, instincts which have been overlaid by the false beliefs of the modern age:

These are my ultimate attitudes towards life; the soils for the seeds of doctrine. These in some dark way I thought before I could write, and felt before I could think: that we may proceed more easily afterwards, I will roughly recapitulate them now. I felt in my bones; first, that world does not explain itself. It may be miracle with a supernatural explanation; it may be a conjuring trick, with a natural explanation. But the explanation of the conjuring trick, if it is to satisfy me, will have to be better than the natural explanations I have heard. The thing is magic, true or false. Second, I came to feel as if magic must have a meaning, and meaning must have some one to mean it. There was something personal in the world, as in a work of art; whatever it meant it meant violently. Third, I thought this purpose beautiful in its old design, in spite of its defects, such as dragons. Fourth, that the proper form of thanks to it is some form of humility and restraint: we should thank God for beer and Burgundy by not drinking too much of them. We owed, also, an obedience to whatever made us. And last, and strangest, there had come into my mind a vague and vast impression that in some way all good was a remnant to be stored and held sacred out of some primordial ruin. Man had saved his good as Crusoe saved his goods: he had saved them from a wreck. All this I felt and the age gave me no encouragement to feel it. And all this time I had not even thought of Christian theology.[95]

There is here, if we seek to identify the successive chapters of *Orthodoxy* with particular stages of Chesterton's own life, a leap forward in time. 'The Ethics of Elfland' seems to be about his childhood. But there is always, in *Orthodoxy*, a conflation of the period recalled with the process of recalling it. The paragraph just quoted has as much to do with Chesterton's memory of his post-Slade digging 'for the submerged sunrise of wonder' as with the sunrise itself; and the chapter is actually, in the end, a remembrance of both periods in Chesterton's life: 'All this I felt and the age gave me no encouragement to feel it' is clearly about the early 1890s, when he was in his late teens, and not about the 1870s. It is worth returning here to Chesterton's own later explication of the process: 'when a memory comes back sharply and suddenly, piercing the protection of oblivion,' he wrote in the *Autobiography*, 'it appears for an instant exactly as it really was. If we think of it often, while its essentials doubtless remain true, it becomes more and more

---

[95] *Collected Works*, i. 268.

our own memory of the thing rather than the thing remembered.'[96] What we have in *Orthodoxy* is a process of multiple remembering, a kind of stratification, in which one layer of remembrance is laid on top of another: thus, this final paragraph of *The Ethics of Elfland* is Chesterton's recollection of his own earlier recollections of childhood. What is striking is that we are left, at the end of this process, not with the impression of an inward-looking, even solipsistic, vision of human life but one which has become broader and more universal in its scope the more it has relied on Chesterton's growing understanding of himself: it is tempting to comment that only a mind whose horizons were so unbounded, a mind, too, so entirely and instinctively prompted by natural humility, could so naturally and so convincingly have assumed the role of Everyman.

The thrilling romance of orthodoxy

The next three chapters, according to A. L. Maycock (one of Gore's successors as Principal of Pusey House), can be 'fairly closely' related to the stages of Chesterton's personal development from the early 1890s up to the period in which he began the composition of *The Man who was Thursday* and *Orthodoxy*. Chapter 5, 'The Flag of the World', Maycock suggests, covers the 'unsettled years' when Chesterton was at the Slade School and starting his first job as a publisher's reader. Chapter 6, 'The Paradoxes of Christianity', belongs to the early years of his married life in Battersea, 'to his first awareness of what Christian orthodoxy was and to his acceptance of it'. In chapter 7, 'The Eternal Revolution', with its passing references to Blatchford, Whistler, Wells, and Tolstoy, we have moved on to the period of *Heretics* and *Charles Dickens*.[97]

It becomes clear, though, if we look at the evidence first of Chesterton's writings from these three periods and then of the contents of these three chapters, that Maycock's chronological account does not fit the biographical facts or the text of *Orthodoxy* except in the broadest way. References to Whistler could belong to any period after the early 1890s; Blatchford and Tolstoy belong just as well (in some ways better), to the early years of Chesterton's marriage (the Blatchford controversy began in mid-1903 and

---

[96] *Autobiography*, 31–2.
[97] A. L. Maycock, *The Man who was Orthodox: A Selection from the Uncollected Writings of G. K. Chesterton* (London, 1963), 58–9.

one of Chesterton's most telling attacks on Tolstoy appeared in 1904, in *England: A Nation*). The argument of chapter 5—in which Chesterton asserts the superiority of an irrational (or supernatural) optimism over both rational optimism and any sort of pessimism—can certainly, in a broad sense, be seen to recall the 1890s, the period in Chesterton's life in which he first struggled with a deadly and depressive pessimism (both in his own life and, as he saw it, in the prevailing culture) and then emerged into the buoyantly optimistic phase described above in Chapter 4. The notion of the superiority of irrational optimism can be traced back to circa 1893: his Slade notebook asserts that 'the mistake of optimism was that it tried to make us admire the world as rational. Anyone who has ever stared long at a tree or a baby knows that the world should be admired as irrational. It is just the queer, incredible look of it, that should make us feel we are in a fairytale. It is the best of all impossible worlds.'[98] We need to note, however, that Chesterton's argument in chapter 5 draws also on later insights. 'My acceptance of the universe is not optimism,' he asserts, 'it is more like patriotism. It is a matter of primary loyalty. The world is . . . the fortress of our family, with the flag flying on the turret, and the more miserable it is the less we should leave it.'[99] But this is an idea which appears for the first time in his thinking only later; he was not writing or thinking about patriotism in this way—either politically or metaphorically—before the outbreak of the Boer War. Similarly, the basis for his defence in *Orthodoxy* of his own 'supernatural' optimism—on the ground that unlike the materialists' 'natural' optimism (which 'leads to stagnation') it leads to reform—belongs not to the 1890s but to the early years of the new century; it appears for the first time in his rebuttal, in the second edition of *The Defendant* (1902), of Masterman's accusation that he was too optimistic by half, and that optimism was generally a conservative force. 'These essays, Chesterton replied, ' . . . seek to remind men that things must be loved first and improved afterwards.'[100] Or as he put it six years later in *Orthodoxy*, '[n]oone doubts that an ordinary man can get on with this world: but . . . Can he hate it enough to change it, and yet love it enough to think it worth changing?'[101] Finally, we can observe that Chesterton's distinction between 'natural' and 'supernatural' optimism, though it is certainly implicit in his writings from the early years of the century, appears for the first time in *Orthodoxy* itself.

[98] Chesterton, 'From the Notebooks of G.K.C.'.   [99] *Collected Works*, i. 270.
[100] G. K. Chesterton, *The Defendant* (London, 1902), 8.
[101] *Collected Works*, i. 275.

Thus, the broad correspondence of these chapters with successive periods in Chesterton's life should not lead us to suppose that we are being offered anything like a simple reprise of his intellectual history. Certainly, as he ponders his earlier life, Chesterton presents his later reflections as though he had arrived at them at the time. Is this a conscious sleight of hand? Or is it the same unconscious process we sometimes observe in the *Autobiography*— notably, for instance, in the projection (already noted[102]) of his later hostility to socialism onto his memories of adolescence and youth? The answer scarcely matters; what matters is the attained completion of these meditations on his earlier life. *Orthodoxy*, it emerges, is very far from being simply a 'slovenly autobiography': it is, as well, a series of new reflections about life and religion, reflections certainly prompted by Chesterton's nostalgic ruminations about his own spiritual history, but conveying also fresh thinking about the nature of his faith and the origins of his own beliefs. What, for instance, was the final meaning of Chesterton's story 'Homesick at Home' (*c*.1896)? Most obviously, as we have already suggested, the story was about the need to rediscover as though it were new what has become stale and jaded (a recurrent Chestertonian theme): but what else could it mean? That notion of 'homesickness' remained latent in Chesterton's imagination for years; so did his memory of the newly recovered optimism of his early twenties: but only now, it seems—despite everything that he had written in defence of his new faith in the intervening years—did the further implications of all that fall into place within the framework of his mature grasp of basic Christian doctrine, in a way which freshly illuminated both maturity and childhood:

all the optimism of the age had been false and disheartening for this reason, that it had always been trying to prove that we fit in to the world.... The optimist's pleasure was prosaic, for it dwelt on the naturalness of everything; the Christian pleasure was poetic, for it dwelt on the unnaturalness of everything in the light of the supernatural. The modern philosopher had told me again and again that I was in the right place, and I had still felt depressed even in acquiescence. But I had heard that I was in the *wrong* place, and my soul sang for joy, like a bird in spring. The knowledge found out and illuminated forgotten chambers in the dark house of infancy. I knew now why grass had always seemed to me as queer as the green beard of a giant, and why I could feel homesick at home.[103]

Chesterton's technique of thus presenting the final result of a complex process of remembrance and meditation—as though it belonged, not to the present in which he has brought it to its conclusion, but to the past time whose recollection had set the process in train—is only confusing if we try to read *Orthodoxy* as conventional autobiography (however 'slovenly'). Chapter 5 'corresponds' to Chesterton's life in the 1890s, for instance: but the ruminations set in train by his optimism of the late 1890s went on for the next decade at least (and in some ways for the rest of his life). At what period in his life, for instance, did he really first propound the following supposedly 1890s questionings?

Had Christianity felt what I felt, but could not (and cannot) express—this need for a first loyalty to things, and then for a ruinous reform of things? Then I remembered that it was actually the charge against Christianity that it combined these two things which I was wildly trying to combine. Christianity was accused, at one and the same time, of being too optimistic about the universe and of being too pessimistic about the world. The coincidence made me suddenly stand still.[104]

Chesterton, we need always to remember, is telling a story. *Orthodoxy* is a 'set of mental pictures', a sequence of almost theatrical scenes of intellectual life: it is a kind of one-man performance. Part of the book's very powerful appeal to those who first responded positively to it was precisely that it held the attention as a personal drama: as Wilfrid Ward put it, 'the story of one who was brought up without Christian faith . . . and had the earnestness and activity of mind to formulate for himself many of its underlying principles . . . makes us recognise [the primary sources of the life-giving power of our religion] explicitly. . . . To see [the great thoughts of Christianity] strike with all the force of youth on a gifted mind makes them young again to us.'[105] It is one of the primary aims of *Orthodoxy* to show that Christian dogma is the very opposite of a constriction of the human spirit, to set the Christian creeds flying in the wind like great banners above a conquering army of liberation. Timing in the theatre is everything: thus, it is in chapter 5, well out of sequence, that Chesterton judges it right to present one of the book's most memorable and histrionic moments, the equivalent, almost, of the dramatic moment in the *Apologia* in which Newman recounts how the words *securus judicat orbis terrarum* brought him to realise for the first time the true nature of the Church and the falseness of his own position: it is the point at which, having realised Christianity's power to reconcile opposites without any loss of their integrity, Chesterton suddenly realises that the claims of Christian

---

[104] *Collected Works*, 277–8.   [105] Ward, 'Mr Chesterton among the Prophets', 6.

doctrine have an exact correspondence with the problems posed by the human condition. This realisation is presented, not as an intellectual conclusion, but—in an intensely visual sequence of almost cinematic images—as a theatrical denouement; and yet again, the scene ends with an evocation of his childhood's 'sunrise of wonder':

And then followed an experience impossible to describe. It was as if I had been blundering about since my birth with two huge and unmanageable machines, of different shapes and without apparent connection—the world and the Christian tradition. I had found this hole in the world: the fact that one must somehow find a way of loving the world without trusting it; somehow one must love the world without being worldly. I found this projecting feature of Christian theology, like a sort of hard spike, the dogmatic insistence that God was personal, and had made a world separate from Himself. The spike of dogma fitted exactly into the hole in the world—it had evidently been meant to go there—and then the strange thing began to happen. When once these two parts of the two machines had come together, one after another, all the other parts fitted and fell in with an eerie exactitude. I could hear bolt after bolt over all the machinery falling into its place with a kind of click of relief. Having got one part right, all the other parts were repeating that rectitude, as clock after clock strikes noon. Instinct after instinct was answered by doctrine after doctrine. Or, to vary the metaphor, I was like one who had advanced into a hostile country to take one high fortress. And when that fort had fallen the whole country surrendered and turned solid behind me. The whole land was lit up, as it were, back to the first fields of my childhood.[106]

The next chapter, 'The Paradoxes of Christianity', according to Maycock, corresponds with the years of Chesterton's 'first awareness of orthodoxy'. Certainly, in some ways it does correspond approximately with the years 1900–3; but as we have seen, Chesterton has just destroyed this chronology by anticipating his 'discovery of orthodoxy' by several years. What we can say, however, is that in this chapter he does come to certain conclusions about the implications of his 'discovery of orthodoxy'; though alas for any lingering hankerings after autobiographical appropriateness, these too belong not to the supposed period of the chapter, but to a later time, to the present in which *Orthodoxy* was being written. In this chapter Chesterton attains, in fact, the intellectual and dramatic summit of the book; and though later chapters contain strong writing and powerful argumentation, there is about them a certain sense of contained anticlimax, of a gradual descent to the plain.

[106] *Collected Works*, i. 282–3.

In this as in much else, Wilfrid Ward's piece in the *Dublin Review* was more perceptive, not only than anything else written at the time but also than most writing about *Orthodoxy* since. 'The Paradoxes of Christianity', he asserted, 'contains . . . the most valuable writing of the whole book.' His article was significantly entitled 'Mr Chesterton among the Prophets'; and in it he had insisted that far from being, as some of the book's reviewers supposed, 'a purveyor of acrobatic feats of the intellect . . . not to be taken seriously', Chesterton was, in fact a substantial writer of real stature:

> They class him with brilliant writers of the hour, such as Mr Wells, who have no claim to teaching the age a serious lesson. . . . I associate him with those writers of the past who have decried mere ingenuity in theorizing, and striven to find the path of philosophy traced by Nature herself. I class his thought—though not his manner— with that of such men as Burke, Butler and Coleridge.[107]

Ward now strikingly compares Chesterton with another prophetic figure, one on which he had some authority to speak—John Henry Newman: in 'The Paradoxes of Christianity', argues Ward, 'here again he has rediscovered the path already travelled by a great thinker. For he gives us a rough and unphilosophical expression of the line of reasoning in a book which he has, perhaps, never read—Cardinal Newman's *Essay in Aid of a Grammar of Assent*. He tells us, in popular language that it is by the cumulative argument, by the "illative sense," which cannot express all the latent reasons which influence its decision, that he, like others really reached his conclusions.' The 'illative sense' is a gift for natural inference, a faculty of reason which—in contrast with the operation of logical proof—can, according to Newman, give rise to certitude by drawing together different strands of argument, separately inconclusive but decisive together. Ward quotes the following passage from 'The Paradoxes of Christianity' to illustrate his comparison:

> a man is not really convinced of a philosophic theory when he finds that something proves it. He is only really convinced when he finds that everything proves it. And the more converging reasons he finds pointing to this conviction, the more bewildered he is if asked suddenly to sum them up. Thus, if one asked an ordinary intelligent man, on the spur of the moment, 'Why do you prefer civilization to savagery?' he would look wildly round at object after object, and would only be able to answer vaguely, 'Why, there is that bookcase . . . and the coals in the coal-scuttle . . . and pianos . . . and policemen.' The whole case for civilization is that the case for it is complex. It has

---

[107] Ward, 'Mr Chesterton among the Prophets', 1.

done so many things. But that very multiplicity of proof which ought to make reply overwhelming makes reply impossible.[108]

In one of his most penetrating, and characteristic, uses of paradox—not as a clever verbal trick but as a way of conveying that some received belief is based on the precise diametric opposite of the truth—Chesterton has already argued that it is not an argument against the Christian tradition to say that its theology is too complex, for life itself is complex in precisely the same way. The argument that a supposedly simple faith like Christianity is unsuited to the modern world is in fact the reverse of the truth: 'The complication of our modern world proves the truth of the creed more perfectly than any of the plain problems of the ages of faith. . . . A stick might fit a hole or a stone a hollow by accident. But a key and a lock are both complex. And if a key fits a lock, you know it is the right key.'[109]

Truth, he goes on to say—in the passage whose argument is compared by Ward to Newman's use of the 'illative sense'—is cumulative, and therefore unwieldy: 'that very multiplicity of proof which ought to make reply overwhelming makes reply impossible. There is, therefore, about all complete conviction a kind of huge helplessness.' It is here that the conventions of the autobiographical mode, not for the first time, come to Chesterton's aid: he returns to the method of describing the various 'mystical coincidences' which have, for him, brought about some sudden clearing of the fog of unbelief. Having weakened his target's defences at one strategic point he now attacks them from another. He has argued, like Newman, that spiritual certitude is a matter of the accumulation of inferences rather than of direct rational proof. He now renews the assault on mere rationality, by attacking the rationalists themselves: this he does by returning to the point in his life at which, having considered 'all the non-Christian or anti-Christian accounts of the faith, from Huxley to Bradlaugh', he comes to a realisation of the incoherences and internal contradictions their arguments embody: 'a slow and awful impression grew gradually but graphically upon my mind—the impression that Christianity must be a most extraordinary thing. For not only (as I understood) had Christianity the most flaming vices, but it had apparently a mystical talent for combining vices which seemed inconsistent with each other. It was attacked on all sides and for all contradictory reasons.'

[108] *Collected Works*, i. 287.   [109] Ibid. 286–7.

Thus, for instance, I was much moved by the eloquent attack on Christianity as a thing of inhuman gloom. . . . if Christianity was, as these people said, a thing purely pessimistic and opposed to life, then I was quite prepared to blow up St. Paul's Cathedral. But the extraordinary thing is this. They did prove to me . . . that Christianity was too pessimistic; and then . . . they began to prove to me that it was a great deal too optimistic. One accusation against Christianity was that it prevented men, by morbid tears and terrors, from seeking joy and liberty in the bosom of Nature. But another accusation was that it comforted men with a fictitious providence. . . . One rationalist had hardly done calling Christianity a nightmare before another began to call it a fool's paradise. . . . This puzzled me; the charges seemed inconsistent. . . . The state of the Christian could not be at once so comfortable that he was a coward to cling to it, and so uncomfortable that he was a fool to stand it.[110]

Chesterton has by this stage in the chapter assembled his arguments so as to be within striking distance of his objective. He now deploys them in an unexpected direction. It has seemed that his tactic is to show the weakness of the opponents of Christianity: now he shows that they have failed less because of their own weakness and inconsistency, than because of an unexpected strength in their opponent. The rationalist attack is inconsistent because it says now one thing then its opposite: what it cannot do, and what Christianity triumphantly succeeds in doing, is to hold opposites together by saying that both are true: not partly, so that truth may be an accommodation between them, but completely and without compromise. 'Paganism declared that virtue was in a balance; Christianity declared it was in a conflict: the collision of two passions apparently opposite.' These passions are not in fact really inconsistent; but they may be difficult to hold together. Chesterton gives the example of courage, which is almost 'a contradiction in terms. It means a strong desire to live taking the form of a readiness to die. "He that will lose his life, the same shall save it," is not a piece of mysticism for saints and heroes. It is a piece of everyday advice for sailors or mountaineers. . . . A man cut off by the sea may save his life if he will risk it on the precipice.'[111] This is not unlike Chesterton's earliest defence of his use of paradox in *The Speaker*: 'courage is a paradox, and can best and most easily be expressed by a paradox. I have only to say, "Courage involves the power of being frightened," and you have a paradox and a matter of plain common sense.'[112]

These reflections lead him to an important discovery. 'And now', he reminisces in *Orthodoxy*, 'I began to find that this duplex passion was the

[110] *Collected Works*, 289–90.   [111] Ibid. 297.
[112] 'G.K.C.', 'Bacon and Beastliness', *The Speaker* (8 Feb. 1902), 532.

Christian key to ethics everywhere. Everywhere the creed made a moderation out of the still crash of two impetuous emotions.' He considers the example of modesty. The average pagan says that he is content with himself, but not self-satisfied, that there are many better and many worse. This is, says Chesterton, a rational position, but hardly inspiring: it is a 'dilution of two things', it is neither true pride nor true humility: '[t]his proper pride does not lift the heart like the tongue of trumpets. . . . On the other hand, this mild rationalist modesty does not cleanse the soul with fire and make it clear like crystal; it does not . . . make a man as a little child. . . . It does not make him look up and see marvels.'[113]

Chesterton now embarks on an extended series of examples of what he has called Christianity's 'duplex passion' for a dramatic but sometimes perilous balance between opposites, rather than for a murky accommodation between them. Again and again, Christianity is shown to be urging paradox rather than compromise. 'In one way Man was to be haughtier than he had ever been before; in another way he was to be humbler than he had ever been before.'[114] 'Charity [too] is a paradox, like modesty and courage. . . . We must be much more angry with theft than before, and yet much kinder to thieves than before.'[115] 'The ordinary aesthetic anarchist . . . breaks away from home limits to follow poetry. But in ceasing to feel home limits he has ceased to feel the *Odyssey*. He is free from national prejudices and outside patriotism. But being outside patriotism he is outside *Henry V*. Such a literary man is simply outside all literature: he is more of a prisoner than any bigot.'[116] 'St. Francis, in praising all good, could be a more shouting optimist than Walt Whitman. St. Jerome, in denouncing all evil, could paint the world blacker than Schopenhauer. Both passions were free because both were kept in their place.'[117] By defining its main doctrine, argues Chesterton, 'the Church not only kept seemingly inconsistent things side by side, but, what was more, allowed them to break out in a sort of artistic violence otherwise possible only to anarchists. Meekness grew more dramatic than madness. Historic Christianity rose into a high and strange *coup de théâtre* of morality—things that are to virtue what the crimes of Nero are to vice.'[118] '[T]he historic Church', he insists, ' . . . hates that combination of two colours which is the feeble expedient of the philosophers. It hates that evolution of black into white which is tantamount to a dirty gray. . . . Christianity sought in most of these cases to keep two colours

---

[113] *Collected Works*, i. 297–8.   [114] Ibid. 298.   [115] Ibid. 299–300.
[116] Ibid. 300.   [117] Ibid.   [118] Ibid. 301.

coexistent but pure.'[119] Orthodox theology had, in particular, 'specially insisted that Christ was not a being apart from God and man, like an elf, nor yet a being half human and half not, like a centaur, but both things at once and both things thoroughly, very man and very God'.[120]

Chesterton now approaches the climax of his argument, the climax, indeed, of the book itself; arguably, even, the climax of his literary career thus far, in the famous passage which ends this chapter. Most important of all, he insists, is the fact that here is the explanation of what it is that most repels the modern world in the teaching of the Church (for it has by now become clear that it is the Catholic tradition—rather than some version of basic or 'mere' Christianity—that he is defending). It is this 'equipoise' of balancing opposites which explains 'what is so inexplicable to all the modern critics of the history of Christianity' (a line of argument directed as much against 'the New Theology' as against the secularism of contemporary culture)—'I mean the monstrous wars about small points of theology, the earthquakes of emotion about a gesture or a word':[121] '[t]he Church could not afford to swerve a hair's breadth on some things if she was to continue her great and daring experiment of the irregular equilibrium. Once let one idea become less powerful and some other idea would become too powerful.'[122] The Church went in for dangerous ideas, 'terrible and devouring doctrines': the death of a divine being, the forgiveness of sins, the fulfilment of prophecies, all ideas which 'any one can see, need but a touch to turn them into something blasphemous or ferocious'. Doctrines, says Chesterton, 'had to be defined within strict limits, even in order that man might enjoy general human liberties. The Church had to be careful, if only that the world might be careless.' This brings us to what is certainly the most quoted passage from *Orthodoxy*, and perhaps one of the most quoted passages in all Chesterton's works. Though it is often described, sometimes dismissively, as a 'purple passage' it is important to insist that this is not only writing of considerable dramatic power; it contains, too, the essence of Chesterton's case for the Christian tradition—here evoked with a sure sense of historical reference: that it satisfies profoundly the universal need for what he had called, at the beginning of his journey, a 'life of practical romance; the combination of something that is strange with something that is secure'. It exemplifies as well as articulating the Christian paradox of courage (including intellectual courage), that it is only by taking risks that one can

---

[119] *Collected Works*, 302.   [120] Ibid. 296.   [121] Ibid. 304.   [122] Ibid.

truly be safe. Finally, it allows us to grasp how it was that the book had such an impact on so many at the time, an impact most memorably conveyed, perhaps, by Ward's infectious excitement at the 'spectacle of this intensely active and earnest modern intellect... of Mr Chesterton's whole forcible, energising self, with its strength and its defects, fired by the Christian dogma and ethics, as though he had lived in the days of Nero or Marcus Aurelius'.[123] The passage should always be (but rarely is) quoted in full:

This is the thrilling romance of Orthodoxy. People have fallen into a foolish habit of speaking of orthodoxy as something heavy, humdrum, and safe. There never was anything so perilous or so exciting as orthodoxy. It was sanity: and to be sane is more dramatic than to be mad. It was the equilibrium of a man behind madly rushing horses, seeming to stoop this way and to sway that, yet in every attitude having the grace of statuary and the accuracy of arithmetic. The Church in its early days went fierce and fast with any warhorse; yet it is utterly unhistoric to say that she merely went mad along one idea, like a vulgar fanaticism. She swerved to left and right, so exactly as to avoid enormous obstacles. She left on one hand the huge bulk of Arianism, buttressed by all the worldly powers to make Christianity too worldly. The next instant she was swerving to avoid an orientalism, which would have made it too unworldly. The orthodox Church never took the tame course or accepted the conventions; the orthodox Church was never respectable. It would have been easier to have accepted the earthly power of the Arians. It would have been easy, in the Calvinistic seventeenth century, to fall into the bottomless pit of predestination. It is easy to be a madman: it is easy to be a heretic. It is always easy to let the age have its head; the difficult thing is to keep one's own. It is always easy to be a modernist; as it is easy to be a snob. To have fallen into any of those open traps of error and exaggeration which fashion after fashion and sect after sect set along the historic path of Christendom—that would indeed have been simple. It is always simple to fall; there are an infinity of angles at which one falls, only one at which one stands. To have fallen into any one of the fads from Gnosticism to Christian Science would indeed have been obvious and tame. But to have avoided them all has been one whirling adventure; and in my vision the heavenly chariot flies thundering through the ages, the dull heresies sprawling and prostrate, the wild truth reeling but erect.[124]

---

[123] Ward, 'Mr Chesterton among the Prophets', 7.   [124] *Collected Works*, i. 305–6.

Epilogue

In February 1908—the same month that Chesterton published *The Man who was Thursday*—George Bernard Shaw brought forth the Chesterbelloc, the fabulous beast whose hind legs were Chesterton's, and whose forelegs were Belloc's. Ironically, this bizarre conception (the 'twiformed monster' as Chesterton called it),[1] which ever since has perpetuated the notion that Chesterton's ideas are indistinguishable (or at least inseparable) from Belloc's, was intended by Shaw to indicate the exact reverse: 'a pantomime animal with two men in it is a mistake when the two men are not very carefully paired. . . . Chesterton and Belloc are so unlike that they get frightfully into one another's way. . . . They are unlike in everything except the specific literary genius and delight in play-acting that is common to them and that threw them into one another's arms.'[2] The Chesterbelloc, thus portrayed as a farcical impossibility, was Shaw's response to a series of articles in the socialist weekly *New Age* in which Belloc's arguments and Chesterton's had become to some extent confused: hence, given Shaw's instinctive liking for Chesterton and lack of sympathy with Belloc, his anxiety to disentangle them. The debate had begun two months before with an attack on various modern ideas, including socialism, by Belloc. Four weeks later, the *New Age* published a piece by Chesterton agreeing with Belloc about socialism; the following week, H. G. Wells responded with an article ('About Chesterton and Belloc') disagreeing with them both, but insisting nevertheless that 'Chesterton and Belloc agree with the socialist that the present world doesn't give at all what they want', and that 'in the fight against human selfishness and narrowness and for a finer, juster law, we are brothers'.[3] In the years that followed, Shaw and Wells often debated with Belloc and Chesterton on the public platform; but the real

---

[1] *Autobiography*, 117.
[2] G. B. Shaw, 'Belloc and Chesterton', *New Age* (15 Feb. 1908), 309.
[3] H. G. Wells, 'About Chesterton and Belloc', *New Age* (11 Jan. 1908), 210.

debate, the one that caught the public imagination, was that between Chesterton and Shaw. Their public confrontations, according to Michael Holroyd, Shaw's biographer, began in 1911;[4] but this cannot be accurate, since Shaw's Chesterbelloc piece refers to 'a recent occasion' on which he and Chesterton had debated the question of miracles.[5] This debate had taken place at Clifford's Inn, probably in late 1907 or early 1908, and Shaw referred to it again in December 1908 (the *New Age* controversy went on well into the following year before running out of steam), claiming that he had 'deflated' Chesterton by asking him about a particular miracle in which '[n]obody believed'.[6] The 'incredible' miracle was the annual liquefaction of the blood of St Januarius, and Chesterton responded by denying that he had been deflated by Shaw's question, and by insisting that the question of whether or not the blood of St Januarius liquefied was a simple matter of logic and evidence: it was Shaw the rationalist who had fallen back on mere prejudice; in contrast, wrote Chesterton, 'reason is permitted to a Catholic Christian; it is forbidden to a follower of Shaw. Shaw does not retire into his inner consciousness to find out if blood is shed at Smithfield. Why should he do it to find out if blood is liquefied in Italy? The answer is that he has become a man who denies rational truth.'[7] Shaw delighted in their exchanges, and in the spirit in which their debates through the years were conducted; 'I enjoyed him,' Shaw wrote after Chesterton's death, 'and nothing could have been more generous than his treatment of me.'[8] These feelings were entirely reciprocated. 'It is not easy', wrote Chesterton in his *Autobiography*, 'to dispute violently with a man for twenty years, about sex, about sin, about sacraments, about personal points of honour, about all the most sacred or delicate essentials of existence, without sometimes being irritated or feeling that he hits unfair blows or employs discreditable ingenuities. And I can testify that I have never read a reply by Bernard Shaw that did not leave me in a better and not a worse temper or frame of mind; which did not seem to come out of inexhaustible fountains of fair-mindedness and intellectual geniality.... It is necessary to disagree with him as much as I do, in order to admire him as much as I do; and I am proud of him as a foe even more than as a friend.'[9]

[4] Michael Holroyd, *Bernard Shaw: The One-Volume Definitive Edition* (London, 1997), 372.
[5] Shaw, 'Belloc and Chesterton', 310.
[6] G. B. Shaw, 'On Miracles: A Retort on Mr Chesterton', *New Age* (10 Dec. 1908),129.
[7] G. K. Chesterton, 'A Summary of Sects', *New Age* (25 Feb. 1909), 362.
[8] Holroyd, *Bernard Shaw*, 373.
[9] *Autobiography*, 234.

The friendship began in splendidly picturesque circumstances: on a visit to Paris in August 1906 in the studio of Auguste Rodin, where Shaw was sitting for a portrait bust. Shaw, at that stage in their lives, was the great man and Chesterton the rising young writer. He had published *Heretics* two months before; but there is no indication, from the account of the event by Chesterton's brother-in-law, Lucian Oldershaw, that Shaw was aware of its attack on him. When Chesterton and Oldershaw entered Rodin's studio, he was talking volubly in broken French. Rodin's secretary told them that Shaw had been 'endeavouring to explain at some length the nature of the Salvation Army' (*Major Barbara* had been performed for the first time the year before). At the end of the explanation, Rodin's secretary remarked—to a rather apologetic Shaw—'The Master says you have not much French but you impose yourself.'[10] Oldershaw's memory was that Shaw 'talked Gilbert down'; '[t]hat the famous man should talk more than the beginner is hardly surprising', comments Maisie Ward; she adds that 'Chesterton was one of the few great conversationalists —perhaps the only one—who would really rather listen than talk'.

When it came to public debate, however, Chesterton was not to be 'talked down', even by Shaw. 'Their jousting over the years', observes Michael Holroyd, 'developed into a perfect balance of contrasting styles, with breathtaking displays of analogy and tricks of paradox. Chesterton's bulky swaying presence matched the immense range of illustration he gave his ideas, lit up by a spirit of enjoyment and comic inventiveness. Shaw was more incisive, his emphatic eyebrows like two supplementary moustaches, an assured and wiry figure standing with arms folded who could speak with a force thrilling to all who heard it.'[11] Their final (and best documented) public debate took place in October 1927 at Kingsway Hall and was organised by the Distributist League, which had been formed the previous year. The debate was broadcast by the infant BBC; crowds struggled to get into the hall. During the debate, proceedings were interrupted by persistent knocking at the doors by ticket-holders who, through some misunderstanding, had been locked out. Belloc, who was chairman, had the doors opened, and order was restored, partly by Belloc and partly by Shaw, who quietened the audience by proclaiming, 'Ladies and Gentlemen, I must go on because, as you see, if I don't begin to talk everybody else does.'[12] Despite Shaw's

---

[10] Ward, 136.   [11] Holroyd, *Bernard Shaw*, 374.
[12] G. B. Shaw and G. K. Chesterton, *Do We Agree?* (London, 1928), 10–11.

telling the audience that he suspected that they did 'not really care much what we debate about provided we entertain you by talking in our characteristic manners', Chesterton, at least—though, as always, with a light touch—talked of profoundly serious matters; five years before the election of Hitler as Chancellor of Germany, he went prophetically to the heart of the terrible events that were to dominate the remaining years of the century by articulating his fears about collectivisms of both left and right, fears which in 1927 had (unknown to most Englishmen) already become reality in the Soviet Union:

when you have vast systems...you do in fact find that those who rule are the few.... We say there ought to be in the world a great mass of scattered powers, privileges, limits, points of resistance, so that the mass of the Commons may resist tyranny. And we say that there is a permanent possibility of that central direction...becoming a tyranny. I do not think it would be difficult to suggest a way in which it could happen.[13]

The debate between Shaw and Chesterton came to encapsulate in the public mind two great overlapping intellectual conflicts of the twentieth century: first, that between the Christian tradition and modern rationalism, and then—beginning with the two men's articles in the *New Age*—between family and property and individual liberty on the one hand and collectivism on the other. Their political differences, however, were in one sense outside the political mainstream. Chesterton's hostility to socialism (by no means shared by his friends within the Christian Social Union) was not the result of any conservative instinct that would be remotely recognisable as such within the English political tradition. By now, indeed, his political instincts were fundamentally to reject that tradition; there would be no more canvassing for Liberal candidates. There was, he wrote in *The Daily News* in October 1907, a 'fundamental absurdity in our political institutions':

It has existed ever since somebody started that idiotic habit of dividing men, not by what they thought or wanted, but on the theory that there are some people who want to alter things, and some other people who want to keep things as they are. Of course there are no people who want to keep things as they are.... [and] if a magician...from Mars told us that when we woke up next morning we should find things very much altered, we should go to bed with disturbed feelings. Yet the present Liberal and Conservative parties are based upon this unthinkable fantasy.[14]

[13] Ibid. 22–5.
[14] G. K. Chesterton, 'The Last of the Conservatives', *The Daily News* (5 Oct. 1907).

It may be doubted, however, whether he had ever been enthusiastic about 'our political institutions'. He had never lost his boyhood enthusiasm for the French revolutionary tradition, and it survived his conversion to a form of Catholic Christianity; indeed, he seems to have believed that orthodox Christianity was by no means incompatible with a predisposition to bloody revolution. His reaction to the first Russian Revolution (1905–7) is instructive. 'It is clear', he wrote in May 1907, 'that in some way there is a Revolution of some kind going on in Russia; and that ought to be enough to make any healthy man happy. Revolution is certainly the divine part of man; "Behold, I make all things new".'[15] His poem about the people of England, 'The Secret People', was written at about this time and shows that events in Russia were arousing within him not the reactions of a natural conservative, but rather a hankering for the same thing to happen in England, if possible with a little more violence ('It may be we shall rise the last as Frenchmen rose the first, | Our wrath come after Russia's wrath and our wrath be the worst'[16]).

Chesterton's political articulation of his hostility to collectivism, based on his deep belief in the instincts of the common man, became known as distributism only later; the word, indeed, was not yet invented when he wrote, in this landmark year of 1908, that

No part of the community is so specially fixed in those forms and feelings which are opposite to the tone of most Socialists [as the mass of the common people]; the privacy of homes, the control of one's own children, the minding of one's own business.... I believe I could make up a sort of creed... believed strongly by the overwhelming mass of men and women.... For instance, that an Englishman's house is his castle... that marriage is a real bond... that vegetarianism and all pitting of animal against human rights is a silly fad...[17]

These are ideas which need no particular theological rationale; but they dovetail exactly with Belloc's expression of hostility to socialism, published in the *New Age* the previous month, the origins of which are openly Roman Catholic (the qualification is necessary, since Chesterton was at this time regularly describing his beliefs as 'Catholic', as we have seen a self-description normal among Anglicans of his kind). Belloc insists on a specifically, indeed triumphalistically, religious critique of socialism:

---

[15] G. K. Chesterton, 'The Indispensable Fire', *The Daily News* (4 May 1907).

[16] *Collected Works*, x. 411.

[17] G. K. Chesterton, 'Why I am not a Socialist', *New Age* (4 Jan. 1908), 190.

The criticism I offer to collectivism is offered by the whole weight and mass of Catholic opinion; in other words, it is the criticism offered by all that is healthy and permanent in the intellectual life of Europe; it is a criticism which has been repeated a hundred times in the French Parliament, and a thousand times in the Irish pulpits throughout the world. The sentiment of property is normal and necessary to a citizen. Exactly the same thing as makes Catholic opinion as a whole to-day, and Catholic countries in the past, the enemies of the rich, of landlordism, and the rest . . . exactly the same self-preserving sense as made Catholic societies reject the beastly economies of industrialism in its beginnings. . . . There is no defence of collectivism save from men who either deny that man is now fixed in a certain moral plan, or from men who deny free-will.[18]

This argument was to be elaborated in *The Servile State* (1912), written under the influence of Pope Leo XIII's *Rerum Novarum* (1891), an encyclical which was equally hostile to large-scale capitalism and to socialism, and which both asserted the rights of labour to organise trade unions, and of the private individual to own property. *The Servile State* later became the bible of the distributist movement. In it, Belloc argued that capitalism was creating, and socialism would create, the kind of society in which power would be concentrated in the hands of a small ruling class, and which would generate a permanent servile class whose economic position would be fixed by the structures of the state. The only alternative to the 'slave' state was a distributist state of small ownership and workers' guilds. Distributists must therefore repudiate modern industrialism in its present form and work for a return to the principles of the medieval past.[19] Chesterton's connection with what was to become the distributist movement began in 1916, when he took his brother's place as editor of the *New Witness*; but it is possible to see much earlier traces of this kind of thinking in his work. In *The Man who was Thursday*, Gabriel Syme points to 'a heavy French peasant . . . cutting wood with a hatchet. His cart stood a few yards off, already half full of timber. . . . his swarthy figure stood dark against a square of sunlight, almost like some allegoric figure of labour frescoed on a ground of gold'; here, says Syme, is someone who could never become an anarchist, 'if only for the reason that he has . . . property to defend'. But Chesterton's belief in property (at this date quite distinct from Belloc's) is as much temperamental as political or religious; it is part of an almost instinctual belief in what he calls, in his own *New Age* attack on socialism, 'the strong sense of English cosiness, the

---

[18] Hilaire Belloc, 'Thoughts about Modern Thought', *New Age* (7 Dec. 1907), 108.
[19] Ian Boyd, *The Novels of G. K. Chesterton: A Study in Art and Propaganda* (London, 1975), 77.

instinct for special festival, the distinction between the dignities of man and woman, responsibility of a man under his roof'.[20]

It is most profoundly, perhaps, in this sense of the 'responsibility of a man under his roof' that we can begin to judge Chesterton's special countervailing relevance to the political mass cultures that were to arise during the twentieth century, most terribly in the years that followed his death in 1936. Prophetic figures are not always heeded when they speak; and we often judge them best when time can lend perspective to our own judgement. Chesterton's predictions were not always borne out in the short term. In *Orthodoxy*, at the end of his 'rough review of recent thought', he pronounced that '[b]y the accident of my present detachment, I can see the inevitable smash of the philosophies of Schopenhauer and Tolstoy, Nietzsche and Shaw, as clearly as an inevitable railway smash could be seen from a balloon.' Of these four names, three at least were very far from the predicted smash. Certainly, Tolstoy the philosopher was soon largely to disappear in the public mind, effaced by his lasting reputation as the greatest of all epic novelists. Shaw's 'philosophy' however—though he is today a purely literary figure whose 'philosophy' time has consigned to a merciful oblivion—was seen at the time as relevant and viable enough. When Chesterton wrote his book on Shaw (1909) he pointed to one sinister element in that philosophy. Nietzsche, he wrote, 'succeeded in putting into [Shaw's] head a new superstition, *which bids fair to be the chief superstition of the dark ages which are possibly in front of us*—I mean the superstition of what is called the Superman' (my italics). As we have seen, this was not his first warning; he had already given a specifically Christian response to the implications of the Superman (without mentioning Nietzsche or Shaw) in the second phase of the Blatchford controversy, asserting that 'if a man came up to us (*as many will soon come up to us*) to say, "I am a new kind of man. I am the super-man. I have abandoned mercy and justice"; we should answer, "Doubtless you are new, but you are not nearer to the perfect man, for he has already been in the mind of God" ' (my italics).[21] In *Heretics* he had upbraided Shaw, 'perhaps the most humane man alive', for being, in one sense, 'inhumane. He has . . . been infected . . . with the primary intellectual weakness of his new master, Nietzsche, [with] the strange notion that the

[20]   Chesterton, 'Why I am not a Socialist', 190.
[21]   G. K. Chesterton, 'We are All Agnostics until—', *The Clarion* (22 July 1904); *Collected Works*, i. 385.

greater and stronger a man was the more he would despise other things.'[22] Nietzsche's influence on the century came to its dreadful climax in the years following Chesterton's death and then, the only one of the four names singled out in *Orthodoxy* to do so, came to the 'inevitable smash' Chesterton had predicted nearly thirty years before.

But Schopenhauer's influence was a different matter; it was to grow throughout the twentieth century more than Chesterton could possibly have imagined; the 'inevitable smash' never took place. Chesterton's distaste for Schopenhauer needs no explanation; two human beings could hardly have been more different in mind and heart. In the *Autobiography*, Chesterton wrote that his life had been 'indefensibly fortunate and happy'.[23] Schopenhauer truly believed that 'no man is happy';[24] he certainly was not. When Chesterton wrote his *Daily News* attack on Schopenhauer in the first year of the new century, he assumed that he was confronting a current literary fashion, 'modern pessimism'. And when, toward the end of his life, he recalled that when he began to write, he 'was full of a new and fiery resolution to write against the Decadents and the Pessimists who ruled the culture of the age', he was looking back on movements and men whose influence he judged to be dead—the Pessimists, Schopenhauer included, as much as the Decadents. Schopenhauer is mentioned three times in *Orthodoxy* (1908) as a still current threat, but not at all in *The Everlasting Man* (1925) or in the *Autobiography* (1936); in *Robert Louis Stevenson* (1928) he saw Stevenson's 'reaction against pessimism' against the background of 'the gigantic shadow of Schopenhauer' which had been 'thrown across all that earth and sky' in the closing decades of the century, a period during which 'we might almost say that pessimism was another name for culture'. Even then, reflected Chesterton in 1928, 'some of us may already have suspected that the shadow was larger than the man'.[25]

His hostility toward 'the Pessimists', however, continued to define his own literary identity; it is one of a complex of ideas that make Chesterton as much a landmark for the culture of the twentieth century as Carlyle and Ruskin had been for the nineteenth, each of them epitomising their own age by prophetically denouncing many of its most characteristic beliefs. Chesterton's denunciations, for the most part, were gentle, even affectionate. His treatment of

---

[22] *Collected Works*, i. 68.   [23] *Autobiography*, 331.
[24] Arthur Schopenhauer, 'The Emptiness of Existence', in *Essays of Schopenhauer*, trans. S. H. Dircks (London, 1897), 56.
[25] *Collected Works*, xviii. 74.

Schopenhauer was an exception. In 1901, he had written that 'of all men whose souls have influenced the world, Schopenhauer seems to me the most contemptible'. But it was not Schopenhauer's fundamental and obsessive belief in 'The Misery of Life' (the title of his most famous essay) that Chesterton thought most contemptible: it was his ingratitude for the gift of his own creation. Chesterton's *Daily News* article (quoted at length in Chapter 5 [26]) is as much an assertion of his own most deeply held convictions as an onslaught on Schopenhauer's. Schopenhauer seemed to believe it would have been better never to have been born: 'He did not realise', wrote Chesterton, 'that the question of whether life contains a preponderance of joy or sorrow is entirely secondary to the fact that life is an experience of a unique and miraculous character, the idea of missing which would be intolerable if it were for one moment conceivable.'[27]

Chesterton's attitude to Schopenhauer, we can say, is a touchstone for his profound and instinctive opposition to what was to become, ever more powerfully, one of the most irresistible currents, perhaps even the mainstream, of twentieth-century culture; it is also a touchstone for his prophetic relevance to that culture. His *Daily News* article begins by accepting that 'the popularity of Schopenhauer at the present day far surpasses the popularity of any of his contemporaries in philosophy'. It was written in the first year of the new century: by the end of that century, Schopenhauer's impact on twentieth-century thought, and particularly on imaginative literature, had been greater than Chesterton himself could ever have foreseen. Brian Magee argues not only that Schopenhauer was a major influence over philosophy (particularly Nietzsche and Wittgenstein) and over psychology (both Freud and Jung) but also that his influence over creative artists in the late nineteenth and twentieth centuries was greater than that of any other philosopher, including Marx; among novelists he includes Tolstoy, Turgenev, Zola, Maupassant, Proust, Hardy, Conrad, and Thomas Mann; among short-story writers, Maugham and Borges. He also influenced, among poets, Rilke and Eliot, and among dramatists, Pirandello and Beckett.[28] The common theme here is the profound disenchantment with human nature and with the human situation itself that is the keynote of so much of the literature of the last century. With hindsight, we can see Chesterton's passionate gratitude for creation and his unconditional love of humanity as indicating from the

[26] See pp. 208–10 above.
[27] G. K. Chesterton, 'The Great Pessimist', *The Daily News* (7 June 1901), 6.
[28] Bryan Magee, *The Philosophy of Schopenhauer* (Oxford, 1997), 403–17.

beginning of his career that his place in twentieth-century culture was inevitably to be one of unremitting insurgency against a civilisation in which, more and more, the human race was to be perceived as inhabiting the heart of darkness.

By the time he wrote *Orthodoxy* his vocation (the word is not out of place) had become clear. 'Mr Chesterton', wrote his brother Cecil, in his own book on his brother's intellectual development up to this pivotal year (it appeared just before *Orthodoxy* itself), 'is not and does not profess to be [a pure artist]. He is primarily . . . the preacher of a definite message to his own time. He is using all the power which his literary capacity gives him to lead the age in a certain direction.'[29] Once we have seen that, we are able to understand much else besides, including Chesterton's continuing relevance to our own age. This has in recent times become much clearer than it once was. Eliot's assessment in 1936 that Chesterton's ideas were '*the* ideas for [the times] that were funda-mentally Christian and Catholic' had become, or so it seemed, by the 1960s and 1970s, a simple dead letter, with a change in fashion—which then seemed final and definitive—about what ought to be considered the ideas for *that* time which were fundamentally Christian and Catholic. To take an important example, Chesterton's defence of what was small against what was large, especially his defence of small nations against their agglomeration into larger empires or other international groupings, had become so unfashionable by the middle of the century as to be almost laughable. Internationalism had become not only 'politically correct' but apparently inevitable, Chesterton's dislike of the 'cosmopolitan' simply quaint. In his book *The Mind of Chesterton* (1970), Christopher Hollis explained that unlike Chesterton, who had been suspicious of the League of Nations, 'in these years after the second world war, the Popes, by their strong support of the League's successor, the United Nations, have shown themselves the champions of the creation of the international author-ity'. Whether Hollis was right about the support of the Popes for 'international authority' is at least doubtful; what is certain is that it is he and not Chesterton who at the beginning of the third millennium looks dated, in his lofty dismissal of Chesterton's defence of small nations and in his supposition, too, that Leo XIII's encyclical *Rerum Novarum* (1891)—the ultimate basis of Chesterton's economic and political thinking during his distributist years—had been super-seded by such documents as Paul VI's *Populorum Progressio* (1967). By the end of the last century, Chesterton's distaste for state socialism, his suspicion of

---

[29] Cecil, p. x.

internationalism, and his support for the independence from imperial domin-
ation of small nations like Poland had once more become understood as being
at the centre of Catholic thinking, and they were validated by the disintegra-
tion of Yugoslavia and the Soviet bloc. *Rerum Novarum* was celebrated and
brought into the new age by John Paul II's encyclical *Centesimus Annus*. The
anti-modernism of *Pascendi* was paralleled by Pope John Paul's counter-
revolution against the theological liberalism of the 1960s and 1970s, a liberalism
even more powerful (as it had also been during the first decade of the century)
within Protestantism; here, too, Chesterton's transcendentalist arguments
against the immanentism of the New Theology seem almost uncannily pres-
cient; as the Oxford theologian Alister McGrath puts it of the century's closing
decades, 'Convinced that nobody (well, nobody who really mattered that is)
could believe in a transcendent God any more, revisionist theologians
launched a makeover of their faith. Ideas such as eternal life, Resurrection,
"a God out there" and any sense of the mysterious were unceremoniously
junked as decrepit embarrassments.'[30] Most relevant of all to the modern age,
perhaps, was Chesterton's instinct to be what John Paul II called on all
Christians to be: a 'sign of contradiction'. Chesterton's ideas on monopoly
capitalism, on marriage and the family, on eugenics, above all on the dignity of
the human person and the central importance of the defence of free will in a
determinist age, were all directly pertinent to modern Catholic teaching.

Thus, Chesterton's religious, cultural, and political ideas were once more,
for the new millennium, what T. S. Eliot had called them so many years
before: '*the* ideas for [the times] that were fundamentally Christian and
Catholic'. Eliot, of course, did not intend the term 'Catholic' in the tri-
umphalist Roman Catholic sense that it acquired during the 1930s, when
Chesterton became seen more and more as what he had always struggled
against becoming: a mere propagandist for an alien religious subculture.
Chesterton's Christianity—before and after his submission to Rome in
1922—was deeply rooted in his Englishness. As Susan Hanssen puts it,
'[h]e interpreted his life as a seamless history, thinking that his new
faith was hardly new to him. . . . Chesterton found orthodoxy inescapable,
wedged into every corner of English life, language, and literature. He
therefore could not consider his acceptance of Roman Catholicism to be
a rejection of English culture.'[31]

---

[30] Alister McGrath, *The Twilight of Atheism* (London, 2005), 78.
[31] Susan Hanssen, 'Chesterton's Reputation as Roman Catholic Convert in the Twentieth
Century', *Chesterton Review*, 31/1–2 (Spring–Summer 2005), 64–5.

Chesterton was a 'sign of contradiction', not because he denied his own culture, but because he believed that it was in the process of denying itself. His anti-modernism was never a mere refusal to engage with the present; it derived always from his vision of some particular truth that was being overwhelmed by a new failure of intellectual or imaginative clarity. Hence his vision of 'orthodoxy' as being the exact reverse of what it was (and is) generally taken to be, an assertion of established ideas and standards: the 'chief merit' of orthodoxy was 'that it is the natural fountain of revolution and reform'.[32] Orthodoxy, he insisted, had functioned historically not as a static principle denying growth, but as a dynamic principle defending sanity: '[i]t is always easy to let the age have its head,' he wrote, in the famous passage in *Orthodoxy* quoted at the end of the last chapter; 'the difficult thing is to keep one's own'.[33]

It is probably true to say that since his death, Chesterton's continuing relevance has never been more apparent than it became towards the beginning of the new millennium. Partly, perhaps, this is because 'the modern age' is now increasingly understood as beginning so much earlier than we have habitually supposed. Chesterton's times were much more like our own than we imagine. To understand the development of his ideas in the context of his own age is not only to begin to understand why Chesterton came to write as he did; it is also to deepen our own understanding of what it is to live in the modern world. For, despite the massive impact on the last century of two world wars and of the rise and fall of the totalitarian idea, the culture from which the modern world was created was largely complete by the time Chesterton wrote *Orthodoxy*. We can say, too, that Chesterton's intellectual life thus far was a direct product of the growth of modernity; and that with *Orthodoxy*, he had completed the intellectual and spiritual armoury with which he was to wage a one-man anti-modernist counter-revolution for the rest of his life. With *Orthodoxy*, that is to say, Chesterton had arrived at a mature and complete expression of the essentially Christian and (as Wilfrid Ward acknowledged) essentially Catholic view of the modern world which animated his entire literary career: in *Orthodoxy*, Ward insisted, Chesterton was doing the Church's work.[34] Attempts from within a Roman Catholic perspective to show that it was only when he came into full communion with the Holy See that his theological understanding reached

---

[32] *Collected Works*, i. 343.   [33] Ibid. 305–6.

[34] Wilfrid Ward, 'Mr Chesterton among the Prophets', *Dublin Review*, 144 (Jan. and Apr. 1909), 32.

full maturity are fundamentally misplaced. Such claims have led to some grotesque misjudgements. Margaret Clarke, for instance, argues that before his conversion to Rome, Chesterton was closer to Gnosticism than to Christianity, that 'Chesterton's propaganda for "Christianity", "Christendom" and "Orthodoxy" [did] not admit of Christ in person. The Gnostics kept away from the Eucharist. The sacramental side of Christianity [was] *conspicuous by its absence* in Chesterton' (my italics).[35] The 'sacramental side of Christianity' is also, of course, conspicuous by its absence from the Catholic creeds; it is only in that sense that we can argue that it is 'absent' from *Orthodoxy*. We can say, too, that in the same sense it is equally absent from *The Everlasting Man*, written after Chesterton's conversion to Rome.

The reasons for such denials of the Catholicity of the pre-Roman Chesterton are understandable. We can to some extent observe the same division between Anglican and Roman Catholic critics over Chesterton's literary career as exists over that of another great convert from Canterbury to Rome, John Henry Newman: Anglicans tend to focus on the works written before conversion, Catholics on those which appeared after it. For the Anglican A. L. Maycock, the decade beginning in 1904, 'the decade of *Heretics* and *Orthodoxy*, of *The Ballad of the White Horse*, of ... the *Charles Dickens*, the first two volumes of *Father Brown*, of *The Victorian Age in Literature* and much else shows him at the summit of his powers'.[36] The view, nevertheless, that Chesterton reached the summit only with *The Everlasting Man*, *St Francis*, and, above all perhaps, with *St Thomas Aquinas*, is probably more generally held. Étienne Gilson, one of the most substantial Thomist scholars of the last century, remarked to a friend of Maisie Ward on the appearance of *St Thomas Aquinas* that 'Chesterton makes one despair. I have been studying St. Thomas all my life and I could never have written such a book.'[37]

---

[35] Margaret Clarke, 'Chesterton the Classicist', *Dublin Review*, 209 (1955), 51–67.

[36] A. L. Maycock, *The Man who was Orthodox* (London, 1963), 32.

[37] Ward, 525. After Chesterton's death, Gilson went further: asked for an appreciation of the book, he replied, 'I consider it as being without possible comparison the best book ever written on St. Thomas. Nothing short of genius can account for such an achievement. Everybody will no doubt admit that it is a "clever" book, but the few readers who have spent twenty or thirty years in studying St. Thomas Aquinas, and who, perhaps, have themselves published two or three volumes on the subject, cannot fail to perceive that the so-called "wit" of Chesterton has put their scholarship to shame. He has guessed all that which they had tried to demonstrate, and he has said all that which they were more or less clumsily attempting to express in academic formulas. Chesterton was one of the deepest thinkers who ever existed; he was deep because he was right; and he could not help being right; but he could not either help being modest and charitable, so he left it to those who could understand him to know that he was right, and deep; to the others, he apologized for being right, and he made up for being deep by being witty. That is all they can see of him' (Ward, 526).

Gilson, nevertheless, also thought *Orthodoxy* 'the best piece of apologetic the century [has] produced', and this is a view that other (Roman) Catholic commentators tend to accept. What puzzles some Roman Catholics unacquainted with the Anglican post-Tractarian intellectual tradition, however, is the question of where Chesterton can possibly have come by such ideas. Partly, this confusion comes from the Anglican Chesterton's obvious warmth towards Rome. He describes himself as a Catholic, as Gore (one of the major influences on *Orthodoxy*) would have done: but Gore was one of those Anglo-Catholics who were intensely hostile to the claims of Rome. When Chesterton talks of the Catholic tradition he sees it as being embodied by European culture. As he says in *Orthodoxy*, 'the very word "romance" has in it the mystery and ancient meaning of Rome'.[38] There is no residual trace in his early Christian writings of his youthful hostility to Roman dogma and priestcraft; on the contrary, these things are now seen as embodying and defending the whole Chestertonian vision of life. Ultimately, he sees 'Rome' and 'Christianity' as synonymous, and the Reformation as a great historical disaster for English culture; as he puts it in *Orthodoxy*:

Those countries in Europe which are still influenced by priests, are exactly the countries where there is still singing and dancing and coloured dresses and art in the open-air. Catholic doctrine and discipline may be walls; but they are the walls of a playground. . . . We might fancy some children playing on the flat grassy top of some tall island in the sea. So long as there was a wall round the cliff's edge they could fling themselves into every frantic game and make the place the noisiest of nurseries. But the walls were knocked down, leaving the naked peril of the precipice. They did not fall over; but when their friends returned to them they were all huddled in terror in the centre of the island; and their song had ceased.[39]

At the end of his anonymous book *Gilbert K. Chesterton: A Criticism* (not only published before *Orthodoxy*, but apparently written without any knowledge of it) Cecil Chesterton quotes Macaulay's epigram about Dr Johnson, that he was 'regarded in his own time as a classic and in ours as a contemporary'. 'Mr. Chesterton', Cecil continues, 'is certainly not regarded as a classic, but will he be a contemporary to our children?' He has already asked the question of what, if anything, of his brother's work thus far would survive. His answer is that some of his best poems, *The Napoleon of Notting Hill*, some of the best essays in *The Defendant*, and *Dickens* would probably

[38] G. K. Chesterton, *Orthodoxy* (London, 1908), p. xx.
[39] *Collected Works*, i. 350.

survive, but that *Heretics*, 'brilliant as much of it is', would not, since it 'deals too largely with transitory phenomena and transitory reputations': 'I do not think', judged Cecil, 'that Mr. Chesterton's work has quite the quality that gives to fugitive themes a permanence of its own. If he lives at all it will be by virtue of those parts of his work which deal with things in their nature eternal.' Cecil, of course, had always argued with his brother over nearly everything, and at this stage in his life was much closer, politically at least, to Shaw: he was a member of the Fabian Society, and from 1907 was a member of the editorial board of the *New Age*. But he became a Roman Catholic in 1912, a decade before Gilbert did; and having abandoned socialism became close to Belloc (closer than his brother), and with him was one of the founding fathers of distributism. His criticisms of his brother's work in *Gilbert K. Chesterton* are of uneven quality: but his judgement that '[i]f he lives . . . it will be by virtue of those parts of his work which deal with things in their nature eternal' was soon to be borne out by the first work of Chesterton's which today would be universally accepted as 'a classic'. Until 1908, Chesterton was still searching for and refining his 'philosophy of life'. Cecil had written of his brother's 'drift to Orthodoxy' over the previous eight years. As we have suggested, the process was a good deal more intellectually strenuous than the word 'drift' implies, but with *Orthodoxy*, the process had run its course. Politically and theologically, Chesterton's journey towards a Catholic vision of life was essentially complete. The question is often asked: why did he take so long actually to submit to Rome? His Roman sympathies were clear enough and openly expressed. When he created one of the great fictional detectives, it was in the persona of a Catholic priest, not an Anglican clergyman, because he felt that Catholic priests understood so much more about sin and evil. Father Brown appeared for the first time in 1911. The same year, addressing undergraduates in Cambridge, he said that 'he was more than ever inclined to think, *though he had not yet been admitted*, that possibly the claims of the Greek and Anglican Churches were less near the truth than the Roman Catholic Church' (my italics).[40] The reason Chesterton delayed so long over his conversion to Rome is difficult to answer with final certainty; the answer undoubtedly had a good deal to do with his worry over whether or not his wife would be hurt by such a decision, and whether or not she would follow him. By 1908, however, the intellectual journey was largely completed; and

---

[40] G. K. Chesterton, *The Future of Religion* (Cambridge, 1911), 21.

when he came into full communion with the Holy See fourteen years later, there was to be little or no further theological development from the position he had arrived at in *Orthodoxy*. There is a parallel here, perhaps, with the conversion of John Henry Newman, who in the *Apologia pro Vita Sua* famously wrote that from the time he became a Catholic,

of course I have no further history of my religious opinions to narrate. In saying this, I do not mean to say that my mind has been idle, or that I have given up thinking on theological subjects; but that I have had no changes to record, and have had no anxiety of heart whatever.... I was not conscious of firmer faith in the fundamental truths of Revelation.[41]

Newman's intellectual journey had taken place, as did Chesterton's, within the Anglican Church. Like so many converts before and since, Chesterton's theological Odyssey was conducted with an Anglican compass and guided by post-Tractarian charts. The difference is that for Chesterton, the milestone at which he had 'no further history of [his] religious opinions to narrate' arrived not on his conversion to Rome but fourteen years before it. *The Everlasting Man* is sometimes seen as a kind of sequel to or completion of *Orthodoxy*; but its theology does not represent in any fundamental way a forward movement away from the equilibrium he had achieved in 1908.

The intellectual chronicle I have in this book attempted to narrate is thus, in this sense, a complete one. Like Newman before him, Chesterton could have said that he 'was not conscious, on [his] conversion, of any inward difference of thought or of temper from what [he] had before'. With *Orthodoxy*, the foundations both of his life and of the mountainous literary oeuvre of the decades to come had been permanently and monumentally laid down.

[41] John Henry Newman, *Apologia pro Vita Sua*, ed. William Oddie (London: Everyman paperback, 1993), 273.

Bibliography

Names of publishers are given only when a work's first edition is not cited.

WORKS BY G. K. CHESTERTON

Works by Chesterton are cited, where possible, in the as yet incomplete Ignatius Press *Collected Works* (San Francisco, 1986–), by volume and page number. The title of the work itself is given in the notes only when it is not evident from the text. Works not yet included in the *Collected Works* are cited in a suitable modern edition, or, if unavailable, in their first edition. Unpublished material from the British Library's Chesterton Papers is cited by catalogue number, and, where relevant, folio reference, with the prefix BL MS. Books by Chesterton quoted in or relevant to the present work are listed below in their first editions. Journalism and other occasional writings quoted are listed separately below. Articles published in the school magazine of which he was a *co-founder, The Debater*, are referred to in the notes by volume and page number (since no dates are given in the bound volumes of the magazine, which do not include the original cover). These are not listed below.

Greybeards at Play (London, 1900).
The Wild Knight and Other Poems (London, 1900).
The Defendant (London, 1901).
—— with W. Robertson Nicoll, *Robert Louis Stevenson* (London, 1902).
Twelve Types (London, 1902).
Robert Browning (London, 1903).
Varied Types (London, 1903).
G. F. Watts (London, 1904).
The Napoleon of Notting Hill (London, 1904).
The Club of Queer Trades (London, 1905).
Heretics (London, 1905).
Charles Dickens (London, 1906).
The Man who was Thursday: A Nightmare (Bristol, 1908).
All Things Considered (London, 1908).
Orthodoxy (London, 1908).
Tremendous Trifles (London, 1909).

George Bernard Shaw (London, 1909).
The Ball and the Cross (London, 1910).
William Blake (London, 1910).
What's Wrong with the World (London, 1910).
The Innocence of Father Brown (London, 1911).
The Future of Religion (Cambridge, 1911).
The Ballad of the White Horse (London, 1911).
Appreciations and Criticisms of the Works of Dickens (London, 1911).
Manalive (London, 1912).
The Victorian Age in Literature (London, 1913).
The Flying Inn (London: Methuen, 1914).
A Short History of England (London, 1917).
The New Jerusalem (London, 1920).
St Francis of Assisi (London, 1923).
The Everlasting Man (London, 1925).
The Catholic Church and Conversion (London, 1926).
St Thomas Aquinas (London, 1933).
The Coloured Lands, ed. Maisie Ward (London and New York, 1938).
A Handful of Authors, ed. Dorothy Collins (London and New York, 1953).
Basil Howe: A Story of Young Love, ed. Denis Conlon (London, 2001).

JOURNALISM AND OTHER OCCASIONAL WRITINGS BY G. K. CHESTERTON

Only those articles cited in or directly relevant to the text have been listed here.

'The Ruskin Reader', *The Academy* (22 June 1895).
'Robert Bridges', *The Academy* (19 Oct. 1895).
'A Picture of Tuesday', *The Quarto*, first series (1896).
'Velasquez and Poussin', *The Bookman* (Dec. 1899).
'A Speech Reported', *The Speaker* (29 Sept. 1900).
'An Election Echo', *The Speaker* (20 Oct. 1900).
'Our Reasonable Imperialist', *The Speaker* (10 Nov. 1900).
'A Defence of Skeletons', *The Speaker* (20 Apr. 1900).
'How the Church Stands Today', *The Speaker* (27 Oct. 1900).
'Buddha versus Buddhism', *The Speaker* (17 Nov. 1900).
'The Literary Portraits of G. F. Watts R.A.', *The Bookman* (Dec. 1900).
'Puritan and Anglican', *The Speaker* (15 Dec. 1900).
'The Christmas Story', *The Speaker* (29 Dec. 1900).
'A Defence of Patriotism', *The Speaker* (4 May 1901).
'Three Books of Verse', *The Daily News* (31 May 1901).
'The Mystery of the Mystics', *The Daily News* (30 Aug. 1901).
'The Great Pessimist', *The Daily News* (7 June 1901).
'The Mystery of the Mystics', *The Daily News* (30 Aug. 1901).

Review of *The Violet Fairy Book* by Andrew Lang, *The Speaker* (12 Oct. 1901).

'The Mystery of Patriotism', *The Commonwealth* (Jan. 1902).

'Bacon and "G.G.G." ', *The Speaker* (22 Feb. 1902).

'Mr Stopford Brooke's "Browning" ', *The Daily News* (25 Sept. 1902).

'The Return of the Angels', *The Daily News* (14 Mar. 1903).

'The Dogmas of Free Thought: I', *The Commonwealth* (July 1903).

'On Calling a Spade a Spade', *The Daily News* (Saturday, 11 July 1903).

'The Dogmas of Free Thought: II', *The Commonwealth* (Aug. 1903).

'Mr Blatchford and Free Will', *The Clarion* (7 Aug. 1903).

'The Dogmas of Free Thought: III', *The Commonwealth* (Sept. 1903).

'The Dogmas of Free Thought: IV', *The Commonwealth* (Oct. 1903).

'The Dogmas of Free Thought: V', *The Commonwealth* (Nov. 1903).

'Mr Blatchford and my Neighbour', *The Daily News* (14 Nov. 1903).

'Mr Blatchford, Persecution and Other Things', *The Clarion* (20 Nov. 1903).

'Faith and the Fantastic', *The Daily News* (28 Nov. 1903).

'A Universal Relevance', *The Daily News* (12 Dec. 1903).

'What Happens to Rational Persons', *The Daily News* (12 Dec. 1903).

'On Irrelevancy', *The Daily News* (19 Dec. 1903).

'The Feast of Christmas Day', *The Daily News* (26 Dec. 1903).

'The Dogmas of Free Thought: VI', *The Commonwealth* (Dec. 1903).

'The Two Compromises', *The Commonwealth* (June 1904).

'Christianity and Rationalism', *The Clarion* (22 July 1904).

'We are All Agnostics until—', *The Clarion* (29 July 1904).

'Mr Blatchford's Religion', *The Clarion* (5 Aug. 1904).

'A Discussion Somewhat in the Air', *The Commonwealth* (Mar. 1905).

'Canvassing in Elections', *Illustrated London News* (13 Jan. 1906).

'The Root of the Quarrel', *The Daily News* (13 Jan. 1906).

'One Last Remark I Wish to Make', *The Daily News* (27 Jan. 1906).

'On Certain Politicians', *The Daily News* (10 Feb. 1906).

'On Believing in Oneself', *The Daily News* (19 Mar. 1906).

'The God of the Tribe', *The Daily News* (14 Apr. 1906).

'Something to Avoid', *The Daily News* (28 Apr. 1906).

'The New Hypocrite', *The Daily News* (9 June 1906).

'The Grave-digger', *The Daily News* (26 Jan. 1907).

'Common Sense in Politics', *The Daily News* (16 Mar. 1907).

'The Indispensable Fire', *The Daily News* (4 May 1907).

'A Plea for Popular Philosophy', *The Daily News* (22 June 1907).

'The Riddle of the Ivy', *The Daily News* (6 July 1907).

'The Last of the Conservatives', *The Daily News* (5 Oct. 1907).

'The Diabolist', *The Daily News* (9 Nov. 1907).

'Why I am not a Socialist', *New Age* (4 Jan. 1908).

'A Summary of Sects', *New Age* (25 Feb. 1909).

Introduction to C. Creighton Mandell and Edward Shanks, *Hilaire Belloc: The Man and his Work* (London, 1916).

Introduction to Greville M. MacDonald, *George MacDonald and his Wife* (London, 1924).

'From the Note-books of G.K.C.', *The Tablet* (4 Apr. 1953), 270–1.

'The History of Kids', *G. K. Chesterton Quarterly*, 1 (Oct. 1996), 1–2.

GENERAL BIBLIOGRAPHY

Ackroyd, Peter, *Dickens* (London, 2002).

Aytoun, William Edmonstoune, *Lays of the Scottish Cavaliers and Other Poems* (Edinburgh, 1849).

Barker, Dudley, *G. K. Chesterton: A Biography* (London, 1973).

Belloc, Hilaire, 'Thoughts about Modern Thought', *New Age* (7 Dec. 1907).

—— Signed obituary, *The Observer* (21 June 1936).

—— *On the Place of Gilbert Chesterton in English Letters* (London, 1940).

Bentley, Edmund Clerihew, *Those Days* (London, 1940).

—— *Biography for Beginners* (London, 1905).

—— *The Complete Clerihews of E. Clerihew Bentley* (Oxford, 1981).

Blake, William, *Songs of Innocence*, ed. Michael Mason (Oxford, 1994).

Blatchford, Robert, 'Religion and Science', *The Clarion* (27 Mar. 1903).

—— 'A Wolf in Lamb's Clothing', *The Clarion* (10 July 1903).

—— 'Wolf!! Wolf!! Wolf!!', *The Clarion* (18 July 1903).

—— 'Christianity before Christ', *The Clarion* (28 Aug. 1903).

—— 'Clerical Logic', *The Clarion* (13 Nov. 1903).

—— 'A Few Arrears', *The Clarion* (4 Dec. 1903).

—— *God and my Neighbour* (London, 1904).

Blodgett, H. W., *Walt Whitman in England* (Ithaca, NY, 1934).

Boyd, Ian, *The Novels of G. K. Chesterton: A Study in Art and Propaganda* (London, 1975).

Brooke, Stopford A., *Theology in the English Poets* (London, 1874).

—— *Short Sermons* (London, 1892).

—— *God and Christ* (London, 1894).

—— *Jesus and Modern Thought* (London, 1894).

Campbell, R. J., *The New Theology* (London, 1907).

Carlyle, Thomas, *The French Revolution* (Cambridge, Mass., 1884).

Carpenter, James, *Gore: A Study in Liberal Catholic Thought* (London, 1960).

Chesterton, Ada, *The Chestertons* (London, 1941).

Chesterton, Cecil, unsigned review, *Vanity Fair* (7 Apr. 1904).

Chesterton, Edward, *The Wonderful Story of Dunder van Haeden* (London, 1902).

Christophers, R. A., 'The G. K. Chesterton Papers in the British Library', *G. K. Chesterton Quarterly*, 17 (Winter 2000), 1–4.

—— *The British Library Catalogue of Additions to the Manuscripts: The G. K. Chesterton Papers* (London, 2001).

Clarke, Margaret, 'Chesterton the Classicist', *Dublin Review*, 209 (1955), 51–67.

Clayborough, Arthur, *The Grotesque in English Literature* (Oxford, 1965).

Coates, John D., *Chesterton and the Edwardian Cultural Crisis* (Hull, 1984).

Coleridge, S. T., *Biographia Literaria*, ed. with his aesthetical essays by J. Shawcross (Oxford, 1954).

Conlon, D. J. (ed.), *G. K. Chesterton: A Half Century of Views* (Oxford, 1987).

Coren, Michael, *Gilbert: The Man who was Chesterton* (London, 1989).

Corrin, Jay P., *G. K. Chesterton & Hilaire Belloc: The Battle against Modernity* (Athens, Oh., 1981).

Crowther, Ian, *Chesterton* (London, 1991).

Dale, Alzina Stone, *The Outline of Sanity* (Grand Rapids, Mich., 1982).

Davidson, J. Morrison, *The Gospel of the Poor* (London, 1893).

Dooley, David, foreword, *Collected Works*, i. 9.

Douglas, James, 'Personality in Literature', *The Bookman* (July 1903).

Eliot, T. S., signed obituary, *The Tablet* (20 June 1936), 785.

Ellman, Richard, *Oscar Wilde* (London, 1987).

Evans, B. Ifor, *W. P. Ker as a Critic of Literature* (Glasgow, 1955).

Evans, David, 'The Making of G. K. Chesterton's *Heretics*', *Yearbook of English Studies*, 5 (1975), 207–13.

Evans, Maurice, *G. K. Chesterton* (Cambridge, 1939).

Ffinch, Michael, *G. K. Chesterton: A Biography* (London, 1986).

Finlayson, Iain, *Browning: A Private Life* (London, 2004).

Gaunt, William, *The Aesthetic Adventure* (London, 1957).

Gilbert, W. S., *The Bab Ballads* (London, 1869).

Gore, Charles, *The Clergy and the Creeds* (London, 1887).

—— *The Permanent Creed and the Christian Idea of Sin* (London, 1905).

—— *The Old Theology and the New Religion* (London, 1907).

Hanssen, Susan, 'Chesterton's Reputation as Roman Catholic Convert in the Twentieth Century', *Chesterton Review*, 31/1–2 (Spring–Summer 2005), 64–5.

Holland, Henry Scott, 'Theologies Old and New', *The Commonwealth* (Mar. 1907).

Hollis, Christopher, *The Mind of Chesterton* (London, 1970).

Holroyd, Michael, *Bernard Shaw: The One-Volume Definitive Edition* (London, 1997).

Ingrams, Richard, introduction to Aidan Mackey, *Mr Chesterton Comes to Tea* (Cambridge, 1978).

Jacks, Lawrence Pearsall, *The Life and Letters of Stopford Brooke* (London, 1917).

Jackson, Holbrook, *The Eighteen Nineties* (London, 1913).

Jaki, Stanley L., 'Chesterton's Landmark Year: The Blatchford–Chesterton Debate of 1903–4', *Chesterton Review*, 10/4 (Nov. 1984), 409–23.

Johnson, Edgar, *Charles Dickens: His Triumph and Tragedy* (New York, 1952).

Jones, Henry, *Browning as a Philosophical and Religious Teacher* (London, 1891).

Jung, C. G., *Memories, Dreams, Reflections* (New York, 1961).

Keats, John, *Keats' Letters*, compiled and annotated by Tohru Matsuura (Tokyo, 1969).

Kenner, Hugh, *Paradox in Chesterton* (London, 1948).

Ker, Ian, *The Catholic Revival in English Literature, 1845–1961* (Notre Dame, Ind., 2003).

Knight, Mark, *Chesterton and Evil* (New York, 2004).

Lane, Lauriat, Jr., 'Dickens and Criticism', in George H. Ford and Lauriat Lane Jr. (eds.), *The Dickens Critics* (Ithaca, NY, 1961), 1–18.

Lilley, A. L., 'The Encyclical "Pascendi" ', *The Commonwealth* (Dec. 1907).

Lyttelton, E., *The Mind and Character of Henry Scott Holland* (London, 1926).

MacDonald, George, *The Princess and the Goblin* (London, 1996).

McGrath, Alister, *The Twilight of Atheism* (London, 2005).

Mackey, Aidan, 'Books from G. K. Chesterton's Library' (unpublished).

—— 'Note on Gilbert and Frances Chesterton' (unpublished).

—— *Mr Chesterton Comes to Tea* (Cambridge, 1978) (with illustrations by Chesterton).

McLuhan, Marshall, introduction to Hugh Kenner, *Paradox in Chesterton* (London, 1948).

Magee, Bryan, *The Philosophy of Schopenhauer* (Oxford, 1997).

Masterman, C. G. F., 'The Blasphemy of Opinion', *The Speaker* (26 Apr. 1902).

Maycock, A. L. (ed.), *The Man who was Orthodox: A Selection from the Uncollected Writings of G. K. Chesterton* (London, 1963).

Moore, George, *Modern Painting* (London, 1893).

—— *Confessions of a Young Man* (London, 1888).

Morris, William, and Hyndman, H. M., *A Summary of the Principles of Socialism* (London, 1884).

Mozley, J. K., *Some Tendencies in British Theology* (London, 1951).

Newman, John Henry, *Apologia pro Vita Sua*, ed. William Oddie (London: Everyman paperback, 1993).

O'Connor, John, *Father Brown on Chesterton* (London, 1938).

Oldershaw, Lucian (ed.), *England: A Nation* (London, 1904).

Pater, Walter, *Studies in the History of the Renaissance* (London, 1873).

Pearce, Joseph, *Wisdom & Innocence: A Life of G. K. Chesterton* (London, 1996).

Pius X, *Pascendi Dominici Gregis* (Rome, 1907).

Ramsey, Michael, *From Gore to Temple* (London, 1960).

Sams, H. A., *Pauline and Old Pauline* (Cambridge, 1933).

Savage, Allan, 'George Tyrrell: Modernist Theologian, 1861–1909: What he Said he Said', *Quodlibet Journal*, 4/1 (Winter 2002), <http://www.Quodlibet.net>.

Schopenhauer, Arthur, 'The Emptiness of Existence', in *Essays of Schopenhauer*, trans. S. H. Dircks (London, 1897).

Shaw, G. B., 'Belloc and Chesterton', *New Age* (15 Feb. 1908).

—— 'On Miracles: A Retort on Mr Chesterton', *New Age* (10 Dec. 1908).

—— and Chesterton, G. K., *Do We Agree?* (London, 1928).

Stevenson, R. L., *Essays in the Art of Writing* (London, 1905).

—— *Memories and Portraits* (Glasgow: Drew, 1990).

Sullivan, John, *G. K. Chesterton: A Bibliography* (London, 1958).

—— *G. K. Chesterton: A Centenary Appraisal, 1874–1974* (London, 1974).

Titterton, W. R., *G. K. Chesterton: A Portrait* (London, 1936).

Tyrrell, George, *Lex Credendi: A Sequel to Lex Orandi* (London, 1906).

Ward, Wilfrid, 'Mr Chesterton among the Prophets', *Dublin Review*, 144 (Jan. and Apr. 1909), 1–32.

Wells, H. G., 'About Chesterton and Belloc', *New Age* (11 Jan. 1908).

Whitman, Walt, *Leaves of Grass*, ed. Ernest Rhys [The 'Canterbury' Edition] (London, 1886).

Wilde, Oscar, *Collected Works* (London: Collins Classics, 1994).

Wills, Garry, *Chesterton: Man and Mask* (London, 1961).

Wilson, A. N., *Hilaire Belloc* (London, 1997).

Wilson, Edmund, 'Dickens: The Two Scrooges', in *The Wound and the Bow* (London, 1941).

Woodifield, Robert, 'Conrad Noel', in Maurice B. Reckitt (ed.), *For Christ and the People* (London, 1968).

Wright, Thomas, *The Life of Charles Dickens* (London, 1935).

Yeats, W. B., introduction to *The Oxford Book of Modern Verse* (Oxford, 1936).

Index